Management Education for Global Sustainability

A volume in
Research in Management Education and Development

Series Editor:
Charles Wankel, *St. John's University*

Research in Management Education and Development

Charles Wankel, Series Editor

Management Education for Global Sustainability (2009)
edited by Charles Wankel and James A. F. Stoner

University and Corporate Innovations in Lifelong Learning (2008)
edited by Charles Wankel and Robert DeFillippi

New Visions of Graduate Management Education (2006)
edited by Charles Wankel and Robert DeFillippi

The Cutting Edge of International Management Education (2006)
edited by Charles Wankel and Robert DeFillippi

Educating Managers Through Real World Projects (2005)
edited by Charles Wankel and Robert DeFillippi

Educating Managers With Tomorrow's Technologies (2003)
edited by Charles Wankel and Robert DeFillippi

Rethinking Management Education for the 21st Century (2002)
edited by Charles Wankel and Robert DeFillippi

Management Education for Global Sustainability

edited by

Charles Wankel
St. John's University

and

James A. F. Stoner
Fordham University

in collaboration with

Kevin Heater
Shaun Malleck
Matthew Marovich
Carolyn F. Stoner
and
Melissa Leviste

Information Age Publishing, Inc.
Charlotte, North Carolina • www.infoagepub.com

HF
1106
.M27
2009

Library of Congress Cataloging-in-Publication Data

Management education for global sustainability / edited by Charles Wankel and James A.F. Stoner.
    p. cm. -- (Research in management education and development)
    Includes bibliographical references.
    ISBN 978-1-60752-234-8 (pbk.) -- ISBN 978-1-60752-235-5 (hardcover) 1. Management--
Study and teaching (Graduate) 2. Sustainable development. I. Wankel, Charles. II. Stoner,
James Arthur Finch, 1935-

    HF1106.M27 2009
    658.4'0830711--dc22
                            2009030521

Editorial Review Board

CONTENTS

PART I

**MANAGEMENT EDUCATION FOR
GLOBAL SUSTAINABILITY:
PAST EVOLUTION AND SOME FUTURE POSIBIILITES**

CHAPTER 1

THE ONLY GAME BIG ENOUGH FOR US TO PLAY

James A. F. Stoner and Charles Wankel

Management education can contribute greatly to dealing with the dangers inherent in the global ecosystem's current trajectory. The authors in this volume grapple with the task of transforming management education from being part of the problem to being a significant part of the solution. To a very large extent our management education enterprise has provided the tools, mindsets, and ethical perspectives to encourage, empower, and justify actions that continue to destroy the capacity of the planet to support our species and many others. The task of transforming our system of management education and contributing to the development of business, government, not-for-profit, and political leaders and followers is the challenge facing all of us, professors and students, whether or not we care to admit it. This chapter provides an overview of the diverse ways that that challenge might be taken up. These themes and initiatives represent exciting possibilities for student learning and offer potentially important avenues toward transforming management education into an endeavor that is part of the solution to global sustainability and away from its being part of the problem.

Management Education for Global Sustainability, pp. 3–17
Copyright © 2009 by Information Age Publishing

Alternate Scenarios

As we were "crossing the i's and dotting the t's" on this volume (yes, "crossing the i's and dotting the t's"—sometimes wrapping up a volume can be a bit stressful when life forgets to get out of the way), ABC-TV aired Bob Woodruff's *Earth 2100* (ABC-TV, 2009). *Earth 2100* contains two scenarios for the next 9 decades: one realistically pessimistic and one optimistically hopeful—perhaps not sufficiently realistically pessimistic and perhaps too optimistically hopeful—but still, very engrossing.

In the first scenario, pessimism arises from at least two sources: our global ecosystem's progress toward collapse and our historical behaviors at all levels, from individual to corporate to national to international, in recognizing and responding to this unfolding crisis. Some of the factors contributing to the first source of pessimism, the possibility of global ecosystem collapse, include climate change, resource depletion, deforestation, endangered water supplies, species extinctions, and enormous income inequalities. The second source of pessimism arises from *Earth 2100's* implicit recognition of our past individual, corporate, and political performance as we have, in most instances, failed to recognize and to take the actions needed to deal with global environmental, social, and political problems—problems that can now no longer be denied by people of good faith and good intentions.

Earth 2100's evolving decade-by-decade scenario is both tragic to watch and all too likely if we, as a species, fail to act with a wisdom and a commitment we have probably never exhibited in the past. This scenario does include multiple, successive actions of a moderately palliative nature, and some optimistic technological developments are included, but they supply far less global healing than is needed.

In the second scenario, logical and sensible actions are taken. Many of the actions are ones that have been urged upon us for decades, but which we have lacked the political will and leadership in business, government, the not-for-profit sector, and academe to make happen. The 9-decade-later results of taking those actions are very attractive and the journey toward them is not appreciably painful. In fact, the journey probably offers the possibility of being far more rewarding than our current daily journeys, since those alternative journeys toward 2100 have a purpose and a commitment to the future and to others lacking in the ways so many of us are currently living our lives.

Obviously there will have been many criticisms and perhaps some appreciations of *Earth 2100* by the time this book is available for the Academy of Management Annual Meeting in August 2009, but the reality of two broad sets of scenarios is very difficult to gainsay. Either the vast majority of us around the world will continue living our lives and pursuing our careers and dreams with the expectation that someone else will solve the global sustainability crisis for us—if there really is any such thing to worry about, or vast numbers of us will commit to learning "what's so" with our global ecosystem, what can be done on a broad scale, what we individually and collectively can do in particular, and then get to work doing it.

To deal with the dangers inherent in the global ecosystem trajectory we are currently on, each of us has a contribution to make—perhaps many contributions. Surely one of the major areas of contribution is in the broad domain of education, and—for many of the readers of this volume—the domain of management education.

The authors of the chapters in this volume are all grappling with the task of how we can transform management education from—as it is currently being produced almost everywhere—being part of the problem to being a significant part of the solution. To a very large extent our management education enterprise has provided the tools, mindsets, and ethical perspectives to encourage, empower, and justify actions that continue to destroy the capacity of the planet to support our species and many others. The task of transforming our system of management education and contributing to the development of business, government, not-for-profit, and political leaders and followers is the challenge facing all of us—professors and students—whether or not we care to admit it. The authors of the chapters in this volume are all taking up that challenge, even if, perhaps, they might not be comfortable phrasing that challenge of our global and individual situations as dramatically—or perhaps melodramatically—as we have done.

Whether or not you, the reader, agrees with the seriousness of the situation we allude to, and that *Earth 2100* describes, we invite you to consider that the transformation of management education is, for many of us and hopefully for you, the only game big enough for us to play.

PART I: MANAGEMENT EDUCATION FOR GLOBAL SUSTAINABILITY: PAST EVOLUTION AND SOME FUTURE POSIBIILITES

This first chapter of Part I "provides an overview of the 4 parts and 18 chapters in the book. It attempts to highlight aspects of each chapter that the chapter authors particularly wish to call to readers' attention.

The remaining chapters of Part I address ways in which management education for global sustainability has been evolving and might evolve in the future: first, how it has been evolving in recent years in North America (chapter 2); then the valuable role an integrative metatheory of global sustainability might play in guiding the future evolution of management education and what such a metatheory might look like (chapter 3); and finally, how much thousands of years of largely overlooked Chinese innovations in management theory and practice in general, and environmental management theory and practice in particular, can contribute to that continuing evolution ... and the dangers that exist if all of us (the Chinese, in particular, and also the 1.2 billion citizens of India) fail to heed the valuable lessons of the past (chapter 4).

In chapter 2, "The Short and Glorious History of Sustainability in North American Management Education," Gordon Rands and Mark Starik, key contributors to the evolution of management education in North America and beyond, describe the history of attention to sustainability in North American management education, addressing key events that influenced the development of such attention. They report on curriculum development initiatives, the creation of academically oriented organizations focusing on business and sustainability, the emergence of special journal issues on the topic, the emergence of databases of curriculum materials in the area, and the issuance of reports ranking business schools on their attention to the environment.

They then review the current status of sustainability-oriented business degree options, such as certificates, concentrations, dual degree programs, and sustainability-focused MBA programs. While the development of such options has rapidly grown in recent years and is likely to continue to do so, they suggest that there is a need to begin to identify what works well in management sustainability education, and suggest a number of questions that can guide our study of educational effectiveness in this area.

Given the critical nature of the unsustainable path that global society is on, they then identify five areas that will require careful consideration, and action, as attention to sustainability in management education continues to develop in the future. They conclude by observing that while the growth in attention to sustainability in North American management education over the past two decades has been in one sense remarkably glorious, far greater growth in the future is absolutely essential, and suggest that we must move from discussing "sustainability IN management education" to a future in which "management education FOR sustainability" becomes the norm.

Mark Edward's chapter 3: "Visions of Sustainability: An Integrative Metatheory for Management Education," addresses the lack of a coherent theory of global sustainability that can be used to guide management education. He discusses the relevance of metatheory for dealing with the theoretical pluralism and the growing fragmentation that characterizes sustainability theory. Edwards shows how metatheoretical research not only provides a more integrative response to the diversity of theories and research paradigms, but also allows for the development of a critical overview of the relative importance of theories of sustainability. Metatheorizing across multiple paradigms raises awareness of the range of explanations and understandings that have been, and are being developed.

To demonstrate the opportunities for creative theory building that metatheory opens up, Edwards describes a number of common conceptual lenses that can be used to explore sustainability issues. When these lenses are combined to develop integrative frameworks, new insights and innovative reframings can be developed for exploring sustainability issues. As with other disciplines and professional fields, metatheory has been neglected in management education and Edwards shows how metatheory can contribute to the development of more critical and more expansive forms of learning in general and for global sustainability in particular.

In chapter 4, "Taoism and Innovation in China; Recovering the Legacy of Environmentally Sustainable Enterprise," John Hollwitz calls attention to how, in the past two decades, China and the West have developed extensive mutual sources of supply, production, and markets. These developments have heightened risks of irreversible damage to the natural environment. He warns that western management education cannot treat new global opportunities or risks without appreciating the nature and extent of Chinese development. His chapter summarizes an extraordinary array of strategic and operational innovations in Chinese history. It also addresses systems at the heart of Chinese enterprise, particularly Taoism, which for millennia have made environmental sustainability the prerequisite for successful social, economic, and military success.

The chapter urges us as educators to heed advice offered to the West in nineteenth century China, at the peak of the Western industrial revolution. That advice provides a model, based on Taoist traditions, of how extraordinary innovation must proceed in line with moral, practical, and highly productive commitments to natural ecology.

Hollwitz emphasizes that management education cannot be complete and fully effective without appreciating the extent of these Taoist influences on Asian practice. It is also true that Asia is equally at risk if it overlooks these influences. Something has changed in China itself, and the priority to environmental order at the heart of Taoism may be vanishing in the industrialization of Asia. Loss of these Taoist influences risks more than the loss of a historical sense. It risks the loss of a powerful and historically proven model for enterprise as a whole.

PART II: APPROACHES TO BRINGING GLOBAL
SUSTAINABILITY INTO MANAGEMENT EDUCATION

The four chapters in Part II present four ways of bringing global sustainability into management education: taking an artistic point of view (chapter 5), building systems thinking much more deeply into teaching for sustainability (chapter 6), immersing learners in the issues of sustainability through intensive on-site field experiences (chapter 7), and bringing a stakeholder approach to viewing and acting upon global sustainability issues in general, and poverty alleviation in particular (chapter 8).

Ralph Bathurst and Margot Edwards note in chapter 5, "Developing a Sustainability Consciousness through Engagement with Art," that predicting climate change and many other global sustainability issues are explored by an exacting science that relies on computer modeling and other techniques to predict the state of the planet over the next century. Because of the complex, sophisticated, and scientific nature of such forecasting a distance is created between researchers and society and barriers to understanding are not easily overcome. Thus, reports of alarming situations uncovered by science-based work frequently lack the visceral impact needed to energize commitment and action.

Bathurst and Edwards demonstrate the value of stepping back from the science and taking an artful approach. They inquire into the power of art to provoke and challenge, and describe this power as a catalytic jolt that results in a shift in consciousness on the part of those viewing works of art. They argue that this kind of visceral response is a necessary precursor in developing a sustainable approach to business development. They make their argument concrete by using the example of war, an occasionally overlooked aspect of the broad global sustainability issue.

Works of art by-pass intellect, they initiate emotional responses within perceivers, and while art is invitational, it does not necessarily evoke warm feelings of affirmation. Sometimes art puzzles us, confounds our ability to make any sense of the artist's intention and may even make us angry. With this in mind, Bathurst and Edwards' chapter presents the painting *The Carbon Footprint of War and the Pollution of Religion* by the Australasian artist Tom Mutch. Using exemplars from Dali and Picasso, they explore Mutch's painting and offer the view that unless we in the global community grapple with the problem of war, our attempts at developing sustainable business practices are futile. The painting asks us all to inquire into the relationships among political forces, global business enterprises, and religion and to critique those alliances.

In chapter 6, "Education in Sustainability through Systems Thinking," José-Rodrigo Córdoba and Terry Porter discuss how systems theory is contributing and can contribute even more, to the continuing evolution of management education described in Part 1. Cordoba and Porter suggest the use of systems thinking to facilitate sustainability education. Their experience in the United Kingdom and United States leads them to propose the language and concepts of systems as a vehicle to enable educators and students to explore the complexities of sustainability. The chapter overviews three different schools of thought in systems thinking, as well as their corresponding methodological approaches. Their conclusions point out the importance of critical reflection about sustainability as a modern condition that influences our identities as human beings. Reflection is needed to encourage us to think of who we want to become as practitioners or academics in sustainability.

Phil Mirvis describes taking corporate executives and young leaders out of the classroom and immersing them in the realities of the unsustainable world they and we inhabit in chapter 7, "Educating for Sustainability: The Power of Learning Journeys to Raise Consciousness." Focusing on raising business leaders and students consciousness about the world in which they live and do business, the chapter describes a set of journeys where executives and students opened their eyes and hearts to the economic, social, and environmental aspects of commerce in different parts of the world. Mirvis discusses *e* "design" of journeys—picking a locale, readying the organization and executives, "themeing" the experience to make it relevant to business leaders, facilitating reflections, and deepening learning.

In chapter 8, "The Challenges of Businesses' Intervention in Areas with High Poverty and Environmental Deterioration: Promoting an Integrated Stakeholders' Approach in Management Education," Diego A. Vázquez-Brust, José A. Plaza-Ubeda, Claudia E. Natenzon, and Jerónimo de Burgos-Jiménez describe a current conceptual gap—both in management theory and in education—in teaching future managers how to address a major challenge to sustainable development. That challenge is the "vicious circle" between poverty, environmental deterioration, and unsustainable business strategies. The chapter emphasizes the need for educators to alert students and managers to the importance and difficulty of developing business intervention strategies in regions with high levels of social vulnerability and environmental deterioration, and to give them a framework for conceptualizing how such situations can be analyzed, addressed, and ultimately improved.

The chapter aims to help educators do so by introducing a framework and intervention model developed as part of an ongoing international multidisciplinary research project involving researchers from seven European and Latin-American universities: "Environmental impact of businesses, social vulnerability, and poverty in Latin America." The authors propose that the framework and model presented can be used in management education not only to address the challenge highlighted in the chapter but also to show why sustainability problems and solutions are inherently multidimensional and how existing concepts and theories of management can be combined with other fields of knowledge, helping to shift management education from subject-based teaching to a more holistic approach.

The framework and intervention model uses stakeholders' theory to integrate concepts from sociology, management, and natural sciences. The need for a holistic approach is emphasized; hence environmental deterioration and poverty are framed in terms of vulnerability to environmental and economic risk. Increasing the influence of stakeholders in company decision-making will lead to increased adaptive capabilities and a decrease in vulnerability to environmental and economic risk. Sustainable entrepreneurship is seen as the key mechanism to increase stakeholder adaptive capabilities. A key idea to be transmitted in the classroom is the understanding that "performance" within the organization should be less focused on short term financial performance, and more concerned with the long term survival of the company. In turn, a key value to be infused is that voluntary actions of the business community must consistently contribute to strengthening the adaptive capacity of social systems, considered as stakeholder networks existing in a context of equity–development, freedom, democracy, and harmony with nature.

PART III: INSTITUTIONAL AND PROGRAM LEVEL INNOVATIONS IN MANAGEMENT EDUCATION FOR GLOBAL SUSTAINABILITY

Part III reports on a series of program and institutional level initiatives that, in some cases have already been very successful, and in others are quite new, but show great promise. Part III opens with reports of two new programs for developing leaders in global sustainability—one of which involved starting an entirely new educational institution. Chapter 9 describes the emergence of that new educational institution as it created an MBA program in sustainability from a clean slate, unencumbered by previous institutional obligations or momentum. Chapter 10 reports on another new sustainability MBA program that integrates ocean and climate science with MBA education for sustainability. Chapter 11 traces the evolution of the French educational system's progress in bringing sustainability into higher education in France, and chapter 12 focuses on undergraduate business education for global sustainability in liberal arts colleges.

In Chapter 9, "Building the Bainbridge Graduate Institute (BGI): Pioneering Management Education for Global Sustainability," Jill Bamburg and Lorinda Rowledge paint a vivid picture of a remarkable institution created to revolutionize business education. BGI's mission is "to prepare students from diverse backgrounds to build enterprises that are financially successful, socially responsible, and environmentally sustainable." Beyond serving the needs of students, the vision of the school is "to infuse environmentally and socially responsible business innovation into general business practice by transforming business education." In just 6 years BGI succeeded, not only in incubating new management curricula aimed at leveraging business' role in solving global problems, but also in demonstrating to other business schools that there is a demand and market for business education that integrates sustainability.

Bamburg and Rowledge tell the story of BGI's conception and development from a far-reaching idea to an award-winning program with hundreds of people enthralled with the power of BGI's program and its potential to make change in the world. In addition to describing core elements of BGI's purpose, people, program, and process, the authors convey the power and magic that is BGI. They provide a sense of what it felt like to "build the bicycle while riding it" as they engaged multiple stakeholders in defining learning objectives relevant for transformational leaders, co-created a sustainability-infused program and curriculum, assembled BGI's national faculty academy of sustainability academics and expert practitioners, built distance learning platforms to support the hybrid delivery model, designed a unique orientation at an eco-retreat center, consciously built a powerful learning community, and implemented action learning projects and industry concentrations as core elements of the MBA program. The reader is given a glimpse into the monthly "intensives" where mid-career students assemble from around the country to learn and discover ways to make business more sustainable. The sense of deeper purpose, vibrancy, and foundation of authentic relationships is tangible. Already BGI graduates and students are making a significant impact in the world: inside multi-national corporations, as leaders of not-for-profits, and as entrepreneurs of sustainable ventures and social enterprises. As one of the leading institutions in sustainable business, BGI promises to continue to make an impact and to serve as a model for other institutions and programs.

Bradley Moran, Mark M. Higgins, and Deborah E. Rosen discuss how universities in general and graduate management schools in particular, need to align their educational offerings with the move toward a globally sustainable world. In chapter 10, "Educating Future Business Leaders in the Strategic Management of Global Change Opportunities: The Blue MBA," they describe a new MBA-MO (Master of Oceanography) dual-degree designed for students with undergraduate training in science and engineering who aim to develop management skills and prepare themselves for the opportunities and challenges of a globally sustainable world. The central rationale for this novel graduate degree is that climate change represents a major challenge and opportunity to a broad range of businesses and to the global economy. Whereas "sustainability" is increasingly part of business schools' curricula, climate science has only recently begun to be formally included in management education programs. This unique program contributes to the growing focus on global sustainability and facilitates interaction between faculty and graduate students with corporate executives needing to adapt their management practices to address real-world environmental and social challenges. The authors note that The Blue MBA will be particularly beneficial to those pursuing management careers in growth markets such as renewable energy, energy efficiency, ocean technology and engineering, hazard risk management, water resources management, fisheries, and ocean and human health.

In Chapter 11, "The Contribution of French Business and Management Education to the Development of Key Skills in Sustainable Development" Vera Ivanaj and John R. McIntyre discuss the recent contribution of the French business and management education system to training key skills for sustainable development management. The authors describe the French political and institutional context and the role it plays in the development of an overall sustainability policy, leading to the emergence of new initiatives such as training courses in the field. These courses and programs adopt a multidisciplinary approach and integrate all aspects of sustainable development: environmental, economic, and societal questions.

Ivanaj and McIntyre show that business and management establishments account for a significant part of the pedagogical content available at the master's level. They offer SD (sustainable development) courses involving a wide range of training for professional-level students and executives, keeping their main focus on strategic and operational issues. The teaching methods emphasize the concrete and practical side of training and seek to bring the teaching as close as possible to the issues faced by companies. Teaching is carried out through a balanced mix of full-time professors, company professionals, and SD specialists employing interactive pedagogical methods whenever possible.

The authors analyze pedagogical contents and philosophy and note that SD courses are generally open to highly motivated students and professionals with a wide variety of academic and work profiles: engineers, company legal advisors, economists, literature students, politicians, and so forth. Following a course of training, students have access to various career opportunities in key organizational positions such as SD projects manager, ethical fund manager, SD auditor, eco-conception specialist, risk manager, compliance officer, ethical supervisor, and so forth.

In chapter 12, "Undergraduate Management Education for Sustainability: A Perspective from the Liberal Arts," Kirk R. Karwan, Robert L. Underwood, and Thomas I. Smythe describe the unique strategy Furman University followed in integrating sustainability concepts and management theory and practice with knowledge from a broad liberal arts tradition (e.g., history, philosophy, political science, psychology, and the sciences). The chapter details Furman's university-wide commitment to sustainability; and highlights specific sustainability initiatives instituted by the Department of Business and Accounting.

The primary goal of the department is to infuse a culture of sustainability awareness and engagement among faculty and students via an array of curriculum and co-curriculum programs. These activities include, most prominently, new sustainability-focused courses and external engagement opportunities with business leaders. Departmental courses entitled "The Sustainable Corporation" and "Ethics and Corporate Social Responsibility" require students to address strategically the operational, ethical, and stakeholder concerns of a firm's triple bottom line. In true liberal arts fashion, these two electives are open to students from throughout the University; promoting an interesting breadth of perspective that fosters meaningful discussion. Additionally, traditional marketing and management course offerings have been significantly altered to incorporate sustainability as a fundamental dimension of new product development and strategic planning projects.

External engagement with business leaders is achieved through an executive lecture series, internships and sponsored events for the University's traditional cultural learning program. Major firms such as BMW, Caterpillar, Home Depot, Interface, and Milliken have visited Furman to participate in these programs and share their expertise concerning global sustainability.

PART IV: CREATING SUCCESSFUL MANAGEMENT COURSES IN GLOBAL SUSTAINABILITY

The final set of six chapters report on course-level initiatives to bring global sustainability into and in some cases, outside of, the management classroom. They all have a common theme of grounding sustainability in reality by the way the courses are designed and on having the courses draw heavily on the creativity and initiative of the student course members. In many of these chapters, the authors share their personal and professional experiences in creating and conducting the courses they have delivered and continue to develop.

Chapter 13 takes the reader through an introductory course focused on creating and investing in sustainable enterprises. Chapter 13, 14, and 15 describe approaches to bringing sustainability into the classroom that lead the students to build their own business cases for corporate sustainability initiatives, approaches that have considerable similarities to the approach described in chapter 13. Chapter 16 shows how a course based on service learning projects is enabling students to learn about global sustainability. The authors advocate for the value of service learning in general and for its value in creating sustainability learning opportunities and experiences in particular. Chapter 17 introduces readers to a project-oriented course in developing sustainable enterprises that is being used to create a management education capstone course experience, and chapter 18 brings the book to a close by reporting on the challenges three professors faced and met in bringing three different approaches to teaching about sustainability into their universities' business curricula, and what they learned from their attempts to do so.

In chapter 13, "Investing in a Sustainable Future," Mark White and Edeltraud Günther describe their experiences developing and delivering a cross-disciplinary, cross-cultural, collaborative capstone course. Drawing on recent pedagogical research emphasizing experiential learning and synergies between different learning objectives, the authors propose a structured approach to the analysis of sustainability challenges. Students work in groups to identify, evaluate, and apply solutions to a "sustainable investment project"—a real-world situation facing a business or other organization.

Students are expected to evaluate their proposed alternatives for sustainability, using various frameworks, for example, the ecological footprint, The Natural Step, triple bottom line, cradle-to-cradle, life cycle analysis, and so forth. Proposals must also be assessed for strategic fit within the sponsoring organizations, using Porter's "five forces" or SWOT analysis. Alternatives passing these screens are then evaluated for their economic viability (using cost-benefit analysis, and/or traditional financial techniques such as NPV and IRR), and finally, students identify and evaluate important practical hurdles impeding their implementation. These four screens—sustainability, strategic fit, financial viability, and practicality—form the core of their approach.

To facilitate and engage students in this hands-on learning experience, White and Günther developed numerous experiential learning assignments and exercises, a number of which are described in their chapter. They report excellent success with their course and suggest that a multidisciplinary, hands-on, collaborative approach is particularly effective in helping business students acquire an understanding of sustainability challenges.

Wendy Stubbs and Ed Lockhart describe how corporate sustainability is taught to MBA students at Monash University in chapter 14, "The Sustainability Business Case: Educating MBAS in Sustainability." The learning unit, "Corporate Sustainability: The Business Case," is structured to facilitate learning on three dimensions: knowledge, skills, and attitudes.

The first part of the unit develops students' understanding of sustainability from environmental, social, and economic perspectives through lectures, videos, discussion forums, industry case studies, and guest speakers from organizations that are sustainability leaders. The lecturers present a sustainability framework to help the students understand and reconcile the different sustainability perspectives. The framework aims to stimulate and broaden business students' understanding of sustainability and shift their thinking beyond the dominant neoclassical economic paradigm.

Building on the knowledge gained in part one, part two of the unit is an interactive workshop where students use a SPIR (Situation-Problem-Implication-Response) tool to articulate the business case for sustainability, and develop skills to formulate strategic responses. In small groups, the students apply the SPIR tool to analyze sustainability within two industry sectors.

Postulating that organizational change is predicated on personal change, an "inspirational life coach" challenges the students, in the third part of the unit, to reflect on how they will, or will not, "personalize" sustainability in their careers and/or lives. In the quest for affective outcomes, this part of the unit encourages students to examine their own attitudes, values, and behaviors, and reflect on their career and life goals.

Kate Kearins and Eva Colllins describe a student case-writing project that can be used in sustainability, social responsibility, or environmental management course. In chapter 15, "Grounding Sustainability in Reality: Encouraging Students to Make Their Own Case for Action," full guidelines for the unit are provided, but at the same time variations are discussed to allow for maximum teaching flexibility. The project enables students to focus in-depth on just one organization, industry, or situation, evaluate for themselves the key issues, and present an argument and/or a plan for working toward resolution of those issues.

Kearins and Collins use examples to show how students select (and sometimes develop) theory that yields insight into the situations they are analyzing. They also show how students can contribute to enhanced practice by presenting options and/or recommendations for the short, medium, and even long term. To be successful, these options must take into account the complexities faced by the owner/managers, industry bodies, event organizers, or relevant policy-makers in the cases.

Kearins and Collins encourage other instructors to incorporate a case writing assignment into their courses because it can lead to a powerful learning experience for both the students and the organizations involved. Student case writing projects can be an effective way to help students to bridge the divide between theory and practice. Encouraging students to write their own cases allows them to see for themselves the real-world tensions associated with the achievement of sustainability. In addition, by getting students out of the classroom and into the field, student engagement with class content increases significantly.

In chapter 16, "The Integration of Real-World Student Projects Into a Sustainable MBA Program," Robert Sroufe describes how Duquesne University instructors create experiences for MBA students to apply newly learned business management skills to the ethical and profitable management of social and environmental resources. Their case study describes how instructors operate as senior partners for live consulting projects: soliciting clients with problems that complement semester course content, assembling student teams, coordinating faculty mentors, prescribing sound methodology, and overseeing students from the initial stage of negotiating each project's scope to the final stage of providing the project's deliverables to the clients. Information helpful to other faculty developing similar service learning and project management experiences include project examples, excerpts from the course syllabus, stakeholder benefits, scope of work, communication plan, project manager schedule, and evaluation criteria.

Robert Girling's chapter 17, "Teaching Green Business: How to Bring Sustainability Into a Capstone Business Class," delves into why sustainability is an essential topic for students of business and how it might it be incorporated in a capstone business class. The chapter provides practical guidance and examples for doing so. Featured prominently are two students' reports on how they connected the topic of sustainability with their professional lives.

In the final chapter, "Training Managers for Sustainable Development: The Lens of Three Practitioners," Emmanuel Raufflet, Denis Dupré, and Odile Blanchardshare share their experiences teaching sustainable development to business and economics students in three different ways. One involves teaching corporate social responsibility with students wearing different hats and with an innovative approach to business "success." The second way involves teaching ethics in a context of freedom and openness. The third way adopts a problem-based learning approach. The common "paths" of these experiences to make sustainability palpable and relevant to students are learning-by-doing, experiencing, raising awareness, and grounding in local specificities.

Common challenges encountered by the instructors include (1) a cross-functional challenge: sustainable management education is inherently transversal, although our institutions tend to be designed in functional silos; (2) an integration challenge: how to enhance a paradigm of complexity in a context which fosters linear thinking; (3) a problem-solving challenge: how to foster complex problem-solving approaches and skills acquisition in a learning agenda driven by instrumentalist values.

The authors use the five skills identified by Tilbury and Wortman (2004) to compare and assess the relevance of their experiences in terms of education for sustainable development, namely: envisioning, critical thinking and reflection, systemic thinking, building partnerships, and participation in decision making. This framework can be of help to program managers and scholars interested in going beyond traditional discipline-based courses and seeking to foster new skills and competencies.

The authors of the chapters in this book recognize, and in many cases emphasize, that these initiatives are works in progress, However, readers are very likely to recognize that these themes and initiatives represent exciting possibilities for student learning and that they offer potentially important avenues toward transforming management education into an endeavor that is part of the solution to global sustainability and away from its being part of the problem.

REFERENCES

ABC-TV. (2009). *Earth 2100*. Retrieved June 11, 2009, from http://abcnews.go.com/technology/earth2100/

Tilbury, D., & Wortman, D. (2004). *Engaging people in sustainability*. IUCN, Gland: Switzerland.

CHAPTER 2

THE SHORT AND GLORIOUS HISTORY OF SUSTAINABILITY IN NORTH AMERICAN MANAGEMENT EDUCATION

Gordon Rands and Mark Starik

This chapter provides a review of the major events and other salient phenomena that have shaped the emergence of the field of management sustainability education, briefly examines its current status, and considers prospects for its future development.

Attention to sustainability—defined here as long-term environmental, social, and economic (or triple bottom line) quality of life—in management education in North America is a fairly recent phenomenon. While many schools of business have offered courses on a range of socioeconomic topics for several decades, North American business schools began offering courses focusing on environmental topics only about 1990. These new offerings reflect the renewed emphasis on environmental issues accompanying several critical environmental events of the late 1980s and the twentieth anniversary of Earth Day in this region. In addition, efforts to increase attention to the natural environment in business schools; the emergence of several organizations at the interface of business, the environment, and the business academy; and the emergence of special issues of established jour-

Management Education for Global Sustainability, pp. 19–49
Copyright © 2009 by Information Age Publishing
All rights of reproduction in any form reserved.

nals, new dedicated journals, and book series supported this emerging emphasis. In the past decade, attention to environmental sustainability has been extended to include the social justice component of the triple bottom line through attention to the "base of the pyramid." Although attention to sustainability has continued to increase in the past few years, as evidenced by the creation of several sustainability-focused MBA programs, the needs of the planet and of businesses and people, both of the present and the future, demand that we redouble our efforts to increase the speed and effectiveness with which we bring management FOR sustainability into business education.

INTRODUCTION

In his 1973 essay, "The Short and Glorious History of Organizational Theory," Charles Perrow discusses the struggle for theoretical primacy in organizational understanding between advocates of the "mechanical" (i.e., scientific management and administrative principles) and "human relations" schools of management thought. This controversy over how best to understand organizations, Perrow suggests, was the central issue in the development of organizational theory over the preceding 7 decades.

Over the past 4 decades business, and therefore business academia, has been challenged by calls to reconceptualize its views regarding its responsibilities to society. Since about 1990, calls for adopting a new view of business responsibility regarding the natural environment have been particularly influential. The demands for attention to sustainability in management education have met with growing acceptance in recent years, as this volume and others (e.g., Galea, 2004) attest. Despite this growing acceptance, attention to sustainability in management education is, we suggest, woefully inadequate given the sustainability challenges that face organizations, societies, and species. We believe that the breadth and depth of these challenges are such that they pose much more fundamental questions for management education than did the question addressed by Perrow (1973). Thus, as we enter what may be a period of rapid change in how we think about and address sustainability in management education, it may be useful to take stock of the events and factors that have led us to where we are today, and briefly consider where we might go in the future.

The scope and magnitude of the environmental threats facing humanity are familiar to readers of this volume, and will not be reiterated here in detail. Suffice to say that these environmental, social, and economic threats are largely caused by modern organizations and their stakeholders — especially businesses, their suppliers, and their customers—as people produce, distribute, consume, and dispose of their products and services.

Thus, a special need for business educators to engage in education for sustainability is created. In this chapter we provide an overview of some of the key events in the development of management education for sustainability, briefly review its current—although rapidly changing—status, and consider prospects for how it may develop in the future. As the title of this chapter indicates, the authors acknowledge that the observations in this paper largely represent a North American, and especially a U.S. perspective.

A HISTORICAL OVERVIEW OF
SUSTAINABILITY EDUCATION IN BUSINESS SCHOOLS

Facilitating Events

Despite the obvious relationship of business activities and the natural environment, and despite the recognition of this relationship by both business and environmental nongovenmental organization (NGO) sectors, environmental issues garnered very little focused attention from business education in the 1970s and 1980s. However, at least one textbook in this area, with a significant engineering emphasis, was published during this period (Edmunds & Letey, 1973). At some business schools interest in the subject was high among students. For example, the Committee on Corporate Responsibility, a student group at the Stanford Business School, helped sponsor a 1980 conference on corporations and the environment which resulted in the publication of a book (Brunner, Miller, & Stockholm, 1981). But such attention, aside from some discussion in business ethics or business and society classes, appears to have been rare. Several business and society scholars studied and wrote about environmental issues during the 1970s and 1980s, and discussion of environmental issues appeared in most business and society—and some business ethics—texts, readings, and casebooks during this period (e.g., Davis & Blomstrom, 1971; Sethi, 1971; Steiner & Steiner, 1972; Sturdivant & Robinson, 1977; Velasquez, 1982). The importance of this attention cannot be overstated. However, addressing environmental issues solely within these courses may have been interpreted by many students as suggesting that although environmental issues had legal and ethical implications, they had little to do with economic performance, strategic decisions, or day to day business operations, other than as annoying cost factors.

Several events and organizations have contributed to a significant increase in business school attention to the environment since the start of the 1990s. However, five major environmental crises and issues captured widespread public attention during the middle and late 1980s: the Bhopal gas leak in India in 1984, the documentation of the ozone hole over Antarctica in 1985, the major nuclear accident at Chernobyl in 1986, the record breaking heat wave and forest fires in the Western United States of 1988 and the accompanying first wave of media attention to global warming, and the Exxon Valdez oil spill of 1989. Given these events, the twentieth anniversary of Earth Day in 1990 caused attention to the environment to rise significantly. Many business academics and practitioners were becoming convinced that environmental issues were of utmost importance, resulting in publication of numerous books in the early 1990s aimed at practitioners, but also suitable for use in business school courses (e.g., Cairncross, 1992; Hawken, 1993; Makower, 1993; Schmidheiny, 1992; Smart, 1992)

In 1987 the National Wildlife Federation's (NWF) Corporate Conservation Council (CCC) became interested in attention to the environment in management education. The CCC was designed to build bridges between the NWF and industry, and consisted of a few NWF staff members and representatives (generally directors) from the environmental affairs units of about a half dozen corporations. It became concerned about two issues: the degree of understanding of business issues by environmental affairs staff, and the degree of understanding of environmental issues by business school graduates. With respect to the latter topic, CCC staffer Mark Haveman, a University of Michigan MBA graduate, attempted to discover how much coverage there was of environmental issues in MBA curricula. After phone conversations with business faculty members throughout the United States, Haveman concluded that with rare exceptions, coverage seemed to be restricted to courses in business and society and in business ethics. In addition, many faculty members expressed the belief that relatively little in the way of adequate teaching materials on business and the environment existed. As a result, the CCC decided to fund a project designed to increase curricular treatment of environmental topics in the business school.

The CCC's Curriculum Development Project extended from 1988 to 1991. Three management professors in the business and society area— Rogene Buchholz of Loyola University of New Orleans, Alfred Marcus of the University of Minnesota, and James Post of Boston University (along with several graduate students)—worked to identify existing cases and other curriculum materials, develop new cases, and design and offer pilot sustainability courses. These courses were offered at the undergraduate and graduate levels in 1989 and 1990, and revised courses were offered in 1991. The case studies developed by the authors and their colleagues were subsequently published in book form in 1992 (Buchholz, Marcus, & Post, 1992). A textbook by Buchholz appeared the following year (Buchholz, 1993). An unpublished annotated bibliography of approximately

400 articles, books, and cases on business and natural environment topics was also developed. In addition, project team members developed and participated in symposia at meetings sponsored by the Academy of Management, the Center for Business Ethics at Bentley College, and the North American Association for Environmental Education detailing the project's activities and urging increased business school attention to environmental issues (see e.g., Post, 1990; Rands, 1990, 1991).

An underlying assumption of the project was that the creation of pilot courses and course materials would spur faculty attention to environmental issues, resulting in increased exposure of MBA students to environmental issues in their program coursework. Furthermore, the project assumed that such exposure would lead to students developing greater environmental awareness as well as corporate environmental management skills. As students embarked on business careers, the project logic went, they would begin to apply their concern and skills to environmental issues facing their employers, resulting in improved organizational environmental performance (Rands, 1990). Regarding the first assumption, the project was generally viewed as a success. In addition to the two books that resulted from the project, the effort received national media attention and generated substantial requests for information from business school faculty throughout the United States. The second assumption, that environmental education of business students would eventually result in improved organizational environmental performance, has never, to our knowledge, been rigorously examined.

While the CCC project was being conducted, another effort to increase attention to the environment at business schools was initiated. In 1990 the Management Institute for Environment and Business (MEB) was founded by Matthew Arnold. Soon afterwards Dirk Long, like Arnold a former Ivy League graduate business student, joined MEB. Based on the same concerns as the CCC and originally funded by the U.S. EPA, one of MEB's first actions was co-sponsorship—along with the United Nations Environmental Program, Tufts University, and INSEAD—of a conference held in October 1990 at INSEAD in France. This conference brought together faculty, government, NGO and business leaders from the USA and Europe to discuss the state of and prospects for environmental education within business schools (Arnold, 1991). The following year MEB published a resource guide updating the CCC's annotated bibliography of curriculum materials, including a list of business school faculty from various disciplines and nations with environmental interests (Pennell, Choi, & Molinaro, 1992). Over the next few years MEB developed discipline-specific bibliographies (including one on strategy and environment), worked with faculty to generate case studies, and established a pilot project with five business schools to increase attention to the environment

within the curriculum. Then, in 1994, it initiated the Business Environment Learning and Leadership (BELL) program. BELL's activities over
the next decade included providing an electronic newsletter, holding
annual conferences, publishing cases, providing access to curriculum
resources, providing technical assistance to participating schools, creating
opportunities for student teams to consult with environmental entrepreneurs in developing countries, and conducting surveys toward producing
biennial reports on the state of business school environmental education
(Bunch, 2003). Many of these activities significantly expanded after MEB
merged with the World Resources Institute (WRI) in 1996 and became
WRI's Sustainable Enterprise Program (Starik & Dyer, 1999). Included in
these expanded activities was the creation of BELL programs for China
and Latin America (Bunch, 2003). Since the mid-2000s BELL has
decreased its emphasis on promoting business school sustainability education in Europe and North America, focusing instead on China, Brazil,
and Mexico (WRI, 2008).

A third impetus for increased business school attention to environmental issues was provided by the creation of the Greening of Industry Network (GIN). GIN was created by business school scholars in Europe and
North America as a forum for researchers to meet with one another and
practitioners from business, government, and the NGO communities.
GIN's first conference was held in the Netherlands in 1991 and its second
conference in the United States in 1993, with subsequent conferences
alternating between Europe and North America. Asia joined the rotation
in 2001 when GIN held a conference in Thailand. GIN conferences regularly include a number of presentations on environmental education
within business schools and have resulted in books (e.g., Fischer & Schot,
1993), as well as annual issues of *Business Strategy and the Environment*
devoted to papers from the conference (e.g., Sarkis & Gollagher, 2008).

The Organizations and the Natural Environment (ONE) Interest
Group of the Academy of Management (AOM) was established in 1994,
following a 3 year organizing effort. After 12 more years, in 2007, ONE
was upgraded to division status within the AOM. Since 1995, ONE has
provided a forum for presentation of scholarly work on environmental
management as well as symposia and workshop sessions on environmental issues and education. The BELL, GIN, and ONE-AOM meetings have
all provided substantially greater opportunities for faculty and doctoral
students in business schools to meet and exchange ideas about teaching
materials and strategies for incorporating environmental topics into business school education. Of these, BELL was the most education-focused,
GIN the most practice-focused, and ONE the most research-oriented.

With the BELL program's shift in emphasis, two elements of the role
that it had played—providing assistance with course materials and ranking

sustainability oriented business school programs—have been assumed by The Aspen Institute. This organization was created in 1950 by a chairman of the Container Corporation of America, and named after the Colorado (U.S.) resort town whose natural beauty inspired him to create a series of executive seminars on society, values, and culture. The Institute expanded over the next several decades to focus on humanistic studies, adding conference facilities in 1979 near the Chesapeake Bay on Maryland's Eastern Shore (U.S.). Most recently, since the mid-1990s, it developed nearly two dozen programs on numerous "big picture" topics within business and society, energy, and environment, and other areas with a sustainability orientation. Regarding the first area, two efforts worth noting are Caseplace.org and Beyond Grey Pinstripes.

Caseplace.org (Aspen Institute, 2008b) is a free, online library of hundreds of syllabi, cases, articles, and other resources related to business sustainability, covering more than 30 business disciplines and boasting 32,000 registered users. Topics range from business/government relations to technological change and development, with nearly 500 resource items directly related to the topic of sustainability.

Beyond Grey Pinstripes (BGP), is a biennial assessment of business school graduate curricula and faculty research on the topic of social and environmental issues in business. BGP was initiated by the World Resources Institute in 1998, with Aspen assuming responsibility for the project that produces the biennial report (*Beyond Grey Pinstripes*, 2007). The project invited hundreds of accredited business school programs to submit syllabi and research citations related to sustainability topics in order to qualify for recognition in its "Global 100" listing. By inviting applications, the project seeks to advance innovation, inform prospective MBA students, inform business recruiters, and otherwise disseminate best practices in business school scholarship and activity.

Both projects appear to have had a moderate, positive influence toward increasing the quality and quantity of such scholarship and activity by at least focusing attention on business social and environmental issues for the various stakeholders they seek to impact. With Caseplace.org, business faculties less familiar with social and environmental issues have an information resource from which to draw, enabling them to stay abreast of opportunities to incorporate these issues into their curricula. BGP has injected an element of low-level competition into business school teaching and research, with schools commonly citing their BGP rankings. The existence of BGP has more than likely increased the salience of sustainability issues within business academia. Within the past decade, both projects have expanded in size and staff, coinciding with increases in the breadth and depth of sustainability scholarship.

Four other events—three journal special issues and a post-conference event—should also be noted for their impact on business school sustainability education. In 1994 a special double issue of the *Journal of Teaching in International Business* (*JTIB*) (Mintu, Lozada, & Polonsky, 1994) contained nine articles that raised issues and offered suggestions for faculty to consider in incorporating environmental issues into the business curriculum The following year a special post-conference workshop was held after the Organizational Behavior Teaching Society's (OBTS) annual conference, held that year at Bucknell University. Faculty who had incorporated environmental issues into their courses offered suggestions for others considering making this effort. This workshop was significant in that the OBTS was, at that time, one of the two major North American fora devoted to the practice of management education. (The other organization was the Management Education and Development division of the Academy of Management) More recently, the *Journal of Management Education* (*JME* a publication of the OBTS) devoted a special issue to teaching about the natural environment in management education (Egri & Rogers, 2003). The eight articles in this issue provide conceptual frameworks, pedagogical approaches, program implementation case studies, course designs, exercises and activities that faculty can use by faculty in integrating environmental issues into existing business courses or in developing stand alone courses devoted to sustainability. This issue was followed by a special issue of *Business Strategy and the Environment* (*BSE*) in 2005 (Springett & Kearins, 2005) containing four articles, three of which addressed education for sustainability of business graduate students. While many of the same themes and challenges are raised, the level of sophistication in the *JME* and *BSE* articles is far greater than in the *JTIB* articles, reflecting the dramatic expansion in education for sustainability that had occurred in business schools since 1993. Another special issue of *JME* on sustainability education was published in 2009 (Rusinko & Sama, 2009), and a 2010 special issue of the *Academy of Management Learning and Education* journal will also be devoted to the topic.

Courses

While the courses offered by the CCC program participants were the first widely publicized courses devoted to business and the natural environment, others had undoubtedly been offered earlier. Evidence of these courses is provided by other books on the topic that emerged in the early 1990s and was reported to have been piloted by their authors in their own environmental courses (e.g., Stead & Stead, 1992). At some schools, such as the University of Minnesota, adjunct faculty had occasionally been offering electives on business and the natural environment from a variety of perspectives (Rands, 1991). Accompanying—and in the wake of—Earth Day 1990, the number of environmentally focused courses offered in business schools appeared to have dramatically expanded, although we have found no comprehensive studies charting this growth.

Centers and Institutes

In recent years the creation of sustainability centers and institutes focusing on facilitating the development and diffusion of sustainable practices and technologies has emerged as a new means for academic institutions to address sustainability. A recent examination of these centers, *A Closer Look at Applied Sustainability Centers* (Aspen Institute, 2008a) identified 240 different academic applied sustainability centers around the world. Many of these centers focus on agriculture, forestry, minerals, and other engineering and technological topics. An increasing number are focusing on sustainability issues directly relating to business. Most of the business-focused sustainability centers appear to have been established since 2000. However, a few of the more prominent ones—such as the Bren School of Environmental Science and Management at the University of California-Santa Barbara and the Erb Institute for Global Sustainable Enterprise at the University of Michigan—were established in the mid-1990s. The Aspen Institute report examines 20 of the more business-focused centers in some detail, noting emerging trends such as rapid growth, diversity in focus, interdisciplinary and collaborative nature, benefits to sponsoring universities in recruiting faculty and students, and the development of strong and trusted partnerships with the corporate sector (Aspen Institute, 2008a).

RESOURCES FOR
SUSTAINABILITY EDUCATION IN BUSINESS SCHOOLS

Teaching Materials and Methods

Lists of teaching resources are available from several organizations. ONE provides an online list of teaching resources (ONE Teaching Resources, 2008), including a list of course syllabi. WRI's BELL program also provides a list of thirty course syllabi, 20 of which focus on environment and sustainability (WRI, 2008). Currently, the most significant online teaching material resource is, the Aspen Institute's Center for Business Education's CasePlace.org (Aspen Institute, 2008a).

WRI also provides an online annotated directory of cases (WRI, 2006). This directory lists cases from various sources, in various business disciplines: accounting (20 cases listed), business and public policy (75), economics (39), entrepreneurship (14), finance (43), marketing (33), negotiation (23), organizational behavior (29), production and operations management (40), strategy and management (131), and sustainable development (19). While many of the cases are cross-listed in different disciplines, this is nevertheless a rich body of material. It does not, however, list any cases published since 2000. Additional sources of cases include casebooks (e.g., Rowledge, Barton, & Brady, 1999) and books emerging from conferences (e.g., Waage, 2003) and the Aspen Institute (Aspen Institute, 2008a)

In comparison to a decade and a half ago, when *Management for a Small Planet* (Stead & Stead, 1992) and *Principles of Environmental Management* (Buchholz, 1993) were the only environmental management texts readily available in the United States, numerous books are now available. Revised editions of both of these texts have been published, along with several other texts and books of readings (e.g., Piasecki, Fletcher, & Mendelson, 1999; Reinhardt, 2000; Reinhardt & Vietor, 1996; Russo, 1999; Schaltegger, Burritt, & Petersen, 2003; Welford & Starkey, 1996) that can serve as primary readings for a course in environmental management. Numerous trade books, while oriented more toward executives, can also be used in a broadly focused environmental management course (e.g., Elkington, 1998; Frankel, 1998; Freeman, Pierce, & Dodd, 2000; Shrivastava, 1996; Wasik, 1996). Academically oriented treatments of corporate environmentalism that can be used in graduate classes are also available (e.g., Hoffman, 2001; Prakash, 2000). Finally, there are trade oriented books that can be used in more environmentally focused courses directed at subjects such as accounting (e.g., Bennett & James, 2000; Schaltegger & Burritt, 2000), finance (e.g., Bouma, Jeucken, & Klinkers, 2001), environmental marketing (e.g., Fuller, 1999; McKenzie-Mohr & Smith, 1999), purchasing (e.g., Russel, 1998), operations management (e.g., Sarkis, 2001), product design (e.g., Charter & Tischner, 2001; Lewis, Gertsakis, Grant, Morelli, & Sweatman, 2001), and organizational environmental change (e.g., Doppelt, 2003; Dunphy, Griffiths, & Benn, 2003; Nattrass & Altomare, 1999).

Along with the expansion of knowledgeable authors and increased interest by U.S. business practitioners, the expanded book offerings reflect a dramatically increased availability of books from European authors, particularly as the result of the publishing efforts of Greenleaf Press. While sustainable management readings options have increased dramatically, there is still a need for the kind of instructor and student friendly resource materials that exist for core subjects such as organizational behavior, principles of management, and strategy. This reflects the lack of a standardized body of topics and principles for this still emerging field. A particular need exists for sustainability resources dealing with the fields of human resource management, operations management, project management, and the management of information systems. These needs are not surprising, given the size of the market and submarket niches.

Happily, society beyond academia has recently become aware of sustainability issues, particularly those regarding climate crises. As a result, at least compared to a decade or 2 ago, the number of popular magazines and other published sources providing extended coverage of these issues has increased dramatically. For example, even many of the traditional business publications, such as the *Wall Street Journal*, the *Economist*, the *Financial Times*, *Fortune*, and others, have followed *National Geographic*, *Scientific American*, and *New Scientist* in publishing multi-page sections on climate change and related sustainability issues, all of which are potential resources for the sustainability management educator.

In addition, the number of Web sites and YouTube and other online videos that address sustainability management issues continues to expand far faster than any educator or student could possibly absorb. Sites such as http://www.cbsm.com, which focuses on community based social marketing as a way to advance sustainability implementation, are becoming both popular and useful. Over the past decade, sustainability organizations, such as the U.S. Green Building Council, the World Resources Institute, and the World Business Council for Sustainable Development, have continued to expand and improve their respective Web sites to make relevant, timely, and important information available to the sustainability management educator and student. In addition, a number of sustainability oriented databases, particularly those using the Global Reporting Initiative sustainability reporting format, may be useful to sustainability management educators. These databases include the SAS Sustainability Solution and the Zumer database.

One interesting set of materials from which sustainability management educators can draw is the two-volume set of articles from Greenleaf entitled *Teaching Business Sustainability*, edited by Chris Galea (2004, 2007). The first volume, subtitled *From Theory to Practice*, features more than 20 chapters dealing with a diverse set of sustainability management education topics, from mental models and environmental sustainability to whole systems thinking and social sustainability. The diversity of topics in this volume is matched only by the diversity of authors, including academics from around the world, and practitioners and consultants representing multiple business organizations and industries. The second volume, titled *Cases, Simulations, and Experiential Approaches* is similarly diverse, even more practitioner/consultant oriented, and chockfull of interesting sustainability management education approaches and resources. Along these lines, a special issue of the *Academy of Management Learning & Education* focusing on the topic of sustainability in management education, due for publication in September of 2010, will likely include a diversity of authors, topics, approaches, methods, and materials that will hopefully also advance the development of sustainability management education planning, implementation, and evaluation.

Sustainability Management in Business and B-School Academic Research

The recent substantial increase in attention to sustainability management education mirrors similar trends among business practitioners and academic researchers. Over the past few years, businesses from Wal-Mart to the hundreds of members of the World Business Council for Sustainable Business to the several dozen green businesses in the Sustainable Business Network of Washington (DC), have developed and implemented significant programs to advance energy efficiency, pollution prevention, green supply chain management, water conservation, and biodiversity preservation, among many others. These and many more businesses, as well as government agencies and nonprofit organizations, have designed environmental management systems, produced green products and services, and reported on both their social and environmental sustainability programs and results.

Business academic researchers have not been far behind in studying these phenomena, given the increasing number of academic journal special issues, conferences, and case studies that have focused on sustainability management topics in the past 2 years. Perhaps the best example of sustainability management as a salient business academic research theme is the selection of the 2009 Academy of Management annual meetings theme of "Green Management Matters." The Academy of Management boasts about 18,000 faculty, doctoral student, and executive members from 105 countries, more than 9,000 of whom participate in annual meetings, recently generating more than 5,800 research papers at its 2008 annual event. For the 2009 meetings, Academy members have been encouraged to focus on a wide range of sustainability management research topics, including design-for-environment, green-collar work, industrial ecosystems, and voluntary environmental programs.

Environmentally Oriented Rankings of Management Education Programs

While courses on sustainability are now likely offered at hundreds of business schools, a much smaller subset of schools offer official programs that have a particular focus on sustainability. These programs are increasingly the subject of media attention (e.g., Charski, 2008). At least some of this attention is due to the Beyond Grey Pinstripes reports, issued roughly biannually since the late 1990s.

As part of its effort to increase attention to environmental issues in business schools, WRI issued a report entitled *Grey Pinstripes with Green Ties: MBA Programs Where the Environment Matters.* The report identified eight schools based on outstanding curricula and other attention to environmental issues in their MBA programs. The eight schools, which were listed alphabetically, were George Washington University, New York University, Northwestern University, University of Michigan, University of North Carolina—Chapel Hill, University of Tennessee, University of Virginia, and University of Washington (WRI, 1998).

In 1999 WRI partnered with the Aspen Institute in an update of the report. *Beyond Grey Pinstripes: Preparing Managers for Social and Environmental Stewardship* considered not only attention to environmental issues, but to social responsibility as well. Business schools recognized for attention to social issues included those at Case Western, Harvard, Loyola Marymount, Northwestern, Stanford, Michigan, Notre Dame, Pennsylvania, Pittsburgh, and Virginia. Schools recognized for attention to environmental issues were Cornell, George Washington, Rensselaer Polytechnic, Tulane, Michigan, North Carolina, Pennsylvania, Texas and Vanderbilt (WRI, 1999).

The 2001 *Beyond Grey Pinstripes* again listed schools based on attention to either social or environmental issues. Scores were based on three factors: student coursework, institutional support, and faculty research. In terms of both social and environmental attention, schools were listed in two groups: those on the cutting edge, and those showing significant activities. Cutting edge schools for social impact included Harvard, Loyola Marymount, Michigan, North Carolina, and York. Those recognized for significant activity included California—Berkeley, UCLA, Case Western, George Washington, ITESM (Mexico), New Mexico, Pennsylvania, Pittsburgh, Stanford, Wake Forest, and Yale. Twelve universities were recognized for environmental attention: George Washington, Jyvaskyla (Finland), Michigan, North Carolina and Yale at the cutting edge, and California—Berkeley, UCLA, Harvard, Hong Kong Polytechnic (China),

Illinois Institute of Technology, ITESM, Pennsylvania, RPI, Vanderbilt and York at the significant activity level (*Beyond Grey Pinstripes*, 2001).

In 2003, *Beyond Grey Pinstripes* listed schools in three tiers—schools on the cutting edge, schools with significant activity, and schools with moderate activity—but no longer separated them based on social or environmental focus. Another change was that extracurricular activities were considered in the rankings, along with attention to teaching and research. George Washington, Michigan, North Carolina, Stanford, Yale, and York were the six schools in the top group. Nine schools were listed in the second tier, with twenty-one schools listed in the third (*Beyond Grey Pinstripes*, 2003). Most, but not all, of the highly rated schools from 2001 remained on the 2003 list of 36 schools.

Thirty schools were ranked in 2005, this time in simple order rather than in tiers. Rankings were derived from the ratings of programs on four criteria: the number of courses giving attention to social and environmental issues, the percentage of course time devoted to these issues, the degree to which courses emphasized the ability to integrate social/environmental and economic considerations, and the amount of faculty research attention to these issues. George Washington, Michigan, North Carolina, Stanford, and York remained highly ranked, and were joined in the top ten by Cornell, Notre Dame, and Wake Forest, as well as by ESADE of Spain (*Beyond Grey Pinstripes*, 2005).

In recognition of the expansion of attention to social and environmental issues by universities throughout the world, the 2007-8 rankings were dramatically expanded, listing 100 universities (*Beyond Grey Pinstripes*, 2007). Rankings were based on the same four criteria used in 2005. Many of the same schools dominated the upper ranks, but there were some notable new additions. For example, Duquesne University, which had never been ranked in earlier reports, was ranked number eight.

THE CURRENT STATUS OF
SUSTAINABILITY IN MANAGEMENT EDUCATION

Sustainability receives far greater treatment today in management education than it did 2 decades—or even 5 years—ago. Anecdotal evidence suggests that the number of management courses focusing on sustainability has expanded tremendously, although no reliable estimates exist as to how many such courses are taught. *Beyond Grey Pinstripes, 2007–2008* indicates that the 111 schools participating in its survey reported an average of 17 elective courses per school featuring some social and/or environmental content, and an average of 6 largely dedicated to such issues. While the number of elective courses addressing or dedicated to sustainability issues is undoubtedly lower, they are definitely becoming more common in the management curriculum.

Another indication of growing interest in sustainability education in business schools is that the Association to Advance Collegiate Schools of Business (AACSB), the major accrediting body of business schools, has begun to hold annual seminars on sustainability. The first, held in July 2008 in Salt Lake City, Utah, attracted nearly 200 participants from business schools, exceeding organizers' expectations. The conference included presentations from a number of business practitioners regarding the significance of sustainability to the private sector, and a review of some of the ways in which companies are responding to increased demands for triple bottom line sustainability. Presentations were also given by faculty and administrators from a number of business schools, highlighting their efforts to incorporate sustainability into their management education efforts (AACSB, 2008).

One of the clearest indicators of the increased management education attention to sustainability is the growth in the number of specialized graduate business programs that focus, to one degree or another, on the topic. While the total number of such programs may be higher, by late 2008 thirty institutions in the United States and Canada had provided information to the Association for the Advancement of Sustainability in Higher Education (AASHE) indicating that they offered either sustainability focused master's degree programs (11 schools), concentrations, emphases or specializations (16), or certificates (6) in sustainable business (AASHE, 2008). In addition, several joint or dual degree programs exist. Below we provide brief examples of some of each type of program, beginning with certificates.

Certificate Programs

Certificate programs typically consist of a relatively small number of courses, and can be taken either as part of, of separately from, a business degree program. The latter element makes them particularly appealing both to working professionals and to nonbusiness students.

One of the first MBA programs to offer a concentration in environmental management was established in the early 1990s at the University of Washington. While the concentration is no longer in existence, MBA and other graduate students at the university can take six courses (three required courses and three electives) enabling them to receive a graduate certificate in environmental management (University of Washington, 2008).

Stanford's Graduate School of Business (2008) offers MBA students a Certificate in Public Management, which includes attention to environmental issues. Students have a choice of a general public management certificate, or one emphasizing government, nonprofit management, or socially responsible business. Up to four environmentally focused courses may be taken in some of the tracks.

The Stuart School of Business at the Illinois Institute of Technology offers two environmental certificates for nondegree seeking professionals, one in compliance and pollution prevention, and one in sustainable enterprise. Each of the certificate programs consist of four courses from an MS program in environmental management, and courses completed as part of a certificate can be applied to an MS degree (Illinois Institute of Technology, 2008a). Other schools offering certificate programs in business and sustainability include Arizona State, California State University—San Bernardino, Portland State University, and York University (AASHE, 2008).

Concentrations, Emphases, and Specializations

In addition to its certificate programs, the Illinois Institute of Technology has for a number of years offered a fourteen course MS degree in environmental management (Illinois Institute of Technology, 2008c). It has recently added an MBA concentration in sustainable enterprise, which requires six credits of environmentally focused courses in addition to business core courses and additional electives (Illinois Institute of Technology, 2008b).

George Washington University offered an environmental MBA concentration requiring four environmentally focused courses beginning in 1999. Since that time, it has incorporated sustainability content within many of its core courses, given that the overall MBA program has become focused on globally responsible management (GW News Center, 2008). Along with those core courses, GW offers multiple sustainability oriented elective courses, including several that are offered through distance learning and study abroad formats. Students graduating with interests in sustainability have made careers in the government, business, and NGO sectors, both locally and globally.

The University of North Carolina (UNC) at Chapel Hill's Kenan-Flagler Business School offers an MBA concentration in Sustainable Enterprise. While the Sustainable Enterprise concentration originally consisted of the equivalent of eight courses, it is now the equivalent of a four course concentration intended to supplement a more typical concentration such as finance, supply chain management, or management consulting (UNC, 2007).

Vanderbilt offers an environmental management emphasis within its MBA degree. Similar to the program at UNC, the environmental management emphasis is taken in addition to a more traditional concentration. Students are required to take at least one of two environmentally focused courses offered within the Owen Graduate School of Management, and two or three additional environmentally focused courses offered by other departments on campus (VCEMS Environmental Studies, 2008). Vanderbilt also offers a more interdisciplinary Masters in Environmental Science, which requires two environmentally focused management courses.

Other North American universities that offer MBAs or master's in management degrees with sustainability tracks, majors, or concentrations include Aquinas College (Michigan), Benedictine University (Illinois), Brandeis University (Massachusetts), Duke University (North Carolina), the Rochester Institute of Technology (New York), the University of British Columbia, the University of Maine, the University of Oregon, two campuses of the University of South Florida, and York University (AASHE, 2008).

Although no longer in operation, it is worth noting one innovative approach to delivering an MBA concentration in sustainability. From about 1999–2004, the Bren School of Environmental Science and Management at University of California-Santa Barbara offered an MBA Emphasis in Corporate Environmental Management for MBA students from any of the five business schools in the UC system (Berkley, Davis, UCLA, Irvine, and Riverside). Second year MBA students could come to Bren for 3 weekends during each of 2 quarters and take 5 required courses offered by Bren faculty. They could also take an additional one or two electives. The program capstone course was a management practicum in which students worked on an environmental project with an outside organization. The program was funded by a donor with the intent of infusing business schools with a greater understanding of environmental issues. As other units of the University of California system began to attend to these issues—for example, UC-Berkeley now offers an Engineering and Business for Sustainability Certificate Program (University of California–Berkeley, 2008)—the Bren MBA program was judged to have accomplished its goals and was ended. The Bren School continues to offer a master of environmental science and management (MESM) degree program for students attending UCSB in which business sustainability oriented courses are part of the curriculum, with corporate environmental management as one of six specializations available within the program (Bren School, 2008).

Dual and Joint Degrees

Established in 1992, one of the longest running and most well known environmental MBA programs is the University of Michigan's Corporate Environmental Management Program (CEMP). The CEMP program was created by Stuart Hart, who later founded UNC's Sustainable Enterprise program. CEMP is a joint program of the university's College of Business and its School of Natural Resources & the Environment (SNRE). Students enrolled in the 3 year CEMP program must spend three semesters in each college, graduating with not only an MBA, but also with a master of science in natural resources and environment or a master of landscape architecture degree (University of Michigan, 2008).

Yale University has a dual degree program linking the School of Management and the School of Forestry and Environmental Studies. This program, in existence since 1989, has a number of similarities to Michigan's CEMP program: the Yale program is a 3 year program, it results in both an MBA and a MS degree, and the program director, Gary Brewer (himself a former dean of the Michigan School of Natural Resources & the Environment) has a joint appointment in both schools (Yale, 2008). There are seven environmentally focused courses taught by Yale SOM faculty, several of which are cross-listed with forestry and environmental studies.

There are also dual degree programs involving two universities as partners. For example, the Vermont Law School, which is consistently rated as one of the top environmental law programs in the nation, has several dual degree programs. One of these, in which students earn both an MBA and a master of environmental law and policy degree, operates in conjunction with the Tuck School of Business at Dartmouth. In 2008, Vermont Law School added a second dual degree program with Thunderbird School of Global Management, in which students earn both a JD and an MBA in Global Management (Vermont Law School, 2008).

Sustainability Focused Programs

A relatively new and exciting development in management education for sustainability is that of programs offered by institutes specializing only in environmental MBAs. Two such programs exist in the United States: Bainbridge Graduate Institute's MBA in Sustainable Business, and the Presidio School of Management, MBA Graduate Program. Another formerly independent program, the Green MBA once offered by the Institute for Environmental Leadership, is now housed at Dominican University of California (2008).

Bainbridge Graduate Institute, located on Bainbridge Island, near Seattle, Washington (United States) is perhaps the longest operating (since 2002), best-known small business school focused on sustainability. The school offers an MBA in sustainable business, a certificate in sustainable business, and a certificate in sustainable entrepreneurship and intrapreneurship. The MBA is a 2 or 3 year program of 20 courses, while its certificate programs are three courses in length, all offered in hybrid— that is, both in-class and online—formats (Bainbridge Graduate Institute, 2008). The most recent ranking of sustainability and social responsibility offerings by graduate business programs (Net Impact, 2008), which examined 64 programs, ranked BGI first in 5 of 13 categories.

The four-semester long MBA in sustainable management at the Presidio School of Management consists of 16 courses. Four courses are taken from each of four areas—people (organizational behavior, strategy), numbers (accounting, finance, operations management, economics), markets (economics, marketing and a capstone venture project course) and sustainability—with one course being taken from each area every semester (Presidio School of Management, 2008). Sustainability concepts and orientations are infused into every course.

Several previously existing small colleges and universities have recently developed sustainability focused MBA programs. These include Green Mountain College, Marlboro College, Goddard College, Antioch University New England, Dominican University of California, and Maharishi University of Management.

Several of these programs are located in New England. Green Mountain College in Poultney, Vermont, which has won a number of awards for its campus ecology project, began an online sustainable business MBA program in 2006. Drawing on students from across seven U.S. states, including those in both the West and Midwest, the 2-year program features 10 core courses lasting 6 weeks, two short-term residencies, and concentrations in general business and nonprofit organization management consisting of 3 elective courses each. Goddard College, also located in central Vermont, offers a 48 credit "low residency" master of arts program in socially responsible business and sustainable communities. students can also opt for a shorter program that yields a certificate of graduate study (Goddard College, 2008).

Marlboro College, one of the newest (2007) entrants in the small sustainable business program market, is located in Marlboro, Vermont with a graduate center in nearby Brattleboro, Vermont. Its 2-year program consists of 12 courses, also uses a hybrid delivery model, and includes internships, independent studies, and an international study component. Antioch University New England, located in New Hampshire—a school that has long been highly regarded for its environmental studies program

—has also developed an MBA program in organizational and environmental sustainability (Antioch, 2008). As with most of the other small programs, Antioch uses a hybrid delivery program, in which both business and environmental studies faculty members teach courses.

Dominican University of California's MBA in sustainable enterprise program emphasizes business fundamentals, sustainability, and leadership. Dominican also offers two 5-month sustainable enterprise certificate programs. One, "Green Your MBA," allows MBA students at other universities to augment their university's MBA curriculum with sustainability focused courses. The other program, "Green Your Enterprise," is provided on-site at organizations that can guarantee a cohort of 10 individuals (Dominican University of California, 2008). Maharishi University of Management, located in eastern Iowa, offers a residential MBA in sustainability that takes 1 to 2 years to complete, depending on whether students already have an undergraduate business degree. The program addresses five key areas: self sustainability, sustainable entrepreneurship, sustainable business solutions, sustainable management, and sustainable living (Maharishi University of Management, 2008).

The most recent development in management sustainability education programs is that business schools at larger universities, already accredited by AACSB, have begun to offer sustainability infused MBA programs. These include Duquesne University and Colorado State University. Duquesne had for many years offered a part-time MBA, but when it created its first full-time program it decided to make the entire program focus on sustainability. The residential program is 12 months long. Sustainability is integrated into all courses, which are delivered in a modular fashion. In addition to receiving a general MBA with a concentration in sustainability, students may decide to spend extra time in the program to earn an additional concentration in finance, environmental management, or supply chain management (Duquesne University, 2008).

A final sustainability focused program is one offered by Colorado State University (CSU). Although not a traditional residential MBA program, CSU offers several different MBA options. It recently introduced a full-time residential global social and sustainable enterprise (GSSE) master of science in business administration. Although this program is similar to other ones in emphasizing the environmental component, it is unique in the sense that it is aimed more at the social justice component of sustainability. The program is intended to develop students who can assist in the creation of economically successful, environmentally sustainable enterprises contributing to the social welfare of the poor, particularly in the global South (Colorado State University, 2008). The program admits cohorts of 25 students per year, evenly split between U.S. and international students, and draws upon diverse disciplines such as business, engineering, environmental studies, and international development.

Questions Regarding Sustainability Programs

Advocates of attention to sustainability in management education are, as this diversity of programs suggests, experimenting with various approaches by which such attention can be given. Many new approaches will undoubtedly yet emerge. We are nowhere near the point at which the most effective types of approaches can be determined. The need exists to continue creating new programs and refining existing ones, and to disseminate information about materials, teaching methods, and course and program design. While we engage in such innovations, however, we must not neglect their critique and evaluation.

The need for dramatically expanding and increasing the effectiveness of management education for sustainability requires that we continually explore questions such as the following:

- What are the appropriate goals of sustainability courses and programs (Rands, 1993)?
- What knowledge, attitudes and skills do business professionals need to contribute to the creation of environmentally sustainable organizations (Rands, 2009; Starik & Rands, 1995)?
- What types of backgrounds are helpful or perhaps necessary for students to develop these attributes?
- How well do various delivery mechanisms (residential, distance and hybrid) accomplish program goals?
- What are the relative impacts of certificate and concentration approaches versus fully integrated approaches?
- Of what duration must a program be to provide students an adequate education in sustainability in management?
- What is the relative effectiveness of interdisciplinary sustainability programs versus ones in which all courses are taught by business faculty with expertise in sustainability?
- How many environmentally focused courses are necessary, and what business sustainability topics are most important?
- What teaching materials and methods are most effective?
- How do the various dimensions raised above interact? Are there more and less effective program configurations that emerge from these interactions?

These questions are ones that are difficult to answer, and are of the sort usually explored by scholars from schools of education rather than schools of business. It is tempting not to worry about giving them intense examination, particularly when securing any attention at all to sustainability in the management curriculum is, at most schools, still an unrealized goal. But the sustainability challenges we face suggest that we need to pay significant attention to these and similar questions, so we can move rapidly in developing and deploying effective sustainability education efforts. Our consideration of the future of sustainability in management education begins with a review of some of these challenges.

THE FUTURE OF SUSTAINABILITY IN MANAGEMENT EDUCATION

As "glorious" a quest as sustainability management education has become over the past 2 decades, the next 20 years may be even more challenging, both for educators and for students. While a few sustainability indicators—such as surface water quality improvements and reductions of concentrations of ambient lead and other heavy metal toxins in some regions, communities, and ecosystems—point in positive directions, the general trend for many other sustainability indicators is toward ever more urgent and significant sustainability challenges in the future. For example, atmospheric carbon and other greenhouse gas concentrations associated with climate crises are increasing at higher than expected rates worldwide. This is potentially moving us closer to the realization of catastrophic climate change, first and foremost for many of the world's disadvantaged societies. Biodiversity crises, including the extinction of large numbers of valuable animal and plant species, are another significantly worsening sustainability trend. This trend and other similar ones suggest that future generations of humans will likely experience rapidly deteriorating ecosystems, such as fisheries, forests, and coral reefs, including those that have provided humans with a host of important and beneficial resources for millennia. Other sustainability challenges loom, including desertification, the uncontrollable spread of debilitating diseases, falling water tables and increasing groundwater pollution, and the absolute increase of our species' population. An expanding human population means both more people with high consumption lifestyles, and more of our fellow humans subsisting at or below poverty levels. These and many other daunting sustainability challenges portend that management educators and students have only just begun to perceive the scope and depth of these issues of survival and quality of life, and to collectively and individually take positive steps to address them. Below we suggest five areas needing particular attention.

First of all, these trends appear to call for management educators and students to increase the pace, intensity, and strategic orientation of the sustainability management education activities in which they are involved. Sustainability management courses, which likely need to be significantly expanded in number and quality as soon as possible, should also aim to proceed quickly through discussion of why sustainability is important. These courses must move with all due speed toward planning and implementing decisions and actions that will address the most vital sustainability issues. While the science of sustainability is still developing, enough is already known about the scientific bases of many sustainability challenges, such as climate change impacts and ecosystem/species protection, to begin to take action—whether initiated and/or executed by business, government, and nonprofit organizations, or by individuals, households, and communities. As a result, management education may need to emphasize the urgency of sustainability oriented actions, developing and applying organizational and other tools that can be used very quickly and frequently by entities in multiple industries and cultures. Of course, the wider the scope of courses in which these tools can be of some value, the better, since numerous professions and perspectives will likely be necessary in the overall sustainability effort. In addition, given the reality that not all sustainability challenges can be addressed simultaneously by management educators and students, strategic decisions will need to be made by all stakeholders regarding which sustainability issues, tools, and applications should be advanced for immediate attention.

Second, sustainability management education needs to connect more deeply with many more potential educators and students on a continuous basis. If the civil rights, women's rights, antipoverty, peace, and environmental movements are any indication of viable approaches to modern widespread societal change, sustainability management may need to become a movement itself, perhaps linking with several others to form a major societal change effort. In order to attain this uber-movement status, much more creativity and innovation in sustainability management education—including the areas of outreach and marketing; delivery approaches; content substance, form, and style; and follow-through—may be required. As the community-based social marketing field (e.g., McKenzie-Mohr & Smith, 1999) has identified, we face both significant opportunities and limitations for learning how to change as a society. Traditional, mostly one-way, in-class, repetitive lectures, on how greenhouse gases affect the climate, for example, may need to be either complemented or replaced by more modern interactive approaches. This will both reflect our evolving understanding of sustainability and attract more students who can help advance it beyond the classroom and graduation. Some of these approaches may require sustainability management educators to take more risks in exploring new, or as yet little-explored, sustainability topics, such as the usefulness of indigenous sustainability knowledge. They must then present this information in educational yet interesting ways, and engage students in identifying, analyzing, and evaluating sustainability information that can be shared both inside and outside the classroom. Far greater and more effective use of online and video information, for instance, can both broaden and deepen student understanding of sustainability management. It can also provide an increased level of portability and perhaps application, of this information to address sustainability management challenges in multiple venues. Tying this last point to the need for urgency in developing and implementing sustainability solutions suggests that an emphasis on how, when, and where sustainability management education can actually be used by individuals, organizations, and societies to execute sustainability solutions appears to be a major need and obvious next direction of sustainability management education.

Third, sustainability education will likely need to establish stronger external and internal linkages to enable multiple fields, industries, and cultures to contribute to advancing knowledge of sustainability and its role in management education. In addition, the environmental, social, and economic bottom lines of sustainability will need to be better integrated to provide a holistic view of sustainability and of sustainability management education. Regarding external linkages, many fields have yet to be substantively connected to the sustainability concept. These fields include most of the medical sector, much of the infrastructure and engineering sectors, large-scale agriculture, mining, forestry, fishery, and other resource extraction sectors, recreation and athletic sectors, small-to-medium businesses of many kinds, and numerous others. Both in academia and in practice, an apparent massive need exists for transformative leaders, processes, products, relationships, and services—especially information services (i.e., hardware, software, databases, online, and "warmware")—to begin to push these societal and economic drivers toward sustainability orientations. Similarly, internal linkages among the environmental, social, and economic realms of sustainability appear to need far more attention, including both their interaction and their inescapable interdependence, with economies dependent on societies, both of which are dependent on natural environments.

Fourth, future sustainability management educators will also need to find ways to encourage their students to connect with individuals, communities, and small-to-medium enterprises, both down the block and around the world. Focusing on local stakeholders and their potential for advancing sustainability can provide students with a depth of understanding of their own culture, and how quality of life can be improved in their own backyards. Expanding a student's sustainability perspectives to account for and learn from other cultures can provide a breadth of understanding about how sustainability is perceived and encouraged in different cultures with different environmental, social, and economic contexts. Of course, the real challenge of sustainability management educators is to connect these different "glocal" approaches, so that students realize the full range of on the ground opportunities and challenges they are likely to encounter as they attempt to integrate sustainability into their personal and professional lives, as well as throughout their networks, communities, and societies. To this end, sustainability educators should take greater advantage of opportunities to incorporate management sustainability topics into study abroad and international student mobility programs.

Fifth, and similarly, another potential need for sustainability management educators in the future is to integrate the sustainability related actions of the "haves" and "have-nots" in their respective societies. Regarding the first group, the challenge appears to be trying to change over-consumption habits and expectations, so that these consumer/citizens are not setting unsustainable examples for the rest of their respective cultures. Regarding the disadvantaged in our societies, recent consideration of a "green-collar economy" by various North American leaders may be the vanguard of an effort to develop ways to teach or upgrade skills that could be employed in the emerging sustainability sectors of, among many others, energy efficiency, materials recycling, resource conservation, and renewable energy development. These skills could include the entrepreneurial skills to own, startup, and grow these sustainability-related enterprises, skills that might be possessed by the haves but not the have-nots. Again, sustainability management educators will be challenged to find ways to connect the reduction of over-consumption with the expansion of sustainability know-how, opportunity, and success.

CONCLUSION

In this chapter we have attempted to point out the significant progress that has been made in the past 2 decades in attending to sustainability in management education. This period, in reality, has been relatively short, and the recent strides have been extremely satisfying to those who have labored in this field for the past 20 years. However, the critical needs posed by the sustainability challenges outlined above make it clear that the current amount of attention to sustainability in management education is, sadly, far from glorious. These challenges demand that we quickly reach the point where attention to sustainability in management education has become as widespread and as taken for granted as attention to quality, technology, and globalization. Indeed, the discussion must turn from "sustainability IN management education" to "management education FOR sustainability." The needs of the planet and of businesses and people, both of the present and the future, demand this of us. It is our hope that readers of this chapter—and the others in this volume—will redouble their efforts to bring such a vital, and glorious, future into being as rapidly as possible.

ACKNOWLEDGMENT

The authors wish to thank Pamela Rands for editorial assistance.

REFERENCES

AACSB. (2008). *Sustainability conference.* Retrieved October 29, 2008, http://www.aacsb.edu/conferences/events/conferences/sc-jul-08-desc.asp

AASHE. (2008). *Graduate business programs in sustainability.* Retrieved June 3, 2009, from http://www.aashe.org/resources/grad_business.php#masters (access limited to individual or institutional members of AASHE).

Antioch University New England. (2008). *MBA in organizational and environmental sustainability.* Retrieved October 5, 2008, from http://www.antiochne.edu/om/mba/

Arnold, M. (1991). On environmental education for the business manager. In J. H. Baldwin (Ed.), *Confronting environmental challenges in a changing world: Selected papers from the twentieth annual conference of the North American Association for Environmental Education* (pp. 309–312). Troy, OH: North American Association for Environmental Education.

Aspen Institute. (2008a). *A closer look at applied sustainability centers.* Retrieved September 23, 2008, from http://www.aspencbe.org/documents/Applied%20Sustainability%20Centers%20Final.pdf

Aspen Institute. (2008b). *CasePlace.org.* Retrieved September 23, 2008, from http://www.caseplace.org/

Bainbridge Graduate Institute. (2008). *MBA in sustainable business.* Retrieved October 29, 2008, from http://www.bgiedu.org/content/view/9/40/

Bennett, M., & James, P. (Eds.). (2000). *The green bottom line: Environmental accounting for management.* Sheffield, UK: Greenleaf.

Beyond Grey Pinstripes 2001 (2001). Retrieved December 28, 2007, from http://www.aspencbe.org/documents/beyondgreypinstripes2001.pdf

Beyond Grey Pinstripes 2003. (2003). Retrieved December 28, 2007, from http://www.beyondgreypinstripes.org/results/index.cfm

Beyond Grey Pinstripes 2005 (2005). Retrieved December 28, 2007, from http://www.aspencbe.org/documents/bgp_ranking_2005.pdf

Beyond Grey Pinstripes 2007-2008 (2007). Retrieved December 28, 2007, from http://www.beyondgreypinstripes.org/rankings/bgp_2007_2008.pdf

Bouma, J. J., Jeucken, M., & Klinkers, L. (2001). *Sustainable banking: The greening of finance*. Sheffield, UK: Greenleaf.

Bren School. (2008). *Academic Programs—MESM Specialization: Corporate Environmental Management*. Retrieved October 31, 2008, from http://www.bren.ucsb.edu/academics/mesm_specialization/corp_env_mgt.htm

Brunner, D. L., Miller, W., & Stockholm, N. (Eds.). (1981). *Corporations and the environment: How should decisions be made?* Palo Alto, CA: Stanford University Graduate School of Business.

Buchholz, R. A. (1993). *Principles of environmental management: The greening of business*. Englewood Cliffs, NJ: Prentice Hall.

Buchholz, R. A., Marcus, A. A., & Post, J. E. (1992). *Managing environmental issues: A casebook*. Englewood Cliffs, NJ: Prentice Hall.

Bunch, R. (2003). Development of BELL in North America and China. Retrieved December 28, 2003, from http://www.chinaeol.net/bell/brdt/RickBunch.ppt

Cairncross, F. (1992). *Costing the earth: The challenge for governments, the opportunities for business*. Boston: Harvard Business School Press.

Charski, M. (2008). *Business schools teach environmental studies*. Retrieved November 5, 2008, from http://www.usnews.com/articles/education/best-graduate-schools/2008/03/26/business-schools-teach-environmental-studies.html

Charter, M., & Tischner, U. (Eds.). (2001). *Sustainable solutions: Developing products and services for the future*. Sheffield, UK: Greenleaf.

Colorado State University. (2008). *GSSE program overview*. November 5, 2008, from http://www.biz.colostate.edu/ms/GSSE/ProgramOverview/

Davis, K., & Blomstrom, R. L. (1971). *Business, society and environment* (2nd ed.). New York: McGraw-Hill.

Dominican University of California. (2008). *Green MBA*. Retrieved October 5 2008, from http://www.greenmba.com/

Doppelt, B. (2003). *Leading change toward sustainability: A change-management guide for business, government and civil society*. Sheffield, UK: Greenleaf.

Dunphy, E., Griffiths, A., & Benn, S. (2003). *Organizational change for corporate sustainability*. London: Routledge.

Duquesne University. (2008). *Sustainable MBA*. Retrieved September 5, 2008, from http://mba.sustainability.duq.edu/

Edmunds, S., & Letey, J. (1973). *Environmental administration*. New York: McGraw-Hill.

Egri, C. P., & Rogers, K. S. (2003). Teaching about the natural environment in management education: New directions and approaches. *Journal of Management Education, 27*(2), 139–143.

Elkington, J. (1998). *Cannibals with forks: The triple bottom line of 21st century business*. Gabriola Island, BC: New Society.

Fischer, K., & Schot, J. (1993). *Environmental strategies for industry*. Washington, DC: Island Press.

Frankel, C. (1998). *In earth's company: Business, environment and the challenge of sustainability*. Gabriola Island, BC: New Society.

Freeman, R. E., Pierce, J., & Dodd, R. H. (2000). *Environmentalism and the new logic of business: How firms can be profitable and leave our children a living planet.* Oxford, England: Oxford University Press.

Fuller, D. A. (1999.) *Sustainable marketing: Managerial-ecological issues.* Thousand Oaks, CA: SAGE.

Galea, C. (2004). *Teaching business sustainability: From theory to practice.* Sheffield, UK: Greenleaf.

Galea, C. (2007). *Teaching business sustainability: Cases, simulations and experiential approaches.* Sheffield, UK: Greenleaf.

Goddard College. (2008). *MA in socially responsible business and sustainable communities.* Retrieved November 5, 2008, from http://www.goddard.edu/masterarts_businesscommunities

GW News Center. (2008, September 16). *GW School of Business revolutionizes its MBA programs with a focus on ethical leadership in the global marketplace.* Washington, DC: Author.

Hawken, P. (1993). *The ecology of commerce: A declaration of sustainability.* New York: HarperCollins.

Hoffman, A. J. (2001). *From heresy to dogma: An institutional history of corporate environmentalism.* Stanford, CA: Stanford University Press.

Illinois Institute of Technology. (2008a). *Environmental management certificate.* Retrieved October 29, 2008, from http://www.stuart.iit.edu /graduateprograms/certificate/environmental_mgmnt/

Illinois Institute of Technology. (2008b). *MBA program: Concentrations: Sustainable enterprise.* Retrieved October 29, 2008, http://www.stuart.iit.edu /graduateprograms/mba/concentrations/sustainable_enterprise.shtml

Illinois Institute of Technology. (2008c). *MS in environmental management.* Retrieved October 29, 2008, from http://www.stuart.iit.edu/graduateprograms/ms/environmentalmanagement/

Lewis, H., Gertsakis, J., Grant, T., Morelli, N., & Sweatman, A. (2001). *Design + Environment: A global guide to designing greener goods.* Sheffield, UK: Greenleaf.

Makower, J. (1993). *The e-factor: The bottom-line approach to environmentally responsible business.* New York: Times Books.

Maharishi University of Management. (2008). Retrieved November 5, 2008, from http://www.mum.edu/mba/

McKenzie-Mohr, D., & Smith, W. (1999). *Fostering sustainable behavior: An introduction to community-based social marketing.* Gabriola Island, BC: New Society.

Mintu, A. T., Lozada, H. R., & Polonsky, M. J. (1994). Environmental consciousness and the business curricula: Some thoughts. *Journal of Teaching in International Business, 5*(1/2), xv–xviii.

Nattrass, B., & Altomare, M. (1999). *The natural step for business: Wealth, ecology and the evolutionary corporation.* Gabriola Island, BC: New Society.

Net Impact. (2008). *Business as UNusual: The Net Impact student guide to graduate business programs.* San Francisco, CA: Author.

ONE Teaching Resources. (2008). Retrieved September 23, 2008, http://one.aomonline.org/

Pennell, A. A., Choi, P. E., & Molinaro, L. (Eds.). (1992). *Business and the environment: A resource guide.* Washington, DC: Island Press.

Perrow, C. (1973). The short and glorious history of organizational theory. *Organizational Dynamics, 2*(1), 2–15.

Piasecki, B. W., Fletcher, K. A., & Mendelson, F. J. (1999). *Environmental management and business strategy: Leadership skills for the 21st century.* New York: Wiley.

Post, J. E. (1990). Getting the environment into the business school. In W. M. Hoffman, R. E. Frederick, & E. S. Petry, Jr. (Eds.), *The corporation, ethics, and the environment* (pp. 259-267). New York: Quorum Books.

Prakash, A. (2000). *Greening the firm: The politics of corporate environmentalism.* Cambridge: Cambridge University Press.

Presidio School of Management. (2008). MBA Graduate Program: Curriculum. Retrieved October 29, 2008, from http://www.presidioworldcollege.org /programs.php

Rands, G. P. (1990). Environmental attitudes, behaviors and decision making: Implications for management education and development. In W. M. Hoffman, R .E. Frederick, & E. S. Petry, Jr. (Eds.), *The corporation, ethics, and the environment* (pp. 269–286). New York: Quorum Books.

Rands, G. P. (1991). Toward greener business schools: Efforts at management student environmental education. In J. H. Baldwin (Ed.), *Confronting environmental challenges in a changing world: Selected papers from the twentieth annual conference of the North American Association for Environmental Education* (pp. 326–329. Troy, OH: North American Association for Environmental Education.

Rands, G P. (1993). Preparing students to work for sustainability: Teaching as if the earth's future mattered. *Journal of Teaching in International Business, 5*(1/2), 19–46.

Rands, G. P. (2009). A principle-attribute matrix for environmentally sustainable management education and its application: The case for change-oriented service-learning projects. *Journal of Management Education, 33*(3), 296–322.

Reinhardt, F. L. (2000). *Down to earth: Applying business principles to environmental management.* Boston: Harvard Business School Press.

Reinhardt, F. L., & Vietor, R. H. K. (1996). *Business management and the natural environment: Cases & text.* Cincinnati, OH: South-Western.

Rowledge, L. R., Barton, R. S., & Brady, K. S. (1999). *Mapping the journey: Case studies in strategy and action toward sustainable development.* Sheffield, UK: Greenleaf.

Rusinko, C., & Sama, L. (2009). Greening and sustainability across the management curriculum: An extended journey. *Journal of Management Education, 33*(3), 271–275.

Russel, T. (Ed.). (1998). *Greener purchasing: Opportunities and innovations.* Sheffield, UK: Greenleaf.

Russo, M. V. (1999). *Environmental management: Readings and cases.* Boston: Houghton Mifflin.

Sarkis, J. (Ed.). (2001). *Greener manufacturing and operations: From design to delivery and back.* Sheffield, UK: Greenleaf.

Sarkis, J., & Gollagher, M. (2008). Of pyramids, roads and bridges: The 2007 Greening of Industry Network Conference. *Business Strategy and the Environment, 17*(5), 289–293.

Schmidheiny, S. (1992). *Changing course: A global business perspective on development and the environment*. Cambridge, MA: MIT Press.

Sethi, S. P. (1971). *Up against the corporate wall: Modern corporations and social issues of the seventies*. Englewood Cliffs, NJ: Prentice Hall.

Schaltegger, S., & Burritt, R. (2000). *Contemporary environmental accounting: Issues, concepts and practice*. Sheffield, UK: Greenleaf.

Schaltegger, S., Burritt, R., & Petersen, H. (2003). *An introduction to corporate environmental management: Striving for sustainability*. Sheffield, UK: Greenleaf.

Shrivastava, P. (1996). *Greening business: Profiting the corporation and the environment*. Cincinnati, OH: Thomson Executive Press.

Smart, B. (1992). *Beyond compliance: A new industry view of the environment*. Washington, DC: World Resources Institute.

Springett, D., & Kearins, K. (2005). Educating for sustainability: An imperative for action. *Business Strategy and the Environment, 14*(3), 143–145.

Stanford University Graduate School of Business. (2008). *Public management program*. Retrieved October 31, 2008, from http://www.gsb.stanford.edu/pmp/

Starik, M., & Dyer, R. F. (1999, March). The World Resources Institute: WRI—Moving to engage business. GW/KPMG MBA Case Competition.

Starik M., & Rands G. (1995). Weaving an integrated web: Multilevel and multisystem perspectives of ecologically sustainable organizations. *Academy of Management Review, 20*(4), 908–935.

Stead, W. E., & Stead, J. G. (1992). *Management for a small planet*. Newbury Park, CA: SAGE.

Steiner, G. A., & Steiner, J. F. (1972). *Issues in business and society*. New York: Random House.

Sturdivant, F. D., & Robinson, L. M. (1977). *The corporate social challenge: Cases and commentaries*. Homewood, IL: Irwin.

University of California—Berkeley. (2008). *Engineering and business for sustainability*. Retrieved November 5, 2008, from http://sustainable-engineering.berkeley.edu/

University of Michigan. (2008). MBA Sustainability. Retrieved October 30, 2008, from http://www.erb.umich.edu/Education/Masters/MBA-MS/

University of North Carolina UNC. (2007). *Kenan-Flagler Business School: Sustainable enterprise*. Retrieved December 30, 2007, from http://www.kenan-flagler.unc.edu/Programs/MBA/Academics/sustainable-enterprise.cfm

University of Washington. (2008). *Environmental management*. Retrieved September 29, 2008, from http://www.washington.edu/students/gencat/academic/env_mang.html

VCEMS Environmental Studies. (2008). *Environmental management*. Retrieved October 29, 2008, from http://www.vanderbilt.edu/vcems/mba.html

Velasquez, M. G. (1982). *Business ethics: Concepts and cases*. Englewood Cliffs, NJ: Prentice Hall.

Vermont Law School. (2008). *Dual environmental law degree options*. Retrieved November 5, 2008, from http://www.vermontlaw.edu/academic/index.cfm?doc_id=121

Waage, S. (Ed.). (2003). *Ants, Galileo, & Gandhi: Designing the future of business through nature, genius, and compassion*. Sheffield, UK: Greenleaf.

Wasik, J. F. (1996). *Green marketing and management: A global perspective*. Cambridge, MA: Blackwell.

Welford, R., & Starkey, R. (Eds.) (1996). *Business and the environment*. Washington, DC: Taylor & Francis.

WRI. (1998). *News release: Eight business school MBA programs recognized for business curricula and activities focusing on the environment*. Retrieved December 29, 2007, from http://archive.wri.org/item_detail.cfm?id=97&section=newsroom&page=newsrelease_text&z=?

WRI. (1999). *News release: New study Beyond Grey Pinstripes: Preparing MBAs for social and environmental stewardship finds some surprising educational innovators*. Retrieved December 29, 2007, from http://archive.wri.org/item_detail.cfm?id=82&section=newsroom&page=newsrelease_text&z=?

WRI. (2006). *BELL teaching case studies*. Retrieved July 18, 2009, from http://www.wri.org/publication/bell-teaching-case-studies

WRI. (2008). *BELL (Business Environment Learning and Leadership)*. Retrieved September 23, 2008, from http://www.wri.org/project/bell

Yale. (2008). *Center for Business and Environment at Yale: Joint degree program*. Retrieved October 30, 2008, from http://cbey.research.yale.edu/people/joint-degree-program

CHAPTER 3

VISIONS OF SUSTAINABILITY

An Integrative Metatheory for Management Education

Mark G. Edwards

The current global sustainability crisis will require the transformation of organizations on a scale rarely, if ever, seen before. But, how can educational institutions prepare management students to deal with such radical levels of change when the theory base for studying organizational transformation toward sustainability is so fragmented? While the diversity in theories offers a fertile base for innovative policies and programs, it also means that each perspective, in isolation, is partial and may even be contributing to the fragmentation of ideas on sustainable futures, and to the polarization of what might actually be complementary views. The myriad organizational sustainability approaches urgently require an integrative, metatheory-building project that can provide orientating overviews and connecting conceptualizations for how authentic sustainability might be imagined and achieved. The implications for management education of such a project are significant. This chapter proposes a framework for accommodating multiple perspectives within an integrative picture of sustainability—one that is relevant to the important task of presenting sustainability theory in management education.

Management Education for Global Sustainability, pp. 51–91
Copyright © 2009 by Information Age Publishing

51

INTRODUCTION

If we wish our students to contribute to building what Warren Bennis (2000) has described as "delightful organizations," we will have to teach them the theories that describe how they can do so.

—Ghoshal (2005, p. 87)

This book argues that management education must take a global perspective on sustainability. Such a view demands that we draw together environmental, ecological, intergenerational, economic, and social theories of sustainability and try to weave together their disparate threads into some more integrative understanding. Sustainability cannot be compartmentalized into one or two domains of human experience or aspects of the natural environment. Sustainability is truly a global issue that is not just about the natural environment, but also about the social and political worlds. It is not just about economics, but also about justice for the environmental, biological, and social aspects of existence. From the perspective of the long-term implications of our actions, everything is indeed connected (Plater, 1999). Defining sustainability in a meaningful way requires an integrative approach that has the capacity to recognize the theoretical diversity and conceptual complexity of the topic (Mudacumura, Mebratu, & Haque 2006). The moment we admit to this perspective, however, we open a Pandora's box of a multiplicity of paradigms, theories, and contending scientific understandings of what sustainability is, how it might be understood and studied, and what attitudes and actions might be needed to achieve it (either as a goal or as a process). The plurality of perspectives on sustainability and the many theories and interventions that characterize its study creates a great complexity, where each view is also likely to contribute some important insight. Consequently, educators face significant challenges: in situating their courses within the diversity of theoretical approaches, and in equipping their students with ideas that can accommodate the multiplicity of contemporary views about sustainability.

Such issues are not peripheral to the mainstream concerns of preparing management students for the rigors of organizational life. Dealing with the "sustainability imperative" (Vanderheiden, 2008) is quickly becoming a core issue for many organizations. Globalization not only means that trade, financing, and economic concerns are part of the daily reality of organizational life; it also means that environmental and social matters need to be factored into organizational decision-making and planning. Global sustainability will require the transformation of organizations on a scale rarely, if ever, seen before (Cartwright & Craig 2006).

The scope of this needed transformation has important implications for how educational institutions prepare their students to deal with these radical levels of change. A reviewer of the book *Higher Education and the Challenge of Sustainability* has noted that (Clugston, 2004):

> Sustainability challenges universities around the world to rethink their missions and to re-structure their courses, research programs, and the way life on campus is organized. Graduates are increasingly exposed to notions of sustainability which are emotionally, politically, ethically, and scientifically charged. They must be able to deal with conflicting norms and values, uncertain outcomes and futures, and a changing knowledge base. At the same time they will need to be able to contextualize knowledge in an increasingly globalized society. (p. 421)

Now in the "Decade of Education for Sustainable Development (2005–2014)," as it was declared by the United Nations, it is a matter of urgency that educators face the challenge of developing evaluative skills and transformative attitudes in their students and expose them to the potential means for transferring these skills from the classroom to the workplace and other community settings; yet it appears that we are not meeting this challenge. In a seminal article on the teaching of "bad theory" in management programs, Ghoshal (2005, p. 75) proposes that business schools are complicit in some of the worst aspects of contemporary commercial practice. Ghoshal says that business academics are teaching theories that actually create the conditions which bring about such disasters as Enron, Tyco, and HIH insurance. He says that, "many of the worst excesses of recent management practices have their roots in a set of ideas that have emerged from business school academics" (p. 75). For Ghoshal, it is our "theories and ideas" that have failed us and which are in dire need of review. Had Ghoshal lived to see the fallout of the current global credit financial crisis, I am sure he would have felt his opinions to be further supported.

In particular, Ghoshal deplores the type of empirical research that is driven by ideological theories that assume what he calls, following Hayek, the "pretense of knowledge." These are theories that are based on pessimistic and mechanistic assumptions about why people do what they do. Through the reflexive process of the "double hermeneutic" (Giddens 1984), these ideological assumptions actually create the physical and social conditions by which people "dehumanize" (Ghoshal, 2005) one another. Ghoshal calls for a reconnection with forms of theory-building that break away from the ideological dominance of certain economic theories of human nature. Standard theory-testing research, which does not question the fundamental assumptions of its theoretical context, is not capable of this type of critical evaluation and it needs to be rebalanced by generalist forms of scholarship that take an integrative and critical approach toward construction of theory. Ghoshal (2005, p. 82) asks:

> What if, in acknowledgment of the "research benefit to generalists and generalism" (Pfeffer & Fong 2002, p. 88), we granted the generalists tenure, allowed them to groom others like them, and to interact with the scientists at the high table? It would compromise the pretense of knowledge, but would it not create a richer environment for knowledge creation? Would it not help us weed out each other's absurdities in theory and, thereby, reduce the chances of dehumanization of practice?

The questions Ghoshal posed here are metatheoretical in nature. The generalist is someone who sees across the theoretical pluralism of conceptual models and acknowledges the diversity of assumptions and explanatory factors that underpin them. The existing sustainability literature is characterised by diverse explanatory orientations and stands to gain from metatheoretical research that can create "a richer environment for knowledge creation." Such a research environment can identify the partialities and "absurdities in theory" of which Ghoshal is so critical.

Generalist studies are sometimes regarded simply as detailed reviews (Slavin, 1986) but they can be much more than that. The generalist approach to scholarship can be an eclectic gathering and review of different theories, but it can also contribute new knowledge through the comparative analysis and integration of contesting perspectives. Generalist approaches become metatheoretical when, in the process of the comparative analysis, they identify converging and diverging conceptual elements between those theories and use those elements to build pluralistic conceptual frameworks—that is, metatheories that can accommodate multiple theoretical and philosophical perspectives. In this way, the strengths and weaknesses of particular approaches can be more accurately assessed according to the more integrative perspective of the metatheoretical framework. This critical capacity of metatheory is something that is sorely needed within sustainability studies where, rather than being based on critical comparisons of paradigms and theories, the teaching of particular management approaches is often determined by disciplinary specializations or personal preferences.

Ironically, the attempt to develop a greater awareness of sustainability issues within the administration of universities highlights the disparity between espoused values of creating more sustainable institutions and what is actually being taught in the faculties of business, management, and economics. Speaking from the viewpoint of an advocate for sustainability in higher education, Clugston (2004) says of this misalignment:

The major problem for higher education is that it is almost impossible to create a sustainable university in an unsustainable society. David Orr describes our plight as walking north on a southbound train. The train of economic globalization is barrelling south. We, the advocates of sustainability in higher education, have taken significant steps to create a more humane, just, and sustainable path for globalization. But as we walk north, we are still passengers of this accelerating train moving in the opposite direction (Orr, 2003). We urgently need to educate and motivate professionals, citizens, and present and future leaders to change course toward a more sustainable future. (p. x)

As Ghoshal (2005) argues, university schools of business and economics are aligned with, and feeding into, many of the unsustainable practices of commercial society. Both seem to be "barrelling south" in the direction of what Luke (2006) calls "sustainable degradation." Rather than encouraging the transformational perspectives required to meet the challenges of, for example, global environmental problems, business schools are supporting those worldviews that are at the heart of these problems. Nowhere is the task of addressing the global sustainability challenge more worthy of urgent attention than in the field of management education. But how might business schools start this task of educating for sustaining forms of management in a pluralistic world? And which approaches could bring coherency to the theories and research paradigms that make up the organizational sustainability field? This chapter proposes some routes into considering these difficult questions. The chapter also presents a tentative theoretical framework for accommodating these and other perspectives in a more integrative and multidimensional picture of sustainability—one that reflects the interconnected nature of this issue.

THE NEED FOR
A METATHEORETICAL APPROACH TO SUSTAINABILITY

There is a deep polarity present within business and management schools regarding the place of sustainability theory. On the one side, there is the great variety of theoretical approaches used in conceptualizing, researching, critiquing, and working toward sustainable organizations, economies, and societies. On the other side, there is the dominance of a more conservative approach to teaching and researching organizational change issues, one that comes out of the functionalist concern for stability and incremental change rather than transformational change. This more orthodox and, some might say, positivist approach (Hassard & Kelemen 2002; Lewis & Kelemen, 2002) to organization theory and research occupies a central position in many management schools (Clegg & Ross-Smith,

2003; Dehler, Welsh, & Lewis 2001; Mingers, 2003) and, when it does address the theme of sustainability, often does so from a position of "sustaining" economic growth and business practices rather than any focal concern on environmental, social, or intergenerational sustainability. Thus, as Fergus and Rowney (2005) note:

> the meaning of Sustainable Development has been simulated into the language of the dominant scientific-economic paradigm, a language in which the discourse of Sustainable Development becomes more of a debate on scientific facts and methodologies and in which success is measured by the ethic of finance, as opposed to a fully inclusive, integrated discourse based on an ethic of values and diversity. (p. 26)

In contrast, more radical approaches to sustainability delve into such issues as authentic corporate social responsibility (CSR), Triple Bottom Line, organizational governance as transformational, the connection between sustainability and consciousness, issues of culture and sustainability, and the relationship between global issues of poverty, social justice, and sustainability.

These sustainability research paradigms, including those on the periphery and those at the center, offers unique and valuable insights into sustainability, how it might be achieved, how it might add to an organization's basic goals, and how organizations might respond to the growing community demand for sustainable business practices. While this pluralistic diversity offer a fertile base for innovative policies and programs, it also means that, in isolation, each of these approaches is partial and may even be contributing to the fragmentation of ideas on sustainable futures and to the separation of what might actually be complementary views (Korhonen, 2006).

The myriad organizational sustainability approaches urgently requires a metatheory building project that can connect disparate paradigms and theories and identify more integrative conceptualizations of how sustainability can be achieved. The implications for management education of a metatheoretical project are significant. Ghoshal's (2005) views on the damaging consequences of teaching "poor theory" in management studies are also pertinent to the teaching of poor metatheory. The following sections propose a framework for accommodating multiple perspectives within an integrative picture of sustainability—one that has relevance for how theories and metatheories of organizational sustainability are presented in management education.

Metatheory is not only needed for mapping the general landscape of a particular research field; it can also critically examine the relationships between research paradigms and their constituent theories. From their metatheoretical work, Burrell and Morgan (1979) noted 30 years ago that particular organizational paradigms, notably the positivist-functionalist paradigm, occupied a dominant position within the social sciences, while others were neglected or at least marginalized in terms of their academic credibility and impact. Several contemporary theorists argue that this situation has not changed (Hassard & Kelemen, 2002; Mingers, 2006; Schultze & Stabell 2004). Referring to the dominance of positivism within management schools in the United States, Stewart Clegg and Anne Ross-Smith (2003) argue that it has thwarted the development of new perspectives:

> Rather than reflecting a plurality of conceptual frameworks, research approaches, geographic locations, and input from the diverse cultural backgrounds and values of management scholars worldwide, this powerful U.S. construction of management knowledge has imbued it with glacier-like stability of cultural assumptions founded on the local rationalities of the U.S. world. (p. 89)

This chapter argues that the centrality of positivist programs in most management courses needs to be reviewed. However, it also acknowledges that there is nothing particularly unusual or undesirable about some research programs achieving temporary centrality within a field. What is problematic is the entrenching over years and decades of one dominant paradigm whose basic assumptions form an unquestioned foundation for the development of further theory and research. This situation has occurred with the ongoing centrality of positivist-functionalist management theories in, for example, their growth-centered, "homo economicus," "strategic," "hard," and "Chicago school" variants. The crucial issue here is the lack of metatheoretical research and multiparadigm research programs that can, on an ongoing basis, evaluate the relative strengths and weaknesses of paradigms so that no single school becomes as politically and socially entrenched as the positivist-functionalist paradigm has become. Middle-range theory building, empirical research, and their accompanying methodologies cannot, of themselves, perform this important critical work.

RESPONSES TO THEORETICAL PLURALISM

Generalist and metatheoretical studies are ideally suited to investigate the relationship between central and marginal scientific discourses among the throng of vying theoretical positions that characterize sustainability studies. And yet, mainstream academic responses to the growing plurality of views have not yet recognized the potential of more integrative research approaches. The range of research responses to the growing plurality of sustainability theories has included the following:

1. The dominant positivist-functionalist response which relies on functionalist, "hard," and "strategic" theories that support the conventional academic focus on regulatory compliance, the "business case," and the development of "sustainable businesses" rather than on the real transformations needed for authentic sustainability.
2. The inter/multi/cross-disciplinary response which develops inter-disciplinary approaches that bring together multi/cross-disciplinary teams (and hence their theoretical domains) to solve different sustainability problems.
3. The "incommensurate paradigms" response which establishes multiple research silos that represent different research paradigms and programs.

The problem with the positivist-functionalist response is that the embedded centrality of positivist ontologies and modernist epistemologies (Lewis & Kelemen, 2002) is now accepted as evidence of their scientific validity. Alternative explanatory domains are regarded as methodologically or conceptually inadequate. Such a view ensures the ongoing marginalization of alternative paradigms or multiparadigm approaches within management and business schools. From this perspective, the fact that a field is characterized by theoretical plurality is itself regarded as evidence of failure of social science research. The task for the positivist/functionalist approach is to reach a unified state of integration of theories that achieves "theoretical monism" (McLennan, 2002), "integration" (Donaldson, 1997; Donaldson & Dunfee 1994), or "consilience" (Wilson, 1998). This understanding of integration is one in which the many views are supplanted by a single unified theory or research paradigm. Hence, the ongoing dominance of one approach and the permanent marginalization of others is a desirable state for the positivist. In researching sustainability issues, the integrative monism response includes theories based on "the business case," "sustainable business," and strategic CSR approaches. The premise here is to see how sustainability fits in with and contributes to meeting conventional business and management goals such as functional efficiency, productivity, and financial returns.

A second type of business and management school response to theoretical pluralism has been the establishment of a growing number of small centers that specialize in a particular research paradigm. This "research silo" response reinforces the view that these different theoretical orientations are incommensurate with one another. However, although their theoretical contributions, research methods, and practitioner interventions contribute significantly to the development of scientific knowledge, these contributions do not greatly influence the mainstream. This non-integrative pluralism response includes postmodern theories of sustainability that emphasize its multi-faceted nature, the spectrum of alternative explanations, the dominance of some positions over others, and the ultimate incommensurability of the various discourses (Davison, 2008).

Moves to broaden the disciplinary response to theoretical plurality often result in interdisciplinary approaches that bring together researchers from different scientific disciplines. However, the focus of these activities is not on including contending theoretical positions or on giving voice to the plurality of theoretical positions, but on problem solving that cuts across disciplinary boundaries. These problem-solving activities are not necessarily metatheoretical engagements. First, disciplinary diversity is no guarantee for conceptual or theoretical plurality. An interdisciplinary research team that includes psychologists, engineers, economists, and management theorists can still undertake research based on functionalist assumptions. Second, interdisciplinary and cross-disciplinary research might bring multiple approaches to bear on a particular problem, but doing so does not mean that any conceptual integration of views has taken place. Interdisciplinarity can have major benefits in terms of improved efficiency and communication processes without bringing about any metatheoretical development.

None of these responses adequately deals with the issue of diversity in theoretical positions. Theoretical monism either ignores plurality or aims to unify and "integrate" contending views into some functionalist supertheory. The inter/multidisciplinary response has produced temporary benefits in applied problem solving but has failed to develop integrated theoretical frameworks that provide orienting positions for the further development of (meta)theory. Theoretical pluralism has been successful in developing multiple research silos and in developing new understandings within particular theoretical, methodological, and philosophical positions, but has otherwise only reinforced notions of incommensurability. Unfortunately, most researchers coming from postmodern schools, such as interpretivism and social constructionism, have also not recognized the possibility of an integrative pluralism, and they have argued that all types of metatheoretical integration are of the theoretical monistic form (see, e.g., Deetz, 1996; Lyotard, 1984).

These various responses to theoretical pluralism (see Figure 3.1) are a marked feature of the sustainability field (Scholz, Lang, Wiek, Walter, & Stauffacher, 2006). The integrative pluralism response to the diversity of sustainability theories attempts to retain that multiplicity of perspectives while also developing new knowledge that connects their definitive elements. That is, it seeks to identify core conceptual factors and their relationships, and construct metatheoretical frameworks that accommodate those viewpoints. Examples of this approach include multilevel theories of sustainability (Starik & Rands, 1995), integral philosophy (Hochachka, 2006), and systems theory approaches (Clayton & Radcliffe, 1996; Gallopín, 2003). The integrative pluralism response is one that recognizes that environmental, psychological, social, economic, and cultural faces of the sustainability challenge are connected in intimate and interdependent ways (Bell & Morse 2005).

METATHEORY AND PEDAGOGY

A deep polarity is present within management education in its treatment of sustainability theory. This polarity of views comes in response to an important paradox that underlies all issues regarding global sustainability: the growth paradox. It refers to our need for growth as an essential aspect of human development, and to the idea that global growth is unsustainable. One view is that growth is a solution—a necessary pathway, not only to the creation of improved personal and national health and well-being, but also to solving almost all environmental and social issues. The other view is that growth is a problem—a process that contributes to global warming, the collapse of biodiversity, and the economic and social upheavals that result from global environmental degradation.

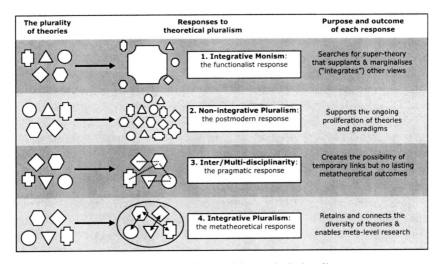

Figure 3.1.   Some responses to the issue of theoretical pluralism.

The need to respond to this powerful paradox has given rise to a paradigmatic split in theories used to address the sustainability challenge. On the one hand, conventional theories look to develop solutions based on continued or increasing levels of growth, institutional development, and economic prosperity; on the other hand, there are perspectives seeking more transformative alternatives based on human values and new paradigms of meaning-making. Such paradoxes create opportunities for developing deeper insights into the way we theorize institutional sustainability and for how we create pedagogical frameworks for explicating those insights. This perspective views paradox as a pedagogical tool. As Dehler et al. (2001) put it:

> Multiple disciplinary or paradigmatic theories may serve as lenses to deepen debates and insights (Bartunek, Gordon, & Weathersby, 1983). Juxtaposing conflicting understandings create a space for learning—an opportunity to recognize how differing perspectives coexist and complicate the learning milieu of organizations. (p. 506)

An integrative pedagogical response to this paradox involves developing students' capacities for taking multiple perspectives through a dialectical process of metatheoretical connection and accommodation. Metatheorizing can be, therefore, not only a means for developing alternative perspectives on old problems, but a transformational learning process of expansion of one's own and one's students' perspectival boundaries. Before describing some overarching perspectives that address these types of paradoxes, I will present a brief introduction to integrative metatheorizing.

METATHEORIZING AS SCIENTIFIC RESEARCH

The scientific importance of metatheory has generally gone unrecognized. However, as George Ritzer (2001) has pointed out, metatheorizing is actually a common activity for many researchers. Wherever theories are reviewed, comparatively evaluated, or analyzed in some way to develop further theory or hypothesis development, that is where metatheorizing is usually occurring. Metatheorizing is part of what might be seen as a spectrum of sense-making procedures (Dervin, 1999). Whereas middle-range theory deals with empirical data and the patterns that arise in that data, metatheory deals with middle-range theories and the patterns that exist between theories. Metatheory is built from the "second-order" (Gioia & Pitre, 1990) conceptual patterns that exist between individual theories. Like other forms of sense-making, metatheorizing attempts to structure and derive meaning from some body of knowledge, information, data, or experience. Unlike other forms of sense-making, its "data," the sources of information it draws on, are other theories or formal models of understanding. As Ritzer (1990) puts it "metatheory takes theory as its subject matter" (p. 3).

George Ritzer (1991) and Paul Colomy (1991) have proposed a number of different types of scientific metatheorizing based on the aims of this type of research. These are:

1. reviewing extant theory and becoming familiar with the range of paradigm assumptions and perspectives (M_U),
2. preparing for the development of middle-range theory (M_P),
3. developing overarching metatheory (M_O), and
4. developing adjudicative metatheory (M_A).

M_O is the most distinctive type of metatheorizing because it results in large-scale conceptual frameworks that help to map out the conceptual landscape of a particular domain of theories. It is important to remember that metatheories are not based on empirical data and therefore cannot be directly tested by empirical research. As Figure 3.2 shows, their "data" are middle-range theories and so they can be evaluated by assessing how well they represent and make sense of the strengths and weaknesses of those theories. This aspect enables metatheorizing to be most useful in contested domains that include many different theoretical positions, enabling metatheory to treat, as Weinstein and Weinstein (1991) say, "the multiplicity of theorizations as an opportunity for multiple operations of analysis and synthesis" (p. 140)

Tsoukas and Knudsen (2003) propose a spectrum of sense-making spectrum in their metatheoretical approach to organization theory. Experiencing, symbolizing, and conceptualizing provide the content for the object level of organizational life. The object level involves everyday sense-making procedures that deal with the lived reality of organizational life. The theory level is where formal theories and models of organizational life are developed and tested. The theory level attempts to provide sense-making contexts for the object level content. The metatheoretical level is where our scientific knowledge about organizational theories themselves are developed, validated, and linked with other levels. Metatheorizing can be regarded as the continuation of the process of sense-making at a more abstract and generalizing order of analysis (cf. Lewis & Kelemen, 2002). This multilevel process is dynamic and interactive in the sense that experiences, symbols, concepts, theories, and metatheories mediate and inform one another. There is an

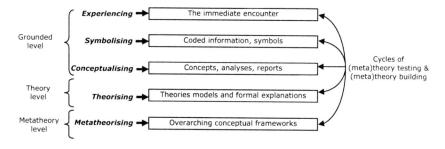

Figure 3.2.   Stylized view of phases of scientific sense-making.

ongoing iteration of influences and mediations between experience, concepts, theories, and metatheoretical perspectives (Tsoukas & Knudsen, 2003).

Figure 3.2 builds on Tsoukas and Knudsen's (2003) perspective on those iterations to develop a multilevel holarchy of sense-making. Metatheorizing, then, should be regarded as a crucial contributor to the development of formal scientific research. In fact, it is an important research activity that can set the context for any theory development and testing. Such a view sees conceptual and empirical research, not as two sides of a dichotomy, but as two phases in the spectrum of knowledge-building processes that, when performed within formal socio-cultural contexts, inform the development of scientific knowledge.

In the case of sustainability research, the holarchy of sense-making, in its theory building phase, moves from:

1.   the grounded level of empirical data such as the measurement of recycling programs, pollution levels, or the well-being of local residents, through to,

2.   the development of formal explanations of patterns of empirical data at the theory level with, for example, the Natural Step sustainability theory (Nattrass & Altomare 1999), through to,

3.   the development of metatheoretical explanations of middle-range (unit-level) theories such as, for example, Brown's (2005) integral sustainable development approach.

This holarchy can be regarded as running in both (meta)theory building and (meta)theory testing cycles. This latter form dominates most scientific research to an unwarranted level, and it is during times of turmoil that metatheorizing becomes particularly important to the emergence of new ideas (Trim & Lee 2004).

In summary, metatheorizing is of crucial importance to the ongoing development of scientific knowledge. Metatheorizing is particularly relevant in social science fields consisting of diverse theoretical orientations and during times of considerable social turbulence. Metatheorizing responds to the need for recognizing and evaluating theoretical diversity with an integrated and pluralistic approach.

METATHEORETICAL LENSES

One crucial element of metatheoretical research is the identification of the fundamental architectonics of unit-level theories. These architectonics, or lenses, are the sets of core assumptions, second-order concepts, and conceptual relationships that constitute the unit-level theories; and it is these conceptual lenses, together with their relationships, that form the building blocks of a metatheory. The metaphor of lens is used here in a dual sense. Conceptual lenses should not be regarded as purely interpretive filters, but also as tools that shape and create social realities. Hence they are not only interpretive, but also enactive. Conceptual lenses might also be described as voices or tools that shape and sometimes distort social structures and patterns of meaning and activity. They function according to the principle of the "double hermeneutic" (Giddens, 1984), and it is this iterative process of both interpreting and shaping reality that creates the self-fulfilling nature of theory (see Figure 3.3). Ghoshal (2005) points out that it is this double hermeneutic that "characterizes the link between theory and practice in social domains" (p. 77). Even more than the subject matter of the physical sciences, social data are "theory laden."

The operation of the double hermeneutic can be seen, for example, when our management theories help us to create and build certain types of industrial organizations and production processes. We then go into those physical and social realities and collect data that we attempt to interpret using our theories and methods. Often this cycle of building and meaning-making goes on in an unconscious manner. One of the reasons metatheorizing is such an important research activity is that it can step outside of this iterative reinforcement of conventional theorizing. To illustrate the value of metatheorizing for management pedagogy in the sustainability field, the following sections provide several integrative forms of metatheory building and the lenses that contribute to a more cohesive understanding of the issues of global sustainability.

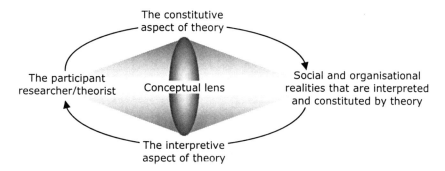

Figure 3.3.   Conceptual lens as both interpreting and constituting social realities.

SOME INTEGRATIVE METATHEORIES FOR SUSTAINABILITY

Several forms of integrative metatheorizing have emerged during the twentieth century, and in recent decades these have been applied within the field of sustainability. Each of these schools of metatheorizing possesses its own particular set of metatheoretical lenses, domains of application, and histories. In the following section, four schools of metatheoretical research will be introduced briefly, and some of their possible contributions to management education for the sustainability field will be described. These are general systems theory, the holistic approach, the multilevel approach, and the integral theory/AQAL framework. Although both general systems theory and integral theory use the word "theory" in their titles, they are better described as true metatheories according to any of the definitional criteria used by metatheorists such as George Ritzer (2001), and David Wagner and Joseph Berger (1986).

The General Systems Theory Approach

Different types of systems theory approaches have been applied to the issue of sustainability. These include complex adaptive systems theory, soft systems theory, living systems theory, open systems theory, complexity theory, and chaordic systems thinking. Because of the diversity of definitions and general complexity of sustainability issues, systems approaches are well-suited to exploring the patterns that exist among the various theoretical systems of sustainability thinking. As Andrew Manderson (2006) says:

> Sustainability's magnitude of vagueness, its scope of contextual application, and its depth of under-expressed complexity makes it particularly amendable to abstract examination through systems principles. (p. 86)

General systems theory (GST) is the "transdisciplinary study of the abstract organization of phenomena" (Manderson 2006, p. 87). Ludwig Bertalanffy, the founding father of the general systems theory approach warned more than half a century ago that:

> humankind has a poor chance to survive if we do not accept a new worldview—as citizens of the entire world rather than of single countries only—and consider the entire biosphere as one organization full of mutually supporting and mutually opposing interdependencies. (as cited in Mulej & Potocan 2007, p. 428)

In the hunt for guiding scientific principles that can support a "new worldview," GST looks for the patterns that exist *between* systems theories irrespective of their disciplinary origin. Hence, GST takes an integrative stance on theoretical pluralism and connects chemical, biological, physiological, and sociological theories of sustainability:

> A systems approach to sustainability entails considering the various agents interacting in the world as systems. Such an approach involves invoking general principles concerning systems to make inferences about likely and actual interactions between the systems under consideration. These principles can also be used to analyze the observed patterns of interactions between systems. (Clayton & Radcliffe, 1996, p. 28)

A systems approach sees sustainability as an essentially dynamic phenomenon. Every complex event can be viewed as an interlocking web of dynamic systems. The symbiotic nature of the relationships between those systems means that any theory of sustainability must include such concepts as adaption, complexity, dynamic equilibrium, and feedback. These are all system theory concepts and they can be used to create general frameworks for bringing together ideas about sustainability. There are many points that can be raised regarding the metatheoretical relevance of GST to management education and sustainability. Drawing on the work of GST thinkers Fred Waelchli (1992) and Vitaly Dubrovsky (2004), the following metatheoretical lenses are useful for drawing out these connections:

The Lens of Systemic Unity

Perhaps the most important lens that we might take from GST is the capacity to see ways of linking theories across physical, chemical, economic, and social understandings of sustainability. In each of these different domains there are many theories of sustainability that contribute to understanding how complex social entities such as organizations can be managed more sustainably. The difficulty is that, within and between these theories, very little coordination of viewpoints toward some more coherent overview exists. GST sees existence as "a unified whole" (Waelchli, 1992) whose patterns are comprehensible to the human mind. GST research uses the notion of systemic unity to "illuminate structural similarities in the laws of the divergent human 'content' disciplines" (Waelchli, 1992, p. 5).

The Lens of Complexity

Complexity within GST is regarded as a counterpart to the notion of unity and simplicity. A definitive quality of all systems is their complexity and the variety of (un)sustainable states that systems can occupy. Whereas the recognition of the unity of patterns across disciplinary domains enables a generalizing framework to be constructed, the lens of complexity requires that framework to be able to accommodate a great variety of unit-level perspectives.

The Lens of Holarchical Order

GST argues that systems exist within "hierarchical" (or "holarchical") orders of complexity and regulation. The term "holarchical order" is preferred here because it also includes heterarchical relations. Within this holarchy there are hierarchical relations of multiple levels of sustainability— for example, between physical, biological, psychological, and sociological levels—and there are heterarchical relations of multiple attractions within levels of sustainability—for example, between many different biological systems. Maccoby (1991) provides a useful discussion of issues of hierarchy and heterarchy in management studies. Through this holarchical lens GST offers a way of accommodating and situating many different sustainability theories within a holarchical modeling system.

The Boundaries Lens (System-Environment)

GST, like all systems theory approaches, offers many different ways of looking at dynamic relationships across system boundaries. Through such tools as positive and negative feedback loops, bifurcation points, far-from-equilibrium states, and near-to-equilibrium states, systems approaches to sustainability can look at the interactions between systems and their environments. The boundaries lens is commonly used by many different theories of sustainability across different domains of scientific research in considering the inputs, throughputs, and outputs that are exchanged across system and environment boundaries.

There are, of course, many other definitive elements of system theory approaches beyond those mentioned here. However, these lenses of system unity, complexity, holarchy, and dynamics are crucial for developing integrative frameworks for theories of sustainability.

The Holistic Approach

The holistic model of sustainability (Barrett & Grizzle, 1999; Bell & Morse 2005; Bell & Morse 2007; Kalland, 2002; Naveh, 2000) seeks integration through exploring those traditional, philosophical, and spiritual worldviews that find deep connections between human and natural worlds. Holism is the philosophical orientation that proposes that parts only exist because of some underlying perception of the whole (Naveh, 2000). This approach is not, however, an assumption that everything can be unequivocally regarded as essentially the same thing. In this regard the integrative holistic approach agrees with Stables and Scott (2002, p. 54) when they emphasize that they are:

> opposed to a holistic approach to [sustainable development education] that assumes we should be aiming for a single and uncontested set of understandings and for complete consensus concerning future action.

Rather, the integrative holism that authors such as Simon Bell and Christopher Barrett refer to seeks a sustainability that identifies the special interests of all stakeholders, including environmental and ecological stakeholders, and accommodates them within a holistic framework. This is a pluralistic, rather than monistic, form of integration. An example of this kind of holism can be seen in Potocan's and Mulej's (2003) work on the multiple dimensions of sustainable development. Their notion of "requisite holism" is their response to the need for a holistic approach to sustainability at a time when scientific research has taken a much narrower approach to the multiplicity of issues involved. As they put it:

> The majority of present investigations about [Sustainable Development] in economy ... have been performed from selected single viewpoints of economic operations. Less research has been devoted so far to the issues of a holistic (and hence interdisciplinary, interdependence-based) understanding, implementation, and application of [Sustainable Development]. (p. 422)

The major lenses that integrative holism contributes include:

The Spirituality Lens

Bell and Morse (2005) propose that the worldviews of theocentrism, cosmocentrism, and anthropocentrism together offer a truly holistic approach to sustainable development. They point out that the spiritual traditions have always had an element of environmental sustainability at the heart of their ethical program. They state that "All of these [spiritual] traditions speak of a far richer vision of the world as an object worthy of sustaining" (p. 413). The spirituality lens is sensitive to the whole moral dimension of how our values and goals generate the unsustainable cycles of production and consumption that drive global growth. Bell and Morse argue that holistic worldviews might connect human spirituality with more integrative notions of sustainability and the means to achieve that state. They speculate that:

> It is perhaps surprising to think that those perhaps best placed to understand and appreciate the complexities of sustainability are those who have striven to understand the human spirit and how we have arrived at where we are today. (p. 413)

Egalitarian Lens

Integrative holism looks across many disparate corners of life—including human, plant, and animal forms—to find an egalitarianism that does not privilege one form of life over another. Chea and Chea (2002) propose a detailed model of integrative holism that connects ecological, economic, social, and global dimensions of sustainability. The authors propose a holistic model that incorporates these domains within a corporate, social, and global context (see Table 3.1). This attempt to deal holistically with the micro-meso-macro nature of sustainability issues is a feature of the multilevel approach that is outlined next.

The Multilevel Approach

All theories of sustainability make inferences about levels—that is about the micro, meso, and/or macro characteristics—of organizations, their members, and their environments (Yammarino, Dionne, Chun, & Dansereau 2005). Microlevel explanations focus on "individuals" and "small social units," and macro explanations focus on "large social units" (Alexander, 1987). Unfortunately, very few theories specifically take account of this multilevel nature of social existence. A recent review found that very few studies adopt theoretical frameworks and research methods that tap into the multilevel nature of phenomena (Yammarino et al., 2005). This finding is particularly relevant for sustainability studies where the multilevel impact of sustainability issues on the personal, organizational, community, and international levels is so relevant.

Table 3.1.   Holistic Integration of Multiple Dimension of Sustainable Development (After Chea & Chea, 2002)

Dimensions	Focus	Corporate Performance Criterion	Societal Performance Criterion	Global Performance Criterion
Economic	Competitiveness	profitability	social wealth	global wealth
Ecological	Habitability	ecological rating	ecological rating	ecological rating
Social	Community	reputation	societal quality-of-life	global quality-of-life
Ethical	moral legitimacy	values	societal values	in values
Legal	legal legitimacy	legal compliance	legal compliance	international law compliance
All dimensions	combined foci	sustainable management index	sustainable management index	sustainable management index

The Multilevel (Micro-Meso-Macro) Lens

Multilevel approaches to sustainability seek to connect the ecological layers of human social involvement across such domains as organizational work and economic activity. Figure 3.4 depicts the holonic or nested quality of levels of organizing. Employees, dyads, teams, departments, organizations, industries, and societies can be seen as levels or wholes within a nested ecological holarchy. Such a view provides a basis for connecting theories regarding sustaining work, organizational sustainability, and, more broadly, sustainable industries. The nested nature of holarchies means theories that target, for example, the organizational level of sustainability can be connected with the theories of individual psychology and behavior, team and group dynamics, and organizational subunits. This multilevel approach provides a way of connecting theories at each of these different scales of focus.

The multilevel theorists Mark Starik and Gordon Rands (Starik, 2004; Starik & Rands 1995) have proposed a multilevel and multisystem perspective that takes this nested approach to understanding sustainable organizations. They describe this multilevel orientation in the following way:

> Several authors have suggested and we agree that sustainability and sustainable development have multilevel and multisystem characteristics ... and that the achievement of sustainability requires an effective integration of these multiple levels and systems. For us, integration involves the assumptions that (a) an ecologically sustainable world requires ecologically sustainable societies, cultures, political and economic systems, organizations, and

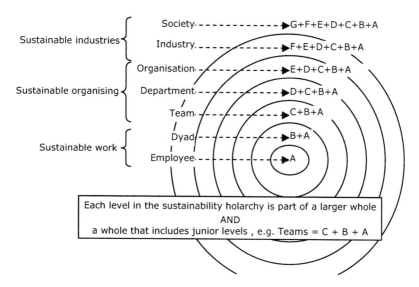

Figure 3.4.   A multilevel sustainability holarchy for organizations.

individuals; and that (b) achievement of sustainability by an entity at any one of these levels requires simultaneously recognizing and addressing the actions of and interactions with entities at each of these levels. (Starik & Rands 1995, p. 909)

Management education for sustainability must take into account these multiple levels of personal and collective interaction. In a globalized world which connects micro, meso, and macro activities in very direct and immediate ways, it is important that managers understand the mutuality between microlevel sustainability (which includes the psychological/cognitive), mesolevel sustainability (which includes the group attitudes and peer relations), and macrolevel sustainability practices. Bridging between these paradigms results in a micro–meso–macro lens that emphasizes the multilevel characteristics of transformation.

The Developmental Approach

Developmental studies have always taken an integrative perspective to their subject matter. Systems often show over time a tendency toward the emergence of greater complexity and differentiation. Because developmental approaches are inherently longitudinal, they are sensitive to the stages of transformation and emergence that social systems exhibit. This principle of development in sustainability conceptualizations has been applied to the management systems field by Marcel van Marrewijk and his colleagues (van Marrewijk & Hardjono 2003; van Marrewijk & Werre 2003). Van Marrewijk and Hardjono state that:

> History demonstrates the emergence of more profound quality management systems over time and especially the current attention for corporate social responsibility (CSR) and Corporate Sustainability (CS), referring to the corporation's new role within society, indicates a much higher level of complexity. (pp. 121–122)

The Developmental Lens

Using a developmental approach from the field of human psychological development, Marrewijk and Werre (2003) have applied developmental principles to the study of sustainability and management. In so doing they have identified a range of sustainability archetypes that can be used to map the transformation of individuals and groups through various sustainability levels. The outcome of this developmental approach is a spectrum of sustainability stages that bears remarkable similarity to other stage-based models of organizational sustainability. In particular, the sustaining organization model of Dunphy, Griffiths, and Benn (2003) describes stages of organizational sustainability that integrate a number of forms of sustainability, including compliance-driven, competition-driven, efficiency-driven, values-driven, and community-driven forms. The use of the developmental lens provides theorists and practitioners with an integrative approach which maps out the transformational pathways that lead to what they call "third wave corporations" or sustaining corporations. Table 3.2 shows how the developmental phases of organizational sustainability can be used as a categorizing tool for situating sustainability theories. Dunphy's et al.'s sustainability phases appear in the left column. The next two columns show the various sustainability theories for human and ecological sustainability. As Dunphy and his colleagues put it, "the phases outline a set of distinct steps organizations take in progressing to sustainability (p. 14).

This type of indexing of theories is a common task in metatheorizing. It not only provides a means for categorizing theories along some useful dimension but also situates those theories relative to each other, thereby drawing out their relationship to one another, their limitations, and areas of focus. Such a process also identifies where there is a lack of middle-range theory and where further theory building and research may be required. Such tools can provide important learning resources for management education by showing how certain theories relate to certain levels of organizational development.

Table 3.2.   Integrating Sustainability Theories

Dunphy's Sustainability Phases	Human Sustainability	Ecological Sustainability
1. Rejection	Theories of employee exploitation	Theories of environmental exploitation
2. Nonresponsiveness	Competition theory, theories of wealth maximization	Theories of environmental commercialization
3. Compliance	Theories of HR compliance	Theories of regulatory compliance, industry compliance
4. Efficiency	The "business case," theories of cost cutting and efficiency	Theories of poor environmental practice as an important source of affordable cost.
5. Committed	Theories of HR development and sustainability— the CSR case	Strategic theories of CSR, theories of competitive advantage
6. The sustaining corporation	Stakeholder theories, community development theories, holistic theories	Global sustainability theories, theories of global governance

The Transformational Lens

This developmental approach emphasizes the task of transformation in the quest for sustainable forms of organizing. For example, transformational processes are required for organizations to move from preconventional to conventional and postconventional forms of sustainability. As Dunphy and his colleagues (2003) state:

> Some traditional organizational values and forms are not sustainable and, unless significantly reshaped, will continue to undermine the sustainability of society and the planet. Corporations have contributed to [sustainability] problems ... and they must therefore be part of the answer. Fortunately their transformation is already underway, driven in part by the changing demands of modern society and also by the leadership of farsighted and responsive people within and outside corporations who see the need for change. (p. 4)

It is interesting to note that the highest stage in the models of Dunphy and van Marrewijk have much in common with the type of sustainability aspired to by theorists taking the holism approach. For example, Dunphy et al. calls the type of consciousness that is required for an authentic form of sustaining corporation "Cosmocentric consciousness, or spiritual intelligence" (p. 272):

This mystical view is also supported by many other leading physicists who have been involved in redefining scientific views of the universe. Jaworski calls this type of awareness unity consciousness. Unity consciousness releases us from the cultural boundaries we have internalized and allows us to experience the interrelatedness of the universe and become part of its unfolding future. (p. 271)

The concordances here with the holistic view are very powerful and once again show that the use of integral approaches enables connections and accommodations to be made which promote sense-making in many, often unpredictable, ways.

The AQAL Approach

The AQAL or integral theory approach was developed by the philosopher Ken Wilber (2000) as a metatheory that attempts to include as many different scientific and cultural lenses as possible. AQAL is an abbreviated acronym for "All Quadrants, All Levels, All Lines, All States, All Types." It has recently been applied to the field of sustainability (Esbjörn-Hargens & Brown, 2006; Hochachka 2006) in an attempt to develop a more cohesive response to the worldwide sustainability crisis (Brown, 2005). Barrett Brown, for example, has developed the "Integral Sustainable Development Approach" which, rather than attempting to find which theories and models are right and which are wrong, asks the question "what kind of universe is it that allows for all these definitions, methodologies, and reasons to arise in the first place?" (p. 6). Referring to the frequent calls for a more cooperative research response to sustainability issues, Brown describes integral sustainable development as a:

> response to these calls for an end to the age of fragmentation in [the sustainability] field. It is a first attempt to create a context for deploying knowledge from the full spectrum of established disciplines in order to address local and global social environmental problems. This fragmentation in the sustainable development (SD_v) arena is evidenced by, among other things, the multiple definitions of SD_v, the myriad frameworks and methodologies for enacting SD_v, and the vastly different motivations for why we should pursue a sustainable future. (pp. 5-6)

There are many lenses included within the AQAL approach to sustainability. The most important being (1) the quadrants and (2) the levels of development.

The Quadrants Lens

A basic feature of integral sustainable development is the quadrants. These are developmental domains that arise from the intersection of two metatheoretical lenses: interior-exterior and individual-collective. Their combination forms four fundamental domains of existence—experience, culture, behavior, and systems. In terms of sustainability theories, a comprehensive approach will need to include theories that address each of these four domains. Hilary Bradbury (2003) has, for example, drawn attention to the need for greater emphasis on the interior domains of experience and culture in the direct theorizing on sustainability, particularly within management education approaches.

Because AQAL has a reflexive approach in its epistemology—in the sense that it includes first-, second-, and third-person experience—it can be used to develop learning that includes not only third-person theoretical maps but also first- and second-person learning aids. Bradbury (2003) used AQAL to develop her whole-action framework for teaching about sustainability (see Figure 3.5). This program was a course for management students that brought together experiential, behavioral, cultural, and systems learning elements for the development of a comprehensive educational program. The experiential component involved reflection on the sustainability of students' personal lifestyles. The behavioral component consisted of mapping students' personal eco-footprint and listing "the stuff" that students used in daily life. The cultural quadrant was included through an experience of the "vision-quest," an exploration of the natural world through the indigenous American ritual of a personal encounter with nature. The systems quadrant was covered by learning some systems-based approaches to sustainability. This "All-Quadrants" approach provided a comprehensive framework for management students to explore some core domains of sustainable living.

The Spectrum of Developmental Lens

The AQAL framework employs a sophisticated developmental lens to map out the basic structures of stage-based growth models. Brown (2006) has summarized the spectrum of development to the following levels: egocentric, traditional, modern, postmodern, and integral. This spectrum of development can apply to both individuals and collectives and is relevant for both subjective and behavioral aspects of growth. The developmental lens can be combined with the quadrants lens to derive a model of sustainable development that systematically connects the realms of subjective experience, behavior, culture, and social realities as they emerge through on-going periods of transformative change (see Figure 3.6).

Figure 3.6 shows the spectrum of development as it might appear in conjunction with the quadrant lenses. The parallels between AQAL's devel-

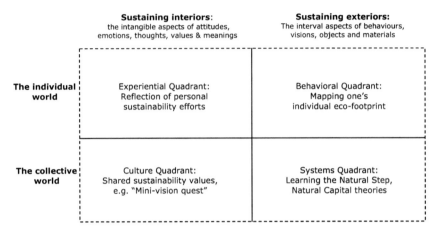

Figure 3.5.   Bradbury's whole-action framework for teaching about sustainability.

opmental lens and the layout of organizational theorists such as Dexter Dunphy and Marcel van Marrewijk are evident. Figure 3.6 juxtaposes the AQAL and organizational development stages to provide an integrative model of sustainability that might be applied in both subjective and objective individual and collective spheres of organizational life. It is this creative, but also evidence-based, combining of lenses that enables integrative metatheorizing to be an innovative and flexible research approach.

INTEGRATIVE METATHEORIZING FOR SUSTAINABILITY

Building upon the preceding outline of several integrative approaches to sustainability, some general features of metatheoretical research that can guide the development of overarching frameworks in this field can now be described.

"The Holism Case for Sustainability"

A scientific approach to metatheorizing gathers together evidenced-based lenses from the theoretical and practitioner literature, identifies the relationships between them, and explores new combinations of lenses to develop and evaluate metatheoretical frameworks. In the preceding sections a number of lenses were identified and these included: systemic unity, complexity, holarchical order, system boundaries, spirituality, egalitarian, multilevel, stage-based developmental, transformation, quadrants

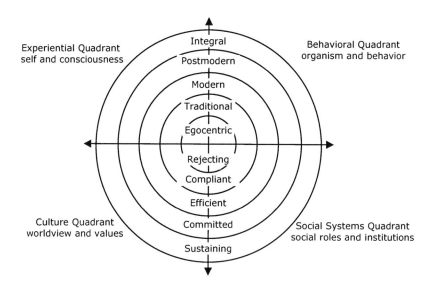

Figure 3.6.   Levels of development through all four quadrants.

(interior-exterior and individual-collective), and the spectrum of development. Several of these lenses show significant conceptual redundancy—e.g. holarchical order and the developmental lens. Part of the task of this type of research is to refine our lenses so that only the most parsimonious and generalizable set is retained (see Wacker, 1998 for further discussion on evaluative criteria for meta/theory building).

In this section several of these and other lenses are used to develop integrative frameworks for describing and exploring a more embracing and more cohesive *big picture* view of the sustainability field in a number of its variations. Such a view opens up innovative ways of connecting theories and generating new visions for sustainable metatheorizing which can provide what Hilary Bradbury (2003) calls "the holism case for sustainability." The developmental, interior-exterior, and system-environment (boundaries) lenses offer a matrix that can be used for indexing many different types of sustainability theories.

Table 3.3 shows the spectrum of forms of sustainability in combination with the interior-exterior and system-environment lenses. When these lenses are used to categorize theories of sustainability, we can build a matrix that locates many different approaches. This matrix brings coherency to what may appear to students of sustainability to be an incoherent diversity of unconnected views. As Bradbury (2003) says, the contribution of such an approach lies in providing "a conceptual framework that helps integrate rational and emotional material ... thereby connecting systems of thinking with an action or experiential approach to learning" (p. 173). Table 3.3 connects theories of management with the values and motivations that underlie different approaches to sustainability. For example, traditional values appear to be associated with compliancy approaches which respond to market-based motivational drivers. These associations provide fertile territory for the development of middle-range theories that can then be tested in the field. But the key point here is that metatheorizing of this kind can generate connection and patterns that will not otherwise be noticed either by researchers or by students in their efforts to make sense of these complex fields of study.

The multilevel or micro-meso-macro lens is particularly important for recognizing how theories and paradigms of sustainability might be accommodated within larger frameworks. For example, the issues of a "sustainable working life" are increasingly becoming relevant to a more global understanding of sustainability (Docherty, Kira, & Shani 2008; Kira, 2003). The multilevel lens can be used to bring together definitions that apply to the micro, meso, macro, and macro-macro levels of personal, organizational, and environmental sustainability. Such an approach is found in the work of Starik and Rands (1995) where sustainability is considered at the individual level all the way through to the global level.

There are some important metatheoretical points that can be made about the application of this lens for defining sustainability in working life. First, the multilevel lens is not essentially a bipolar factor with indi-

Table 3.3.   Form of Organizational Sustainability, Interior-Exterior Characteristics and Systemic Environmental Relations

Developmental Lens	Interior-Exterior Lens		System-Environment Lens	
Form of organizational sustainability	Theories of the subjective interiors	Theories of the objective exterior	Theories of internal motivation	Theories of sustainability management
Sustaining II	Integrated Holism	Global	Consciousness-driven	Integrative
Sustaining I	Synergism	Networking	Values-driven	Developmental
Caring	Pluralism	Cooperative	Stakeholder-driven	Consultative
Economizing	Pragmatism	Technological	Market-driven	Efficiency
Complying	Traditionalism	Conforming		Productive
Avoiding	Egocentrism	Competitive	Profit-driven	Coercive
Rejecting	Hedonism	Conflict		Exploitative

viduals at one pole and collectives at the other (as it is treated by Wilber and many other metatheorists). It has many possible gradations; for example, as we have seen, it can be divided into individual, dyad, triad, small group, organization, industry, etc. Second, the meso level of the group plays a crucial role within this ecological spectrum. Decision-making teams and committees are vital in the life of an organization, particularly where change is involved. Third, a multilevel lens does not stop at an organization's boundary but includes interorganizational, industry-level, environmental, societal, and global levels.

Sustaining Work Life

These macro and macro-macro levels are the key determinants in structuring the basic form of an individual's working life, and so this lens sets the points of connections between the sustainability of one's own working life and that of the wider circles of involvement. For example, working hours and many other employment conditions are subject to government regulation and statutory obligations. Industry standards, benchmarking, and self-regulation all play a role in defining many of the core features of a sustaining work-life and how it links into the sustainability of other natural and social ecological systems. All these distinctions are lost when we think of an organization's multilevel ecology simply as an individual-collective polarity.

In a similar way, the developmental lens could be applied to integrate definitions related to the physical, emotional, rational, meaning-making, existential, and spiritual aspects of defining sustainability in working life. The literature on quality of working life tends to focus on the more basic levels of need with, for example, a focus on occupational health and safety, ergonomic needs, and on emotional security with such things as bullying and harassment. While attention is being given to the rational and psychological needs of meaningful and enjoyable work, there is still a relative lack of research on the higher-level needs of spiritual development, as well as a sense of contributing to the common good of one's community and, more generally, to global welfare. The multilevel and developmental lenses are so crucial in sustainability because they involve an integrative understanding of space and time respectively. With regard to the space dimension, multilevel sustainability involves the local, the personal, the communal, the organizational, and the global. The developmental lens integrates the temporal dimension in both personal and collective development and provides a window into seeing how an authentic sustainability may emerge through the comparative study of innovation.

Bringing both these lenses to bear on the issue of sustainable working life might be useful in a pedagogical sense in that it connects students' own personal experience of work with more objective understandings of sustainability. Taking the multilevel lens in terms of circles of identification, we might look at, for example, those things that sustain workers in their own sense of personal well-being, that of their work colleagues, that of their families, their local communities, their countries, and their global communities. With the developmental lens the circle of identification moves from somatic identity to affective identity, to the membership self of peer-group belongingness, to egoic-rational identity, to existential and meaning-making identity, and to cosmo-centric identity (Wilber, 2005). The resultant matrix offers a guide for assessing the balance that might exist in a truly comprehensive view of the sustaining work life. Table 3.4 describes the multifarious facets of a sustaining working life as seen through the developmental and multilevel lenses.

A few cells in Table 3.4's sustainability matrix are highlighted to show how this matrix might be used in an educational setting.

1. *Shares a sense of emotional safety at work:* this cell refers to the need for emotional sustenance at work, such as not being bullied, coerced, or affronted by demanding bosses and irate customers. This aspect of sustainability is crucial for emotional well-being and the sense of security in one's relationships at work.

2. *Supports belongingness to community:* this cell refers to work as something that contributes to a community and its sense of belonging to place, to community, and to one's identification within a geographical region. In Western Australia, large mining concerns fly whole workforces in and out of a particular mining operation. In the process of using the "fly in and fly out" option, these companies can impact negatively on existing communities or do away with the idea of community completely. In this sense, the workplace is unsustainable as a community endeavour.

3. *Encourages community-based education:* work should contribute to the educational and intellectual life of the community in which it occurs. Many unions have programs of educational and cultural development that are based within communities and within workplaces. Companies can offer in-house training programs which develop the skills and competencies of their employees, and these skills in turn add to the skill base of the community. These enhanced skills enable a sustainable level of competency to be maintained at the community level.

Table 3.4. The Circles of Sustaining Work: As Seen Through the Developmental and Multilevel Lenses

Circles of Developmental Identification	*Circles of Ecological Identification for Sustaining Work*							
	work sustains the personal circle	work sustains the collegial circle	work sustains the familial circle	work sustains the communal circle	work sustains the societal circle	work sustains the national circle	work sustains the global circle	work sustains the universal circle
Physical	biochemical health	workplace environmental health	the biochemical health of family & its location	biological health of the communal environment	ecological health of biosocial systems	national environmental sustainability		
Somatic	health of the functioning body	OH&S, shared sense of physical security	provides for basic family health needs	basic community infrastructure	physical results build positive social outcomes	contributes to healthy national infrastructure	sustains the global environment	sustains all universal aspects of bio-physical health
Affective	emotional health	**shared sense of emotional safety at work**	enhances emotional health within the family	community's psychological health	produces positive emotional climate in society	encourages national sense of emotional health	contributes to global emotional well-being	supports universal ethic of care/ compassion
Peer-member-ship	belongingness	freedom to associate & belong at work	enhances families sense of belonging	**supports belongingness to community**	supports social cohesion & solidarity	adds to healthy sense of national identity	fosters sense of global citizenry	enhances feeling of universal belongingness

Table continues on next page.

Table 3.4. Continued

Circles of Ecological Identification for Sustaining Work

Circles of Developmental Identification								
Rational-egoic	cognitive health	intellectual exchange is encouraged	provides for educational needs of family	**encourages community-based education**	adds to the intellectual capital of society	supports national educative goals	contributes to international education	contributes to a universe-centred education
Pluralist-Existential	healthy values and purpose	shared meaning & values in the workplace	enhances the family's identity with community	helps to build cultural identity in the community	support multicultural and pluralistic society	**contributes to nation's role as a global member**	international adoption of human rights	
Spiritual	deep meaning and purpose	spiritual connectivity with colleagues	supports spiritual life of the family	fosters spiritual well-being within community	contributes to social sense of connectedness	supports growth in spiritual value of the nation	global communal sense of deep purpose	enriches a spirituality that is both universal and particular

4. *Contributes to nation's role as a global member:* one's work can contribute to the global economy in a positive or negative way. For example, those who work on a Japanese whaling ship are contributing in a negative way to the overall perspective that the international community has of this Japanese industry. In a globalized economy, work has a relationship with an international understanding of sustainability, and it can contribute in a positive or negative way to that understanding.

These few brief explications show how the grid in Table 3.4 might be used in a learning setting to unwrap the many ways in which people (e.g., management students) can see the relevance of sustainability for their working lives, and how those sustaining qualities can be linked with much wider circles of identification. Of course there are many other lenses that might be included within this type of metatheorizing; for example, the discussion has not yet explored the lens of power or of how decision-making, control, management, and governance issues play out within a sustainability context. Because a decision-making or governance/power lens is of central importance in the metatheoretical examination of sustainability theories, a brief discussion of this lens might be useful at this point.

The Governance Lens

People are essentially self-sustaining, especially when surrounded by a supportive community that recognizes their connectedness as well as distinctiveness. It may be that the most important thing organizational management can do in supporting this autopoietic capacity is to provide a physical and emotional climate of openness to creativity, trust, and enthusiasm. This importance, of course brings into sharp relief the inherent paradox between top-down control and bottom-up emergence in the way one envisages management. A more integrative understanding of this paradox assumes that decision-making power and governance are a multilevel phenomena. Management is something that all employees inherently do in their working day. A multilevel understanding of management, leadership, and governance is one possible lens that an organization possesses for generating sustaining work. This lens has been a particular focus for postmodern theorists of management studies and of the ongoing problems with the development of authentic forms of sustainable development (Deetz, 2007; Luke, 2006).

All leaders are followers and all followers are leaders in some way. CEOs need to listen to and follow just as much as they need to lead and direct; likewise, customer reception staff must manage their work and make decisions at a critical point of interface for an organization. So at any level within the organization we have individuals who are both leaders and followers in various capacities. This is a holonic understanding of decision making and management that recognizes the autopoietic capacities of any level and of any individual in an organization. To regard leadership and management as residing in the upper levels of an organization is of course customary, but it also simply serves to reproduce unsustaining and unfulfilling forms of work. The top-down view of leadership and governance is also an inherently reductive understanding of organizational decision making. There are some understandings of management and leadership—for example, servant leadership and reciprocal leadership, which take steps in the direction of a more holarchical conception of organizational governance (defined here in the broad sense of an organization's capacity to self-regulate). Both (1) top-down, control-based understandings and (2) bottom-up, participatory-based conceptualizations of management are partial forms of a management or governance holarchy that recognizes each layer to be both leader and follower, exercising both directive and receptive competencies in the workplace.

Although new management models are being tried, the mechanistic approaches to organizational design, such as scientific management, remain the mainstream management model. That model superimposes a reductive, and thereby distorted, version of this holarchy over more balanced decision-making capacities. Although the bottom-up participatory approach that comes in reaction to the top-down control model of management is offered as a countering balance to the excesses of scientific management, it simply replaces one reductionist model of governance with its mirror opposite. A full integration of these approaches—one that recognizes the need for both control and participation, for leadership and followership, and for multilevel governance and decision making—is only possible through a holarchical re-conception of governance.

The governance lens does not deny that there are multiple levels of decision making within an organization, or that these different levels represent different modes of expression and scope of influence. What it does do is recognize that all levels and all members and teams are self-regulating and self-managing in definitive ways. From this perspective the tools which enable management processes to be truly supportive of sustaining work need to be embedded and utilized from every level of the organization.

CONCLUSION

This chapter has argued for a greater recognition of metatheoretical research in management education. Integrative metatheorizing is valuable both as a form of scientific research, which responds to the problem of theoretical pluralism, and as a learning tool for developing experiential insight and awareness about the need for multiple perspective taking. Several integrative forms of metatheorizing have been described, and their relevance to exploring sustainability issues and theories were outlined. In particular, a number of important metatheoretical lenses were used to develop an innovative metatheory for sustainability—the "circles of sustaining work" (see Table 3.4). This comprehensive model of sustaining work-life combines developmental and multilevel lenses to create a more connective vision of sustainability.

What might be the implications for management education of metatheoretical models such as the "circles of sustaining work" framework? First, it challenges us to deal directly with the issue of how to connect the multiple views that currently exist in the literature. Metatheoretical frameworks are inherently complex and demand multiparadigm thinking that challenges the easier path of staying with the known (Weaver & Gioia 1994). It also means that we take a position on how that diversity could be integrated. Without that metatheoretical stance, multiparadigm inquiry never moves beyond the review of different paradigms and theories and fails to develop a critical basis for linking those findings.

A second implication of metatheorizing sustainability is that it brings into stark relief the degree of transformation that is required to develop truly sustainable vision for the future. To talk of sustaining organizations (within sustaining industries within sustaining economies within) is to propose a fundamentally radical transformation from the mainstream systems of organizing of compliance and efficiency-based understandings to more committed and globalized views of sustainability (Dunphy et al. 2003). That transformation will not be an easy one and will not come about without corresponding transformations in such things as organizational governance, goals, and relationships with communities, markets, industry groups, and governments. This degree of change is rather daunting, but authentic sustainability inevitably leads to the consideration of radical social transformation. Sustainability loses almost all meaning unless it is set within this transformational and metatheoretical context. Consequently, we need ways for conceptualizing how that transformational process might come about and what characteristics it might possess. This need, above all, is an important implication of the metatheoretical approach to sustainability for management education. Metatheoretical research raises our awareness of the true extent of the transformations required to produce sustainable forms of organizing, production, and consumption.

A third implication of metatheorizing for management education is the inherently critical nature of this type of research. Metatheorizing is inherently critical because its surveys of the broad landscape of a field of research identify the gaps, weaknesses, distortions, and imbalances that exist within a particular field. As noted in an earlier section, Colomy (1991) calls this the "adjudicative" capacity of metatheorizing. For example, one particularly important task in considering theories of sustainability is how some less challenging perspectives (those that require translational as opposed to transformational change) move to the center of mainstream research while other, perhaps more confronting, theories become marginalized. These latter theories of sustainability can prove to be threatening concepts to status quo perspectives. Referring to this tendency for transformational change notions to evoke anxiety, Fergus and Rowney remark, "the consequences of such a change in cognitive process are likely to appear quite radical to many people operating within the dominant paradigms" (Fergus & Rowney, 2005, p. 205).

Centers of academic orthodoxy are inherently conservative because they have a justifiable need to ensure the stability and survival of their schools of scientific knowledge. However, this conservatism also influences the way research and practitioner communities conceptualize sustainability and the way it is pursued at the broader community level. For example, there has been a shift in defining sustainability from concerns about environmental, ecological, intergenerational, and social justice toward a focus on economic, financial, and performance "sustainability" (Springett, 2003). This type of reframing of the term "sustainable" evidences a reaction against the need for transformation and toward concerns that organizations are more aligned with—sustainable profitability, sustainable work force recruitment, sustainable growth, and organizational sustainability. Any academic database search on "sustainability" will find as many articles concerned with the sustainability of organizational profit margin, sales, and market share as there are ones addressing environmental or social sustainability. Metatheorizing challenges this type of status quo science. Weinstein and Weinstein (1991, pp. 143-144) refer to this capacity of metatheoretical research to critique status quo positions:

> metatheory, by taking up a reflexive position toward theory, tends to level the playing field by treating less popular or less successful theoretical alternatives as elements in the field, granting them legitimacy by analyzing their structure and presuppositions, and explaining, at least in part, their lack of success in terms of social conditions—for example, disciplinary power, and status structures.

The notion of "sustainability" appears to be particularly vulnerable to this type of reframing (Lakoff, 2004). It goes without saying that organizations need to sustain themselves and their employees. But the reframing of sustainability language toward traditional organizational concerns dilutes the transformation imperative and deflects the challenge of radical change that authentic sustainability calls for. The transformative imperative to shift to new forms of organizing gets reframed into the translational imperative for merely growing profits, providing more jobs, and sustaining the (conventional) developmental goals of the organization. Luke (2006) calls this "sustainable degradation" and the morphing of definitions of sustainability reflect this shift from transformational to translation concerns. It is management students' immersion in this type of dominant theoretical ideology that Sumantra Ghoshal was so critical of. This immersion in the poison of "bad theory" has several anecdotes within the tools of scientific research and one of those tools is rigorous metatheorizing. There is perhaps no more urgent challenge in the field of management education than that presented by the sustainability issue; however, without the inclusion of a critical metatheoretical perspective there will be significantly less likelihood of our successfully meeting that challenge.

REFERENCES

Alexander, J. C. (1987). Action and its environments. In J. C. Alexander, G. Bernard, R. Münch & N. J. Smelser (Eds.), *The micro-macro link* (pp. 289–318). Los Angeles: University of California Press.

Barrett, C. B., & Grizzle, R. (1999). A holistic approach to sustainability based on pluralism stewardship. *Environmental Ethics, 21*(1), 23.

Bartunek, J. M., Gordon, J. R., & Weathersby, R. P. (1983). Developing complicated understanding in administrators. *Academy of Management Review, 8*(2), 273–284.

Bell, S., & Morse, S. (2005). Holism and understanding sustainability. *Systemic Practice and Action Research, 18*(4), 409–426.

Bell, S., & Morse, S. (2007). Problem structuring methods: theorizing the benefits of deconstructing sustainable development projects. *The Journal of the Operational Research Society, 58*(5), 576–587.

Bennis, W. 2000. *Managing the dream: Reflections on leadership and change.* New York: Perseus.

Bradbury, H. (2003). Sustaining inner and outer worlds: A whole-systems approach to developing sustainable business practices in management. *Journal of Management Education, 27*(2), 172.

Brown, B. C. (2006). Theory and practice of integral sustainable development—An overview (Part 1): Quadrants and the practitioner. *AQAL Journal of Integral Theory and Practice, 1*(2), 366–405

Burrell, G., & Morgan, G. (1979). *Sociological paradigms and organisational analysis*. Heinemann, Portsmouth, NH.

Cartwright, W & Craig, JL (2006). 'Sustainability: Aligning corporate governance, strategy and operations with the planet', *Business Process Management Journal*, vol. 12, no. 6, p. 741.

Chea, H-B., & Chea, M. (2002). Sustainable development and sustainable management. In U. Haley & J. Richter (Ed.), *Asian post crises management* (pp. 396–435). New York: Pelgrave.

Clayton, A. M. H., & Radcliffe, N. J. (1996). *Sustainability: A systems approach*, Boulder, CO: Westview Press.

Clegg, S. R., & Ross-Smith, A. (2003). Revising the boundaries: Management education and learning in a postpositivist world. *Academy of Management Learning & Education*, 2(1), 85.

Clugston, R. M. (2004). Foreword. In *Higher education and the challenge of sustainability: Problematics, promise, and practice* (pp. ix–xii). Boston: Dordrecht.

Colomy, P. (1991). Metatheorizing in a postpositivist frame. *Sociological Perspectives*, 34(3), 269–286.

Davison, A. (2008). Contesting sustainability in theory-practice: In praise of ambivalence. *Continuum*, 22(2), 191–199.

Deetz, S. (1996). Describing differences in approaches to organization science: Rethinking Burrell and Morgan and their legacy. *Organization Science*, 7(2), 191–207.

Deetz, S. (2007). Corporate governance, corporate social responsibility, and communication. In S. K. May, G. Cheney, & J. Roper (Eds.), *The debate over corporate social responsibility* (pp. 267–278). New York: Oxford University Press.

Dehler, G. E., Welsh, M. A., & Lewis, M. W. (2001). Critical pedagogy in the "new paradigm." *Management Learning*, 32(4), 493.

Dervin, B. (1999). On studying information-seeking methodologically: The implications of connecting metatheory to method. *Information Processing & Management*, 35(6), 727–750.

Docherty, P., Kira, M., & Shani, A. B. (Eds.). (2008). *Creating sustainable work systems: Developing social sustainability* (2nd ed.) London: Routledge.

Donaldson, L. (1997). A positivist alternative to the structure-action approach', *Organization Studies*, 18(1), 77.

Donaldson, T., & Dunfee, T. W. (1994). Toward a unified conception of business ethics: Integrated social contracts theory. *Academy of Management Review*, 19(2), 252–284.

Dubrovsky, V. (2004). Toward system principles: General system theory and the alternative approach. *Systems Research and Behavioral Science*, 21(2), 109–122.

Dunphy, D., Griffiths, A., & Ben, S. (2003) *Organisational change for corporate sustainability: A guide for leaders and change agents of the future*. London: Routledge.

Esbjörn-Hargens, S., & Brown, B. C. (2005). *Integral ecology and integral sustainability: A brief introduction*. Integral University. Retrieved May 10, 2006, from, www.INTEGARLUNIVERSITY.ORG

Fergus, A. H. T., & Rowney, J. I. A. (2005). Sustainable development: Lost meaning and opportunity? *Journal of Business Ethics*, 60(1), 17.

Gallopín, G. C. (2003). *A systems approach to sustainability and sustainable development*, ECLAC. Santiago, Chile: Sustainable Development and Human Settletments Division.

Ghoshal, S. (2005). Bad management theories are destroying good management practices. *Academy of Management Learning and Education*, *4*(1), 75–91.

Giddens, A. (1984). *The constitution of society.* Cambridge: Polity Press.

Gioia, D. A., & Pitre, E. (1990). Multiparadigm perspectives on theory building. *The Academy of Management Review*, *15*(4), 584–602.

Hassard, J., & Kelemen, M. (2002). Production and consumption in organizational knowledge: The Case of the "Paradigms Debate." *Organization*, *9*(2), 331–355.

Hochachka, G. (2006). *Developing sustainability, developing the self: An integral approach to community and international development*. Drishti Centre for Integral Action. Retrieved July 3, 2006, from http://www.drishti.ca/pdfs/AQAL_integral_int_dev.pdf

Kalland, A. (2002). Holism and sustainability: Lessons from Japan. *Worldviews: Environment Culture Religion*, *6*(2), 145–158.

Kira, M. (2003). *From good work to sustainable development. Human resources consumption and regeneration in the post-bureaucratic working life.* Kungl. Tekniska, Högskolan.

Korhonen, J. (2006). On the paradox of corporate social responsibility: How can we use social science and natural science for a new vision? *Business Ethics: A European Review*, *15*(2), 200–214.

Lakoff, G. (2004). *Don't think of an elephant! Know your values and frame the debate.* Whitet River Junction, VT: Chelsea Green.

Lewis, M. W., & Kelemen, M. L. (2002). Multiparadigm inquiry: Exploring organizational pluralism and paradox. *Human Relations*, *55*(2), 251–275.

Luke, T. W. (2006). The system of sustainable degradation. *Capitalism, Nature, Socialism*, *17*(1), 99–112.

Lyotard, J-F. (1984). *The postmodern condition: A report on knowledge.* Manchester: Manchester University Press.

Maccoby, M. (1991). Move from hierarchy to heterarchy. *Research Technology Management*, *34*(5), 46.

Manderson, A. K. (2006). A systems based framework to examine the multi-contextural application of the sustainability concept. *Environment, Development and Sustainability*, *8*(1), 85.

McLennan, G. G. (2002). Quandaries in meta-theory: Against pluralism. *Economy and Society*, *31*(3), 483–496.

Mingers, J. C. (2003). A classification of the philosophical assumptions of management science methods. *The Journal of the Operational Research Society*, *54*(6), 559.

Mingers, J. C. (2006). A critique of statistical modelling in management science from a critical realist perspective: Its role within multimethodology. *The Journal of the Operational Research Society*, *57*(2), 202.

Mudacumura, G. M., Mebratu, D., & Haque, M. S. (2006), Toward a general theory of sustainability. In *Sustainable Development policy and administration* (pp. 136–159). Pennsylvania: Taylor & Francis.

Mulej, M., & Potocan, V. (2007). Requisite holism—Precondition of reliable business information. *Kybernetes*, *36*(3/4), 319.

Nattrass, B., & Altomare, M. (1999). *The natural step for business; Wealth, ecology, and the evolutionary corporation*. Gabriola Island, BC: New Society.

Naveh, Z. (2000). What is holistic landscape ecology? A conceptual introduction. *Landscape and Urban Planning*, *50*(1–3), 7–26.

Orr, D. (2003). Walking north on a southbound train. *The Journal of the Society for Conservation Biology*, *17*(2), 348–351.

Pfeffer, J., & Fong, C. T. (2002). The end of business schools? Less success than meets the eye. *Academy of Management Learning & Education*, *1*(1), 78–95.

Plater, Z. J. B. (1999). Environmental law and three economies: Navigating a sprawling field of study, practice, and societal governance in which everything is connected to everything else. *The Harvard Environmental Law Review*, *23*(2), 359–392.

Potocan, V., & Mulej, M. (2003). On requisitely holistic understanding of sustainable development from business viewpoints. *Systemic Practice and Action Research*, *16*(6), 85–91.

Ritzer, G. (1990). Metatheorizing in sociology. *Sociological Forum*, *5*(1), 3–15.

Ritzer, G. (1991). *Metatheorizing in sociology*. Toronto: Lexington.

Ritzer, G. (2001). *Explorations in social theory: From metatheorizing to rationalisation*. London: SAGE.

Scholz, R. W., Lang, D. J., Wiek, A., Walter, A. I., & Stauffacher, M. (2006). Transdisciplinary case studies as a means of sustainability learning. *International Journal of Sustainability in Higher Education*, *7*(3), 226–251.

Schultze, U., & Stabell, C. (2004). Knowing what you don't know? Discourses and contradictions in knowledge management research. *Journal of Management Studies*, *41*(4), 549–573.

Slavin, R. E. (1986, February). Best evidence synthesis: An alternative to meta-analytic in traditional reviews. *Educational Researcher*, 5–11.

Springett, D. (2003). Business conceptions of sustainable development: A perspective from critical theory. *Business Strategy and the Environment*, *12*(2), 71.

Stables A. W. G., & Scott W. A. H. (2002). The quest for holism in education for sustainable development. *Environmental Education Research*, *8*(1), 53-60.

Starik, M. (2004). holistic environmental leadership: Living sustainably beyond 9-to-5. *Human ecology review*, *11*(3), 280.

Starik, M., & Rands, G. P. (1995). Weaving an integrated web: Multilevel and multisystem perspectives of ecologically sustainable organizations. *Academy of Management Review*, *20*(4), 908–935.

Trim, P. R. J., & Lee, Y.-I. (2004). A reflection on theory building and the development of management knowledge. *Management Decision*, *42*(3/4), 473.

Tsoukas, H., & Knudsen, C. (Eds.). (2003). *The Oxford Handbook of Organization Theory: Meta-theoretical perspectives*. Oxford, England: Oxford University Press.

van Marrewijk, M., & Hardjono, T. W. (2003). European corporate sustainability framework for managing complexity and corporate transformation. *Journal of Business Ethics*, *5*(2, 3), 121–132.

van Marrewijk, M., & Werre, M. (2003). Multiple levels of corporate sustainability. *Journal of Business Ethics*, *44*(2/3), 107–119.

Vanderheiden, S. (2008). Two conceptions of sustainability. *Political Studies*, *56*(2), 435–455.

Wacker, J. G. (1998). A definition of theory: Research guidelines for different theory-building research methods in operations management. *Journal of Operations Management*, *16*(4), 361.

Waelchli, F. (1992). Eleven theses of general systems theory (GST). *Systems Research*, *9*(4), 1–8.

Wagner, D. G., & Berger, J. (1986). Programs, theory, and metatheory. *The American Journal of Sociology*, *92*(1), 168–182.

Weaver, G. R., & Gioia, D. A. (1994). Paradigms lost: Incommensurability vs structurationist inquiry. *Organization Studies*, *15*(4), 565–590.

Weinstein, D., & Weinstein, M, A. (1991). The postmodern discourse of metatheory. In G Ritzer (Ed.), *Metatheorizing* (pp. 135–150). Newbury Park: SAGE.

Wilber, K. (2000). *Collected works* (Volumes V–VIII). Boston: Shambhala.

Wilber, K. (2005). Introduction to integral theory and practice: IOS basic and the AQAL map. In R. A. Slaughter (Ed.), *Knowledge base of futures studies: Directions and outlooks* (Vol. 3). Brisbane: Foresight International.

Wilson, E. O. (1998). *Consilience: The unity of knowledge* (1st ed.). New York: Knopf.

Yammarino, F. J., Dionne, S. D., Chun, J. U., & Dansereau, F. (2005). Leadership and levels of analysis: A state-of-the-science review. *The Leadership Quarterly*, *16*(6), 879–919.

CHAPTER 4

TAOISM AND INNOVATION IN CHINA

Recovering the Legacy of Environmentally Sustainable Enterprise

John Hollwitz

This is China's century. In the past 2 decades, East Asia and the West have developed mutual sources of supply, production, and markets at a scale never before seen. However, these developments entail heightened environmental risks. Management education in the West has insufficiently understood Chinese traditions in strategy and production, traditions which predated Western technology and commercial (or military) practice by many centuries, sometimes by two millennia. This chapter provides an overview of this situation and its implications for management educators mindful of the potential crisis of environmental devastation.

Management curricula have very little sense of how important environmental sustainability has been as the source of Chinese innovation since the fourth and fifth centuries B.C.E. Though the West understands the importance of Confucianism, we have almost no systematic sense of Taoism, the foundation of systematic thinking about the nature of consumption and about the radical interdependence of innovation and ecological wellness.

Management Education for Global Sustainability, pp. 93–112
Copyright © 2009 by Information Age Publishing
All rights of reproduction in any form reserved.

The chapter argues too that something has changed in China itself, that the environmental order at the heart of Taoism may have been occluded in the industrialization of Asia. This possibility poses extraordinary risks to environmental well-being not just for China and Asia, but also for the world. Management education is incomplete and arguably misleading if it fails to address these traditions and developments.

What puts the Chinese above all the earth's cultures is that their laws, their customs, and even the language spoken by their most learned people have not changed for around four thousand years. Still, this nation and India, the most ancient of those which still exist, which have the largest and most beautiful countries, which invented almost all of the arts before we learned them, have down to today been left out of our so-called "common histories."

—Voltaire, *The Philosophical Dictionary*

China is a vast, inert mass of humanity.

—Walter Gresham
United States Postmaster General, 1883–1884;
Secretary of the Treasury, 1884;
United States Court of Appeals, 7th District, 1884–1892;
United States Secretary of State, 1893–1895

The headlines say that this is China's moment. Recent years have produced an extraordinary expansion of business opportunities between East and West, opportunities hard to imagine even 20 years ago. Management education in Europe and America has worked hard to keep up. Business programs routinely study the emergence of China and its neighbors. We have brought our MBA programs to China; Chinese students are among our students and graduates in the Americas and Europe. The headlines also tell us that this century will determine whether our planet's ecosystem can continue to support us. We do not know when the tipping point will occur (if it has not already) but strong scientific consensus says that it must unless we change how we live and work. And the form that China's continuing emergence takes will play a major, perhaps dominant, role in determining our success or failure in achieving a sustainable way of being on this planet.

In seeking ways to transform how we live and work, China's technological and management history offer valuable lessons for present day China, the West, and the rest of the world. As we shall see, Chinese observers were among the first to warn that the industrial revolution sought economic growth at the risk of survivability, a warning that was scarcely noticed in management and executive training in the twentieth century and is not always present in the thinking and actions of the current Chinese leadership. Long before the industrial revolution, China had business models and technological developments centered on environmental sustainability, 3,500 years of pursuing economic development with a view toward preventing, minimizing, or remediating environmental degradation. Except for a general sense that social norms differ in Asia (cf. Chen, Chen, & Xin, 2004; Farh, Zhong, & Organ, 2004), management education has almost completely neglected this tradition, establishing a void in how we teach people to approach the global marketplace today. As a result, we are less than fully informed about what Chinese practices can contribute to grappling with our current challenges; and if we are less than informed, we are certainly less than effective at preparing people to lead global enterprise, especially at a moment of environmental crisis. Addressing this deficiency by introducing to management education and practice a better and clearer understanding of Asia's and especially of China's history and continuing emergence deserves serious attention.

Historically, Eastern Asia's approach to enterprise and the natural environment differed from that of the West in five ways.

First, Asian enterprise did not distinguish corporate, unit, and individual utilities from the value inherent in the natural environment in which they operate.

Second, historical Asian models saw these utilities as isomorphic, common in structure, potential, and need. This isomorphism shaped how these models defined strategy, tactics, and value. Each of these echoes the others; each level of enterprise echoes the rest.

Third, China historically defined leadership capabilities as ones that had to be effective for all these domains at each level of enterprise. The ideal for successful management was competitive advantage, but not a form of advantage in which returns to one domain could offset deficits in another. All parts of the entity prospered in balance, or all declined.

Fourth, this model of the enterprise and its relationship to the environment had at its core the concept of "harmony," a culturally specific but generalizable balance among people and groups within the natural environment. Harmony in this sense is not a romanticized or utopian ideal. It arose from a hard-headed pragmatic determination to balance interests within systems, even competing systems. In contrast, the West developed the tradition of seeing divergence of interests. Harmony is best described in the many case histories of Chinese innovation, but in simplest terms it is a preference for "both/and" rather than "either/or" ideas about utility, an epistemology which cannot separate individual well-being, economic development, and environmental health.

Fifth, the Asian ideal was neither theoretical nor speculative. It required the commitment to empirical standards for innovation every bit as rigorous as those of the West.

These themes characterized Chinese enterprise from the first millennium BCE almost to the time of Newton, a remarkable period of development scarcely documented in Western professional training and only lately reappearing in the East. China never achieved anything like a full realization of its own best practice traditions. On the contrary, even a cursory glance at the record shows centuries of violence, successions of oppression and insurgency just as brutal as we have experienced in the West. The contrary is more likely true, that environmental damage is an acceptable risk in a game whose jackpot is economic success. The fact that these traditions are largely ignored in current practice does not deny their historical importance. To the contrary: understanding their history shows how pivotal those models might still be. In the pages that follow, we shall offer four propositions about how we train managers for global competition in a natural environment now at profound risk.

ORGANIZATIONAL EFFECTIVENESS AND ENVIRONMENTAL WELL-BEING

First: We have inaccurately described the history of the relationship between organizational effectiveness and environmental well-being. Our texts, casebooks, journals, and practitioner guides are demonstrably incomplete. We are gaining increasing access to information about that history. Without accounting for this information, our pedagogy is at least inefficient, at worst amoral, and in either case inefficient.

Voltaire's dates about Chinese innovations are probably optimistic, but his conclusion was correct. In many ways that matter for environmentally sustainable development, China invented or at least anticipated processes and technologies which we usually associate with the West. From the tenth century B.C.E. to about the sixteenth century C.E., China developed and implemented an extraordinary array of managerial and technological innovations. Some of these made their way West and significantly influenced scientific thought, technology innovation, and organizational design in the Middle East and then Europe. Francis Bacon wrote that gunpowder, the printing press, and the compass, all from China, were the three inventions that most changed the world. We now know of many others.

Chinese innovations were not widely known outside Asia, but they were certainly not secrets. Chinese innovation has been well documented over the centuries. Nearly 50 years ago, the Cambridge scholar Joseph Needham obtained a copy of a volume which Winchester (2008) described as the largest book in the world, the Imperial Chinese Encyclopedia, commissioned around 1,700 to document the comprehensive Chinese history of innovation. The Encyclopedia builds upon enormous records from earlier centuries, including documents from 11,000 to 36,000 volumes long.

Needham's (1954-1994, 1969, 1981) extraordinary work summarizes many of these materials and places them in their historical contexts and modern uses. Digital versions of many of these materials are available from Cambridge University. Columbia University's Loeb edition, some decades old, provides selected translations in strategy, operations, and organizational behavior. Sawyer and Lee-Sawyer's editions and translations identify the interrelationships across defense, agricultural, and public management (Sawyer, 2006, 2007a, 2007b; Sawyer & Lee-Sawyer, 1996). The story of Needham's life and work is described in Simon Winchester's (2008) excellent biography *The Man Who Loved China*.

Needham first visited China just before World War II. In the following decades he and his colleagues systematically documented these developments in encyclopedic volumes of their own. Their inventory traced the origins and continued use of industrial, agricultural, civic, and management innovations. Chinese manuscripts 2,600 years old have much in common with today's textbooks on organizational design, strategy, and behavior. They cover functional and matrix organizational designs, job analysis and design, how to use standardized measures in management development, strategic planning, and how to establish supply chains. The book of *Mo Tzu*, compiled about the fourth century B.C.E., may be the world's first text on the risks to the natural environment posed by toxic byproducts of production and distribution.

Centuries before the Roman empire, Chinese texts discussed team-based job designs in terms similar to those we use in classrooms today. They also discussed managerial inefficiencies like bounded rationality, decisional heuristics, and escalation of commitment, topics for which Kahneman won the Nobel Prize several years ago. By the third century B.C.E., Wei Lao-Tzu described ways to maximize efficiency, minimize involuntary unemployment, and ensure continuous quality improvement in the agricultural sector. He also described teams as the most efficient units for work organization for complex tasks under conditions of uncertainty, but by the third century this was old news. The *Lieh tzu* from the same period proposed an empirical approach to task analysis, outcomes monitoring, and job specialization twenty-two centuries before Fayol and Taylor.

By the first century B.C.E., *The Three Strategies of Huang Shih-Kung* described how to connect job performance and rewards, urging that compensation systems follow logically from an organization's intended pur-

pose. Stephen Kerr did much the same in his Presidential address to the
Academy of Management 35 years ago (Kerr, 1975). *The Three Strategies*
also discussed person-job "fit" and an approach to job motivation recognizable to anyone who is familiar today with path-goal management and
cognitive models of job performance, particularly goal-setting and expectancy theories.

In the first centuries C.E., the *Chou-Li* described how to organize work,
design jobs, conduct strategic and organizational analyses, manage workers, and develop leaders in a nonhereditary system based on professional
education for personnel selection and management development
(Schwartz, 1985; Sawyer, 2006/2007, 2007a, 2007b; Sawyer & Lee-Sawyer,
1996).

Besides producing centuries of scholarship on organizational design
and behavior, Chinese civil engineering produced centuries of innovative
job technologies, many still in use. By the sixth century BCE, Chinese
engineers had derived a method for wrought iron production. Two centuries later, they could produce and distribute tools. By the first century
C.E., Chinese manufacturing used sophisticated smelting processes which
were once thought to have inspired the Bessemer process in England
(Donkin, 2001). In the second century B.C.E., the Chinese were drilling
for natural gas and had begun producing ball bearings. A few decades
later, Chinese medical texts concluded that consumption of saturated fat
and processed sweeteners increased the incidence of what we call insulin-
related disorders.

China originated the use of decimal place numbers in cost accounting
and engineering. It produced the first decimally calibrated calipers to
standardize tolerances in irrigation and civil engineering. By the turn of
the millennium, Chinese organizational theorists understood hierarchical
and functional organizational designs, division of labor, and the efficien-
cies of task specialization, job training, transfer of training, and safety
compliance within hierarchically controlled functional management
structures. By the fifth century B.C.E., China had an annotation system for
harmonic composition. We may yet find that China had the first sheet-
music industry. Needham also discovered ninth century B.C.E. references
to a device whose name translates as something like "mouth-driven,
vibrating reed harmony device"—essentially, a harmonica.

China held the first academic conferences in the first century C.E.
About the same time, Chinese agricultural specialists devised a water
pump capable of siphoning rivers to a height of 15 feet for long-distance
irrigation. The system is still in use. The Dujiangyan irrigation project on
the Min River, dating from the third century B.C.E., still functions. By the
second or third century C.E., China had seismographs and sophisticated
ventures in mining, metallurgy, crop irrigation, and flood control. Our

earliest records of agricultural management and pharmaceutical production date from the same period and probably originated much earlier. Chinese construction firms created the first iron chain suspension bridges (Winchester, 1996, 2008).

Taoist scholars produced the first proof of the hexagonal structure of snowflakes, the first pharmacopeia (seventh century), the first mechanical clock (eighth century), and specifications for a machine whose name translates as "flying conveyance," a propeller-driven aircraft. Chinese mathematicians described formulas which look like wave theories of physics. Liebniz received translations of Taoist and twelfth-century Confucian documents which led him to believe, though incorrectly, that Chinese mathematicians had resolved problems with binary logic with which he was wrestling.

History credits Blaise Pascal for one of the first calculators. However, early in his years in China, Joseph Needham visited a typical tailor's shop and found employees using a device called a *suuan-pan* or *wu-zhu*, which Winchester (2008) (paraphrasing Needham) describes as "a desktop machine, a venerable contraption of heavy teak spheroids and worn brass fixtures," which "predated any calculating engine made in the West" (p. 68). Intrigued, Needham traced the device to somewhere between the second and sixth centuries C.E. to an invention whose name translates as something like "ball-arithmetic-machine."

The record also includes the earliest economic applications of blast furnaces, arched bridges (many still in use), stirrups, crossbows, smallpox vaccinations, personal sanitation, wheelbarrows, and game theories. We know that the Chinese synthesized gunpowder. Explosive technology permitted excavation systems for road construction, flood control, mining, and metallurgy. China had multistage rockets at about the time the Jesuit missionary Matteo Ricci wrote from Beijing to dismiss Chinese astronomers who had proven that the stars are not solid spheres, a belief which lasted in Europe long past Ricci himself.

With infrequent exceptions, China was closed to the West for most of its history. However, the West was aware of its vast market potential at least since the Enlightenment. In 1791, Alexander Hamilton noted in the *Report on Manufactures* that America should consider Asia as a potential customer base. During the nineteenth century we looked to China for labor to construct transportation and commercial infrastructure on the Western frontier. Our interest changed after the recession of 1893. As the American frontier closed, trade with China suddenly seemed very important, doubling between 1895 and 1900 though still representing a small fraction of American exports. These were the years in which America developed an "open door" policy which tried to maintain China as an accessible market instead of segmented parcels of European, Russian, and

Japanese interests. By then, we had begun to consider China as a moral obligation for enlightenment. People probably agreed with Secretary of State Gresham that the Chinese were a "vast inert mass." But they were an inert mass of market opportunity and potential for Western enlightenment. The Progressive movement in the new American politics of the 1900s called for Europe and America to bring China enforced economic enlightenment, to convert the Chinese from "ancestor worship," to change their family-based social order, to mandate education on a Western model, and to "individualize" members of the working class (Ross, 1911).

Then came the Boxer Rebellion, then a new Chinese Republic, then increasing economic contention among China, Japan, and Russia, then interests in oil and commodities, then the two world wars, then Mao, and then ultimately Nixon. If business practice and business education in the West thought about China during the years, we probably thought about it in terms of supply and demand, certainly not as an inspiration or originator for most of the technologies on which Western enterprise depended. By the 1970s, as Needham's volumes were appearing, we knew very little indeed about the history of Chinese enterprise.

Were he writing today, would Voltaire still maintain that Chinese innovations were unknown and unrecorded in the West? On the one hand, we have a far better historical record than he did. On the other hand, that record is hard to find in business curricula. Perhaps it is merely academic to consider who exactly invented "succession planning" or "total quality management" or "wrought iron production" or "hydraulic irrigation" or "natural gas exploration." Those details are interesting, but it is more interesting that they came from a market driven culture which had much to say about the natural environment and people in it, putting the details into a context which we can not ignore.

OVERLOOKING ENVIRONMENTAL SUSTAINABILITY AND ECOLOGICAL WELLNESS

Second: Western management curricula overlook the priority of environmental sustainability and ecological wellness at the source of Chinese innovation.

Traditional China saw "work" and "value" differently from the West. The differences arose from cultural norms. Management education has identified some of these. Our literature discusses Chinese norms of reciprocity such as *ren q'ing*, the complex and highly nuanced sets of expectations governing business and social life (Liu, Friedman, & Chi, 2005). We have not gone much further than this preliminary understanding. When we think about China's normative systems, we almost always narrow our thinking to Confucius. Confucianism has a profound influence upon social organization and management practice. Confucianism, however, was not China's sole founding tradition.

Sometimes complementary, sometimes contradictory, Taoism was at least as important as Confucianism, particularly in the area of technological and process innovation interacting with the natural environment. We would have little reason to think so based upon the literatures in management education and practice. A recent keyword search of management databases produced many references to Confucianism but only passing references to Taoism, none addressing the tradition's vast impact on public and private enterprise in the context of a sustainable natural ecology (Davis, 2003; Egri & Ralston, 2004; Hofstede & Bond, 1988, Liu, Friedman, & Chi, 2005; Lynton & Hogh-Thogersen, 2006; Yang, Chen, Choi, & Zou, 2000). Two of its principles have particular importance for how we can teach about global management: Taoism explicitly equated innovation with sustainability, and it described economic activity in terms of "energy" compatible with practices emerging in the West today.

The Identity of Innovation and Ecological Balance

Taoism emerged out of shamanic traditions in northern Asia by about the sixth or fifth centuries B.C.E., roughly contemporaneous with Confucius (Eliade, 1974; Groot, 1892–1910). "Tao" loosely translates as "the way" or "the course", as in the course of a river. However, a fundamental idea in Taoism is that it cannot be verbally defined and that any verbal definition must by definition be incorrect. The notion, say, of a "river" which "flows" suggests an objective external object with specific physical properties. The Tao is neither. It ontologically exists, but it is not external. Even distinguishing "internal" from "external" is problematic. Taoism is better considered a cosmology of balance. Confucianism developed a norm of social balance; Taoism emphasized alignment with the world conceived as interacting sets of individuals, groups, and the natural environment (Kaptchuk, 2000; Wong, 1997).

This distinction does not suggest that Taoism is uninterested in social order, nor that Confucius ignored individuality. Instead Taoism sees the world and its observable features as isomorphic and radically interdependent, a tradition of organic materialism in which "balance" is the necessary condition for all questions of value. Nature is self-organizing; we function optimally only when individuals, groups, and societies are in step with it. This way of thinking differs radically from Western concepts of goal-directed activity and value. A fundamental premise of Western thinking is Aristotle's law of contradictions which, within his system of meta-physics and ethics, specifies that something cannot at the same time be itself, and also not be itself. For Taoism, things must be *both* themselves and their opposites. It would be impossible to imagine that individuals or societies could "benefit" in any sense if the natural environment were damaged. The distinction is just not comprehensible. This difference in Taoist and Western perspectives was unconcealed for the author in a dia-logue with senior Chinese managers at a conference devoted, among other things, to how our models of professional development and behav-ior diverge without our realizing how, why, or sometimes even when.

Analogies may help. "Shareholder value" does not fit especially well in Taoism, which would probably be more comfortable with the eighteenth century understanding of appreciated gain. Taoism might describe "gain" as a distributed set of outcomes in which any unit's share is something like a piece of a mosaic whose structure, interests, and activities mirror those of larger collections of pieces and ultimately of the mosaic as a whole. "Value" would be the extent to which an "investment" of energy, of money, of outlook preserves or restores this mirroring within the overall natural environment. Economic activity generates value only if collective wealth and health, very hard for Taoism to separate, mirror the resources of the natural world. The reasoning would probably go something like this: gains and losses proceed as a function of time. Unexpected condi-tions determine responses; responses are "valuable" if they produce a net gain, a value at least equal to the resources expended in the face of uncer-tainty. Those resources can be drawn from any level of individual, social, or natural life. The benefits accrue to individuals, societies, and natural life in the form of wellness and prosperity. But if one group expends resources from another and fails to distribute the gain equally, the result will be a progressive degradation of that resource, which will precipitate declining value which no amount of linear strategic thinking can offset. The analogy fails if we try to stretch it to social polity to justify particular distributive economics such as socialism, free market capitalism, or com-munism. Taoism has no interest in doing so, but no problem either with turning a profit. The point is much broader than that, an operation more like natural law than political or legislative ideology.

A domain where Taoist and Western perspectives may start to converge involves risk and uncertainty and value. The interplay of "risk," "uncer-tainty," and "value" is absolutely central to Taoist approaches to strategy. Here, Western professional education may be on to something very important in reviving Knight's (1921) warnings about confounding risk with uncertainty, as evident in a series of new volumes on such things as the "Black Swan" phenomenon (Taleb, 2007). Yet even here there is little evidence to suggest that economists and engineers realize how closely their thinking corresponds to ancient Taoist texts.

"Energy" as a Source and Outcome of Enterprise in Taoism

Another analogy might be a bank account or a portfolio whose units are something like "energy," a term of particular practical importance in Taoism. At the end of the Qin dynasty, the Chinese commentator Yen Fu invited this analogy when he wrote that economic activity is an embodiment of energy, especially in the Western world. (Yen Fu also predicted a century ago that Western economies would face desolation if they continued to ignore the primacy of the natural environment in economic activity (Schwartz, 1964)). "Energy" exists isomorphically in people, groups, social structures, and the natural environment. Properly managed, the account or portfolio sustains "energy" and generates opportunities for increase in each level of the system. Badly managed, the account can be overdrawn or the portfolio imbalanced, increasing risk and ultimately loss. If enough accounts are overdrawn or unsecured, the result will be failure.

Taoism is not a romantic or utopian ideal. It does not consider "energy" to be a metaphor. Its distribution is material, readily observable, and nowhere more conspicuous than in human illness, social disorder, and environmental degradation. If your company is sustaining six percent growth but generates stress-related turnover, the enterprise is failing. Perhaps you would generate 8% growth without the turnover. Perhaps the turnover will prove progressively costly and the return will shrink. Similarly, if your operations produce toxic byproducts which in any way harm people or the natural environment, quarterly shareholder value is a meaningless and even destructive measure of gain. In the intermediate term or the long run, the degradation will vastly outweigh momentary appearance of well-being.

This conception of balance within an economy and between an economy and its natural environment is not entirely alien to the West. Bansal (2002) used a similar metaphor to model "sustainability" as an interdependent imperative at individual, enterprise, and social levels. For Taoist tradition, the model was not a metaphor. It was an ontological fact, an *a priori* given. Cantonese has an aphorism which captures this sense of energy, balance, and value. It translates to something like "earth, people, heavens (or perhaps "cosmos")—they're all the same." All depend on equivalent forms of energy which can be gained, lost, and potentially renewed. Classical Chinese medicine, empirically derived within Taoism, distinguished three primary types of energy.

The first of these, *Qi*, appears in physical activity, especially involuntary movement. It underlies growth and development, but it is not a *cause* of such development. It *is* such development. *Qi* is protective, initially transmitted through conception. It can also be absorbed from the right relationships with the natural environment (assuming appropriate balance). It can be drawn down or exhausted, particularly by imbalance. Uncorrected, this drawing down will have destructive consequences for individual health and collective well-being. The imbalance will not be hard to recognize because it is immediately visible as individual symptomology, as social disruption, and as natural disaster or degradation.

Jin, or "essence," is a second category of energy, specific to organic life, a subtle force described as a kind of soft potential. The classic texts say that it can be felt in contemplative practice, an idea which influenced some forms of Chinese and Japanese Buddhism. Others describe it as an unfolding factor which guides whether potentials can be realized over long periods.

Shen, or "spirit," is the unique texture of human life. It is the capacity for relationships, the kind of energy which moves people together in goal-oriented tasks. It is also the source of the unique human capacity for self-regulation and for reflection upon how activity interacts with the natural world (Kaptchuk, 2000; Wong, 1997).

Taoist empirical science tried to describe how these forces work, what happens when one of them (which means when all of them) go out of balance, and how to address the situation. People in the West have encountered some of these ideas in accounts or experiences of classical Chinese medicine which can be highly effective in treating a number of conditions including stress related disorders, one of the most troubling outcomes (or symptoms) of modern management. But very few in the West have considered how these same forces apply to collective activities such as management.

We do have constructs in organizational behavior which approach some of these same ideas. For example, we traditionally view workplace motivation as persistence over time of goal-directed energy or effort. We are also devoting much attention to workplace well-being. "Balance" is now part of the management vocabulary. Like Taoism, too, we are developing interventions by which management can increase resilience in ways that add value in both Taoist and Western econometric terms. These interventions demonstrably address issues such as job stress, burnout, job design, work-life conflict, self-efficacy, safety compliance, prosocial performance, and employee withdrawal (Bruch & Ghoshal, 2003; Hamel & Valikangas, 2003; Hampden-Turner & Trompenaars, 2001; Luthans, Avolio, & Youssef, 2007; Luthans, Avolio, Walumbwa, & Li, 2005). All may demonstrate how Taoist principles can be directly operationalized and directed toward workplace well-being in modern organizations.

RAISING ISSUES ON WELL-BEING AND SUSTAINABLE DEVELOPMENT

Third: Classical China offers resources by which management education can raise issues on topics relating to well-being and sustainable development.

Two examples illustrate how classical Chinese tradition can inform Western management, particularly regarding environmental sustainability. The first involves the emerging interest in workplace well-being. The second relates to new thinking about how (or whether) to train students to consider optimization as being "sufficiency" in value, the balance point at which enough is enough, beyond which neither individuals nor enterprises can succeed without physiological and environmental damage.

Well-Being, Positive Organizational Development, and Energy

Western economics is comfortable defining economic activity as interactive forms of "energy." As noted earlier, we often describe "worker motivation" as a kind of physical force. Chinese documents from the seventh century B.C.E. used a similar metaphor (Sawyer, 2007a, 2007b). In cross-functional job design and autonomous teams, sociotechnical systems approach the Taoist idea of *shen*. Taoism would recognize the kinds of issues being explored in positive organizational scholarship. It would likely be very interested in our work in employee resilience. In *The Art of War*, possibly the most widely read book in Asia on competitive advantage and strategy, Sun Tzu emphasized leaders' need to cultivate *Qi* energy to sustain high functioning groups.

Chinese tradition also provides a way to generalize the business case for "balance" and "value" to the natural environment. Taoism understands perfectly well that people who expend more energy than they replenish will cease to be well and will eventually cease to exist. It understands that the same dynamic pertains to groups. Those concepts are foundational to Taoist naturalism. But Taoism would probably not say that individuals or businesses are *responsible* for the natural environment, at least in the ways that we tend to discuss corporate social responsibility, sustainability, and leadership ethics in our classrooms. Taoism would make a stronger claim, that the natural environment is the primary measure of true value. Expressed in terms of Western measurement, Taoism would say that environmental sustainability is the ultimate criterion. This criterion is precisely the one Yen Fu urged us to adopt over a century ago, before time runs out on business practices which assume other measures are appropriate. Commercial success, worker well-being, and environmental resilience are the same thing. Managing one is sustaining the others.

SUFFICIENCY IN VALUE, OR WHEN ENOUGH IS ENOUGH

Taoism understands gain and loss. As pragmatic as it is, though, Taoism would have a hard time understanding how neoclassical economics defines productivity as the activities of multiple additive factors in the form of an absolute linear model of growth and well-being. Taoism would probably see "total factor productivity" as the extent to which benefit accrues isomorphically across individual, group, and ecological lines. "Loss" would be the observed decrement if one of these lagged the others. "Productivity" would not be a compensatory operation in which competitive initiatives could offset deficit in one area with greater success in another. If the firm grows while its employees accrue the physiological effects of stress, then the enterprise is a failure no matter how large the annual bonuses might be.

Confucians approached the question differently but reached similar strategic conclusions about behavior and rewards. For them, an enterprise's value is not cumulative growth but rather something like "satiety" or "sufficiency," a situation in which everyone (people, governments, the natural world) has "enough." Confucius was explicit about this in the *Analects*. The successful leader is the one who ensures enough tools, enough food, enough sincerity in enterprise. Beyond "enough," there is very little potential gain. On the other hand, there is a much higher risk of instability. Confucians and neo-Confucians repeatedly described wise leaders as those who cultivate satiety as a virtue, a trait which produces an economy of sufficiency which guarantees social stability and the opportunity for higher pursuits. Leadership without "virtue" produces social failure and strife, conditions far harder to suppress than to prevent. Suppression, frequent in Chinese history, produces ecological devastation, destruction of the agricultural economy, and guaranteed insufficiency. The preventative is simply expressed: Know when enough is enough.

Is this a lesson which China itself can recall? Some express serious doubt, and the implications for global sustainability are ominous (Bosworth & Collins, 2003; Jones, 2002; Krugman, 1994; Tinari & Lam, 1991). Can Western management consider such a norm? It might. Leadership training in some areas of our economy is speaking in terms similar to Confucius' and his followers', particularly in defense and public safety. We have ample classroom resources to explore questions of right behavior, executive compensation, competing interests, and appropriate levels of regulation. Maslow's or Alderfer's motivational models appear in almost every primer on leadership, organizational behavior, and the fundamentals of management. The true utility of needs hierarchies in the workplace has been questioned, but their models retain a strong intuitive appeal which a Confucian strategist would instantly understand. The point of satisfying one level of needs is to free "energy" or motivation to pursue others. There is no point in trying to exceed satiety at any particular level. Doing so would have no utility and would not be a sign of effective management. Instead it would be a sure predictor of discord and loss because it would absorb energy which should be available for people to cultivate higher goals.

The classical Chinese traditions help frame such discussions. The historical texts, very many of them now in translation, represent a library of case materials, simulations, and best practice advice. As an example, many centuries ago Wei Liao-Tzu claimed that nature provides all the models we need to understand leadership strategy. He provided a number of case examples in support. Given that these materials are among the best selling business texts in the Pacific Rim, hadn't we better bring them to the attention of Western students? What would it mean to do so? How might the discussions of environmental sustainability change as a result?

SOME CAUTIONS

Four: Despite its traditions, Chinese innovation may ultimately prove a failure and precipitate environmental catastrophe.

Management education is incomplete and inaccurate in its presentation of the historical record. Asian traditions may provide a framework for new ways to think about global enterprise in a sustainable world. However, some cautions are in order. Despite centuries of achievement, we cannot conclude that the Chinese traditions have served China or Asia themselves, at least in recent centuries.

Taoism's empirical pragmatism inspired centuries of technological development; Confucian social principles guided the definition of effective social order. Neither produced utopia. We ought to resist any suggestion that Chinese history shows an evolution of Confucian systems within Taoist and Buddhist ideals. Any such suggestion is utterly inaccurate. China's history shows a successive culture of dynasties interrupted by oppression, lawlessness, natural catastrophes, and insurgencies. It also shows incidents of strategically induced environmental catastrophes such as flooding and agricultural contamination to suppress popular protest. This history does not impugn the intrinsic merit of Taoism, Confucianism, and Chinese Buddhism which offer no moral support whatsoever for such activities. However, the history does demonstrate that normative ideals in Taoism and Confucianism defined Chinese society no more perfectly than Western religions or philosophies defined Western society.

Something happened in China four or five centuries ago to slow technological and process innovation The situation is sometimes called the "Needham question" after a marginal notation in one of Needham's manuscripts asking why Chinese competitive innovation seemed to decline as the West began to move toward the Enlightenment, the industrial revolution, and a uniquely "Western" view of enterprise in the natural order. That something happened seems hard to deny. The evidence for extraordinary enterprise and innovation in China weakens over these centuries. In measurable economic terms, Chinese productivity and real growth shows nearly a linear decline in relationship to Europe during this period. In the fifteenth century, China had an international mercantile fleet as ambitious as those of Portugal and Spain. The fleet was eliminated by imperial decree. China has not yet recovered its naval capacity, a condition of great interest to defense strategists in recent years. Further, the Needham question asks why something so counterproductive as radical global isolation emerged for China as so stringent a global position. That it had done so was no secret to the West. In the eighteenth century, almost as Alexander Hamilton (the leading advocate for centralized banking in the new United States) was suggesting exchange with China, Adam Smith wrote that something had gone very wrong in the East.

In all likelihood, official Chinese policy would emphatically deny that Needham's question had any rational basis. Official policy would probably also challenge the suggestion that Confucian tradition has been other than the continent's guiding premise over the centuries, at least until Marxism (Meyer, 2008; Pan, 2008; Sawyer, 2006/2007; Yiwu, 2008). The argument might be stronger were it to point to the devastating impact of Western colonialism on China's development, especially in the nineteenth century. Winchester (2008) is inclined to see the quiet centuries as a hiatus in three thousand years of remarkable Chinese innovation. Perhaps too the Confucian and Taoist principles which shaped China's economic order had reached an asymptote at the time that Europe and China began maritime commerce. In their own ways, Confucianism and Taoism are ideals of sufficiency, natural order, stability, and balance. They are not expansionist ideologies. Nothing in them imagines a desirable order beyond natural polity in which the natural world is a container for development and not a gameboard for global competition.

Though unanswered, the Needham question is also worth considering because it invites other important questions. One of these is whether and how we can avoid moving global enterprise in ways that Taoism would (correctly) see as calamitous to the natural environment. Another is whether surging Asian economies have perhaps learned Western management too well, particularly regarding the acceptability of environmental destruction in the calculus of profit. Can the lesson be changed (McDonough, 2002)?

Winchester (1996) offers an interesting case in this regard. Southwest China receives considerable precipitation in the form of annual rainfall and snowmelt. In particularly heavy years, the Yangtze River is capable of extraordinary flooding, sometimes producing a tidal wave ten feet high. Such a flooding happened most recently in 1931, when 140,000 people drowned, 28 million were displaced, and seventy thousand square miles were flooded, covering the equivalent in area of New Jersey, New York State, and most of Connecticut. How to control the Yangtze has been a lively concern since the third and fourth centuries B.C.E. The potential for loss of life is great; at the same time, the agricultural economy depends on the Yangtze much as Egypt's depends on the Nile. China had developed sophisticated hydraulic, dike, and levee technology by the first century C.E. The Taoists and the Confucians historically disagreed over how best to use these technologies on the Yangtze.

The Confucians favored large dikes to create a series of reservoirs fed by the river. Their approach accepted the risk of occasional flooding. The social order is ineluctable. The Confucians did not welcome catastrophe, but understood that different rungs of the social ladder would selectively bear the brunt of specific hardships. The Confucian plan had the additional benefits of increased irrigation fed by an expanded reservoir system, permitting greater agricultural opportunities.

The Taoists, on the other hand, supported the gradual development of low levees to permit the river to establish its own distributed course around the points of greatest flood risk, restricting agricultural opportunity but substantially reducing the risk of catastrophic flooding. These alternatives capture important elemental differences between Taoism and Confucianism.

Modern China developed a third alternative, the Three Gorges Dam, whose stated purpose is to control flooding and to produce hydroelectric power. The project initially generated great interest in the international finance community, but much of that interest retreated when consultants from the U.S. Army Corps of Engineers and elsewhere warned that the dam would not prevent flooding and might create extraordinary silt concentrations downriver. China proceeded with the project. The results have been enormous population relocations, the permanent disruption of whole regional economies, threats to species native to the Yangtze, and the possibility that something like an earthquake (and Three Gorges is close to an historic earthquake zone) could unleash flooding and ecological catastrophe unprecedented in recorded history. Winchester (1996) described the outcome as "ruination by pollution, squalor, filth, ugly architecture, wanton tree felling, factory building, and artificially induced land erosion" (p. 277). Were Taoism to use Western concepts, it might describe the results as an unforgivable sin.

Perhaps we should not generalize Three Gorges to China's overall economic, commercial, and environmental aspirations. Even so, Three Gorges begs a question: To what extent might this sort of project reflect a developing economy's drive to emulate the "best practices" of Western development? We have exported management constructs and practices to business education in China (cf. Farh, Zhong, & Organ, 2004; Hui, Lee, & Roussea, 2004). Virtually no evidence shows a reciprocal effect upon Western business education. Further, virtually no evidence suggests that Chinese business education incorporates Taoist traditions any more extensively than we do, despite these traditions' records of achievement and their business models that presume stewardship of natural resources is seamless with individual and social well-being.

We are concerned, and we had better be, with how economic development can proceed consistently with environmental sustainability. The concern is not new, except perhaps in scale and in urgency, given the nearly inarguable precipice of environmental hazard and worker well-being to which we have come. The Asian historical record demonstrates that highly innovative people over many centuries found a way to frame questions important to what we now face and systematically developed and pursued options to address those questions. Among other things, globalization gives us the opportunity and the imperative to reflect deeply on what they thought and did and how it might guide us in training business leaders for a future of risk which our ancestors would immediately have recognized.

REFERENCES

Bansal, P. (2002). The corporate challenges of sustainable development. *Academy of Management Development, 16,* 122–131.

Bosworth, B., & Collins, S. (2003). The empirics of growth: An update. *Brookings Papers on Economic Activity, 2,* 113–179.

Bruch, H., & Ghoshal, S. (2003). Unleashing organizational energy. *MIT/Sloan Management Review, 45*(1), 45–51.

Chen, C. C., Chen, Y-R., & Xin, K. (2004). *Guanxi* practices and trust in management: A procedural justice perspective. *Organization Science, 15,* 200–209.

Davis, D. D. (2003). The Tao of leadership in virtual teams. *Organizational Dynamics, 33*, 47–62.

Donkin, R. (2001). *Blood, sweat and tears: The evolution of work*. London: Texere.

Egri, C., & Ralston, D. (2004). Generation cohorts and personal values: A comparison of China and the United States. *Organization Science, 15*, 210–220

Eliade, M. (1974). *Shamanism*. Princeton: Princeton University Press.

Farh, J. L., Zhong, C. B., & Organ, D. (2004). Organizational citizenship behavior in the People's Republic of China. *Organization Science, 15*, 241–253.

Groot, J. M. (1892–1910). *The religious system of China*. Six volumes. London: Literature House.

Hamel, G., & Valikangas, L. (2003). The quest for resilience. *Harvard Business Review, 85*(9) 52–63.

Hampden-Turner, C., & Trompenaars, H. (2001) *Mastering the infinite game: How East Asian values are transforming business practices*. London: Capstone.

Hofstede, G., & Bond, M. H. (1988). The Confucius connection: From cultural roots to economic growth. *Organizational Dynamics, 16*, 4–21.

Hui, C., Lee, C., & Rousseau, D. M. (2004). Employment relationships in China: Do workers relate to the organization or to people? *Organization Science, 15*, 232-240.

Jones, C. (2002). *Introduction to economic growth* (2nd ed.). New York: Norton.

Kaptchuk, T. (2000). *The web that has no weaver: Understanding Chinese medicine* (2nd ed.). New York: Contemporary Books.

Kerr, S. (1975). On the folly of rewarding A, while hoping for B. *Academy of Management Journal, 18*, 769–783.

Knight, R. C. (1921). *Risk, uncertainty, and profit*. New York: Houghton Mifflin.

Krugman, P. (1994). The myth of Asia's miracle. *Foreign Affairs, 73*, 62–78.

Liu, A. L., Friedman, R. A., & Chi, S-C. (2005). "*Ren qing*" versus the "Big Five": The role of culturally sensitive measures of individual difference in distributive negotiations. *Management and Organization Review, 1*, 225–247.

Luthans, F., Avolio, B. J., & Youssef, F. (2007). *Psychological capital*. Oxford, England: Oxford University Press.

Luthans, F., Avolio, B. J., Walumbwa, F., & Li, W. (2005). The psychological capital of Chinese workers: Exploring the relationship with performance. *Management and Organization Review, 1*, 249-271.

Lynton, N., & Hogh-Thogersen, K. (2006). How China transforms an executive's mind. *Organizational Dynamics, 35*, 170–181.

McDonough, W. (2002). China as a green lab. *Harvard Business Review, 84*(2), 38–39.

Meyer, M. (2008). *The last days of old Beijing*. New York: Walker.

Needham, J. (1954-1994). *Science and civilization in China. 24 volumes*. Cambridge: Cambridge University Press.

Needham, J. (1969). *The grand titration: Science and society in East and West*. London: Allen & Unwin.

Needham, J. (1981). *Science in traditional China: A comparative perspective*. Cambridge: Harvard University Press.

Pan, P. (2008). *Out of Mao's shadow: The struggle for the soul of a new China*. New York: Simon & Schuster.

Ross, E. A. (1911). *The changing Chinese: The conflict of oriental and western cultures in China*. New York: Century Books.

Sawyer, R. D. (2006/2007). Chinese strategic power: Myths, intent, and projections. *Journal of Military and Strategic Studies, 9*, 4–64.

Sawyer, R. D. (2007a). *The Tao of deception*. NewYork: Perseus Books.

Sawyer, R. D. (Trans. and Ed.) (2007b). *The seven military classics of ancient China*. New York: Basic Books.

Sawyer, R. D., & Lee-Sawyer, M-C. (Ed. and Trans.). (1996). *One hundred unorthodox strategies*. Boulder: Westview Press.

Schwartz, B. I. (1964). *In search of wealth and power: Yen-Fu and the west*. Cambridge: Harvard University Press

Schwartz, B. I. (1985). *The world of thought in ancient China*. Cambridge: Harvard University Press.

Taleb, N. N. (2007). *The black swan: The impact of the highly improbable*. New York: Random House.

Tinari, F. D., & Lam, D. (1991). China's resistance to economic reforms. *Contemporary Policy Issues, 9*, 82–92.

Winchester, S. (1996). *The river at the center of the world*. New York: Henry Holt.

Winchester, S. (2008). *The man who loved China*. New York: Harper Collins.

Wong, E. (1997). *Taoism*. Boston: Shambhala.

Yang, N., Chen, C., Choi, J., & Zou, Y. (2000). Sources of work-family conflict: A Sino-U.S. comparison of the effects of work and family demands. *Academy of Management Journal, 43*, 113–123.

Yiwu, L. (2008). *The corpse walker: Real life stories: China from the bottom up*. New York: Pantheon.

PART II

APPROACHES TO BRINGING GLOBAL SUSTAINABILITY INTO MANAGEMENT EDUCATION

CHAPTER 5

DEVELOPING A SUSTAINABILITY CONSCIOUSNESS THROUGH ENGAGEMENT WITH ART

Ralph Bathurst and Margot Edwards

This chapter adopts an artistic view of the issue of sustainability. We identify war as the most significant global barrier to sustainable development. We argue that art offers a means of unmasking the underlying heroic myths of war, a necessary antecedent to developing sustainable business practices. To do so we begin by examining the current literature on sustainability and adopt a critical position of the ideology that seeks a balance between exploitation and preservation. In this light we discuss the role of the artist as social commentator and explore the aesthetic of dissonance using the metaphor of the catalytic jolt. We then examine contemporary art, and in particular an analysis of a work by Australasian artist Tom Mutch, the *Carbon Footprint* and note how this kind of approach can be used as an educational tool in the business studies classroom. Our discussion ends by looking at how our relationship with the planet may be nurtured and, the need to institute sustainable practices that ensure a thriving future.

Management Education for Global Sustainability, pp. 115–137
Copyright © 2009 by Information Age Publishing
All rights of reproduction in any form reserved.

Progress is not determined then by economic conditions, by physical conditions, nor by biological factors solely, but more especially by our capacity for genuine cooperation.

—Mary Parker Follett (1926)

The need for sustainable business practice and concerns about the effect of overuse of the earth's resources is of global importance. However, this is not a new phenomenon. Writing at the end of World War I, the political commentator and management theorist Mary Parker Follett mirrors some of our contemporary anxieties. Within the context of embittered industrial relations and international conflict that the Great War was unable to solve, Follett (1926) bluntly declares that:

> Our political life is stagnating, capital and labor are virtually at war, the nations of Europe are at one another's throats – because we have not yet learned how to live together. The twentieth century must find a new principle of association. Crowd philosophy, crowd government, crowd patriotism must go. The herd is no longer sufficient to enfold us. (p. 1)

Follett could have been addressing us, for, almost a century later we are still grappling with similar kinds of chauvinistic attitudes. The question is still just as provocative: how do we work together productively and creatively so that we can live sustainably?

The global rise of the business school that sees students seeking generic skills that will enable them to run successful businesses within trans-national contexts has yet to succeed in embedding a sustainability consciousness in graduates. Students enroll in courses with a desire to learn marketing techniques, leadership strategies, and the financial skills that will ensure success of their future enterprises. Until very recently, the focus on efficiency and instrumentality has lacked sensitivity to the impact of business on the environment. Now, however, awareness of sustainability and efforts to mitigate impacts on the environment are becoming business imperatives. Public interest and governance pressures for a sustainable future are high with global warming being featured almost daily in the news media.

However, a change in thinking from growth and efficiency to sustainability is difficult to embed. In this chapter we inquire into the nature of sustainability by taking a macro view. We argue that international conflict is a root problem and that eliminating war is a necessary precursor to achieving sustainability. On this basis, we maintain that localized efforts at achieving sustainable business practice stem from and are directly related to this larger context. We explore the role of the artist as provocateur and demonstrate how art, especially painting, can offer new ways of looking at the issue of sustainability.

War's indiscriminate destruction strikes at the heart of social and economic development. The propensity to take up arms to solve conflict is endemic and, as Winter (1981) notes, human history is littered with evidences of this nihilism.

> Human beings have been pushing and shoving each other so much that they have destroyed well over 90% of their own handiwork. Their libraries, their literature, their cities, their works of art are mostly gone. Even what remains from the distant past is riddled with evidences of a strange and pervasive evil that has grotesquely distorted man's potential. This is strange because apparently no other species of life treats its own with such deadly malignant hatred. The oldest skulls bear mute witness that they were bashed in and roasted to deliver their contents as food for still other human beings. (p. 137)

As our destructive abilities have grown in sophistication more of the earth's resources are extracted for harmful purposes. For, as Cooper and Vargas (2008) declare, "war, violent civil disorder, and terrorism are the *antithesis* of sustainable development" (p. 1, emphasis added).

And yet we are seemingly powerless to address our predisposition toward annihilation. War correspondent Christopher Hedges (2002) addresses this strange paradox that on the one hand war acts like an intoxicating drug that strangely "give us a purpose, meaning, a reason for living" (p. 3), while on the other takes the very life that we seek.

> War exposes a side of human nature that is usually masked by the unacknowledged coercion and social constraints that glue us together. Our cultivated conventions and little lies of civility lull us into a refined and idealistic view of ourselves. But modern industrial warfare may well be leading us, with each technological advance, a step closer to our own annihilation. We too are strapping explosives around our waists. Do we also have a suicide pact? (pp. 12–13)

In order to provide a language that critiques the effects of war on the sustainability project we turn to art and painting in particular. We argue in this chapter that art offers a means of unmasking the underlying heroic myths of war, a necessary antecedent to developing sustainable business practices. To do so we begin by examining the literature on sustainability and adopt a critical position of current ideology that seeks a balance between exploitation and preservation. We then turn to a discussion on the role of the artist as social commentator and explore the aesthetic of dissonance using the metaphor of the catalytic jolt. We then turn to a discussion of contemporary art, and in particular an analysis of a work by

Australasian artist Tom Mutch, the *Carbon Footprint*. Our discussion ends back where we began by looking at how our relationship with the planet and the need to institute sustainable practices that ensure a successful future may be nurtured.

SUSTAINABILITY

Discussing the pros and cons of adopting a particular position and offering comprehensive information is a vexed issue when it comes to studying global sustainability. Kellstedt, Zahran, and Vedlitz (2008) present a fascinating study on attitudes people show toward global warming and climate change after being exposed to scientific ideas about the disastrous consequences of failing to take remedial action. They offer the paradoxical finding that "the more information a person has about global warming, the less responsible he or she feels for it" (p. 122). How can this passivity be explained? We think that it is the way in which information is presented that can account for this disconnect between knowledge and action.

The problem begins with the ways in which the issues of global sustainability have been described. Definitions of sustainability necessarily incorporate the rubric of corporate social responsibility (CSR). Classically CSR "is about seriously considering the impact of the company's actions on society" (Carroll & Buchholtz, 2003, p. 30). The definition and scope of the term "society," though, is somewhat fluid among organizational leaders trying to balance the needs of their growing businesses, the demands of shareholders, and ultimately the requirements of stakeholders. Hence Dyllick and Hockerts' (2002) definition of corporate sustainability as "meeting the needs of a firm's direct and indirect stakeholders (such as shareholders, employees, clients, pressure groups, communities etc.), without compromising its ability to meet the needs of future stakeholders as well" (p. 131) presents a rationale which enables a business to proceed to exploit available resources so long as sufficient assets are left for upcoming generations. A popular method of accounting for this kind of sustainable approach is by the so-called "triple bottom line" (Dyllick & Hockerts, 2002) where economic, environmental, and social dimensions are kept in a healthy balance.

A simplified and often clichéd approach such as the triple bottom line concept inevitably leads to parsimonious attempts at creating sustainable practices. In their provocative exploration of the metaphor of *journey* that is deployed to assuage fears of living unsustainably, Milne, Kearins, and Walton (2006) note that business leaders who proclaim they are "on the way to being sustainable" are using the metaphor to mask their continu-ing exploitation of the Earth's resources. They argue that

> by portraying themselves as "on the path to" or "moving toward" sustain-able development, businesses can avoid the stigma of being seen to be doing nothing and wedded to the old-fashioned paradigm of economic exploitation, while at the same time deflecting attention away from debating about what kind of (radically different) performance is needed to provide a sustainable future. (p. 822)

The views that Milne et al. espouse are important because they critique a concept that sees the planet as a resource to be exploited rather than being a core part of our life-support system and therefore a necessary ele-ment in our continuing future. It is important that we interrogate our beliefs about the nature of our relationship with the planet and examine the perfunctory attitude toward sustainability that Milne et al. expose. Perhaps it is the notion of the earth is a resource *for*, rather than a partner *in* our existence that underpins the underlying reluctance of contempo-rary business leaders to become proactive in creating a sustainable future.

Therefore, in order to take the radical steps necessary to become sus-tainable we need an entirely different approach: one that wakes us out of our slumbering complacency and challenges us to transform dramatically the ways in which we conceive of, and practice, business in the twenty-first century. We argue that it is the artist who offers the social critique and impetus needed to courageously confront realities we would sometimes rather ignore.

ARTISTS IN SOCIETY

Artists provide ways of looking at the world that challenge social mores and accepted practices. Following Henri Bergson (1935), we argue that art strips away "everything that veils reality from us, in order to bring us face-to-face with reality itself" (p. 157). Therefore, rather than mollifying and comforting us, the artistic agenda exposes us to issues that disturb and challenge.

Because of its symbolic form, art moves us beyond mere intellectual engagement, enabling us to *feel* at a deeper level the issues that a work might provoke (Dean, Ottensmeyer, & Ramirez, 1997, p. 422). It is as if the work of art talks back to us challenging our world view and requiring a response. For, "when we look hard enough [at a painting], it can feel as though *we're* the ones being scrutinised" (Paton, 2006, p. 21, emphasis added), as the unspeakable becomes spoken.

According to Susanne Langer (1942/1960), this heightened emotional response is generated by an interplay of "tensions and resolutions" (p. 227) that move us emotionally. Therefore, when engaging with works of art, a process of transformation occurs. Some may describe this as an epiphany or a moment of realization that captivates the imagination. Warren (2008) uses the term "trigger" (p. 560) to describe this moment in which the viewer's awareness is provoked, often turning into conversations with others where new insights are gained. Schama (2006) thinks of it as a "puncturing of routine" (p. 395) which challenges us to take action.

We adopt the term *catalytic jolt* to describe this heightened emotional response that provides the motivation for radical change. The jolt is more than a trigger event because it implies a dramatic change in perceptions and behavior. We argue that without this shock, the kinds of changes in consciousness and the social action necessary for creating a sustainable future will not occur.

Our use of this term is derived from our experience of the science laboratory where adding certain chemicals reduces reaction times. The *Oxford English Dictionary* describes a catalyst as "a substance which when present in small amounts increases the rate of a chemical reaction or process but which is chemically unchanged by the reaction" (*Oxford English Dictionary*, 2009). Typically, catalysts in chemical reactions are always material rather than existing just in the forms of light or heat. Of the three kinds of catalysts (homogeneous, heterogeneous and enzyme), those involving enzymes are the closest to our metaphoric use. Where enzymes act as catalysts, there is a "transformation of matter in living organisms [which] occur as an elaborate sequence of reactions" (Burwell & Haller, 1992, p. 557). In the case of aesthetic engagement, it is the work of art that causes a heightened reaction within the viewer setting off a chain of responses. Although the art work itself remains unchanged, the viewer is transformed, leading him or her to take further action. It should be noted here, however, that not all reactions will be positive. Some may respond to an art work by doggedly maintaining their beliefs thereby causing the effect of the catalytic agent to dissipate.

At a microlevel, the use of the catalyst metaphor is familiar to organizational scholars who see it as a way of describing the change process. In this regard, conflict (Lehman & Linsky, 2008) and culturally diverse staff (Stevens, Plaut, & Sanchez-Burks, 2008) are seen as catalytic agents within organizations. However, these illustrations do not adequately describe the ways in which catalysts offer change at a systemic level.

Our use takes this concept even further by adding the word *jolt* to the frame. Paradoxically, although the original agent remains unchanged, sufficient impetus is generated by the catalyst to bring sustained change. The art work itself does not change; the catalyst has acted on the viewer, and in this instance it is the artist in creating the work who sets in motion the reflective processes that guide thinking about sustainable practices and subsequent action. The jolt provides a moment of shock that lets the work "look right back at [us]" (Paton, 2006, p. 21) with a questioning gaze. It asks us what *we* are going to do about *this* situation. Artists recognize that it takes something extraordinary, a fresh and totally original perspective, to push the viewer to feel and think about the need for something new to occur.

However, we are tempted to deal with these uncomfortable senses of dissonance, and sometimes dislocation, by dismissing the work of art itself, deeming it to be at fault by being poorly executed or just plain ugly.

In her *New York Times* commentary on why works of art are sometimes attacked, mutilated and destroyed by those unwilling to let the piece peel back our protective ideologies, Roberta Smith (2004) argues that there is often a

> simple refusal to entertain paradox, to see art as a coalescence of gray areas, ambiguities and multiple interpretations. Art's job is to provoke thought in ways that are difficult to resolve and uncomfortable; it's a relatively neutral place to experience the irresolvable issues that dominate real life, to practice a kind of abstract flexibility that might move us toward resolution in real life. (para. 9)

Thus, we are challenged more than we are entertained and in that confrontation we are disturbed from our complacency and forced to deal with our discomfort by actively engaging with the work. It is not surprising, then, that totalitarian regimes find ways of silencing those voices either by forcing artists into exile or by imprisonment or even execution.

War Themes

We demonstrate how this catalytic jolt may occur by exploring two paintings: Dali's *Soft Construction with Boiled Beans: Premonitions of Civil War* (1936) and Picasso's *Guernica* (1937). We offer these as seminal exemplars that provoke political consciousness and set the scene for our examination of a contemporary work that offers a similar critique.

Although representing opposing ends of the political spectrum, both Dali and Picasso ruminate on the disastrous results of the Spanish Civil War (1936–1939) and challenge our complacency about accepting war as the ordinary outcome of political machinations.

Notwithstanding his estrangement from the surrealist community for his support of Franco in the Spanish Civil War, in his 1936 work *Soft Construction with Boiled Beans* with the explanatory subtitle *Premonitions of Civil*

War, Dali is clearly deeply troubled about the effects of the war on Spain. Almost as a visual lament to the destruction of humanity, the central image of the painting is a body dismembering itself while at the same time screaming in agony. In concert with this planned destruction, the clouds darken and their turbulence suggests nature's protestations at the merciless "deconstruction of the human" by the human (O'Donovan, 2007, p. 17).

Although we might be caught up in these dramatic depictions, all the while the tiny figure of a man looks over the left hand of the mutilated body as if in dazed reflection of the destruction. Who is this man? Is it Dali himself or are we the viewers invited by the artist to be that man and to become more than just casual passing observers? We gain a sense of Dali's visceral impotence, the soft beans conveying a sense of flaccid response to the events that seem to overtake this small figure almost against his will. But at the same time we are challenged with our own emasculation as we become bystanders of events that appear too big and difficult for us to resist.

> We encourage you to take a look at this painting and to consider your responses. The work hangs in the Philadelphia Museum of Art. You can also see it online at a number of different sites. Visit http://www.virtualdali.com/36SoftConstructionWithCookedBeans.html. Enter into dialogue with the work by discussing it with friends and by making your own responses to current events that threaten global sustainability.

Figure 5.1.   *Soft Beans* student discussion.

Like Dali, Picasso was also troubled by the Spanish Civil War. Courted by both sides of Spain's political divide, he remained aloof and politically agnostic in his early years by establishing his reputation as an artist of choice for wealthy elites. Schama (2006) notes that Picasso

> shrugged off any suggestion that painting might be polemical. "I'll continue to be aesthetic," he said. "I'll continue to make art without preoccupying myself with the question of whether it humanizes life." (p. 355)

Events in the spring of 1937 soon compromised Picasso's neutrality. In a bid to tame the Basque region that had fiercely resisted his advancing army, Franco recruited the favors of Hitler's Luffwaffe. On April 26th German planes crossed into Spain and firebombed the quiet country town of Guernica. Although it had no strategic significance, the obliteration of Guernica provided the German Air force with a dress rehearsal in readiness for future bombing raids on other European cities.

This atrocity galvanized Picasso and he immediately began working on a large mural which was to be exhibited in the Spanish Pavilion at the

Paris International Exhibition July 1937. No longer sitting on the fence as a quietist aesthete, he produced a work that has been called the twentieth century's "most iconic antiwar protest" (O'Donovan, 2007, p. 17).

Living in Paris at the time, Picasso had read accounts of the Guernica massacre in newspaper reports. He translates the discursive accounts into a matching monochromatic black and white work that underpins the stark reality of war's total destruction. We are confronted with screaming figures in their death throes: men, women and babies encapsulated in the horse's dying screech as it reaches up in resistance to the dominating light of technology whose omnipresence snuffs out all life. The open palm of the fallen man at the bottom left of the mural showing signs of the crucified Christ's stigmata, is reminiscent of Goya's (1814) sacrificial victim *The Third of May, 1808*. The only hope of redemption that Picasso offers is the single candle light being held toward the ubiquitous evil eye as it casts its curse on Spain.

As with Dali's painting we encourage you to linger over Picasso's *Guernica* considering your responses. The work hangs in Madrid at the Museo Nacional Centro de Arte Reina Sofia. You can see it online at URL http://www.artquotes.net/masters/picasso/picasso_guernica1937.jpg Enter into dialogue with the work by discussing it with friends and by making your own responses to current events that threaten global sustainability. There is also a full sized tapestry reproduction in the United Nations building New York.

Compare *Guernica* with Goya's *Third of May, 1808*. A reproduction of this painting can be seen at http://www.artchive.com/artchive/G/goya/may_3rd.jpg.html

---

Figure 5.2.   *Guernica* student discussion.

How do contemporary artists engage with the disastrous effects of war and advocate for forms of international diplomatic relations that consider non-destructive alternatives? We argue that this is achieved as artists peel back layers of rhetoric that seek to justify destructive practices evidenced in the Spain of the 1930s.

Franco's declaration that "to save Spain from socialism and atheism he would, if necessary, shoot half the country" (Schama, 2006, p. 371) was an ominous prophecy repeated some 36 years later by an American major to Vietnam War correspondent Peter Arnett that "it became necessary to destroy the town to save it." Known as Ben Tre Logic where an idea is put forth to destroy something to better it (Clark, 2008). Today, another 40 years later, we are confronted with a similar *non sequitur*: "How much of our planet must we destroy in order to become economically sustainable?"

How, though, does this confrontation with reality occur and what responses can we make once the artist has stripped back the veils and revealed a world less familiar? In order to address these questions we inquire into the life and work of a contemporary Australasian artist, Tom Mutch. Tom has worked as a professional artist since 1983 and although he is most celebrated as a painter, with over 40 solo and 70 group shows, he also creates silkscreen prints and sculptures, writes novels and produces short films (see Tom's Web site for reproductions of his works http://www.tommutch.com/). His production, *The Birth of Superbird*, won the New York Independent Film Festival Grand Jury Award for Best Animation in 2005. Tom's paintings demonstrate his highly developed skills and utilize strikingly colourful symbolic and allegorical imagery to explore his neo-realistic messages. Furthermore, Tom is a successful entrepreneur, having founded Bird's Nest Studio in 1996, and in rejecting the more typical artist-gallery relationships, has developed a critical perspective toward the art-business nexus. It is our belief that Tom's entrepreneurial talents, in combination with his commitment to environmental sustainability, provide valuable and challenging perspectives for business students.

Tom's painting philosophy reflects his affinity to nature – he believes that once the seed of an idea is planted in his mind, it grows if he nurtures it, keeps it warm and feeds it with his fertile mind (Webster, 2004). Early in his career, Tom was simply inspired to paint images of the natural world to record what he saw before him; but as his career matured he became more interested in the darker underbelly of the landscape and in exposing serious abuses of the environment in the name of social prosperity. For example in his *Highway Series*, Tom was concerned with the juxtaposition of commercial greed and sustainability and strove to highlight the "importance of our symbiotic relationship with all living things" (p. 106). Tom's environmental crusade rose to a new height in 2002 when he began work on his *Superbird Series*—a large body of works that focuses on issues of sustainability and the relationship between humans and natural ecology. Superbird was invented by Tom as an ecological super-hero designed to protect the world from the negative effects of rampant consumerism. Similarly, Tom's most recent works are interwoven with symbolic messages that connect global warming with the arms race. He critiques political and religious institutional forms and their links to contemporary business culture, depicting them in an unholy alliance.

Tom's work provides a "visionary, poetic and metaphorical treatment" of his subjects (Klingsöhr-Leroy, 2004, p. 14), mirroring the surrealist philosophy that arose between the World Wars of 1915 and 1939, and made popular during the Great Depression. Mutch's paintings display many of the techniques described as *veristic surrealism*. Rather than being works with images cobbled together from unrelated sources, veristic surrealism eschews self-indulgent expression in favor of a much more provocative social critique that directly engages with audiences. Veristic surrealism is distinguished from all other forms of art in its "symbolic, prismatic colour, disparate juxtapositions of representational imagery, concern for the audience, personal content, and classical technique and modelling" (Bell, 1984, p. 251). The call-to-action implied in this artistic form is evident in Bell's assertion that "it matters less how the work came to be created than what we see and what it means to us" (p. 248). Hence the latitude of interpretation available to the reader is important, more so even than the artist's or instructor's opinions. Significantly, in the interpretation of veristic surrealism, particularly that which is subcategorized as *social surrealism* by Fort (1982), there exists considerable opportunities for emotional debates because the subject matter elevates the suffering and hypocrisy inherent in culturally created sociopolitical issues.

Through his paintings, Mutch reveals a deep concern with sustainability. However, as his works depict, sustainability needs to occur at the macro level. Mutch's paintings critique the alliances between global organizations and nation-states that resist and impair any move toward achieving sustainable practice on a local scale.

ENGAGING WITH *THE CARBON FOOTPRINT*

Having scoped Tom Mutch's life and focused on his motivation as an artist, we now turn to an examination of his 2007 painting the *Carbon Footprint of War and the Pollution of Religion*. Although Mutch has a well-articulated ideology, some of which we have explored above, he holds no influence over us, the viewers of his work. In this instance the author (the painter) is no longer in control of the text (the painting), and, quoting Roland Barthes (1977), he is "dead." We are left to locate the clues that Mutch has left behind in his work and try to make sense of these ideas for ourselves.

To this end Mitchell (1987) argues that as perceivers become cognisant of structural elements within a painting by the "artful planting of certain clues" (p. 41) placed there by the artist, the viewer makes coherent meaning of the *evident*, as well as the *implied*, elements within the work. Furthermore, Mitchell claims paradoxically that "we can never understand a picture unless we grasp the ways in which it shows what *cannot* be seen" (p. 39, emphasis added).

Issues that could be considered when viewing a painting include how the artist has constructed perspective and depth of field. Further, how the colors interact and the interplay between background and foreground shapes and figures are all reading strategies open to us as we critically examine works. These elements help in our analysis of the overt symbols and assist us to narrate our own meanings. Before reading any further we encourage you to spend a few minutes looking at Figure 5.3 the *Carbon*

Footprint examining it in its entirety. Take note of the images that disturb you, analyzing what it is about them that are provocative.

In the *Carbon Footprint* we are immediately confronted with starkly contrasting images. A black and white stylized image of the Madonna and Child on the left sits alongside a man in a suit and a skeletal head. These two dominant images present an immediate dissonance as we ask, "Why is the pursuit of spiritual enlightenment placed alongside brute images of business and war?" It appears on first reading that these polar opposites present two alternative visions of the world.

The left half of the painting is rich in biblical symbolism. The mountain in the top left background and the trees at its base are reminiscent of both the spiritual journey (Moses receiving the Decalogue from God on Mt. Sinai) and innocence (the Tree of Life at the center of the Garden of Eden in its pre-fall state), while in the foreground we are invited to celebrate the Eucharistic Feast. For an example of a medieval painting that contains this kind of symbolism see Sassetta's *Meeting of St Anthony and St Paul* (1440). (See Figure 5.4).

We are comforted, redeemed, safe in our lifestyles and assured in this optimistic and perpetual state of green and blue. And yet there is some-

Figure 5.3.   *The Carbon Footprint of War and the Pollution of Religion.*

The Sassetta painting can be viewed online at http://www.oceansbridge.com/
artist-lists/sassetta/The-Meeting-Of-St-Anthony-And-St-Paul-1440.php Notice the hills, trees
and cave that are images Tom Mutch appropriates in the *Carbon Footprint*.

Figure 5.4.   An example of a Medieval religious painting.

thing that disturbs our ease. As we look further at the prominent image
of the Madonna and Child we are shaken out of our self-satisfied slum-
ber. The child is muscular and challenging. Rather than pointing across
to the book as in traditional icons, here he glares with an arrogance
that springs from his prosperity. Rather than prefiguring his sacrificial
crucifixion, this child is intimidating, daring us to challenge his preco-
cious dominance. Rather than being the source of good news, the book
is held well out of sight, away from the critique of those who would dare
contradict his control. He is firmly in the embrace of his mother,
enfolded in her voluptuous robe and is reassured as his right hand fits
snugly into hers. Here is a partnership of ominous proportions as the
mother, with eyes turned to the right, seeks integration with the
machineries of war and destruction.

To compare Mutch's appropriation of iconography with works of that
religious genre see the icon *Our Lady of Perpetual Help*.

The icon *Our Lady of Perpetual Help* can be viewed at number of different Internet sites. Try
http://www.ewtnreligiouscatalogue.com/shop.axd/Search?keywords=The+icon+Our+Lady+of
+Perpetual+Help+&x=32&y=9
Type the name of the icon into your search engine to locate an image. Notice the sorrowful
Madonna compared with Mutch's self-satisfied mother. Also observe how the child's eyes are
diverted to the Gospel text delivered by the Archangel Gabriel in contrast to Mutch's self-
satisfied child.

Figure 5.5.   Traditional iconography.

On the right half of the *Carbon Footprint* the image of a death figure
dressed in a business suit dominates the foreground. Shrapnel from
exploding bombs emanate as darkened bolts from his body. There is no
offer of redeeming light here; just the darkness of war's destructive force.
Dr Death, as we might label him, is being fed with matériel, not by a ter-
rorist but rather by another man in a suit in the right background. Here is
the corporation in cahoots with the instruments of war and death. War
planes swoop, fuelled by the oil which in turn explodes in our faces as the
aftershocks reach out of the painting pulling us, the viewers, into the
action. The all-encompassing effect of war's nihilism gathers us into its
embrace with the blood red curved sky. No one escapes from the effects of
war: our destruction is assured.

As our eyes toggle between the two large images we are gradually drawn to the two small symbols in the center of the painting. Although smaller in proportion a crown of thorns and a starving child take front of stage. How can these two images be interpreted?

The starving child staggers under the weight of the aggression, his left hand begging for us to stop. We feel his sadness and his suffering is ours. We are emaciated, lacking the resources to reverse the madness of war.

The crown of thorns is ambiguous. Does it represent the connecting point between the two embraces: stylized Madonna and red sky? Or does it imply that there is a way forward beyond mutually assured destruction as war engulfs and squanders all the earth's resources?

The crown of thorns links unsustainable systemic practices with each individual. We are invited to wear this crown, to suffer the ignominy of sacrifice in order to save the planet for future generations. This dialectic is not displayed in the two halves of the painting; rather, the two sides are features of the *same* stories of domination and exploitation. The antithesis of the dialectic is found in the begging child and crown of thorns. Here is the true Christ Child set in opposition to the hegemonic relationship forged between religion and business and their collaborative exploitation of the Earth's resources.

But here the painting turns and interrogates us the viewers, compelling us to make a response. We are not entirely powerless but the solutions will involve each individual in a sacrificial response. By offering an individual challenge, the painting strikes at the heart of the problem of sustainability. We need to make both systemic and individual changes and we need to think and act *glocally* if business is going to offer the planet sustainable practice. The painting asks us to set aside our quietist responses and encourages us to challenge prevailing ideologies and theologies that have in the past both salved our guilt and stymied action.

For us as scholars, the ability to make significant change begins in the classroom because it is here that a creative dialogue can begin.

SUSTAINABILITY IN THE CLASSROOM

The classroom is a place where the beginnings of a dialogue of possibilities for the planet's future can be mapped. Furthermore, the academic environment where students learn to test their theories is an ideal venue to practice the kind of cooperation necessary to institute business sustainability. Therefore, rather than pitting one against the other, we need the kind of discussion that contains the seeds of revisionary practice. For, as Follett (1926) argues:

We must learn to think of discussion not as a struggle but as experiment in cooperation. We must learn cooperative thinking, intellectual team-work. There is a secret here which is going to revolutionize the world. (p. 97)

Hence the complexities illustrated in Mutch's painting closely reflect the multifaceted challenges facing business leaders in the 21st twenty-first century. There is a growing body of literature dedicated to strategic sustainability and the application of management systems designed to create a better global future that can be used as classroom resources. For example, Sroufe and Sarkis (2007) provide a range of interesting case studies based on companies that strive for environmentally responsible products and services as demanded by many customers. And, although such cases present important examples for use in education for sustainable development (ESD), we think equal importance should be given to the choice of pedagogic strategies most appropriate to optimal learning opportunities (Wheeler, 2007).

The problem faced by business schools, therefore, is how to find the best fit between the imperative goal of teaching sustainability and the most effective pedagogical approach.

In the first years of some business programs, students are taught, in a conventional manner, the basic tenets of sustainable development, which is meeting the needs of the present without compromising those of the future (UNCED, 2004; UNESCO, 2002). However, there is some uncertainty about the depth of this learning and the consequent application of such information at a later stage. It appears that "deep learning" (Wheeler, 2007) is best achieved when several criteria are met. These criteria are summarized as: exchanging or cross-fertilizing across specialist areas of knowledge (change management, knowledge management and learning management); identifying and challenging deeply ingrained assumptions about business practices and approaches; expending energy to build social capital and collaborative networks; and fostering learning individuals and organizations.

There is always the concern, when dealing with such lofty goals, that the classroom setting may prove inadequate for such grand intentions. However, because the ultimate aim of ESD involves learning transferred from individuals to organizations and ultimately to wider society, it is our belief that interactive pedagogies will make a difference. We agree with Wheeler's (2007) assertion that "organizations learn only through individuals who learn. Individual learning does not guarantee organizational learning: but without it, no organizational learning can take place" (p. 49). Therefore, in terms of the classroom experience, deep learning for sustainable solutions is an essential goal.

As new generations of managers graduate, they need to be equipped with thinking tools to locate unsustainable practices and the insights into how to chart ways forward that offer alternatives to unbridled consumption and growth. Given the power of its highly colored allegorical images in the *Carbon Footprint,* we suggest that students are drawn to the image with a willingness that contrasts sharply to their response to more typical non-interactive learning processes. The value of participatory engagement is highlighted by O'Donoghue and Russo's (2004) review of materials and methods used in environmental education. They argue that the presentation of "abstracting ideals" in combination with a situation which creates "axes of tension and reflexive processes" can increase sustainability consciousness (p. 348).

Thus, it is not our interpretation of the painting that matters; it is the process of "meaning-making interactions" (O'Donoghue & Russo, 2004, p. 336), the struggle to engage with and to interpret the image, and the emotional connectedness to that process (Heimlich, 2007) that cracks the foundations prior to the catalytic jolt. Our interpretation, and indeed that of the artist, is therefore secondary to each individual's struggle for meaning and comprehension.

The key pedagogical approach is therefore, *facilitation,* rather than lecturing (Wheeler, 2007). Such an incorporation of learning through experience is in concert with the approach discussed by Svoboda and Whalen (2007) who use an "ecological" learning model which "treats the person as a complex living system" (p. 172) and see this way of learning involving action, reflection, reframing and application. As commonly seen in experiential activities, feedback between action and reflection is the crucial element as students get to explore the results and consequences of their actions. The reframing stage allows students to weigh the impact of their actions and this weighing of the impact enables them to challenge and/or change their underlying assumptions. The application stage, then, offers students the tools to make linkages between the artificial classroom activity and the societal issues under investigation. The opportunity for group discussion is also an important element in the process because students can have opportunities to learn with colleagues from different backgrounds—a skill which has immediate application in the business environment with its multiple and often conflicting stakeholder interests (Svoboda & Whalen, 2007).

It is important that the interpretation of the art work is a collaborative multileveled process, involving the instructor, the learners and, on some occasions, the artist. While it has never been our intention to underestimate the artist's contribution, we believe that providing answers to the puzzle defeats the challenge and reduces the participatory aspect of the learning process. For example, Mutch cites history in his representation of

---

LESSON PLAN FOR OPTIONAL CLASSROOM LEARNING ACTIVITY

Preparation: The instructor chooses an appropriate artist and painting for the activity. Alternatively this responsibility can be given to a group of students. A short biography of the artist, a digital copy of the artwork and an interpretation of the artwork are required.

Phase One: INTRODUCTION (20 minutes)

The artist is introduced.

The chosen image is presented on a large screen.

Students write a 100–200 word paragraph about the image to answer the question: 'What do you think the artist is communicating?'

Phase Two: IDENTIFICATION OF THEMES (20 MINUTES)

Students share their written reflections with each other in groups of 4–5 people.

Findings from each group are collated into broad themes and recorded on large paper charts on a side wall of the room. (It is best if each group gives one theme, in turn, until no new ones emerge.)

The instructor records students' emotions and attitudes. They also note any counter arguments that emerge. These will be of use in the final phase.

Phase Three: REFLECTIONS (20 MINUTES)

An open class discussion about the key issues is facilitated by the instructor. Groups are re-formed and asked to prioritise the themes/issues arising from Phase Two.

Phase Four: CATALYTIC JOLT (20–30 minutes)

Counter arguments noted in Phase Two are discussed. Alternative evidence can be provided by the instructor or the students.

The groups are asked to re-form and re-prioritize the major themes and issues based on their consideration of the counter arguments.

An open class discussion is held to discuss beliefs and attitudes evident from earlier phases. These may include:

- Hopes and fears for the future
- Optimism and pessimism and the consequences of both positions.

The activity closes with a facilitated discussion on future strategies and action plans.

Figure 5.6.   Lesson plan for optional classroom learning activity.

the men in suits in the *Carbon Footprint* and identifies figures not necessarily recognizable to many students who have grown up in a different generation. Tom Mutch claims Mr. Bomb, the small suited figure in the right background, can be identified as

Edward Teller, a former colleague of Robert Oppenheimer (who was the father of the atomic bomb). There was a fall-out (pardon the pun) between them—Teller testified against Oppenheimer and accused him of being a communist. One version of the story is that Oppenheimer knew the bomb was not stable. He argued that it couldn't just be magnified in strength, as

132 R. BATHURST and M. EDWARDS

Teller advocated. So Teller and his colleagues set about discrediting Oppenheimer. (personal communication, May 27, 2008)

Furthermore, Dr Death can be identified as any political leader who uses war as a tool to reinforce dominance on the international stage.

An important phase of the managed learning activity is the introduction of the counterargument—an exploration of "contradictions inherent in sustainable living" (Vare & Scott, 2007, p. 194). Skepticism is accomplished through the presentation of Lomborg's (2001) alternative view on the state of the world which attacks cultural pessimists and insists that "if we are to make the best decisions for our future, we should base our prioritizations not on fear but on facts" (p. 327). For example, much of the global warming evidence is largely derived from "computer-aided storytelling" and many experts believe more accurate models will not be available for some time (de Vries et al., 2000). The problematic nature of such modelling was highlighted over a decade ago by Yohe and Neumann (1997) who argued that the prediction of rising sea levels required the immediate revisions of business strategies, something market-based economies would be reluctant to consider. Thus, facilitating counterarguments provides an opportunity for students to consider their attitudes toward "traditional scientific" knowledge, and the meanings of fact, truth, logic and evidence, while at the same time recognizing the importance of values in adding to this understanding (Maxwell, 1992).

If values, along with prior understandings and assumptions are explored, we are likely to get closer to attaining the type of wisdom defined by Maxwell (1992) as "the desire, the active endeavour, and the capacity to discover and achieve what is desirable and of value in life, both for oneself and for others" (p. 219). This development of wisdom involves critically assessing possible solutions and nurturing the motivation to execute that action.

The portrayal of a large number of global issues in Mutch's work is fundamental because the need to prioritize actions and produce a united plan for change is of primary importance. Our choice of painting, the *Carbon Footprint*, along with a range of sustainability issues, has avoided the temptation to focus on just one issue at the expense of others as, for example, placing the impending threat of global warming over the inequitable production and supply of the world's food resources. Mutch's inclusion of the starving child places the spotlight clearly on poverty as one of the key issues for global redress (Lomborg, 2001; Maxwell, 1992), and the process of prioritization uncovers students' underlying assumptions about sociopolitical issues. The difficulties uncovered by the process of prioritization also highlight attitudinal differences centring on a continuum of optimism to pessimism. Lomborg emphasizes the danger that pessimism can be linked to apathy and indifference and argues that creating an optimistic view of the future (eliminating indifference) helps students to develop a sustainability consciousness that can then pervade decision-making in all contexts.

FUTURE DIRECTIONS

As we, the authors, have worked with you the readers, we together arrive at a pause in our narratives. While our discussion of Tom Mutch and his contribution has jolted us into a sustainability consciousness, we now have to turn to face the future. For, although this chapter will soon end, the business sustainability project still continues. We are all provoked by our own individual and collective need to work together for a sustainable future.

These closing reflections offer a way forward in our own separate quests for business practices that consider the planet we occupy. Adding his voice to this quest, cosmologist and theologian Thomas Berry (2000) seeks a new kind of peace on Earth. He argues that:

> What we look for is no longer the Pax Romana, the peace of imperial Rome, nor is it simply the Pax Humana, the peace among humans, but the Pax Gaia, the peace of Earth and every being on the Earth. (para. 10)

Such a peace, though, is to be found in our sense of interconnectedness. For, Berry (2000) suggests, it is the Earth that sustains us and that, "as humans we are born of the Earth, nourished by the Earth, healed by the Earth" (para. 11). Berry's polemic causes us to reflect on and question our exploitation of the Earth's provisions for the sake of spurious notions of growth and profit in the business sector.

Our exposé of Tom Mutch's artwork is motivated from a belief that it is important to engage with and be challenged by the insights that he offers in the *Carbon Footprint*, regardless of how uncomfortable and disturbed we feel. Artists will continue to fulfill their prophetic role and the art of one generation will have continuing currency in the next. In this regard we explored two particularly important works which critique and challenge the propensity of human beings to take up arms against each other in the illogical defense that it is necessary to destroy in order to preserve.

Picasso's *Guernica* is a landmark work that speaks to each generation. So powerful is it that we are still challenged by its powerful message. A reproduction of this work today hangs in the Security Council Chamber at the United Nations headquarters in New York. On February 5, 2003, then Secretary of State for the United States of America, Colin Powell, delivered a speech justifying military action in Iraq. But his presentation was to be conducted in front of Picasso's reproduction. Officials recognizing the potency of Picasso's work quickly covered the reproduction lest the images of a screaming horse and dying women and children somehow tainted Powell's message.

This act of denial—denying the horrors of war, denying the destructive influences of armed international conflict and denying the abuse of the earth's resources—flies in the face of concerted action to reverse the destruction and to allow for the kind of reconciliation between earth and human kind that Thomas Berry advocates.

Berry's (2000) views are based on a notion that our relationship with the planet is forever bound to our interpersonal relationships. The intimate human contact we crave with each other is predicated, he argues, by our care of the earth and on our ability to see the self and the earth in a mutually sustaining relationship.

> We are just discovering that the human project is itself a component of the Earth project; that our intimacy with the Earth is our way to intimacy with each other. Such are the foundations of our journey into the future. (para. 20)

Tom Mutch's art is a reflection of this kind of relationship that Berry foreshadows. While the *Carbon Footprint* presents a critique of existing power arrangements between religion and business, he also offers a way forward through our mutual compassion for the starving child. This child's hand is open inviting us into the kind of relationship that recognizes the immorality of rampant consumerism (Taylor, 1977) and the insanity of war's destructive power.

To this end we agree with Wheeler's (2007) assertion that the ultimate goal of education for sustainable development is that it snowballs as it "begins within ourselves and extends to our relationship with others, our communities, and all of our social networks" (p. 49).

Thus art offers sustainability the "attention-catching and emotionally-engaging informational interventions" (Weber, 2006, p. 116) believed to activate individual or collective responses to global sustainability. This move away from computer modeling and objective scientific analysis toward aesthetic engagement offers the kind of catalytic jolt required to make significant lifestyle changes necessary to live at peace with the earth and each other.

To end where we began, Mary Parker Follett, called by some a "prophet of management" (Graham, 1996), deems war to be a sign of weakness and an inability to creatively explore the many alternatives to violence that are present in any disagreement. She declares that:

War is the easy way: we take to war because we have not enough vitality for the far more difficult job of agreeing. (Follett, 1926, p. 103)

Our assent of Follett's pronouncement in this chapter summarizes this view and proposes that the artful approach allows for both intellectual and emotional involvement with the problems of business sustainability, and in so doing offers us the chance to preserve the earth's resources for the generations to come.

REFERENCES

Barthes, R. (1977). The death of the author (S. Heath, Trans.). In *Image, music, text* (pp. 142–148). London: Fontana Press.

Bell, M. S. (1984). Surrealism—An alternative approach: Veristic attitudes in the work and writings of contemporary surrealists. *Leonardo, 17*(4), 247–252.

Bergson, H. (1935). *Laughter: An essay on the meaning of the comic* (C. Brereton & F. Rothwell, Trans.). London: MacMillan.

Berry, T. (2000). Evening thoughts [Electronic Version]. *EarthLight library: The magazine of spiritual ecology*. Retrieved June 4, 2009, from http://www.earthlight.org/essay39_berry.html

Burwell, R. L., & Haller, G. L. (1992). Catalysis. In *McGraw-Hill encyclopedia of science & technology* (10th ed., pp. 556–558). New York: McGraw-Hill.

Carroll, A. B., & Buchholtz, A. K. (2003). *Business & society: Ethics and stakeholder management*. Mason, OH: Thomson.

Clark, S. R. L. (2008). Deconstructing the laws of logic. *Philosophy, 83,* 25–53

Cooper, P. J., & Vargas, C. M. (2008). *Sustainable development in crisis conditions: Challenges of war, terrorism, and civil disorder*. Lanham, MA: Rowman & Littlefield.

de Vries, B., Bollen, J., Bouwman, L., den Elzen, M., Janssen, M., & Kreileman, E. (2000). Greenhouse gas emissions in an equity-, environment- and service-oriented world: An IMAGE-based scenario for the 21st century. *Technological Forecasting and Social Change, 63,* 137–174.

Dean, J. W., Ottensmeyer, E., & Ramirez, R. (1997). An aesthetic perspective on organizations. In C. L. Cooper & S. E. Jackson (Eds.), *Creating tomorrow's organizations: A handbook for future research in organizational behavior* (pp. 419–437). New York: Wiley.

Dyllick, T., & Hockerts, K. (2002). Beyond the business case for corporate sustainability. *Business Strategy and the Environment, 11*(2), 130–141.

Follett, M. P. (1926). *The new state: Group organization the solution of popular government*. New York: Longmans, Green & Co.

Fort, I. S. (1982). American social surrealism. *Archives of American Art Journal, 22*(3), 8–20.

Graham, P. (1996). Mary Parker Follett: A pioneering life. In P. Graham (Ed.), *Mary Parker Follett—Prophet of management: A celebration of writings from the 1920s* (pp. 11–32). Boston: Harvard Business School Press.

Hedges, C. (2002). *War is a force that gives us meaning*. New York: PublicAffairs.

Heimlich, J. E. (2007). Research trends in the United States: EE to ESD. *Journal of Education for Sustainable Development, 1*(2), 219–227.

Kellstedt, P. M., Zahran, S., & Vedlitz, A. (2008). Personal efficacy, the information environment, and attitudes toward global warming and climate change in the United States. *Risk Analysis, 28*(1), 113–126.

Klingsöhr-Leroy, C. (2004). A new declaration of the rights of man. In U. Grosenick (Ed.), *Surrealism* (pp. 6–25). Cologne: Taschen.

Langer, S. K. (1960). *Philosophy in a new key: A study in the symbolism of reason, rite, and art*. Cambridge, Massachusetts: Harvard University Press. (Original work published 1942)

Lehman, K., & Linsky, M. (2008). Using conflict as a catalyst for change. *Harvard Management Update, 13*(4), 3–5.

Lomborg, B. (2001). *The skeptical environmentalist: Measuring the real state of the world*. Cambridge: Cambridge University Press.

Maxwell, N. (1992). What kind of inquiry can best help us create a good world? *Science Technology Human Values, 17*(2), 205–227.

Milne, M. J., Kearins, K., & Walton, S. (2006). Creating adventures in Wonderland: The journey metaphor and environmental sustainability. *Organization, 13*(6), 801–839.

Mitchell, W. J. T. (1987). *Iconology: Image, text, ideology*. Chicago: The University of Chicago Press.

O'Donoghue, R., & Russo, V. (2004). Emerging patterns of abstraction in environmental education: A review of materials, methods and professional development perspectives. *Environmental Education Research, 10*(3), 331–351.

O'Donovan, L. J. (2007). Imagining our defeat: Some 20th-century artists reflect on war. *America, 196*(6), 16–17.

Oxford English Dictionary. (2009). *Catalyst*. Oxford, England: Oxford University Press. Retrieved June 4, 2009 from http://dictionary.oed.com

Paton, J. (2006). *How to look at a painting*. Wellington: Awa Press.

Schama, S. (2006). *The power of art*. New York: HarperCollins.

Smith, R. (2004, 13 May). Why attack art? Its role is to be helpful. *New York Times* Retrieved May 13, 2004, from http://query.nytimes.com/gst/abstract.html?res=F00F12FC3A580C708DDDAC0894DC404482

Sroufe, R., & Sarkis, J. (2007). *Strategic sustainability: The state of the art in corporate environmental management systems*. Sheffield, England: Greenleaf.

Stevens, F. G., Plaut, V. C., & Sanchez-Burks, J. (2008). Unlocking the benefits of diversity. *Journal of Applied Behavioral Science, 44*(1), 116–133.

Svoboda, S., & Whalen, J. (2007). Using experiential simulation to teach sustainability. In C. Galea (Ed.), *Teaching business sustainability: Cases, simulations and experiential approaches* (Vol. 2, pp. 171–179). Sheffield: Greenleaf.

Taylor, J. V. (1977). *Enough is enough: A biblical call for moderation in a consumer-oriented society*. Minneapolis, MN: Augsburg.

UNCED. (2004, December 15). *Promoting education, public awareness and training*. Retrieved June 4, 2009, from http://www.un.org/esa/sustdev/documents/agenda21/english/agenda21chapter36.htm

UNESCO. (2002, May 1). *Développment durable*. Retrieved May 20, 2008, from http://portal.unesco.org/fr/ev
.php-URL_ID=3994&URL_DO=DO_TOPIC&URL_SECTION=201.html

Vare, P., & Scott, W. (2007). Learning for a change: Exploring the relationship between education and sustainable development. *Journal of Education for Sustainable Development, 1*(2), 191–198.

Warren, S. (2008). Empirical challenges in organizational aesthetics research: Towards a sensual methodology. *Organization Studies, 29*(4), 559–580.

Weber, E. U. (2006). Experience-based and description-based perceptions of long-term risk: Why global warming does not scare us (yet). *Climatic Change, 77*, 103–120.

Webster, K. (2004). *Tom Mutch antipodean artist*. Auckland: David Bateman.

Wheeler, K. A. (2007). Learning for deep change. *Journal of Education for Sustainable Development, 1*(1), 45–50.

Winter, R. D. (1981). The kingdom strikes back: The ten epochs of redemptive history. In R. D. Winter & S. C. Hawthorne (Eds.), *Perspectives on the world Christian movement* (pp. 137–155). Pasadena, CA: William Carey Library.

Yohe, G., & Neumann, J. (1997). Planning for sea level rise and shore protection under climate uncertainty. *Climatic Change, 37*, 243–210.

CHAPTER 6

EDUCATION IN SUSTAINABILITY THROUGH SYSTEMS THINKING

José-Rodrigo Córdoba and Terry Porter

In the twenty-first century, the world has become a global entity which needs to be protected and looked after. In this global arena, profit and not-for-profit organizations need to attend to a variety of demands. Their governments encourage them to be socially responsible and sustainable at the same time. Their employees demand better working conditions, and their customers want products and services of quality. The interactions between organizations and their environments gain special attention when we look at how organizations can address these and other demands.

Systems thinking is an evolving discipline that can help management educators and students explore relations between organizations and the natural environment (Midgley, 2000) and address issues of sustainability (Senge, Aleiner, Roberts, Ross, & Smith, 1994; Stead & Stead, 2004). Systems thinking can also help students bring seemingly disparate issues together and better understand the impacts of any action on a variety of domains (Reason, 2007).

This chapter draws on key contributions of systems thinkers and highlights some differences between three different notions and uses of systems, with particular attention to their pedagogical applications in business edu-

Management Education for Global Sustainability, pp. 139–158
Copyright © 2009 by Information Age Publishing

cation. The three different approaches to systems thinking have differing cultural overtones that can influence the insights they offer. The implications of these overtones are discussed as the chapter examines the three systems schools in a holistic and systematic fashion: focusing on theory, research, and practice; and, most importantly, drawing implications for learning and teaching practice.

INTRODUCTION

How have we come to talk about sustainability in almost every business forum or every business plan that we come across as educators, employees, managers, and policymakers? In the twenty-first century, the world has become a global entity that needs to be protected and looked after. In this global arena, profit and not-for-profit organizations need to attend to a variety of demands. Organizations are now addressing sustainability as a way of satisfying current demands while caring for the world in which future generations are to live.

For many managers and employees a commitment to sustainability merely adds more demands to business strategies or practices. What was done in the past needs now to be reviewed so that all practices consider how best to satisfy sustainability requirements. For others, sustainability is more of an ideal toward which to work. Since the landmark "Earth Summit" meeting in Rio in 1992, there has been an imperative for achieving sustainable development, but it is only now that this imperative has become a necessity in the international arena. The imperative has meant being able to satisfy the needs of current generations without compromising the capacity of future generations to meet their needs (UNCED, 1992). In areas like economic development, this imperative is now included in discussions of many issues, including poverty, social exclusion, and environmental degradation.

Organizations and their members are now asking themselves how to address the sustainability imperative in ways that still enable them to fulfill their traditional purposes. Doing so may require important transformations in organizations and society at different levels (Agyeman, Morris, & Bishop, 1996), transformations that could be made more difficult to reconcile if they are looked at or treated separately. Management education contributes to this difficulty by separating education into "silo" subjects which look at organizations as slices, not as wholes. Most of education practices are intended to encourage better and fair management (Jackson, 2003), but this silo type of mentality contributes on the whole to making business education less relevant to the needs of business, people, and society in general (Ghoshal, 2005; Mintzberg, 2004).

A possible way out of this difficulty involves promoting more holistic thinking based on seeing organizations as "whole systems" which interact continuously with their environments (Ackoff, 1981). Systems thinking has been promoted as a reaction to the mechanistic, silo, and functionalistic ways of thinking which see organizations strictly as goal-seeking entities (Jackson, 2003). The idea of organizations as systems has become popular and has been found to be very useful in supporting studies on more human-oriented issues such as motivation, work conditions, and societal responsibilities. Despite this initial acceptance, however, organizational theory and business education still tend to confine systems thinking to a role supporting either instrumental design, seeing organizations as systems made up of parts designed solely to achieve profitability, or to a set of erudite yet impractical ideologies.

This chapter extends what appears to be a common understanding of the notion of "system" and considers its implications for education in sustainability. Three different notions of systems are presented, all of which are still very influential and used in management science. We discuss their applications to business education in general, with particular attention to business education in sustainability. Numerous examples are provided of how these three systems' notions can be used in management education for global sustainability.

THE FIRST NOTION: OPTIMIZING SYSTEMS

The history of systems thinking in the West is fascinating, although difficult to follow. There are accounts tracing it to Aristotle, the Greeks, and their efforts to understand how society could be steered by adequate governance and participation of the people (Jackson, 2003). The relationship between management science and systems thinking appears to become more established after the Second World War. Up to then, studies in biology, psychology, and other areas had led to the development of general systems theory, a set of principles supported by empirical evidence on how systems operated (von Bertalanffy, 1968). With the advent of the war, these studies were redirected to facilitate better understandings of communication and control processes in human beings and machines in order to support the war effort.

The war saw many military successes derived from the modeling and representing of communication processes within "systems." At that time, the notion of a system was that of a definable entity which existed "out there." Once a system was identified, complementary notions of information, feedback, inputs, and outputs allowed researchers to structure systems to predict and to manage their behaviors. This approach included, for instance, the modeling of anti-aircraft systems which facilitated the representation of interactions between airplanes and detection devices. Successes obtained in this field led to the popularity of the optimizing approach to systems, and with it the birth of disciplines like cybernetics and operations research in the United States, the United Kingdom, and other countries.

The idea behind this approach involves seeking to optimize the behavior of a system so as to accomplish a predefined set of goals. An anti-aircraft detection system is oriented to meet the defined goal of accurately identifying targets. The same could be said about a production system of an organization, and, as will be presented later on, an environmentally friendly organization. Once the system is modelled—with its inputs, main parts, outputs, and behavior defined—elements and combinations of elements may be reconfigured, and the model may be retested in terms of desired outputs. The aim is to generate the desired outputs as efficiently and effectively as possible.

SYSTEMS OPTIMIZATION IN SUSTAINABILITY EDUCATION

Systems life cycle analysis and related approaches can be operationalized in terms of sustainability goals such as pollution reduction, managing waste, recycling, or any other environmental or social parameter. Optimizing techniques can then be applied to achieve desired targets. This approach is particularly well suited to the case of regulation compliance, especially for regulations that allow countries and companies to trade aspects of their environmental footprint for some form of environmental offsets. Through systems analysis and reconfiguration, firms may meet compliance goals without needing to make radical transformations of their existing business model and practices.

Traditional operational research methods and techniques support this approach of modeling systems to be optimized toward sustainability goals. As Figure 6.1 illustrates, revised models of business operations can be built and used to assess the impact of policies and plans on the environment (Bloemhof-Ruwaard, Van Beek, Hordijk, & Van Wassenhove, 1995). In this way, supply chain designs can be extended to account for waste activities and to model "whole" systems to reduce waste or to optimize production of items "from cradle to grave." Similarly, simulations can be conducted for business operations to assess the probability of particular optimal scenarios occurring, and what actions are to be taken into account to achieve those optima.

With this approach to systems optimization, a number of existing models can be used to assess the sustainability of systems. For example, systems

Supply Chain

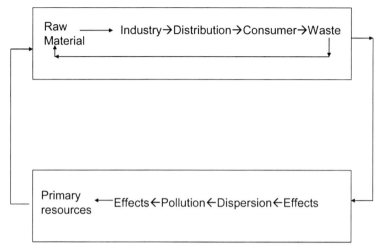

Environmental Chain

Figure 6.1.   An extended "chain" of business operations to include issues of sustainability in business education (Bloemhof-Ruwaard et al. (1995).

dynamics has been used to model the impact of population growth and consumption on the availability of natural resources, leading to previously unforeseen strong impacts on the Western way of life (Meadows, Meadows, & Randers, 1972; Meadows, Meadows, & Randers, 1992). Along the same lines, educational approaches that utilize concrete measures of risk assessment, environmental appraisal, and analysis of costs and benefits can also use this systems notion. For instance, life cycles can be modeled and assessed, and simulations with new environmentally-friendly technologies can be conducted to generate optimized combinations of different types of activities in the generation of desired outputs.

STRENGTHS AND WEAKNESSES OF SYSTEMS OPTIMIZATION

The optimizing approach is very popular, and does not require profound transformations in the ways in which business education is traditionally conducted. Existing subjects like environmental economics, environmental accounting, and sustainable business development are currently presented in business school curricula in just this way. This approach implicitly assumes that systems can be identified, modeled, and optimized, and that sustainability indicators can be incorporated into such models. Indeed, in this era of silo-oriented business education, some institutions and educators find it appealing and easy to include the environment as a constraint that can now be incorporated into existing or new models. Students then benefit from learning to represent environmental situations in concrete terms, discuss different approaches to solve specified problems, and learn to become competent in finding the best solutions according to these models.

The trouble with this approach arises when the system to be optimized cannot be defined as a single entity. Churchman (1968, 1970) and Ackoff (1981) recognized the limitations of traditional operational research when it came to defining human problems. Such problems defy delimitation because legitimacy and valuation become contested issues:

> However, as one moves to consideration of larger [bigger] systems, the problems of complexity become enormous. This can be seen most clearly in the measure of performance of a system ... the larger the system becomes, the more parts interact, the more difficult it is to understand environmental constraints ... the more difficult becomes the problem of the legitimate values of the system. (Churchman, 1968, pp. 76–77)

Churchman (1968) was concerned about the human *values* that guide the definition of systems and operational goals. In organizations, these values typically support the optimization of a particular business activity. But if the notion of a business system is extended to account for the larger social and environmental systems in which it is embedded, there arise a number of competing values such as benefiting the local community or protecting the physical environment. To some, these values can be addressed simply by enlarging optimizing models. To others, however, it is necessary to bring a new dimension of critical reflection to the analysis of systems. Specifically, who defines the system in question? Whose interests are being served by this definition and whose are neglected? And what are the underlying reasons behind one systems configuration versus another? These considerations lead to the consideration of the second notion of a system.

THE SECOND NOTION: SYSTEMS TO LEARN ABOUT SITUATIONS

The initial success of systems analysis for optimizing contrasted with its subsequent failures during the 70s and 80s in tackling ill-structured and complex problems. It was gradually recognized that the difficulties first pointed out by Churchman and others about "enlarging" the definition of a system also refer to its subjective nature. That is, meeting predefined goals was at odds with the continuous and individualized nature of human systems goals. On both sides of the Atlantic, researchers criticized an impoverishment of traditional systems analysis (Rosenhead, 2006). To some this impoverishment arose from focusing on solving rightly the wrong problems rather than defining relevant problems to be solved (Churchman, 1968).

These and other issues motivated researchers like Ackoff and Checkland to propose different ways of developing the systems discipline to contribute more effectively to humanizing the use of systems thinking. For Ackoff (1981), it became clear that organizations were part of larger systems, and thus that their goals needed to fit with the goals of the larger systems. Introducing an approach termed "idealized design of the future," he argued that existing problems could not only be resolved or solved but also dissolved. This perspective would also mean that organizations as systems needed to contribute to the development of human beings and humanized values, not only to economic profit and short-term growth. Checkland's (1981) approach was to employ traditional systems thinking to learn how to tackle ill-structured problems, which he characterized as "messes." In his view, the diversity of perceptions about what is considered relevant and meaningful to tackle in such problems could be used to structure debate about change.

Ackoff (1981) and Checkland (1981) define methodologies to guide people in learning about complex situations, thus ensuring that their organizations would function as "accommodation" systems for meaningful human activity. The differing goals of stakeholders, including those implicit in such larger systems as the natural and social environment, could be reconciled if more meaningful and desirable futures for all are defined as system goals. Their methodologies provide guidance by encouraging the definition of systems models that help in appreciating connections between issues, human activities, and the values that guide decisions in these activities. The important thing in using these models is not defining and finding the best solution to a particular problem; rather, it is to work collectively to arrive at appropriate arrangements and plans which could improve the quality of life of the people involved. Such arrangements would reflect what people consider meaningful to do and would support them in being active participants (citizens) in larger human and non-human systems or "wholes."

Checkland (1981) was explicit in shifting the focus of systems analysis from the world "out there" to the *process of inquiry* about it. His work shows how the notion of systems becomes that of a tool used to *represent and describe* situations, with a view toward learning how to improve them on a continuing basis. He proposed a methodology for inquiring into situations which can be developed iteratively and continuously as a learning process. The process, called soft systems methodology (SSM), uses systems models to enable people to generate insights about meaningful human activities that, if present, could improve the current situation. A comparison takes place between the model and the actual situation, and debate can be structured so that people can explore possibilities for change. The use of human-activity systems models generates new and unforeseen possibilities derived from both the model and from the actual situation and its norms, culture, social roles, and power relations.

SYSTEMS FOR LEARNING IN SUSTAINABILITY EDUCATION

The ideas behind approaches like Checkland's (1981) methodology have inspired educators and students to consider engagement with sustainability as a learning and participative process (Bradbury, 2003; Collins & Kearins, 2004; Leal-Filho, 1999). Here the goal is collaborative development of interpretations and understandings of potential changes and ways in which they may impact systems and organizations, including changes arising from taking sustainability seriously (Roome & Oates, 1996). Learning by engagement is an ongoing process, as it involves students continually interacting with involved stakeholders to check the adequacy of their understandings about a situation as it unfolds.

Using this notion of a system as a learning device, students are encouraged to consider the wider context that surrounds business. As Bradbury (2003) suggests, this encouragement can be developed by asking them to become part of the world they are observing—to represent what they hear and talk about regarding sustainability. Activity centers on the mutual elaboration and application of models about the world from which students and stakeholders can learn together. Techniques of inquiring, dialoguing, and representing people's perceptions are useful ways to enable students to reflect on the world around them, and to recognize a diversity of perspectives on a single issue. Other techniques involving negotiation between stakeholders can help students represent and engage with issues and tradeoffs that emerge when different people's perceptions and issues with sustainability need to be considered and managed (Collins & Kearins, 2004).

Through collaborative research projects, students can define their own sustainability agenda and test it in dialogue and debate with relevant stakeholders. These stakeholders can include government officers, company representatives, community members, or people undertaking sustainability projects. For instance, this rationale guided Córdoba and Campbell's (2008) educational approach to sustainability in their community. They laid out a collaborative project for student groups with the aim of investigating sustainability in the city of Hull, United Kingdom. Students were required to identify and select more than two relevant sustainability issues in the city, provide evidence that related these issues to human or environmental problems, and use one of several systems-based problem-solving methodologies to arrive at insights to improve the situation of the city and its regional stakeholders. To find evidence to justify the classification of their chosen issues as "problematic", students had to engage with and talk to each other in groups, as well as go outside the University and talk to other people about these issues.

According to Córdoba and Campbell (2008), collaborative projects involving student learners and relevant stakeholders may be accompanied by the application of systems methodologies such as Ackoff's (1981) interactive planning (IP) and Checkland's (1981) soft systems methodology (SSM). These frameworks can help students in the following activities:

1. Identifying and representing a complex set of issues related to sustainability in a particular geographical area: Exploring these issues can be helped by using SSM's "rich picture technique" which allows students to identify and model a problematic situation in terms of existing activities, organizational structures involved, and the feelings and attitudes of involved stakeholders.

2. Debating with other students about which subset of issues requires attention: These debates can be supported by SSM's second stage, which encourages people to name relevant systems or systems whose activities currently generate or include multiple identified issues.

3. Using systems definitions and models to define activities and other types of responses to the complex situation at hand: Ackoff's (1981) IP stage of idealized design can also help students to define a number of properties of a "system" whose activity would help people to satisfy their desires to develop their full potential as human beings in relation to a larger system (e.g., society).

4. Exploring possibilities for change: Soft systems methodology's "comparison" and "debate" stages, or the "means-planning" stage of interactive planning, can enable students to formulate a number of possible changes in a situation—changes derived from the models created by the students as well as changes suggested by observing perceived reality on the ground. The idea is to identify a number of possibilities in different areas which, together, could constitute an agenda for action. Students then take their models and the identified possible actions to relevant stakeholders and

Thus, social design is a value-laden effort, and planners consciously or unconsciously tend to incorporate their own values when undertaking design decisions and defining boundaries. Consequently, values may unwittingly determine whom to include within the boundaries and what to privilege. Hence, debate about boundaries in inquiry and design becomes an ethical debate in relation to inclusion and exclusion of issues and people, bringing forth different ethical stances and priorities. To address this aspect of systems thinking, the processes involved in setting up system boundaries need to be opened to critique, so that the values behind a set of boundaries are made explicit and subject to debate. In this way different groups of individuals can take part in a debate characterized by openness and the possibility of revising system boundaries to achieve a more equitable arrangement. Ulrich (1983, 1987, 2001) provides a methodological approach to structure inquiry about systems boundaries and their values. The approach is called critical systems heuristics (CSH), and consists of 12 questions which can be used by people to inquire about the implicit boundaries in any sustainability situation. A summary of the ought mode (to be explained later) is presented in Table 6.1 (Ulrich, 1983).

Table 6.1.   Critical Systems Heuristics Questions (Ulrich, 2001)

Who ought to be the client (beneficiary) of the system S to be designed or improved?

What ought to be the purpose of S; i.e. what goals states ought S be able to achieve so as to serve the client?

What ought to be S's measure of success? (or improvement?)

Who ought to be the decision maker, that is, has the power to change S's measure of improvement?

What components (resources and constraints) of S ought to be controlled by the decision maker?

What resources and conditions ought to be part of S's environment, i.e. should not be controlled by S's decision maker?

Who ought to be involved as designer of S?

What kind of expertise ought to flow into the design of S; i.e. who ought to be considered an expert and what should be his/her role?

Who ought to be the guarantor of S; i.e. where ought the designer seek the guarantee that his/her design will be implemented and will prove successful, judged by S's measure of success (or improvement)?

Who ought to belong to the witnesses representing the concerns of the citizens that will or might be affected by the design of S? That is to say, who among the affected ought to be involved?

To what degree and in what way ought the "affected" be given the chance of emancipation from the premises and promises of the involved?

Upon what worldviews of either the involved or the affected ought S's design be based?

Ulrich emphasizes the need to ask these questions in two modes: The "is" mode and the "ought" model. For Ulrich (1983), both theoretical reason and practical reason should be used. Theoretical reason refers to the "what is" about reality whereas practical reason refers to the "what ought to be". In following the Critical Systems Heuristics approach, the "is" mode refers to an inquiry into how a situation is currently perceived by different groups of participants. The "ought" mode refers to how a situation should be designed if improvement is pursued as an ideal in practice. Methodologically, either of the two modes can be used in a collaborative inquiry about a social design to foster awareness and critique on the conditions that make a design inclusive for different groups. Midgley (2000) offers an alternative way of asking the "is" and "ought" questions, suggesting that the "is" mode is more appropriate to foster the clarification of certain values among a group of participants involved in a design. The "ought" mode might be more useful as a method to foster debate, negotiation, consensus formation, and compromise.

The questions of CSH focus on the *context* in which systems, boundaries, and decisions are embedded. As such, they can help people plan proactively and/or review and challenge the decisions of managers and other decision makers, to reveal the values that underlie decisions about what/who is (to be) included or excluded from consideration. With values and boundaries thus identified, discussion and debate can proceed to explore new possibilities for including issues and people into decision making, ideally permitting decisions to be more collectively constructed and accepted. Since boundaries and decisions are inevitably concerned with the "environment" surrounding a system, sustainability concerns frequently arise in this approach to systems analysis (Ulrich, 1993).

Ulrich's (1993) CSH questions provide a template for probing into the values and boundaries behind complex sustainability issues that affect many stakeholders. What remains, *however*, is a means to understand the dynamics and tensions that often emerge in multi-stakeholder discussions, and how these conflicts are embedded in the wider environment. Building upon Ulrich's work, Midgley (1992, 2000) explores the conflicts that may arise when two different groups of people identify different boundaries for the same situation. The situation can be characterized by the existence of a "boundary conflict," as shown in Figure 6.2. The three concentric circles in Figure 6.2 represent the currently defined system in the center, the immediate surroundings of marginalized elements, people, and values in the next ring, and an outer circle representing the wider macro-environment of the system and its stakeholders. The purpose of this arrangement is to depict the way in which each group of people—both included and marginalized—privileges different boundaries with their corresponding values and ethics. Oftentimes, of course, the biggest tensions are between the values of included groups and those who are marginalized. Midgley (2000) thus provides a way to diagram these tensions so they may be productively addressed in discussion.

Midgley (1992) stresses that the situation can be stabilized only by the imposition of either a "sacred" or "profane" status on the elements, issues, or people lying in between the inner and outer rings of Figure 6.2. This labeling takes place through symbolic or "ritual" processes, in which the status of both types of boundaries (sacred and profane) is confirmed. As a result, the diagram schematically displays which marginal elements have or have not been included in the system and relevant decision making. Conflict may be temporarily stabilized by adopting a single boundary until "further notice", meaning that the tension continues between sacred and profane elements, or that new boundaries become more important to be considered as a situation unfolds.

Midgley (1992, 2000) suggests that the above type of representation helps people reflect on the implications of adopting one type of boundary or another to guide decision making and action. These implications will have to do with reinforcing or challenging existing plans or policies, including or excluding issues and people, or generating desirable or undesirable impacts. Implications can be considered and dealt with by using other systems methodologies and approaches to define sustainable improvements, including those which could benefit present and future generations.

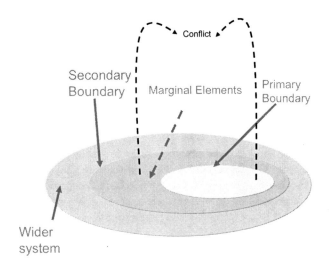

Figure 6.2.   Primary and secondary boundaries of systems (Midgley, 1992).

SYSTEMS BOUNDARIES IN SUSTAINABILITY EDUCATION

The notion of boundary critique as portrayed by Ulrich (1993) and Midgley (2000) can be used to explore which issues and people have been privileged or marginalized in sustainability plans, policies, and programs. Boundary critique invites people to formulate *questions* about decisions, plans, or situations, and also to explore and interpret the origins and manifestations of tensions between the "sacred" and the "profane". With boundary critique, students can identify elements of a situation that are being privileged and marginalized to further their own understandings and to formulate some critical accounts about what they perceive. Córdoba (2002) and Córdoba and Midgley (2008) suggest using questions to identify sacred and profane elements. Some of the questions include:

- What/who has been important to include?
- What about elements which have recently become marginalized? Why?
- From whose point of view are these designations made?
- What issues of concern can be shared among groups so as to find a common ground to orient further decision making?

These and other questions (including those of CSH) can help students produce their own understandings of a situation. If the students have an opportunity to engage with involved or affected stakeholders, the questions can also promote critical reflection about elements that are being included or marginalized. Reflection can help students and/or other people involved in a situation work together in proposing and defining improvements. This reflection can be complemented with the use of other types of systems methodologies to analyze the situation and to arrive at improvements that would make sense, even if the improvements cannot incorporate the value systems of all the marginalized elements.

The example of our course Córdoba and Campbell (2008) offered earlier shows how students were asked to apply the "systems as boundaries" approach to identify and unravel a complex sustainability problem. The insights obtained from the investigation of local sustainability issues in the city of Hull, United Kingdom show that some groups of students went "beyond" what was expected of them. Students recognized that we had drawn some boundaries of participation by allocating them into groups, and therefore privileging their participation on the "inside." However, given the possibility of engagement, some students went further and talked to local decision makers, residents, and business people on the topic of sustainability. One of the student groups found out that the local city council, despite promoting improvements in the quality of life of the city inhabitants via different initiatives, had at the same time been privileging the attracting of big chain supermarkets to local neighborhoods to the detriment of existing small local businesses. In other words, the local council was making non-local business "sacred," while confirming the status of local businesses as "profane." This process had been ritualized via policy documents, the issuing of local licenses to non-local businesses, and support for rapid establishment of non-local business in key areas of the city. This situation is depicted in Figure 6.3.

Although it was not part of the students' assignment in this case, the above issue could have been explored further—for example, to investigate why the council had adopted such a mentality; whether or not there were any historical events leading to this situation; what the implications of marginalization of these local businesses would be; and how existing tensions were being managed by the council, business representatives, and the community in general.

This experience suggests that identification and exploration of boundaries can lead students to reflect on themselves as individuals whose *identity* is being created continuously by adopting these boundaries (Córdoba, 2006; Porter, 2005). In this case, students were being taught other business subjects in order to become competent and knowledgeable managers in the future, professionals who would possibly be working in organizations which require them to privilege certain boundaries (e.g., efficiency, economic goals) at the expense of others (e.g., social responsibility). Their

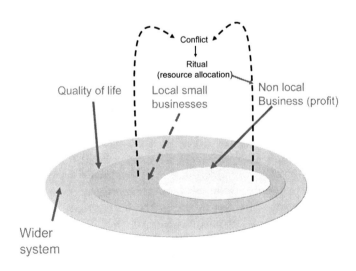

Figure 6.3.   An example of boundaries in sustainability.

experience identifying systems boundaries during their coursework provides them with a framework through which to consider ethical dilemmas for managers as individuals; the framework also invites them to reflect on their own value commitments.

Building on self-reflections on personal value systems, our educational approaches to sustainability could be enhanced by encouraging our students to become their own persons on their own terms. This possibility does not mean that they would need to adopt or abandon sets of values that differ radically from their own; rather, it means that they would gain important skills by learning how to operate within the contours of given boundaries and values, so that they can still become the type of individuals they want to become as managers.

Skill building of this type also requires students to learn to identify the power relations and dynamics in a sustainability situation, and how power manifests itself in the adoption or rejection of certain boundaries to guide decision making. In this domain, the work of Michel Foucault complements the use of systems approaches and the notion of systems boundaries. Foucault (1977, 1982, 1984a, 1984b) offers ways for individuals to identify how they came to be the "subjects" they are. These ways can enrich and enhance the process of identifying boundaries and exploring how decision makers relate to boundaries in their activities, including those related to sustainability. Following Foucault, students could then decide what type of subject they want to become, and use the power available to them to create or recreate their desired identity as individuals while still acting within existing or prescribed boundaries. This level of learning presents challenges not only for students, but also for educators, as the focus shifts from sustainability as an external issue to sustainability as an internal ethical issue for individuals. Such explorations may have great value for those students who, later in their careers, experience pressures from their organizations to act in ways contrary to their personal values.

CONCLUDING REMARKS

This chapter presented three different notions of systems for business education in sustainability. It started by presenting a notion of "system" which can be adopted without changing business practices or business education very much. It then moved to present a more engaging notion of system that could help individuals reflect on the world around them and how they live sustainability as a learning process. Finally the chapter laid out foundations for a more critical approach to sustainability education in which boundaries that guide decision making can be identified and explored further. This exploration can lead students and educators to reflect on themselves as individuals, encouraging them to decide what type of individuals they want to become. In combination with SSM's root definition and conceptual models, Ulrich's (1993) critical systems heuristics (CSH) questions about the "ought to be" of a system can help students define and structure a set of human activities whose impact would improve the current situation. And, they can see what they can contribute as individuals to bringing those improvements into being. These systems-thinking-inspired approaches could be a new lens for sustainability and for education as we see the possibility of encouraging people to become more ethically aware. We hope the ideas in this chapter inspire educators, students, and practitioners to consider how we have become subjects of sustainability and what we can do about it.

REFERENCES

Ackoff, R. (1981). *Creating the corporate future: Plan or to be planned for.* New York: Wiley.

Agyeman, J., Morris, J., & Bishop, J. (1996). Local government's educational role in LA21. In J. Huckle & S. Sterling (Eds.), *Educating for sustainability.* (pp. 181–194). London: Earthscan.

Bloemhof-Ruwaard, J., Van Beek, P., Hordijk, L., & Van Wassenhove, L. (1995). Interactions between operational research and environmental management. *European Journal of Operational Research, 85,* 229–243.

Bradbury, H. (2003). Sustaining inner and outer worlds: A whole systems approach to developing sustainable business practices in management. *Journal of Management Education, 27*(2), 172–187.

Checkland, P. (1981). *Systems thinking, systems practice.* London: Wiley.

Churchman, C. W. (1968). *The systems approach.* New York: Delacorte Press.

Churchman, C. W. (1970). Operations research as a profession. *Management Science, 17,* b37–b53.

Collins, E., & Kearins, K. (2004, August). *Stakeholder negotiation exercises in the classroom: Learning relationships for sustainability.* Paper presented at the Creating Actionable Knowledge: Academy of Management annual meeting, New Orleans, LA.

Córdoba, J. R. (2002). *A critical systems thinking approach for the planning of information technology in the information society.* Unpublished doctoral dissertation, University of Hull, United Kingdom.

Córdoba, J. R. (2006). Using Foucault to analyse ethics in the practice of problem structuring methods. *Journal of the Operational Research Society, 57*(9), 1027–1034.

Córdoba, J. R., & Campbell, T. (2008). Learning to deal with CSR in the classroom. *Systems Research and Behavioral Science, 25*(3), 427–437.

Córdoba, J., & Midgley, G. (2008). Beyond organisational agendas: Using boundary critique to facilitate the inclusion of societal concerns in information systems planning. *European Journal of Information Systems*, *17*, 125–142.

Foucault, M. (1977). *The history of sexuality volume one: The will to knowledge*. London: Penguin.

Foucault, M. (1982). On the genealogy of ethics: An overview of work in progress. In P. Rabinow (Ed.), *The Foucault reader: An introduction to Foucault's thought* (pp. 340–372). London: Penguin.

Foucault, M. (1984a). The ethics of the concern of the self as a practice of freedom. In P. Rabinow (Ed.), *Michel Foucault: Ethics, subjectivity, and truth: Essential works of Foucault 1954-1984* (pp. 281–301). London: Penguin.

Foucault, M. (1984b). What is enlightenment? In P. Rabinow (Ed.), *The Foucault Reader: An introduction to Foucault's thought* (pp. 32-50). London: Penguin.

Ghoshal, S. (2005). Bad management theories are destroying good management practices. *Academy of Management Learning and Education*, *4*, 75–91.

Jackson, M. C. (2003). *Creative holism: Systems thinking for managers*. Chichester: Wiley.

Leal-Filho, W. (1999). Getting people involved. In S. Buckingham-Hatfield, & S. Percy (Eds.), *Constructing local environmental agendas: People, places and participation* (pp. 33–41). London: Routledge.

Meadows, D., Meadows, H., & Randers, J. (1972). *The limits to growth: A report of the Club of Rome's project on the predicament of mankind*. London: Pan Books.

Meadows, D. H., Meadows, D. L., & Randers, J. (1992). *Beyond the limits: Global collapse or a sustainable future*. London: Earthscan in assoc. with the World Wide Fund for Nature.

Midgley, G. (1992). The sacred and profane in critical systems thinking. *Systems Practice*, *5*, 5–16.

Midgley, G. (2000). *Systemic intervention: Philosophy, methodology and practice*. New York: Kluwer Academic/Plenum.

Mintzberg, H. (2004). *Managers not MBAs*. Indianapolis, IN: Financial Times Prentice Hall.

Porter, T. (2005). Identity subtexts in the discursive construction of sustainability. *Electronic Journal of Radical Organization Theory*, *9*(1).

Reason, P. (2007). Education for ecology: Science, aesthetics, spirit, and ceremony. *Management Learning*, *38*(1), 27–44.

Roome, N., & Oates, A. (1996). Corporate greening. In J. Huckle & S. Sterling (Eds.), *Education for sustainability* (pp. 165–180). London: Earthscan.

Rosenhead, J. (2006). Past, present and future of problem structuring methods. *Journal of the Operational Research Society*, *57*(7), 759–765.

Senge, P., Aleiner, A., Roberts, C., Ross, R., & Smith, B. (1994). *The fifth discipline fieldbook: Strategies and tools for building a learning organization*. New York: Doubleday.

Stead, W. E., & Stead, J. (2004). *Sustainable strategic management*. London: M. E. Sharpe.

Ulrich, W. (1983). *Critical heuristics of social planning: A new approach to practical philosophy*. Berne: Haupt.

Ulrich, W. (1987). Critical heuristics of social systems design. *European Journal of Operational Research*, *31*, 276–283.

Ulrich, W. (1993). Some difficulties of ecological thinking, considered from a critical systems perspective: A plea for critical holism. *Systems Practice*, *6*(6), 583–611.

Ulrich, W. (2001). Critically systemic discourse: A discursive approach to reflective practice in ISD (part 2). *Journal of Information Technology Theory and Application*, *3*(3), 85–106.

UNCED. (1992). Earth Summit '92: The United Nations Conference on Environment and Development Rio de Janeiro 1992. In J. Quarrie (Ed.), *United Nations Conference on Environment and Development* (pp. 1–270). Rio de Janeiro: Author.

von Bertalanffy, L. (1968). *General system theory: Foundations, development, applications*. New York: George Braziller.

CHAPTER 7

EDUCATING FOR SUSTAINABILITY

The Power of
Learning Journeys to Raise Consciousness

Philip H. Mirvis

How do you wake people up to the importance and relevance of sustainable business practices? This paper looks at how learning journeys—to see first-hand the health of economies, societies, and natural environment around the world—can serve to raise consciousness about and motivate action toward sustainability. It describes three such journeys of corporate executives and reports observations from the author along with reflections from executives who participated in them. In so doing, it demonstrates the impact of consciousness raising experiences on executive's self awareness, understanding of others, dealings with diversity, and engagement with the larger world. The paper concludes with some considerations in the design of experiences aimed at educating executives for sustainability.

Fifty private equity specialists, participants in a global leadership program, meet with the leaders of Emirates Airlines, the Palm, World, and other real

---

Management Education for Global Sustainability, pp. 159–174
Copyright © 2009 by Information Age Publishing

estate developments, the stock exchange, and officials responsible for developing higher education, transportation, health services, and other aspects of the infrastructure that bloom the desert in Dubai. Their focus is on economic development of the emirate with an eye to the theme of commercial ambition. The achievements they study are significant but equal attention is given, in meetings with nongovernment organization (NGO) and civic leaders, to the environmental and social impact of such sweeping development, matters of employment diversity and the role of women in the society, and the overall sustainability of the economic boom.

Twenty-eight young leaders from 13 Asian countries, members of a leadership development community, travel to Sarawak, Malaysia with senior leaders to view environmental degradation and human displacement resulting from deforestation in the teak rainforests. They meet with the Penan people, former hunter-gatherers who now live in tin-huts in a village, their hunting grounds largely denuded of trees and game. A day-long walk and communal feast with the Penan opens the leaders' eyes to the spoils of industrialization and their hearts to the plight of indigenous peoples.

Thirty-two vice presidents, as part of their executive development program, meet with community health centers in Sao Paulo Brazil that range from a world-class cancer hospital for children to an urban hospital serving 10,000 people a day to a makeshift clinic in a favela. The subject is "access to health" but the shared caregiving and conversation concerns the import of passion in providing health care and dilemmas faced in the allocation of costly medicines, technology, and other health resources. The next day the executives meet with high government officials in Brasilia to talk about the role of government versus private initiatives in meeting health needs in the country.

In each of these vignettes, executives move from the relative comfort of the corporate classroom into unfamiliar territory, where they encounter people and problems seemingly far removed from the day-to-day scope and concerns of business life. Yet, they come away with powerful and relevant lessons. "The economic development in Dubai is breathtaking," said one of the financiers, "but this looks essentially like a real estate play. What about development of the society?" This question led to a sobering discussion of "responsible" economic development and what social obligations, if any, it places on private investors.

On his Brazilian experiences, one manager reported,

Dr. Petrilli of the cancer clinic said something that touched me deeply. "We open our doors to all children, no matter their insurance or what their families can pay. We use state of the art technology and cure many of them. Still, some die. I want these children to know they are dying because of their disease, not because they are Brazilians."

The doctor's noble motivations raised questions for the executives about what kind of leadership was needed to transform their company into a global pharmaceutical business with a significant presence in emerging markets. The encounters with the Penan tribe, in turn, led the Asian company leaders to debate the benefits and costs of economic growth in the region; One concluded, "This reminds us that we have strong social responsibilities ... to help protect the environment, to relieve poverty."

While each case's venues and lessons are unique, these development programs all feature the consciousness raising of executive learners about the state of the world, specifically the social, economic, and environmental impact of commerce, and about their own role in business today and tomorrow (Mirvis, 2008). Based on the first-hand involvement of the author and observations from participants, this paper looks at the design and impact of such consciousness raising experiences in executive development programs in the three companies cited. To begin, consider first some facts about the state of the world.

THE TWENTY-FIRST CENTURY OPERATING ENVIRONMENT

A few decades ago, it was possible for most senior executives to do their jobs blissfully unaware of issues pertaining to community welfare, the natural environment, the healthcare and work-life concerns of employees, and human rights in nascent global supply chains, as well as numerous other issues. And, they were largely unaffected by activist NGOs and shareholder resolutions and the threat of boycotts and protests, not to mention by calls for greater transparency and the dramatic increase in exposure provided by the Internet. No more. Ironically, these changes in the operating environment arose, in part, because of the dramatic increase in the scale, reach, and influence of business, particularly large corporations.

Globalization and Business Power

The last quarter of the twenty-first century saw a dramatic surge in the relative power of the private sector as the globalization of the world's economy opened up new opportunities for global businesses (cf. Gabel & Bruner, 2003; Anderson & Cavanaugh, 2000). In the past 15 years, the number of multinational corporations doubled (from roughly 36,000 in 1990 to over 72,000 in 2006). In the same period, the number of their foreign operations and affiliates nearly tripled (from about 240,000 to over 700,000). Today, two hundred corporations account for 23% of the world's GDP, and 51 of the top 100 economies in the world are corporations.

The integration of a global marketplace, the internationalization of capital and labor markets, and the retraction of the public sector in the United States and abroad have spurred this unprecedented growth in business activity. Increased productivity, due to innovation and specialization, has improved competitiveness and efficiency; greater market opportunities worldwide have raised revenues and expanded the scope of business opportunity; and access to cheaper sources of labor and raw materials continually lowers costs. These advantages have raised the power position of business, often beyond that of national governments. They have also produced undeniable economic, social, and environmental costs.

Social and Environmental Issues

In past 25 years, the gap between the average per-capita GDP in the 20 richest and poorest countries has doubled; and, today, 3 billion people live on less than $2.50 per day (World Bank, 2000, 2007). Some 2.4 billion people lack adequate sanitation facilities, even simple latrines, and 1.1 billion lack access to clean water. This combination has dire consequences for the world's poor. It is estimated that close to half of all people in developing countries suffer, at any given time, from health problems caused by water and sanitation deficits. Two million, 90% of them children, die annually from infectious diarrhea. These gaps raise challenges for corporations concerning wealth distribution, access to health care and technology, and their license to operate in developing and emerging countries.

On the environmental side apart from global warming, one in four mammal species is in serious decline, mainly due to human activity; fish stocks are eroding; the world's wetlands and forest cover are declining markedly; and desertification puts some 135 million people worldwide at risk of being driven from their lands (World Business Council for Sustainable Development [WBCSD], 2006). The UN's Environment Programme projects there will be 50 million environmental refugees worldwide by 2010. All of these developments and predictions call for the greening of corporations and raise questions for firms dependent on water, marine life, and timber for doing their business.

Global trends of rising poverty and declining eco-productivity have parallels in the United States, where a fortunate-fifth of the population has seen its earnings grow while the wages of the rest of the workforce stagnate. Wealthy nations have health concerns, too. Europeans and Americans, who constitute just 28% of world population, account for 42% of deaths from cardiovascular diseases and cancers—diseases often triggered by smoking, sedentary lifestyles, and eating foods rich in salt, sugar, and fat. All food-and-beverage purveyors must now attend to the ingredients in their products and how they promote their goods to the public.

Discontent with Business

Today, executives confront a paradox. On the one hand, the public holds business leaders in low regard, mistrusts what they say and the motives behind what they do, and sees big companies as too powerful and far more interested in profits than in the welfare of people or health of the planet. On the other hand, the public has high expectations that business should behave more responsibly, concern itself with environmental sustainability, use its resources and talents to improve society, and address itself to social issues as broad as the gap between the rich and poor and as specific as the spread of HIV/AIDS (Globescan, 2001–2007).

Recent surveys show that, worldwide, most CEOs understand the press of the public's expectations and recognize a need for business to play a more engaged and responsible role in society. A poll of U.S. business leaders found that 75% believe that the public expects them to exceed laws to ensure products are reliable and safe, and 58% believe that the public expects them to exceed laws to protect the environment (Global Education and Research Network [GERN], 2007). On a global scale, another survey (McKinsey, 2006) found that just 16% of executives in 116 countries held the view that business should "focus solely on providing highest possible returns to investors while obeying all laws and regulations." The other 84% agreed with the statement that business should "generate high returns to investors but balance that with contributing to the broader public good."

Powerful New Interests

New agents and forces are bringing these heightened expectations forcefully into business. A growing legion of NGOs, which represent varied social and environmental issues and interests, operate at the nexus of business and society (Hawken, 2007). Since the mid-1980s, over 200,000 new citizen groups have formed worldwide and global NGOs have been rising in numbers, scale, and scope. Amnesty International, for example, has nearly 2 million members in every country where multinational corporations do business and the World Wildlife Fund has over 5 million. Historically, both of these groups, as well as Oxfam, Greenpeace, and thousands more, have acted as corporate "watchdogs" and forced companies to account for their social and environmental inaction or misdeeds. Now, some of these groups are beginning to join with industry in partnerships concerned with human rights, natural resource stocks, climate change, world hunger, and the like.

How are companies reacting to the new operating environment? One response has been embracing new concepts of and frameworks for business management, including the idea that firms have responsibility to multiple stakeholders, not just shareholders, and need to take account of their economic, social, and environmental performance, or the "triple-bottom line" (Elkington, 1997; Freeman, 1984). Over the past 10 years, new models of corporate citizenship and sustainability (and namesakes like social responsibility, corporate responsibility, etc.) have advanced significantly into business in Europe, the United States, and around the world (cf. GERN, 2008; Googins, Mirvis, & Rochlin, 2007). Indeed, growing numbers of firms are building business models aimed at addressing the world's biggest economic, social, and environmental problems.

One challenge for the management educator is to animate these ideas and highlight their relevance for business and business leaders. Certainly corporate citizenship and sustainability are making their way into the MBA curricula and executive development programs in the form of readings, case studies, simulations, and so on. Moreover, information about the state of the world is accessible in many Web sites on the Internet. But the experience of *being there physically* and *seeing first-hand* adds texture to this kind of knowledge and yields memories that increase mindfulness about doing business in the larger world (Wuthnow, 1991). A closer look at these three developmental efforts illustrates their success in exposing business leaders to the world around them, raising consciousness about the need for business to respond, and motivating them to take action.

ON SEEING ECONOMIES

The private equity specialists' journey to Dubai launched their year-long executive development program. Prereadings highlighted the scale and sources of investments in the emirate, previewed select social and environmental issues, and set a context for engaging with this economy. On the ground "business anthropology," had the executives first visit traditional markets, where fish, produce, vegetables, and gold were on offer, much as they had been in prior eras via face-to-face commercial trade, from suppliers to vendors to consumers. The smells of fish and foods, the sounds of mongers promoting goods and bargaining their wares, and the attendant chaos of motor and camel transport infused the senses. Initially, the specialists questioned the purpose of these visits and their relevance

to finance and modern trade. The next day, however, as we visited contemporary traders, operating out of commercial palaces, one local executive remarked,

> I learned to trade from my grandfather in the spice markets: Who to buy
> from; how to care for products; how to treat customers; how much to charge
> and make a profit; how to do business for the long run. These same princi-
> ples apply today.

Subsequent visits to leaders in air, ground, and sea transport, in tourism and trade, and in other essential industries revealed the complexities
of doing business in a royal economy where relationships and linkages to
the royal family enter the commercial calculus. In many companies, members of the royal family have been moved into investment roles and global
operating managers have been hired to set up corporate governance and
control systems, increase transparency, and cope with the complexity of
managing multicultural workforces, including, in one firm, staff from
forty-three countries. "Progress on governance, sustainability, and other
essentials of good management lag behind the economy in Dubai,"
remarked one of the executives on the learning team, adding "There is a
risk that this will slow down economic development. But there's a bigger
risk that if these things don't progress, the whole project implodes."

Later legs of the private equity managers' development journey took
them to the command economy of Vietnam, the more socially-oriented
economies of Brazil and South Africa, and post-communist Bosnia-Herze-
govina. The investors, trained in finance and skilled in deal-making, were
exposed to diverse political economies, regulatory frameworks, and the
varied mix of interests and stakeholders in different parts of the world. It
was surprising to some that the "Anglo-Saxon" model was neither the norm
nor even the desired form of capitalism in other countries and regions.
This finding produced considerable introspection and debate about the
supposed "natural order" of economic exchange posited by neoclassical
economists. The specialists also raised questions about where to draw the
line on facilitation fees and political influence in deal making, the dark side
of global commerce, and how to facilitate progressive arrangements involving, for instance, fair trade provisions, eco-investments, and public-private
partnerships.

ON SEEING THE NATURAL ENVIRONMENT

At their initial meeting in Sarawak (once part of Borneo), the Asian leaders gathered to experience, first-hand, the terrible costs incurred by the

clear-cutting of tropical rainforests. They first learned about the state of Asia's natural environment from a talk by a director of a global natural resources group. Then, to get closer to the scene and symbolically lend a hand, the executives cleaned a nearby beach of industrial flotsam and tourist trash. Afterwards, a trip upriver in hollowed-out wooden canoes took them to the village of the Penan. There, they met villagers and hunters, in their tribal dress and loincloths, talked through translators to the chief, medicine man, and tribesmen, and took a long walk with them through their clear-cut forests.

Along the journey, periodic group reflections opened up hearts and led to earnest discussion of the benefits and costs of economic growth in Asia. This discussion led to calls to incorporate sustainability into strategic plans. The reflections of one leader:

> The beauty of the nature and the majesty of the place helped deepen our insights about our roles as leaders and individuals on this earth. To be in the jungles of Borneo helped us feel and see the potential in this region, almost feel and touch the vision. We were able to move from discovering self to building a mental picture about the future with a clear direction of where you want to go and where you want to be. And it is extremely powerful when you see around you a lot of people sharing the same picture.

The Asian leaders took subsequent journeys to China and India to look at migration from farms to cities and the social side of sustainability, to disaster relief in post-tsunami Sri Lanka, where they helped to care for the distressed and rebuild the commercial supply chain, and to the northern mountains of Vietnam, where they participated in an extended service learning program with the Hmong peoples, teaching them about sanitation, hand washing, and tooth brushing. These journeys raised the consciousness of leaders about the perilous state of agriculture in their region, which lies at the center of the business model and whose problems include water shortages, the loss of family farms, and the toxic side effects of forms of chemical fertilization. Many, motivated by this knowledge, applied it to environmental cleanup projects in their own nations and sustainable certification schemes for their products. Many also took their own teams on consciousness raising journeys (Mirvis & Gunning, 2006).

ON SEEING SOCIETY

In the case of the Brazil journey, the executives were divided into several teams to study the provision of health care in Brazilian communities. They visited with health care specialists, planners, and managers, while dialoging with community members and providing service to people in need. On-site, each team conducted a community diagnosis that analyzed the social setting and service process and considered how their company in particular, and business in general, might be implicated in problems and potential solutions. Many teams also drew upon their community experiences to prepare a roster of lessons that could apply to their company's operations and management. They shared and discussed these findings with fellow leaders and the chief executive, who had also visited the communities. In these reflective forums, individual insights and lessons were shared for collective consideration and learning.

Talking to doctors, caring for patients, and getting first-hand impressions on "access to health" opened up a flood of conversation. In reflecting on the experience, one participant spoke of a doctor's entrepreneurial spirit: "He built a diabetes clinic from nothing. How? Real passion and belief in what he's doing. There was no complaining about resources or roadblocks. Nothing got in the way of his vision and drive." Another spoke of the caring, as opposed to strictly clinical, approach to patients, "At the hospital, the nurses didn't feel sorry for the children. They held them, laughed with them, and treated their illnesses aggressively. They taught the children how to win."

Subsequent talk, late into the night, stressed the importance of vision, passion, and purpose in leading their own business and especially in achieving their company's commitment to defeat disease. "We could learn from the Brazilians," remarked one vice president. "Seeing how much people can do if they set their minds to it, how much can be accomplished and how many resources can be mobilized in a developing country. With limited public and patient funding, but lots of volunteers and donations and a desire to change the world, two doctors had each built a world-class hospital for children, each full of fun and games, despite hardship." These executives could see how their business might be implicated in, and could take positive steps to address, problems of access to health. Many took these lessons home with them by helping to support and staff village-level clinics in impoverished and disease stricken areas throughout the world and by working with local manufacturers to make their medicines more affordable to those in need.

JOURNEYS AS CONSCIOUSNESS RAISING EXPERIENCES

On the surface, the idea of achieving consciousness raising for business executives through a journey may seem rather far afield. Yet, the case can be made that it is very applicable to the development of leaders and their companies. First, there is increased emphasis on self-awareness in leadership and scholarship programs (Goleman, Boyatzis, & McKee, 2002;

Quinn, 1996). This emphasis is amply evident in the wide-ranging use of self-assessment tools, in the widespread interest in emotional intelligence, in the growing practice of self-reflection in personal and professional development, and in the experimentation among executives with meditation, martial arts, yoga, and other forms of "soul work" (cf. Bolman & Deal, 1995; Schön, 1983). On consciousness raising journeys, executives confront their personal beliefs about, as well as the social costs and benefits of, economic activity and the state of the environment. Their very identity as business leaders is open to introspection.

Second, business leaders, long encouraged to develop social awareness and interpersonal skills, are being challenged today to go beyond simply understanding others to empathizing with and connecting to them deeply. These ideas, first formulated in the era of human relations management, are stressed in contemporary theories of resonant leadership and in the application of positive psychology to organizations (Boyatzis & McKee, 2005; Frost, 2003). In addition, leaders are now tasked to work sensitively and effectively with people of different ethnic, racial, and socio-economic backgrounds and from different cultures. This expectation applies to their dealings with employees, to be sure, but as well as to interactions with customers, suppliers, and NGOS, and in the communities in which they do business. Earley and Peterson (2004) thus regard "cultural intelligence" as essential to contemporary executive development. Certainly the mix of peoples they encounter on these journeys broadens their appreciation of the complexity and diversity of humanity.

Third, leaders are being urged to apply their business acumen to the scramble of fast-paced changes in the world around them and, in particular, to come to grips with the social, moral, and environmental impact of their organizations. Answering this call means, among other things, becoming "global citizens" and developing a point of view about the role of business in society (Tichy, Brimm, Charan, & Takeuchi, 1992; Waddock, 2002). On these counts, exposure to a broader array of socioenvironmental stimuli and situations can stretch and deepen a leader's world view. Mintzberg and Gosling (2002) refer to this broadly as "educating managers beyond borders." They and their colleagues incorporated consciousness raising experiences and self-reflection into a multi-country Executive MBA program and later designed the overall leadership development program for the private equity specialists, emphasizing the "five minds" of a manager (Gosling & Mintzberg, 2003).

DESIGNING A LEARNING JOURNEY

While assembling a large number of executives to travel to faraway lands may be beyond the scope and interests of many educators, there are growing numbers of these types of programs in companies, universities, and training institutions. Consider:

- Global university-based programs where MBA and executive learners travel to emerging markets, meet with business leaders and companies, and deepen their appreciation of global business;
- Corporate university programs where high performers and developing managers visit the operations of their own company and others firms, and meet counterparts in local business and government as part of their developmental journey;
- Corporate sponsored service learning programs where select managers work in NGOs or small businesses for 1-to-6 months to sharpen their cultural awareness and global business acumen;
- Independent service learning programs where leaders from several sectors come together to work-and-learn in developing countries.

The design principles for journeys have relevance in these and almost any program, which seek to raise consciousness among people about themselves and the world around them. In my experience, modestly-scaled journeys, involving, for instance, time spent in the natural environment, service learning in local hospitals, an orphanage, or community centers, and two-way interaction with other leaders, operators, and customers in another line of work, can also open minds and stimulate fresh thinking about new personal and collective directions.

What are the key design considerations? In each of the companies cited here, program managers in executive education built relationships with top executives, external faculty, and community groups and helped executive learners prepare for and follow up on their service learning assignments. Some key design elements:

Top-Level Buy-In

Needless to say, not all executives warm to the idea of global forays and service learning, are comfortable with exercises in self-disclosure, or embrace the overall connection to corporate citizenship and sustainability. However, when superiors self-disclose and speak to the link between service and citizenship, some resistance lessens. It is worth noting that, in the programs described, the CEOs typically joined their company teams and community members at each locale.

Preparing to Learn

Prior to a journey, it is useful to cue executives on its pedagogical purposes. As an example, some discussion of one's life history, or perhaps some autobiographical writing, followed by discussion of it with colleagues can help prepare leaders, operationally and emotionally, to meet people with different life experiences and stories to tell. It is also useful to preview how learning goals—such as self-awareness or dealing with diversity—will be explored during a journey.

To sharpen perspectives on economic, social, and political factors, some prereading, talks by subject matter experts, and open discussion help ready the mind for thoughtful questions and the senses for what is to be seen and heard. A workbook to organize thoughts and record observations can be helpful as well. Community members can also use workbooks, thereby making observation and analysis a joint activity.

Learning as a Group

Individuals can gain from a journey and even make significant contributions to the service setting as solo participants. In the cases described here, the executives, as participants in developmental programs, entered into learning as a group. Learning as a group has several advantages. First, otherwise reluctant individuals can be pulled into engagement by the group-as-a-whole and, in any case, find safety-in-numbers. Second, peer learners can be a source of orientation, stimulation and social support, and aid in interpreting what's going on and considering any implications. Third, the cohort effect, whereby a group begins to see itself and is seen by others as having a unifying identity, is a prerequisite to taking common action.

Setting Learning Objectives

The journeys' learning goals—increased self-awareness, an improved ability to understand and relate to others, and heightened sensitivity to how social, political, and economic forces interplay in the service setting – are, to some extent, organic byproducts of service learning. They do not have to be fully engineered. At the same time, the design and facilitation of the learning experience can enhance the likelihood of achieving these goals.

In the cases here, detailed designs called for individual, small group, and whole system activities. Reams have been written on how to design meaningful learning experiences at each of these levels, but it is in the choice of activities and in reflection that specific learning objectives come to life (cf. Kolenko, Porter, Wheatley, & Colby, 1996). For example, service learning programs involving house construction, painting, trash pickup, and such are useful for stimulating informal interaction, building bonds, and illustrating vividly the social and economic cleavages between business and society. These programs also demonstrate, substantively and symbolically, what can be accomplished when business and community people work together. In comparison, the experiences described here were biased toward person-to-person interaction. Given the cited journeys' focus on leadership development, primary emphasis was given to connecting executives both personally and professionally with leaders in a community as well as with the people they serve. Reflections, in turn, stressed personal insights and takeaways.

The Learning Experience

Journeys run the risk of seeming to be or looking like "corporate tourism." Thus, it is important to emphasize learning within and from the experience. My own preferences are for action learning; it is the pedagogy behind almost every step in a journey, which means there is little] explanation or theorizing before we embark on an activity, though there is a lot of individual and collective reflecting afterwards.

Attention to atmospherics, staging, and the flow of energy throughout the experience–all part of experience management—were carefully considered in the design of such programs. The aim was to create a multisensory experience and stimulate leaders' heads and hearts. In addition, learning content was, to some extent, "themed" to relevant issues in the firm's leadership development programs (e.g., self-knowledge, storytelling, learning from others, diversity) and to strategic considerations of the business (e.g., economic returns, environmental sustainability, corporate citizenship, access to health, core purpose).

Reflections: Before, During, Afterwards

Many studies suggest that focus on effective reflection is a primary enforcer of the power of service learning. Where self-awareness and consciousness raising are intentions of a service learning engagement, it is essential to make personal, as well as group, reflection an integral and ongoing part of the program. There are a variety of tools that can aid reflection, including materials and practice in journaling, "time outs" for note taking, and episodic group reflection.

It can be helpful for groups to use the principles of dialogue where they speak to the "group as a whole" and build on others' comments to develop collective thinking. Sitting in a circle can signify that there is no individual leader in charge of the conversation but rather a collective body at work (Mirvis & Ayas, 2003).

Interpretive Content

For program faculty, it is helpful to bring interpretive frameworks and content into reflective activities throughout a journey. Some material of particular relevance:

- *Issue Identification.* When leaders see myriad economic, social, political, and environmental conditions along a journey, it can help to have them categorize the "issues" in terms of, say, their relevance as *risks versus oppor*tunities for their business, or in terms of the *extent and likelihood* of their impact on the firm. These kinds of 2 x 2 grids are familiar to most business leaders and faculty alike.
- *Stakeholder Mapping.* Likewise, a mapping of relevant stakeholders in a country can highlight the diversity of interests, their relative support for or opposition to particular aspects of commerce and corporations, and the potential impact. Either, or both, of these reflective exercises can segue into the development of company "action plans"—whether as a developmental exercises or for real-time application.
- *Country/Market Analyses.* These exercises, plus case material and background reading, can inform development of a company's market entry or expansion strategy, and inform its social and environmental profile. These analyses were "takeaways" in each of the learning journeys highlighted here.
- *Personal & Group Development.* The journeys can also stimulate content-driven inner-exploration. Deep reflection on one's own personal reactions to a country's economic, social, and environmental conditions, for instance, can inform self-assessment of one's readiness to lead and operate in a global business and can help in identifying needed development targets. Feedback from peers, as well as from leaders met along a journey, can also stimulate further thinking about one's strengths and weaknesses. The same applies to learning groups.

Finally, it is important to recall Weick's (1995) commentary that "Experiences are not what happens to us, but what we do to what happens to us." This quote reminds us that journey experiences themselves do not engage participants, stretch them, or instruct them. The onus of transforming activities into mind-expanding, heart-rending, and soul-stirring encounters is on the participants. They do the work and learning of asking provocative questions, challenging assumptions, surfacing contradictions, and confronting themselves and one another. And, the educator plays the important role as a facilitator of their real-time learning.

REFERENCES

Anderson, S., & Cavanaugh, J. (2000, December). Top 200: The rise of corporate global power. *The Institute for Policy Studies*. Retrieved July, 19, 2008 from http://www.attac-bern.ch/fileadmin/dokumente/infos/top200-Multis.pdf

Bolman, L. G., & Deal, T. E. (1995). *Leading with soul: An uncommon journey of spirit.* San Francisco: Jossey-Bass.

Boston College Center for Corporate Citizenship. (2007). *The state of corporate citizenship in the U.S.: Rhetoric versus reality in 2007.* Boston: BCCCC.

Boyatzis, R., & McKee, A. (2005). *Resonant leadership.* Boston: Harvard Business School Press.

Earley, P. C., & Peterson, R. S. (2004). The elusive cultural chameleon: Cultural intelligence as a new approach to intercultural training for the global manager. *Academy of Management Learning & Education, 3*(1), 100–115.

Elkington, J. (1997). *Cannibals with forks: The triple-bottom line of 21st century business.* London: Capstone/John Wiley.

Freeman, R. E. (1984). *Strategic management: A stakeholder approach.* Boston: Pitman.

Frost, P. (2003). *Toxic emotions at work: How compassionate managers handle pain and conflict* Boston: Harvard Business School Press.

Gabel, M., & Bruner, H. (2003). *Globalinc: An atlas of the multinational corporation.* New York: The New York Press.

Global Education and Research Network. (2008). *Corporate citizenship around the world.* Boston: BCCCC.

Globescan. (2001–2007). *Corporate social responsibility monitor.* Retrieved from www.globescan.com

Goleman, D., Boyatzis, R., & McKee, A. (2002). *Primal leadership.* Boston: Harvard Business School Press.

Googins, B., Mirvis, P. H., & Rochlin, S. (2007). *Beyond good company: Next generation corporate citizenship.* New York: Palgrave-McMillan.

Gosling, J., & Mintzberg, H. (2003, November). The five minds of a manager. *Harvard Business Review,* pp. 1–9.

Hawken, P. (2007). *Blessed unrest.* New York: Viking.

Kolenko, T. A., Porter, G., Wheatley, W., & Colby, M. (1996). A critique of service-learning projects in management education: Pedagogical foundations, barriers, and guidelines. *Journal of Business Ethics*, *15*, 133–142.

McKinsey Quarterly Global Survey. (2006, January). Retrieved from www.Mckinsey.com

Mintzberg, H., & Gosling, J. (2002). Educating managers beyond borders. *Academy of Management Learning & Education, 1*(1), 64–76.

Mirvis, P. H. (2008). Executive development through consciousness raising experiences. *Academy of Management Learning & Education. 7*(2), 173–188.

Mirvis, P. H., & Ayas, K. (2003). Reflective dialogue, life stories, and leadership development. *Reflections, 4*(4) 39–48.

Mirvis, P. H., & Gunning, W. L. (2006). Creating a community of leaders. *Organizational Dynamics, 35*(1), 69´82.

Quinn, R. E. (1996). *Deep change: Discovering the leader within*. San Francisco: Jossey-Bass.

Schön, D. (1983*). The reflective practitioner*. New York: Basic Books.

Tichy, N. M., Brimm, M. I., & Takeuchi, H. (1991). *Leadership development as a lever for global transformation* (DRSBA Working Paper 668). Retrieved July 19, 2009, from http://deepblue.lib.umich.edu/bitstream/ 2027.42/36208/2/b1572490.0001.001.pdf

Waddock, S. (2002). *Leading corporate citizens: Visions, values, and value added*. New York: McGraw Hill.

Weick, K. E. (1995). *Sensemaking in organizations*. Thousand Oaks, CA: SAGE.

World Bank. (2000). *PREM Economic Policy Group and Development Economics Group. "Assessing Globalization" at worldbank.org*. Retrieved June 4, 2009, from http:// www.wbcsd.org/plugins/DocSearch/details.asp? type=DocDet&ObjectId=MTgyMTM

World Bank (2007). *World Development Indicators, at worldbank.org*. Retrieved June 4, 2009, from http://web.worldbank.org/WBSITE/EXTERNAL/ DATASTATISTICS/0,, contentMDK:21298138~pagePK:64133150~piPK:64133175~ theSitePK:239419,00.htm

World Business Council for Sustainable Development (2006). *From challenge to opportunity: The role of business in tomorrow's society*. Retrieved from www.wbcsd.org

Wuthnow, R. (1991). *Acts of compassion: Caring for others and helping ourselves*. Princeton, NJ: Princeton University Press.

CHAPTER 8

THE CHALLENGES OF BUSINESSES' INTERVENTION IN AREAS WITH HIGH POVERTY AND ENVIRONMENTAL DETERIORATION

Promoting an Integrated Stakeholders' Approach in Management Education

**Diego A. Vázquez-Brust, José A. Plaza-Ubeda,
Claudia E. Natenzon, and Jerónimo de Burgos-Jiménez**

"Sustainability is inherently a multidimensional concept" (Foot & Ross, 2004, p. 109). Therefore, teaching about sustainability requires not only understanding the "language" and ideas of sustainability but also moving from subject-based teaching to a more integrated approach (Eber, 2007). This chapter highlights the current conceptual gap in sustainability education when addressing the "vicious circle" between poverty and environmen-

Management Education for Global Sustainability, pp. 175–203
Copyright © 2009 by Information Age Publishing
All rights of reproduction in any form reserved.

tal deterioration—a major challenge to sustainable development for businesses and all societies. The chapter emphasizes the need for a more holistic approach to the poverty-environmental deterioration problem and the need for students, managers, and educators to adopt new mindsets and roles in addressing this challenge. Stressing the importance of taking proactive management strategies, it provides a framework for teachers, students, and managers to use in conceptualizing the relationship between poverty and environmental deterioration, identifies factors that can be brought to bear on it, and summarizes different types of company approaches to this challenge—distinguishing between strong and weak sustainability actions by companies. Emphasizing the importance of understanding the roles vulnerability, adaptability, entrepreneurship, and stakeholders can play in seeking solutions to this problem, the chapter concludes with recommendations directed at students, teachers, managers, and other stakeholders committed to breaking the vicious circle of poverty and environmental deterioration.

INTRODUCTION

Education helps societies to become more sustainable (UNRISD, 2000; McIntosh Leipziger, Jones, & Coleman, 1998). The way people and organizations behave is a result of how they see the world according to their knowledge, beliefs, and values (D'Andrade, 1984). Education and training influences the regulative, normative, and cognitive aspects of organizations and institutions (Scott, 1995). Management education can contribute to sustainable development by raising awareness of the diversity and complexity of challenges facing our planet, by embedding sustainability values and principles in managers and students (Galea, 2004), and by showing ways to address these challenges.

"Sustainability is inherently a multidimensional concept" (Foot & Ross, 2004, p. 109). Therefore, delivering sustainability in business teaching requires not only understanding the "language" and ideas of sustainability but also moving from subject-based teaching to a more integrated approach (Eber, 2007) This chapter highlights the current conceptual gap in business education when addressing the "vicious circle" between poverty and environmental deterioration—a major challenge to sustainable development. More concretely, the chapter emphasizes the need for students, educators, and managers to take a more holistic approach to understanding and addressing this challenge, and it stresses the special need for proactive management strategies in regions with high levels of social vulnerability.

Increasing efforts are being made in management education to transmit the importance of sustainability, environmental management, and corporate social responsibility (CSR) for the future of life on the planet

(Adams, 2004). However, the interdependence between poverty and environmental damage and the effect that social vulnerability has on the relationship between environment and companies have not been fully addressed. Although management education has made some progress in recognizing the importance of stakeholder engagement in the delivery of business solutions to social and environmental problems in general, it has made little progress doing so for areas with high social and environmental vulnerability. This chapter begins by identifying the conceptual bases required to address this issue and presents an integrated framework for the analysis of business interventions aimed at breaking this "vicious circle." This framework can be used in management education to show why sustainability problems and solutions are inherently multidimensional (Foot & Ross, 2004), and how existing concepts and theories of management can be combined with other fields of knowledge, shifting from subject-based teaching to a more holistic approach. Later sections of the chapter suggest teaching strategies, directed at instilling key conceptual issues and practices (Meyer & Scott, 1983).

THE "VICIOUS CIRCLE" BETWEEN POVERTY AND ENVIRONMENTAL DETERIORATION: A GLOBAL CHALLENGE

The "vicious circle" between poverty and environmental deterioration is a main challenge for global sustainability (Kandachar & Halme, 2008). Poverty causes environmental deterioration (Hart, 1995) and, at the same time, environmental deterioration increases poverty of populations living in vulnerable environments (water shortages, destruction of ecosystems) or in those highly contaminated by human activity, where the productivity of the land decreases or the costs of protecting health increase (Gray & Moseley, 2005).

Poverty increases environmental deterioration both in rural and urban areas. In poor rural areas, intensive agriculture, overuse of fertilizers, and tree cutting produce deforestation, topsoil erosion, and water contamination. These effects are exacerbated by communities' incapacity to invest in the environment and by demographic pressure (birth rate rises as income falls) (Hart, 1997). Moreover, in poor urban areas environmental regulation is weaker (Pargal & Wheeler, 1996) because the poor tend to be less informed of the risks, have limited capability to press for a better environment, and assign the environment a lower relative value compared to the possibility of a job (Dasgupta, Lucas, & Wheeler, 1998). These factors lead to a higher density of "dirty" and inefficient industries and to higher pollution levels (Hettige, Mani, & Wheeler, 1998).

At the same time, poverty reduction obtained at the cost of environmental damage is deceptive, and in the longer term generates higher social inequality. On one hand, higher incomes increase environmental deterioration because of the higher emissions and use of natural resources associated with creating the higher incomes (Murphy, 1994). On the other hand, when economic growth is achieved by avoiding or limiting environmental regulations in "dirty" sectors, there is a growing risk of pollution and industrial accidents, which threaten the health, lifestyle and economic standards of the neighboring population. (Dasgupta et al., 1998). In turn, these factors increase the effective poorness of those who have limited resources to protect themselves from environmental diseases, thus affecting their lifestyles and depriving them of job opportunities and ways to contribute to family subsistence (Waelkens, Doors, & Criel, 2005)

The well-being of populations living in hotspots with high environmental deterioration and social vulnerability is diminished in terms of health, education, employment, life expectancy and opportunities to develop (Martinez-Alier, 2002). The cause-effect relationship between environmental illnesses and poverty is an example of the mechanics of vicious circles: as much as 24% of all diseases (and 33% of illnesses in children under the age of 5) has been attributed to environmental deterioration (Prüss-Ustün & Corvalán, 2004). If the poor pay for care, even during short periods of ill-health, their poverty increases (maybe forcing them to sell land or animals), and so does their vulnerability to illness (due to malnutrition and lack of defences). If they do not get care, they lose working days due to illness, thus seeing their income fall and their vulnerability increase (Waelkens et al., 2005). Similar processes can explain the relationships between poverty and degradation of land by deforestation or extensive use of pesticides (Yapa, 2002), environmental degradation and access to education, or even environmental pollution and criminality (Masters, 1997).

Social and economic vulnerability operates also as a barrier to the development of firms' sustainable environmental strategies (De Jongh, 2004). Companies working in vulnerable areas tend to be subjected to stringent cost-based constraints, have fewer resources to invest in the environment owing to the urgency of reaching a minimal level of economic performance, and experience limited regulatory or social pressures to conduct themselves in ways that support sustainability (Dasgupta et al., 1998). Even proactive environmental solutions may have unforeseen negative social effects when implemented in vulnerable communities. Cleaner processes, for example, tend to use fewer workers, which increases unemployment. Recycling and waste minimization can affect marginal groups living on informal recycling (Furedy, 1984)

THEORETICAL FRAMEWORK: AN INTEGRATIVE APPROACH TO SUSTAINABILITY AND VULNERABILITY

The previous section described the problem addressed in this chapter: environmental deterioration and poverty are not only linked, but they feed on one another. The effectiveness of the different approaches used so far by management to address this interconnected problem are described next and initiatives that seek to solve part of the problem without considering the effects on the other part, are shown not to be true solutions.

Relationships Between Companies and the Natural Environment: Sustainability, Eco-Modernization, and Environmental Strategies

The incorporation of the sustainability concept in mainstream managerial practices has come forward mainly through the so-called eco-modernization discourse (Dryzek, 1997; Prasad & Elmes, 2005), which acknowledges the need for more integration of environmental issues within corporate management strategy (Welford, 1995) and encourages companies to balance the "triple bottom line" (Elkington & Fennel, 1998) of economic, environmental, and social interests.

In practice, eco-modernization encompasses a continuum of strategies ranging from "weak" to "strong" versions according to its likely efficacy in terms of promoting sustainability (Christoff, 2000; Dryzek, 1997). "Weak" eco-modernization has a technical-economic focus on improving the environmental efficiency of production through ongoing innovation and environmental management, aiming at maximizing profit while minimizing environmental costs (Springett, 2003) Social issues such as poverty or social vulnerability are hardly ever considered. In contrast, "strong" eco-modernization seeks not only to minimise the production of risks but also to prevent their unfair externalization in space and time, thus highlighting social and political aspects linked to the environmental conflict. (Christoff, 2000; Dryzek, 1997; Hajer, 1995).

"Strong" eco-modernization intervention strategies, such as industrial ecology, natural capitalism (Hawken, Lovins, & Lovins, 1999), cradle to cradle (McDonough & Braungart, 2002), or biosphere rules (Unruh, 2008) are gradually being accepted by companies embracing corporate sustainability more proactively. Their widespread acceptance would help to redefine responsibilities and possiblities for industry to contribute to changing production and consumption structures in ways that would decrease environmental deterioration. However, so far as offering comprehensive solutions for the problem addressed by this chapter, they are not completely satisfactory because they do not include the management of social aspects in their strategic toolkit (Dyllick & Hockerts, 2002)

The need for further research into practical aspects of "social corporate sustainability" is often mentioned in the strong eco-modernization literature (Elkington & Fennel, 1998; Hart, 1997; Senge, 1999). However, insights into social strategies rarely go beyond a general normative framework, indicating intervention areas (Dyllick & Hockerts, 2002; Hart, 1997; Sharma & Ruud, 2003). They also do not go into detail about how to develop specific strategies and practices to enhance social sustainability by applying economic and natural capital to the greater societal good (Dyllick & Hockerts, 2002).

Relationships Between Firms and Vulnerable Populations: Poverty Alleviation Strategies

The integration of poverty alleviation policies within corporate environmental strategies is an issue where strong ecological-modernization and corporate sustainability are still wanting (Myers, 2008; Robbins, 2001). However, since the UN "Millenium Development Goals" put poverty at center stage of global agendas, there has been a growing pressure for a higher profile role of business in the matter. This pressure is triggering a variety of initiatives, some of them already existing in companies long before poverty became a corporate challenge (Jain & Vachani, 2006; van Tulder & Kolk, 2008). Although the issue is still in the early development phase of its life-cycle (van Tulder & Kolk, 2008) three businesses approaches to deal with poverty reduction can be identified: the donor model, the legitimacy model, and the market model.

The *donor* model sees the company as a good citizen with a moral responsibility to share part of its economic gains with society, thus helping the poor with philanthropic activities channelled through charities or foundations. The *legitimacy* model sees poverty alleviation from a more utilitarian perspective. Their socially responsible behaviors seek to achieve of long-term business survival (Gond & Mullenbach-Servayre, 2004). It argues that businesses require a "social license" to operate and seeks to maintain such license by earning society's goodwill through acts of corporate social responsibility (CSR). CSR is defined as the voluntary inclusion of environmental and social concerns?such as poverty—in the companies' strategies, transactions, and interactions with stakeholders (European Commission, 2006) Finally, *Market* models frame the relationship between the companies and the poor as a business opportunity. The most widespread version of these models is the "Base of the Pyramid"

(BoP) framework which seeks to "eradicate poverty through profit" and sees lack of investment in certain social sectors and areas of the planet as the main cause of poverty (Prahalad & Hammond, 2002). Other well-known market models are "sustainable livelihoods" which defines the poor as consumers and entrepreneurs affected by economic and social injustice (Kirchgeorg & Winn, 2006) and "social enterprises" where commercial strategies are used to achieve social goals rather than high profits.

These models, as they are currently being executed, all give rise to controversy concerning their contributions toward reducing widespread poverty (Crabtree, 2007; Sachs, 2005; Jenkins, 2005; Karnani, 2007; Porter & Kramer, 2006; Kircheorg & Winn, 2006). At their best, they are seen by many as contributing to the development of what Dyllick & Hockert (2002) call "welfare islands" surrounding a company. Jenkins (2005) provides a detailed account of the limitations of direct aid, CSR, BoP, and sustainable livelihoods approaches to fighting poverty.

Both legitimacy and market approaches have been redrafted to increase their efficiency in combating poverty (Brugmann & Prahalad, 2007; Kirchgeorg & Winn, 2006). Yet, their greatest problems are that they still misunderstand the dynamics and importance of vulnerability and environmental issues and therefore suggest solutions that are dissociated from the potential environmental impacts generated by a rise in production and consumption (Michaelis, 2003). Ultimately, such "solutions" reinforce the vicious poverty-vulnerability circle (Kandachar & Halme, 2008).

The approaches to sustainability management or poverty alleviation described in the previous section are neither designed nor able to offer holistic solutions for overcoming the vicious circle of poverty-environmental deterioration. Corporate sustainability approaches, although valuable in terms of ecological sustainability, are limited by their superficial consideration of social aspects (Dyllick & Hockert, 2002; Sharma & Ruud, 2003), and the approaches to confront poverty have flaws in terms of ecological sustainability (Kirchgeorg & Winn, 2006).

Although these approaches are gradually being incorporated into subjects studied in management education (especially in the area of environmental management), they still do not stress the connection between sustainable environmental practices and poverty. A possible strategy for addressing this shortcoming in the classroom is to use economic models that take into account and recreate different scenarios for the environmental-deterioration/poverty-vulnerability interaction and to combine these economic models with business simulation tools (Yaron & Moyini, 2004) and active-learning teaching exercises. Conducting environmental and social assessments for community organizations in areas with high social and environmental vulnerability—"getting the students out there"

(Fowler & Engel-Cox, 2007) will elicit emotional responses. These approaches can reinforce the moral obligation to take into consideration the impact of environmental and poverty related actions and highlight the normative elements of the relationship between the two (Scott, 1995).

CONCEPTUAL FRAMEWORK

One of the purposes of this chapter is to provide guidance on classroom material to help students understand the necessity and added difficulty of developing proactive company strategies offering solutions to problems of environmental sustainability and poverty reduction. This section reviews theoretical contributions that can be helpful in guiding intervention strategies, discusses how such concepts can be taught in business schools, and integrates the contributions into a conceptual framework for application in present-day society.

Stakeholder Theory

Stakeholder theory holds firms responsible for delivering benefits to all their stakeholders rather than only to shareholders and customers, defining stakeholders as "the individuals and constituencies that contribute, either voluntarily or involuntarily, to firms' wealth-creating capacity and activities, and that are therefore its potential beneficiaries and/or risk bearers" (Post, Preston, & Sachs, 2002, p. 19).

The stakeholder approach can play a very relevant role in breaking the environmental impact-poverty vicious circle. Stakeholder theory has been applied to analyze both environmental and social issues. A strong body of research has been devoted to analyze the motivations, evolution, and consequences of environmental strategies and management (Bremmers, Omta, Kemp, & Haverkamp, 2007; Buysse & Verbeke, 2003; Delmas & Toffel, 2004; Post et al., 2002; Sharma & Henriques, 2005). Similarly, there is abundance of stakeholder theory research on firms' social responsibilities, in particular on health, security and human rights (Clarkson, 1991, 1995; Jones, 1995; Post et al., 2002; Weaver, Treviño, & Cochran, 1999). However, practical examples of the use of stakeholder theory to propose solutions related to poverty and vulnerability are scarcer (see, for instance, De Jongh, 2004; Pater & van Lierop, 2006).

In agreement with Post et al. (2002) we can identify three basic components in stakeholder theory that will be used in the framework we develop.

(a) Flows of benefits between companies and stakeholders.
(b) Stakeholders' networks and roles.
(c) Varied and discrepant issues or interests.

Nakao, Amano, Matsamura, Kenba, and Nakano (2007) emphasize how challenging it is for companies to make social and economic benefits compatible in the long term. Not only may benefits not be attained by all stakeholders but certain groups, such as those who are particularly vulnerable, may be negatively affected by a firm's activities (Walley & Whitehead, 1994). However, if the vulnerable stakeholders are "engaged" in entrepreneurial initiatives, their cooperation and honest adaptation can influence companies to make their economic goals more compatible with those stakeholders' needs (Wall & Marzan, 2006). To this end, it is necessary and urgent for more vulnerable groups to join proactively with the rest of stakeholders and with the companies themselves in directing company activities toward cooperative actions (Pater & van Lierop, 2006).

Numerous studies have pointed out the importance of stakeholder networks (Rowley, 1997; Roloff, 2008) and their influence strategies (Frooman, 1999) in determining company behavior. Therefore, if a company is to contribute to breaking the poverty-environmental vicious circle, the stakeholder management model it uses must have integrated and entrepreneurial perspectives in responding to stakeholder networks and influence strategies. These perspectives must give priority to innovative solutions that reduce both environmental deterioration and social vulnerability. The quantity and quality of entrepreneurship within the stakeholder networks is a key resource developing innovative and sustainable solutions (Bruggman & Prahalad, 2007; UNCPSD, 2005).

Post et al. (2002) make a crucial distinction between what they call "the management of stakeholders" and "stakeholder management" in firms' strategies for stakeholder engagement. The management of stakeholders is primarily a morally neutral practice (Greenwood, 2007) that assumes relationships with stakeholders must be arranged in ways that support specific interests of the company, and puts forward a more "manipulative" strategy aimed at convincing or "guiding" stakeholders to align themselves with the company (Polonsky, 1995). On the other hand, stakeholder management is based on a change in management philosophy that involves the inclusion of stakeholder interests in the firms' processes of strategy-making and execution (Post et al., 2002). Aiming simultaneously at current business success and long term survival of the company, this approach has a moral motivation, based on the rightful consideration and integration of stakeholder interests into business decision making (Sirgy, 2002). When the interests of various stakeholder groups differ, the key to settling those discrepancies lies in identifying which social and environmental approaches allow a better use of a company's resources and have a better set of impacts on the interests of the different stakeholder groups (Pater & van Lierop, 2006).

The first point of the framework being presented, consequently, postulates the use of the stakeholder management perspective as a general basis for understanding the roles that stakeholders and companies must play in order to combine traditional management goals with sustainable strategies for the reduction of poverty and environmental deterioration.

Teaching of stakeholder management is widespread within management education, usually integrated in subjects such as "strategic management," "project management," and in courses about CSR. To develop their knowledge of the environmental-poverty challenge, students can be presented with practical exercises and cases, where they seek strategies to deal with discrepant demands from different stakeholder groups. The use of innovative methods, such as role-playing, is especially useful in assisting students to see the diversity of demands from stakeholders and the difficulties in making those demands compatible. The utilization of specific software for stakeholder relationship management (Bourne, 2008) can help to reinforce the legitimacy of stakeholder management practices (Scott, 1995) that the students may choose to apply later in their professional activities.

Crucially, management education should highlight the importance of including ethical and moral components as inseparable from the application of stakeholder management. The same vocabulary is often used to express different ideas and "stakeholder management" has been used in the literature and education interchangeably with "management of stakeholders" (Post et al., 2002). However, as the previous section highlighted, the conceptual difference between these two terms is substantial and it should be clear to teachers and managers that only stakeholder management is conducive to sustainable development. It is important to encourage development of this approach because only stakeholder management is a moral practice and one that is likely to contribute to reducing both environmental and social vulnerability as companies simultaneously seek fulfilment of their economic objectives.

Social Theories of Risk and Vulnerability

The UN defines vulnerability as "conditions determined by physical, social, economic and environmental factors or processes which increase the susceptibility of a community to the impact of hazards" (UN/ISDR, 2004). Social theories of risk define risk as the probability of a potentially harmful phenomenon (threat or hazard) resulting in damage for a certain social system (Downing et al., 2001). Natenzon et al. (2005) see risk as a function of four independent factors: the hazardousness of the threat, the level of exposure of the social system to such threat or its "environmental vulnerability," the system's social vulnerability, and scientific uncertainty.

Environmental vulnerability is a state of susceptibility to harm, powerlessness, or marginality stemming from the physical system hosting the community (e.g., flood-prone areas). In turn, social vulnerability is an inherent characteristic of human systems which makes certain communities more likely to suffer economic or human life losses as a consequence of environmental hazards such as shocks (for example, floods caused by climate change) or stress (such as exposure to polluted rivers), Adger, Brooks, Bentham, and Eriksen (2004). For instance, communities that lack adequate sanitary and drinking water infrastructure are more environmentally vulnerable and prone to suffer harm from pollution (Crichton, 1999).

Cardona (2005) links social vulnerability to socioeconomic weakness (poverty; inequity; unemployment and debt; access to food, insurance, and credit) and lack of resilience, or of ability to endure negative impacts (marginality; limited access to education; poor quality housing; inadequate infrastructure of services and welfare; low life expectancy, lack of social security). Although social vulnerability is not a function of the risks to which the system is exposed, the characteristics of a system make it more vulnerable to some hazards than to others. For example, good quality housing reduces vulnerability to wind storms but has no impact on vulnerability to industrial pollution.

This concept has guided normative study of actions intended to enhance well-being through the reduction of risk in general (Adger, Brooks, Bentham, & Eriksen, 2004.) and also to economic risk (Yapa, 2002, Scott, 2006). Morduch (1994) defines a state of *vulnerability to poverty* in terms of economic risk. For example, communities where a saving culture is nonexistent are more vulnerable to poverty, thus more likely to go through important changes in their lifestyle as a consequence of an economic recession. Calandrino and Michelle (2003) and Minujín (1999) see poverty as a complex phenomenon defining a continuum between those practically invulnerable—the rich—and those extremely vulnerable —the chronically poor for whom prevention must integrate the reduction of both social and environmental vulnerabilities (Filgueira & Peri, 2004).

Vulnerability underlies both environmental deterioration and poverty. Scott (2006) believes that social vulnerability and environmental risk are two of the key factors in the construction of poverty, while Hart (1997) considers that environmental deterioration originates because of poverty, technology, and population rise. Siegel and Alwang (1999) found a vicious circle of vulnerability where social vulnerability results in lower

economic productivity and higher vulnerability to poverty. Further connections were exposed by Dilley, Chen, Deichmann, and Lerne-Lam
(2005), who found that areas with low gross product per person and low
density are more vulnerable to both economic and environmental risks.

*The second part of our conceptual framework introduces the concept of vulnera-
bility to encourage framing the vicious circle of poverty-environmental deterioration as a single problem: vulnerability to economic-environmental risk.*

Teaching of vulnerability issues is usually done in economics and sociology, but not widespread in the management field. The growing body of
studies of stakeholder management offers an opportunity to include the
teaching of vulnerability in management courses as a conceptual tool to
put in context the legitimacy and urgency of basic social demands. In this
sense, it is essential to shift teaching from the prevailing mental model of
business benefit toward a "social sustainability of the business" framing
(Adams, 2004).

Walker (2007) emphasizes the importance of eliciting emotional
responses from students in turning learning into action. Such emotional
responses can be triggered by the interaction of students with vulnerable
communities. Pedagogic activities carried out to familiarize students with
the integration of stakeholders into company processes are a good opportunity to deepen their knowledge of vulnerability and to catalyze emotional responses (Clarke & Chenoweth, 2006; Walker, 2007). Since most
critical cases on this issue are in developing countries, "Getting the students out there" is not always a realistic option. Critical analysis of real
cases and videos that portray how some companies create problems for
vulnerable local communities are a very useful teaching tool to raise students' awareness of vulnerability. However, there is a need for more didac-
tic materials, focusing, from the manager's point of view, on the
repercussions of company actions on the most vulnerable social agents.

Adaptation and Adaptive Capability

The importance of the concepts of adaptation and the ability to adapt
is highlighted by researchers studying vulnerability to environmental risks
(Adger et al., 2004; Eakin & Lemos, 2006; Yamin, Rahman, & Huq,
2005), poverty (Morduch, 1994; Sen, 1981; Yapa, 2002), and the two risks
jointly (Archer, Crocker, & Shogren, 2006; Calandrino & Michelle, 2003;
Kelly & Adger, 2000; Scott, 2006).

The concept of adaptation has nuances that are different in natural science and in social science. In natural science, adaptation means maintaining life, whereas in social science this meaning is not sufficient. In social
systems adaptation is not resignation but implies keeping life in dignified

conditions. Such conditions depend on factors linked to the development process and to the democratic quality of the social system. Adequate planning can facilitate adaptation but effective adaptation requires social systems to have capacity to respond effectively to surprises and shocks.

A social system's adaptive capacity can be defined as the ability to plan and implement adaptation processes, or, more generally, as the capacity of a human system to modify itself to improve, or at least maintain, its member's quality of life against a range of present and future disruptions in their physical or social environment (Gallopin, 2006).

The importance of reinforcing the communities' adaptive capacities to reduce environmental or economic vulnerability is becoming more and more evident in our present society. A human system's adaptive capacity depends to a great extent on coordinated collective and institutional actions whose efficiency can be enhanced by developing social capital -- mutual trust, social integration, community networks, rules, consensus, and the information flow used by individuals both to their own benefit and to that of the community (Allen, 2003) Other factors that influence it include income level; saving capacity; technology and infrastructure; knowledge and abilities; equity; quality and power of its institutions; and access to credit, insurance and employment (Yapa, 2002).

Reinforcement of adaptive capacity is the third part of our theoretical-conceptual framework. We postulate that the actions of the entrepreneurial community must consistently contribute to strengthening the adaptive capacity of social systems which in turn are considered to be stakeholder networks existing within a framework of equity (development) and freedom (democracy).

Adaptive capacity is an ability that, in contrast with the previous issue (vulnerability), is usually present in management training programs. Because it occurs in such topics as organizational development and change, creating learning organizations, and strategy implementation, no additional effort to bring it into management curricula is required. In the domain of sustainability, this theme has been widely used to address topics such as environmental protection (Hart, 1995), integration of stakeholders (Sharma & Vredenburg, 1998), and CSR (Wall & Marzall, 2006). Tools such as brainstorming, negotiation techniques, and quality management methods are known by business school students and can be used to develop adaptive capacity. The goal in this context to continue to promote their use and to integrate them more explicitly with the theme of vulnerability,

Entrepreneurship

Dean and McMullen (2007) claim that entrepreneurship can reduce environmental degradation problems. Environmental problems such as

shock or stress can be seen as results of unregulated market imperfections, and since entrepreneurs are by definition those who have the veloc-
ity of response and innovating capacity needed to create business
opportunities out of market imperfections, simply supporting entrepreneurs to exploit the inherent opportunities can help move the global
economy toward sustainability.

Similarly, the United Nations Commission on the Private Sector and
Development (UNCPSD) concluded that promoting entrepreneurship
can be a more effective solution for global poverty than economic humanitarian aid. The commission reckons that the actions of entrepreneurs,
adequately supported by a solid institutional framework, fortify all dimensions of adaptive capacity. They create opportunities for saving, employment, and innovation, take into account local conditions, and integrate
marginal groups. However, their actions can potentially reduce natural
capital (UNCPSD, 2005).

Dean and McMullen (2007) note that entrepreneurs are able to exploit
opportunities arising from a shock in part because certain barriers prevent other stakeholders (for instance, large firms) from making use of
those opportunities. Bruggman and Prahalad (2007) explain that in vulnerable social systems, such barriers include lack of information within
large firms about the dynamics of social systems in the affected communities. In such communities, perceptions of risk, adaptive capacity, and
social acceptance are key factors in determining the acceptance of a new
product. Just as engaging vulnerable stakeholders in entrepreneurs' initiatives can bring resources to those communities, building partnerships
with large firms can do the same by helping firms overcome barriers to
exploiting opportunities.

Another barrier inhibiting efforts by large firms to exploit environmental or social market opportunities is the tendency of many managers to fil-
ter market signals that imply a need for change, particularly on
environmental issues (Halme, 2002). Hence, the companies engaging in
partnerships with local entrepreneurs must at the same time try to promote internal environmental entrepreneurship. Political and institutional
obstacles can also frustrate the exploitation of opportunities, raising
transactional costs (payments to intermediaries, corruption, bureaucratic
delays). A broad definition of "institutional entrepreneurs" and political
entrepreneurs suggests they are important stakeholders to integrate into
company alliances. Institutional entrepreneurs include lawyers who can
collectively represent all those affected by an environmental catastrophe
and it even can be stretched to include technologies such as the "chemical
digital fingerprint" that provides evidence of the originator of a communication. Political entrepreneurs include government employees who can

modify subsidy or tax systems and who can influence political and economic systems (Dean & McMullen, 2007).

To provide a theoretical link between risk, vulnerability, and entrepreneurial activity, the definition of environmental entrepreneurship coined by Dean and McMullen (2007) is adapted by adding social concerns into the following definition of sustainable entrepreneurship: "the process of discovery, evaluation and exploitation of economic opportunities present in market flaws, including those related to environmental and social issues, hindering sustainable development."

The fourth element of this framework is the emphasis on promoting sustainable entrepreneurship, with proactive managerial strategies, as links and levers between companies and their stakeholders.

Entrepreneurship is a subject present in the great majority of management programs, usually associated with the development of new products, opening of new markets, and forming new enterprises (Srivastava & Lee, 2005). The most useful formative activity to develop entrepreneurship is the presentation and defence of an idea or business project that will have to be submitted to public scrutiny (such as to a tribunal or in a business plan competition). Such activities offer very promising opportunities to combine and apply the previous elements: stakeholder integration, vulnerability, and adaptation capability.

This part of the chapter has laid the basis for different theoretical approaches that will help explain a sustainability model in social and environmental terms. On one hand, social theories of risk help to show the relationship between poverty and environment, as suggested by Hart (1997). They also offer a guide to the types of interventions that can contribute to breaking the vicious circle between poverty and environmental deterioration. In a similar vein, theories of adaptation and entrepreneurship can help explain the importance of proactive behavior from company and stakeholders. Finally, stakeholder theory presents itself as a modern management theory that can help all these complex goals to be compatible in the future.

INTERVENTION MODEL TO DECREASE ENVIRONMENTAL DETERIORATION AND POVERTY

The next two sections incorporate the elements presented just discussed into an intervention model aimed at reducing vulnerability and environmental impact.

The suggested interaction model focuses on maximizing benefits of *genuine voluntary entrepreneurial actions*, without relying on instrumental motivation to generate actions to reduce environmental and social problems (Ulrich, 2002). The company is seen as a corporative citizen who, for altruistic or political reasons, wants to progress from "doing no harm" to "doing good" (Matten & Crane, 2005; RESPONSE, 2007). In this context, the model uses normative approaches based on responsibility and necessity (Greeno & Robinson, 1992) which change the approach from reaction to stakeholder's pressure, to the analysis of the "right thing to" do by the company as a political actor in the formation of willpower and contribution to the general welfare (Scherer & Palazzo, 2007).

The "right thing to do" regarding the poverty-environment vicious circle requires an entrepreneurial strategy that integrates economic growth, satisfaction of social necessities through the reduction of vulnerability, and, of course, nature conservation (Hay & Mimura, 2006). Stakeholder theory (and the utilization of basic processes in its application, such as engagement, cooperation, transparency and participation) appears as the ideal academic framework to transmit the importance of this triple target. Lépineux (2005) stresses that stakeholder management must seek to reinforce social cohesion. The model shown in Figure 8.1 recommends that the target of sustainable stakeholder management should be the reinforcement of socionatural cohesion., (i.e., strengthening the bounds and relations that keep individuals together in society while preserving harmony with nature) In doing so, it complements the work of Lépineux integrating the natural environment within a normative context (Starik & Rands, 1995).

The model in Figure 8.1 frames the relation between companies and stakeholders in terms of stakeholder management, collaboration, and integration. Necessary inputs from the firm are knowledge, engagement and transparent participation of managers and employees with processes for integrating stakeholder needs, and with the deliberative design of practices to "do the right thing." The philosophical base for the model is Habermas' (1996) deliberative democracy: the use of dialogue and reasoned argumentation to foster mutual understanding, delivering collective decision-making through the best possible genuine democratic decisions, reflecting the diversity of interests, and minimizing the interference of political power, money, or strategizing (Dryzek, 1997; Scherer & Palazzo, 2007).

The types of actions to be implemented will depend on the internal relationships of power and entrepreneurship among stakeholders they develop social and environmental strategies. Global Compact (2008) identifies four priority areas to be worked on to help improve social actors' performance in implementing sustainable strategies in cooperation with companies:

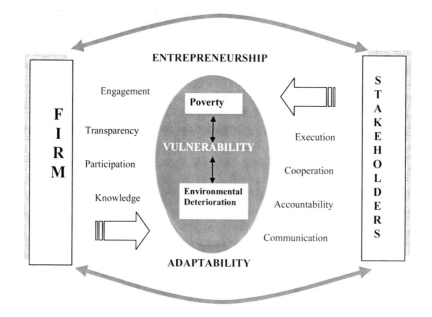

Source: Own elaboration.

Figure 8.1.   Firms strategies to decrease environmental deterioration and poverty.

- Accountability: Commitment of the social actor to achieving defined partnership goals.
- Adaptability: Ability of the social actor to complement, and utilize the expertise of the company in pursuit of the partnership goals.
- Execution: Capacity of the social actor to convert plans and intentions into successful projects.
- Communication: Performance of the social actor in providing high-quality, timely, and concise information throughout the partnership.

Adaptation and entrepreneurship have particular importance in Figure 8.1. Successful interventions require dignified adaptation of those stakeholders more vulnerable to physical changes in their environment and mutual adaptation of companies and stakeholders to maximize the results from cooperation and to make their interests as compatible as possible in the future. Companies and stakeholders should jointly develop practices that will make it possible to improve "their adaptability" or their adaptive capacity for dealing with possible future changes in their environments.

Although some adaptation processes can be planned, their impact on risk reduction for the more vulnerable sectors of society is limited when compared to that of spontaneous processes of individual or community adaptation toward new lifestyles and use of resources (Adger, 2001, 2006). Spontaneous adaptation processes emerge only in communities that have some adaptive capacity, where entrepreneurs play a key role. Similarly, the existence of entrepreneurs within the company triggers the firm's processes of adaptation to changes in the external environment and improves the company's performance in the relationships with stakeholders.

Sustainable entrepreneurship entails the discovery, evaluation and exploitation of the economic opportunities present in market imperfections hindering sustainable development. The promotion of sustainable entrepreneurship within a company requires the development of recruiting, evaluation, and compensation mechanisms allowing the discovery and promotion of sustainable entrepreneurs. A key skill to be selected and rewarded in managers is "ambidexterity," the ability to manage seemingly opposing tasks such as preserving existing business while at the same time aiming for entrepreneurial opportunities and alignment with society's expectations (Kollmann & Stockman, 2008). To promote sustainable entrepreneurship among stakeholders, the firms should develop standards for suppliers and distributors that will not inhibit entrepreneurship and that will foster communication with communities, NGOs, and universities. It is also important to identify and train potential entrepreneurs, implementing sponsorship and mentorship programmes to reward entrepreneurs who promote the objectives of sustainability and who help to improve access to capital for more vulnerable communities.

In summary, it is necessary that firms and stakeholders develop collaborative practices of dialogue and adaptation, while promoting entrepreneurship, so the new sustainability challenges rapidly arising in the competitive global environment can be faced successfully.

The model in Figure 8.1 can be used in shifting management-teaching from subject-based teaching to a more integrated approach (Eber, 2007) by demonstrating why sustainability problems and solutions are inherently multidimensional (Foot & Ross, 2004) and how existing concepts and theories of management can be combined with other fields of knowledge.

Moving from theory to practice, it is possible to recommend specific activities and intervention strategies for companies working in communities with high social and environmental vulnerability. Business schools should create awareness in students of such strategies and cooperate closely with companies that show exemplary behavior combining the four elements of stakeholder integration, vulnerability, adaptation, and entrepreneurship. Thus, students can analyze cases of companies that apply stakeholder integration in environments where vulnerability and sustainability are crucial. They can also be assisted by their universities in seeking internships with companies characterized by excellent performance.

Intervention Strategies

Strategic Targets

Successful implementation of the model presented in the previous section requires that firms allocate resources to achieving the following targets:

- Promoting the use of dialogue and communication tools between the main environmental pollution agents and groups who are especially vulnerable.
- Promoting engagement and mutual knowledge between firms and stakeholders (especially those more underprivileged and NGOs
- Improving the capacity to undertake activities and projects in areas that are more vulnerable to environmental impacts and to adverse socioeconomic conditions.
- Setting up adaptation mechanisms for both firms and stakeholders, to work together to reconcile their interests and objectives in the short and in the long term.
- Recognizing sustainable entrepreneurs as the leverage for developing proactive company strategies, and setting-up alliances with stakeholders and creating new markets by supporting entrepreneurs, both within the organization and in the social and institutional context, as part of the strategic vision of the firm's commitment to sustainability.
- Developing new technologies and practices adapted to the resources available in areas with vulnerable communities

Some vulnerable stakeholders (for example, the environment) have no voice of their own, or lack the organizational capacities or the knowledge required to get effectively involved in and profit from these collaborative processes. Hence, vulnerable stakeholders frequently require the support or the representation of their cause by other stakeholders, such as NGOs (Fassin, 2008). However, they run the risk of their interests not always being correctly interpreted or negotiated (Moody, 2007). The model this chapter draws attention to the fundamental role played by NGOs in the defence of vulnerable stakeholders, but it emphasizes that the ideal scenario would be that of the stakeholders themselves being involved proactively and being selected through democratic and market processes.

Stakeholder Integration Strategies

The more vulnerable sectors, although underprivileged, are not unimportant for firms, quite the opposite; they sometimes become key allies for the success of initiatives. (De Jongh, 2004). Participation of all stakeholders should be guaranteed by firms when developing and implementing strategies to deal with the harms and hazards affecting them. Deliberation helps balance contradictory stakeholder claims and enhances corporate legitimacy (Roloff, 2008). A deliberative environment requires transparency in the discourse, monitoring mechanisms, enforcement of compliance with compromises, comparability of information and standards, and implementation of mechanisms to guarantee the least powerful stakeholders are fully involved in the discourse.

- A formal participation methodology should be established to give stakeholder viewpoints and opinions the correct effect.
- All stakeholders should be identified in an objective and systematic manner to guarantee that important stakeholders are not ignored.
- In many cases, it may be necessary to choose representative stakeholders and recognize them officially through appropriate documents or reports.
- All the representative stakeholders should be able to communicate about identified harms and hazards as part of the methodology developed during the process of problem definition.
- Stakeholders should provide a written reply to any noticeable deviation in the recommended politics and procedures.
- A process should be established and implemented to manage all identified hazards appropriately and in an integrated manner.

All the stakeholders and, in particular, the most vulnerable ones, along with NGOs, must have adaptation capability to join in dialogue with the company (Wustenhagen, Hamschmidt, Sharma, & Starik, 2008). In this context, adaptation capability is redefined as the "ability of the social actor to complement, and utilize the expertise of, the company in pursuit of the partnership goals" (Global Compact, 2008, p. 13). Predisposition to dialogue, communicative skills, entrepreneurship, as well as the quantity and quality of the relationships among the stakeholders, all reinforce stakeholders' ability to adapt.

CONCLUDING REMARKS

There is pressing need to infuse business leaders with the key concepts behind sustainability and to provide them with ideas and strategies to address its challenges (Galea, 2004). This chapter highlights a current conceptual gap—both in management theory and in education—in teaching future managers how to address a major challenge to sustainable development. That challenge is the "vicious circle" between poverty, environmental deterioration, and unsustainable business strategies. This chapter emphasizes the need for educators to alert students and managers to the importance and difficulty of developing an environmentally proactive management strategy, especially in regions with high levels of social vulnerability, and to give them a framework for conceptualizing how such situations can be analyzed, addressed, and ultimately improved.

It also stresses the great need to equip management educators with suitable tools to infuse such knowledge and motivate current or future managers to engage with sustainable business practices (Galea, 2004). The chapter aims to help them do so by introducing some key concepts and theories required to build a conceptual understanding of the problem. The need for a holistic approach is emphasized, hence environmental deterioration and poverty are framed in terms of *vulnerability* to environmental and economic risk. Stakeholder theory is proposed as a normative and an instrumental guideline to integrate those concepts. A key idea to be transmitted in the classroom is the understanding that "performance" within the organization should be less focused on short term financial performance and more concerned with the long term and with the survival of the company (Burchell & Cook, 2008; Longo & Mura, 2008). In turn, a key value to be infused is that voluntary actions of the business community must consistently contribute to strengthening the adaptive capacity of social systems, considered as stakeholder networks existing in a context of equity –development, and freedom—democracy. (Black & Hartel, 2004; Martin, 2004).

The chapter further proposed a conceptual framework and intervention model to exemplify how these concepts can integrated around stakeholder theory to provide a rationale and guidance for intervention. Increased integration of stakeholders in company decision-making will lead to increased adaptive capabilities and a decrease in vulnerability to environmental and economic risk. Sustainable entrepreneurship is seen as the key mechanism to increase stakeholder adaptive capabilities without affecting firms' economic viability. The framework and model presented can be used in management education to show why sustainability problems and solutions are inherently multidimensional (Foot & Ross, 2004) and how existing concepts and theories of management can be combined with other fields of knowledge, helping to shift management education from subject-based teaching to a more holistic approach.

We recommend that more education efforts be aimed at transmitting to managers, students, and stakeholders in general the necessity of thinking about the importance of integrating the stakeholder approach into strategic management and the importance of improving the environmental, economic, and social conditions of vulnerable stakeholders, in particular, through sustainable entrepreneurship and adaptation.

Management education can provide the necessary legitimacy to the designing and implementing of management practices that address environmental sustainability and vulnerability. The contribution of management education to each of the three pillars (regulative, normative, and cognitive) that sustain this legitimacy is different for each pillar. Management education's contribution is limited in the domain of the regulative pillar, and that contribution tends to focus on the use of coercive mechanisms (laws and fines) which belong to governments. However, management education can play an important part within the normative and cognitive pillars. The development of role-play activities, where students take the role of stakeholders under vulnerability and/or environmental risk, encourages their identification with those groups and reinforces the normative pillar: where decisions and actions are morally governed. The cognitive pillar, which is often taken for granted, can be strengthened by arranging the active participation of students in practical activities (such as case studies, exercises, business simulations, and work experiences) where the four proposed theoretical elements are considered jointly. Doing so may make it possible for these for elements to be actively considered and then blended into the students' future professional activities.

ACKNOWLEDGMENTS

The model presented in this chapter was developed as part of an International Research Project called "Environmental impact of businesses, social vulnerability and poverty in Latin America: Interaction, analysis and diagnosis of areas potentially at risk," financed by the Spanish Agency of International Cooperation (AECI) 2008–2009, the Centre for Business Relationships, Accountability, Sustainability and Society (BRASS, United Kingdom) and The Spanish Ministry of Science and Education/European Fund for Regional Development (reference (reference ECO2008-03445/ECON).

REFERENCES

Adams, J. (2004). Mental models at work: Implications for teaching sustainability. In C. Galea (Ed.), *Teaching business sustainability: From theory to practice* (Vol. 1, pp. 20–33). Sheffield, UK: Greenleaf.

Adger, W. (2001). Scales of governance and environmental justice for adaptation and mitigation of climate change. *Journal of International Development, 13,* 921–931.

Adger, W. (2006). Vulnerability. *Global Environmental Change, 16,* 268–281.

Adger, W., Brooks, N., Bentham, G., & Eriksen, S. (2004). *New indicators of vulnerability and adaptive capacity* (Technical Report 7). United Kingdom: Tyndall Centre for Climate Change Research.

Allen, K. (2003). Vulnerability reduction and the community-based approach. In M. Pelling (Ed.), *Natural disasters and development in a globalising world* (pp. 170–184). London: Routledge.

Archer, D., Crocker, T., & Shogren, J. (2006). Choosing children's environmental risk. *Environment and resource economics, 33,* 347–369.

Black, L. D., & Hartel, C. S. J. (2004). The five capabilities of socially responsible companies. *Journal of Public Affairs, 4,* 25–144.

Bourne, L. M. (2008). Stakeholder relationship management maturity. *PMI Global Congress, EMEA.* St. Julians, Malta: Project Management Institute based in Europe in Brussels Belgium.

Bremmers, H., Omta, O., Kemp, R., & Haverkamp, D. (2007). Do stakeholder groups influence environmental management system development in the Dutch agri-food sector? *Business Strategy and the Environment, 16,* 214–231.

Brugmann, J., & Prahalad, C. K. (2007). Co-creating business's new social compact. *Harvard Business Review, 85*(2), 80–90.

Burchell, J., & Cook, J. (2008). Stakeholder dialogue and organisational learning: changing relationships between companies and NGOs. *Journal of Business Ethics, 17,* 35–46.

Buysse, K., & Verbeke, A. (2003). Proactive environmental strategies: A stakeholder management perspective. *Strategic Management Journal, 24,* 453–470.

Calandrino, N., & Michelle, M (2003). Vulnerability and chronic poverty in rural Sichuan, *World Development, 31*(3), 611–628.

Cardona, O. D. (2005). *Indicators of disaster risk and risk management. Summary report. IDB/IDEA Program on Indicators for Disaster Risk Management.* Washington DC: Inter-American Development Bank, Sustainable Development Department Environment Division.

Christoff, P. (2000). Ecological modernisation, ecological modernities. In S. Young (Ed.), *The emergence of ecological modernisation.* London: Routledge.

Clarke, S., & Chenoweth, E. (2006). *The politics of vulnerability: Constructing local performance regimes for homeland security.* Paper presented at the annual meeting of the Western Political Science Association, Hyatt Regency, Albuquerque, New Mexico.

Clarkson, M. B. E. (1991). Defining, evaluating, and managing corporate social performance: A stakeholder management model. In J. E. Post. (Ed.), *Research in corporate social performance and policy.* Greenwich, CT: JAI Press.

Clarkson, M. B. E. (1995). A stakeholder framework for analyzing and evaluating corporate social performance. *Academy Of Management Review, 20,* 92–117.

Crabtree, A. (2007). *Evaluating the bottom of the pyramid from a fundamental capabilities perspective.* Retrieved from http://www.cbs.dk/content/view/pub/38201

Crichton, D. (1999). The risk triangle. In J. Ingleton (Ed.), *Natural disaster management*. London: Tudor Rose.

D'Andrade, R. G. (1984). Cultural meaning systems. In R. A. Shweder & R. A. Levine (Ed.), *Culture theory: Essays on mind, self, and emotion*. Cambridge, UK: Cambridge University Press.

Dasgupta, S., Lucas, E. B., & Wheeler, D. (1998). *Small plants, industrial pollution and poverty, evidence from Brazil and Mexico* (Working Paper 2029). Washington: World Bank Development Research Group.

De Jongh, D. (2004). A stakeholder perspective on managing social risk in South Africa: Responsibility or accountability? *The Journal of Corporate Citizenship, 15*, 27–31.

Dean, T., & McMullen, J. (2007). Toward a theory of sustainable entrepreneurship: Reducing environmental degradation through entrepreneurial action. *Journal of Business Venturing, 22*, 50–76.

Delmas, M., & Toffel, M. (2004). Stakeholders and environmental management practices: An institutional framework. *Business Strategy and the Environment, 13*, 209–222.

Dilley, M., Chen, S., Deichmann, U., & Lerner-Lam, L. (2005). *Natural disaster hotspots: a global risk analysis*. Washington, DC: World Bank.

Downing, T. E., Butterfield, R., Cohen, S., Huq, S., Moss, R, Rahman, A., et al. (2001). *Vulnerability indices: climate change, impacts and adaptation*. Nairobi: UNEP Policy Series.

Dryzek, J. S. (1997). *The politics of the earth, environmental discourses*. Oxford, England: Oxford University Press.

Dyllick, T., & Hockerts, K. (2002). Beyond the business case for corporate sustainability. *Business Strategy and The Environment, 11*, 130–141.

Eakin, H., &. Lemos, M. C. (2006). Adaptation and the state: Latin America and the challenge of capacity building under globalization. *Global Environmental Change, 16*, 7–18.

Eber, S. (2007). Sustainability in business education: The leisure and tourism curriculum. In C. Galea (Ed.), *Teaching business sustainability: Cases, simulations and experiential approaches* (Vol. 2, pp. 42–55). Sheffield, UK: Greenleaf.

Elkington, J., & Fennel, S. (1998). Partners for sustainability. *Greener Management International, 24*, 48–60.

European Commission. (2006). *European commission's communication on corporate social responsibility* (CSR). Retrieved from http://ec.europa.eu/entreprise/csr/policy.htm

Fassin, Y. (2008). The stakeholders model refined. *Journal of Business Ethics, 84*(1), 113–135.

Filgueira, C., & Andres, P. (2004). *América Latina: Los rostros de la pobreza y sus causas determinantes* [The faces of poverty and its determinants]. Santiago de Chile: CELADE/ CEPAL.

Foot, D., & Ross, S. (2004). Social sustainability. In C. Galea, (Ed.), *Teaching business sustainability: From theory to practice* (Vol. 1, pp. 107‑125). Sheffield, UK: Greenleaf.

Fowler, K., & Engel-Cox, D. (2007). Getting out there: Incorporating site visits and industry assessments in pollution prevention and sustainability education

In C. Galea (Ed.), *Teaching business sustainability: Cases, simulations and experiential approaches* (Vol. 2, pp. 18–25). Sheffield, UK: Greenleaf.

Frooman, J. (1999). Stakeholder influence strategies. *Academy Of Management Review, 24,* 191–205.

Furedy, C. (1984). Survival strategies of the urban poor: Scavenging and recuperation in Calcutta. *GeoJournal, 8,* 129–136.

Galea, C. (2004). *Teaching business sustainability: Cases, simulations and experiential approaches* (Vol. 1). Sheffield, UK: Greenleaf.

Gallopin, G. (2006). Linkages between vulnerability, resilience, and adaptive capacity. *Global Environmental Change, 56,* 293–303.

Global Compact. (2008). *Business guide to partnering with NGOs and the United Nations.* New York: Global Compact and Dalberg Global Development Advisors.

Gond, J. P., & Mullenbach-Servayre, A. (2004). Les fondements théoriques de la responsabilité sociétale de l'entreprise [The theoretical basis of Corporate Social Responsibility]. *La Revue des Sciences de Gestion: Direction et Gestion, 205,* 93–116.

Gray, L., & Moseley, W. (2005). A geographical perspective on poverty–environment interactions. *Geographical Journal, 171*(1). Retrieved from http://www3.interscience.wiley.com/journal/118643925/issue9–23

Greeno, J. L., & Robinson, S. N. (1992). Rethinking corporate environmental management. *Columbia Journal of World Business, 27,* 222–232.

Greenwood, M. (2007). Stakeholder engagement: Beyond the myth of corporate responsibility. *Journal of Business Ethics, 74,* 315–327.

Habermas, J. (1996). *Between facts and norms: Contributions to a discourse theory of law and democracy.* Cambridge, MA: MIT Press.

Hajer, M. (1995). *The politics of environmental discourse: Modernisation and the policy process.* Oxford, UK: Oxford University Press.

Halme, M. (2002). Corporate environmental paradigms in shift: Learning during the course of action at UPM-Kymmene. *Journal of Management Studies, 39,* 1087–1109.

Hart, S. L. (1995). A natural-resource-based view of the firm. *Academy Of Management Review, 20,* 986–1014.

Hart, S. L. (1997). *Beyond greening: strategies for a sustainable world. Harvard Business Review, 75*(1), 66–76.

Hawken, P., Lovins, A., & Lovins, H. L. (1999). *Natural capitalism: Creating the next industrial revolution.* New York: Little, Brown.

Hay J., & Mimura, N. (2006). Supporting climate change vulnerability and adaptation assessments in the Asia-Pacific region: An example of sustainability science. *Sustainability Science, 1,* 23–35.

Hettige, M., Mani, M., & Wheeler, D. (1998). *Pollution intensity in economic development: Kuznet revisited* (Working Paper 1876). Washington DC: World Bank Development Research.

Jain, S., & Vachani, S. (2006). *Multinational corporations and global poverty reduction.* Cheltemhan, UK: Edward Elgar.

Jenkins, R. (2005). Globalization, corporate social responsibility and poverty. *International Affairs, 81,* 525–540.

Jones, T. M. (1995). Instrumental stakeholder theory: A synthesis of ethics and economics. *Academy of Management Review, 20*, 404–437.

Kandachar, P., & Halme, M. (2008). *Sustainability challenges and solutions at the bottom of the pyramid.* London: Greenleaf.

Karnani, A. (2007). The mirage of marketing to the bottom of the pyramid: How the private sector can help alleviate poverty. *California Management Review, 49*, 90–111.

Kelly, P. M., & Adger, W. N. (2000). Theory and practice in assessing vulnerability to climate change and facilitating adaptation. *Climate Change, 47*(4), 325–352.

Kirchgeorg, M., & Winn, M. I. (2006). Sustainability Marketing for the poorest of the Poor. *Business Strategy and the Environment, 15*, 171–184.

Kollmann, T., & Stockman, C. (2008). Corporate entrepreneurship. In C. Wankel (Ed.), *21st century management: A reference handbook* (pp. 11–21). London: SAGE.

Lépineux, F. (2005). Stakeholder theory, society and social cohesion. *Corporate Governance, 5*, 99–110.

Longo, M., & Mura, M. (2008). Stakeholder management and human resources: development and implementation of a performance measurement system. *Corporate Governance, 8*, 191–213.

Martin, L. (2004). Measuring responsibility with stakeholder interviews. *Corporate Responsibility Management, 1, 34–37.*

Martinez-Alier, J. (2002). *The environmentalism of the poor.* Cheltenham, UK: Edward Elgar.

Masters, R. (1997). Environmental pollution and crime. *Vermont L. Rev., 22*, 359–375.

Matten, D., & Crane, A. (2005). Corporate citizenship: Toward an extended theoretical conceptualization. *Academy of Management Review, 30*(1), 166–179.

McDonough W., & Braungart, M. (2002). *Cradle to cradle: Remaking the way we make things.* New York: North Point Press.

McIntosh, M., Leipziger, D., Jones, K., & Coleman, G. (1998). *Corporate citizenship. Successful strategies for responsible companies*: Financial Times: Pitman.

Meyer, J. W., & Scott, W. R. (1983). Organizational environment: Ritual and rationality. Beverly-Hills, CA: SAGE.

Michaelis, L. (2003). The role of business in sustainable consumption. *Journal of Cleaner production, 11*, 915–921.

Minujín, A. (1999). ¿La gran exclusión? Vulnerabilidad y exclusión en América Latina. In D. Filmus, (Ed.), *Los noventa. Política, sociedad y cultura en América Latin* [The large exclusion? Social and structural vulnerability] (pp. 53–77). Buenos Aires, Argentina: FLACSO/EUDEBA.

Moody, R. (2007). *Rocks and hard places. The globalisation of mining.* London: Zed Books.

Morduch, J. (1994). Poverty and vulnerability. *American Economic Review, 84*, 221–225.

Murphy, R. (1994). *Rationality and nature: A sociological inquiry into a changing relationship.* Colorado: Westview Press.

Myers, G. H. (2008). Sustainable development and environmental justice in African cities. *Geography Compass, 2*, 695–708.

Nakao, Y., Amano, A., Matsamura, K., Kenba, K., & Nakano, M. (2007). Relationship between environmental performance and financial performance: An empirical analysis of Japanese corporations. *Business Strategy and the Environment, 16*(2), 106–119.

Natenzon, C. E., Marlenko, N., González, S., Ríos, D., Barrenechea, J. A. N, Murgida, A. N., et al. (2005). Vulnerabilidad social y estructural [The visible hand: Taking responsibility for social development]. In V. Barros, A. Menéndez, & J. Nagy (Eds.), *El cambio climático en el río de la plata* (pp. 113–118). Buenos Aires, Argentina: AIACC/CIMA.

Pargal, S., & Wheeler, D. (1996). Informal regulation of industrial pollution in developing countries: Evidence from Indonesia. *The Journal of Political Economy, 104*, 1314–1327.

Pater A., & Van Lierop, K. (2006). Sense and sensitivity: The roles of organisation and stakeholders in managing corporate social responsibility. *Business Ethics: A European Review, 15*(4), 339–351.

Polonsky, M. J. (1995). A stakeholder theory approach to designing environmental marketing strategy. *Journal of Business and Industrial Marketing, 10*, 29–46.

Porter, M. E., & Kramer, M. R. (2006). Strategy and society: The link between competitive advantage and Corporate social responsibility. *Harvard Business Review, 84*(12), 78–92.

Post, J. E., Preston, L. E., & Sachs, S. (2002). *Redefining the corporation: stakeholder management and organizational wealth*. Stanford, CA: Stanford University Press.

Prahalad, C. K., & Hammond, A. (2002). Serving the world's poor, profitably. *Harvard Business Review, 80*(9), 48–58.

Prüss-Ustün, A., & Corvalán, J. (2004). *Preventing disease through healthy environments: Towards an estimate of the environmental burden of disease*. Geneva: World Health Organization.

Prasad, P., & Elmes, M. (2005). In the name of the practical: Unearthing the hegemony of pragmatics in the discourse of environmental management. *The Journal of Management Studies, 42*, 845–867.

RESPONSE Project. (2007). *Final Report to European Commission*. Retrieved from www.insead.edu/ibis/responseproject

Robbins, P. T (2001). *Greening the corporation: Management strategy and the environmental challenge*. London: Earthscan.

Roloff, J. (2008). A life cycle model of multi-stakeholder networks. *Business Ethics: An European Review, 17*, 311–325.

Rowley, T. J. (1997). Moving beyond dyadic ties: A network theory of stakeholder influences. *Academy Of Management Review, 22*, 887–910.

Sachs, J. (2005). *The end of poverty: How we can make it happen in our lifetime*. London: Penguin.

Scherer A. G., & Palazzo, G. (2007). Toward a political conception of corporate responsibility. Business and society seen from a Habermasian perspective. *Academy of Management Review, 32*, 1096–1120.

Scott, L. (2006). *Chronic poverty and the environment: A vulnerability perspective*. (Working Paper 62). Manchester, UK: Chronic Poverty Research Centre.

Scott, W. R. (1995). *Institutions and organisations*. Thousand Oaks, CA: SAGE.

Sen, A. (1981). *Poverty and famines: An essay on entitlement and deprivation.* Oxford, UK: Clarendon Press.

Senge, P. (1999). *The dance of change: Mastering the twelve challenges to change in a learning organization.* New York: Doubleday.

Sharma, S., & Henriques, I. (2005). Stakeholder Influences on sustainability practices in the Canadian forest products industry. *Strategic Management Journal, 26,* 159–180.

Sharma, S., & Ruud, A. (2003). On the path to sustainability: Integration of social dimensions into the research and practice of environmental management. *Business Strategy and the Environment, 12,* 205–214.

Sharma, S., & Vredenburg, H. (1998). Proactive environmental strategy and the development of competitively valuable organizational capabilities. *Strategic Management Journal, 19*(8), 729–753.

Siegel, P. B., & Alwang, J. (1999). *An asset based approach to social risk Management: A conceptual framework.* Washington: Discussion Series No 9926, World Bank Social Protection.

Sirgy, M. J. (2002). Measuring corporate performance by building on the stakeholders model of business ethics. *Journal of Business Ethics, 35,* 143-162.

Springett, D. (2003). Business conceptions of sustainable development: A perspective from critical theory. *Business Strategy and the Environment, 12,* 71–86.

Srivastava, A., & Lee, H. (2005). Predicting order and timing of new product moves: the role of top management in corporate entrepreneurship. *Journal of Business Venturing, 20*(4), 459–481.

Starik, M., & Rands, G. P. (1995). Weaving an integrated web: Multilevel and multisystem perspectives of ecologically sustainable organizations. *Academy of Management Review, 20,* 908–925.

Ulrich, P. (2002). Ethics and economics, In L. Zsolnai (Ed.), *Ethics in the economy* (pp. 13–121). Oxford, UK: Peter Lang.

UNCPSD. (2005). *Unleashing entrepreneurship: Making business work for the poor,* New York: United Nations Commission on Private Sector Development.

Unruh, G. C. (2008). The biosphere rules. *Harvard Business Review, 86*(2), 111–138.

UNRISD. (2000). *La mano visible: Asumir la responsabilidad por el desarrollo social* [TRANSSLATION?] Geneva: Author.

UN/ISDR (2004). *Living with risk—A global review of disaster reduction initiatives* (Vol 1). New York and Geneva: United Nation.

Van Tulder, R., & Kolk, A. (2008). Poverty alleviation as a corporate issue, In C.Wankel (Ed.), *21st century management: A reference handbook.* London: SAGE.

Waelkens, M., Doors, W., & Criel, B. (2005). *The role of social health protection in reducing poverty: the case of Africa.* Geneva. ILO: Extension of Social Security Paper No. 22. Retrieved from http://www.shi-conference.de/downl/811sp1.pdf

Walker, P. (2007). Different planets: beliefs, denial and courage. The role of emotion into turning learning into action, In C. Galea (Ed.), *Teaching business sustainability: Cases, simulations and experiential approaches* (Vol. 2, pp. 26–41). Sheffield, UK: Greenleaf.

Wall, E., & Marzall, K. (2006). Adaptive capacity for climate change in Canadian Rural Communities. *Local Environment, 11*(4), 373–397.

Walley, N., & Whitehead, B. (1994). It's not easy being green. *Harvard Business Review, 72,* 46–51.

Weaver, G. R., Treviño, L. K., & Cochran, P. L. (1999). Integrated and decoupled corporate social performance: Management commitments, external Pressures, and corporate ethics practices. *Academy Of Management Journal, 42,* 539–552.

Welford, R. (1995). *Environmental strategy and sustainable development.* London: Routledge

Wustenhagen, R., Hamschmidt, J., Sharma, S., & Starik, M. (2008). *Sustainable innovation and entrepreneurship.* London: Edward Elgar.

Yamin, F., Rahman, A., & Huq, S. (2005). Vulnerability, adaptation and climate disasters: A conceptual overview. *Institute of Development Studies, 36 (4),* 1–14.

Yapa, L. (2002). How the discipline of geography exacerbates poverty in the third world. *Futures: The Journal of Forecasting and Planning, 34,* 33–46.

Yaron, G., & Moyini, Y. (2004). *The role of environment in increasing growth and reducing poverty in Uganda* (Technical Report: Final).Uganda: Gy Associates.

PART III

INSTITUTIONAL AND PROGRAM LEVEL INNOVATIONS IN MANAGEMENT EDUCATION FOR GLOBAL SUSTAINABILITY

CHAPTER 9

BUILDING THE BAINBRIDGE GRADUATE INSTITUTE (BGI)

Pioneering Management Education for Global Sustainability

Jill Bamburg and Lorinda Rowledge

Business is likely THE most important lever for solving the world's problems—so what could be more vital than changing the education of business leaders to embrace global sustainability? In creating the Bainbridge Graduate Institute (BGI) and its pioneering MBA program in sustainable business, the community of founders, faculty, staff, students, and a host of ardent supporters confronted this challenge head-on. Told from the perspective of the founding dean and provost, this chapter describes the purpose, people, program and process behind the success of BGI's "Profound Idea" of preparing business students to build enterprises that are economically successful, socially responsible, and environmentally sustainable.

This chapter describes the evolution of BGI over the first 6 years. During this time, BGI grew from 14 to 200 students; was ranked the past 3 years consecutively as the #1 MBA program in the country by Net Impact (among 63 business schools, including 15 of the top business schools as ranked by the *Wall Street Journal*); and was chosen by *BusinessWeek* for its international

Management Education for Global Sustainability, pp. 207–226

list of Best Design Schools (1 of only 6 business schools) for "Designing Sustainable Leadership." In 2008, BGI was the co-winner of the inaugural Joan Bavaria Award.

INTRODUCTION

In 2002, Elizabeth and Gifford Pinchot, the two lead founders of the Bainbridge Graduate Institute (BGI), were looking for leverage and legacy.

They had spent the last 25 years of their lives consulting to corporate America on creativity, entrepreneurship, and intrapreneurship, working to liberate the creativity of the individual human being trapped inside giant corporations. Contemplating retirement, they decided to do "just one more thing" to try to make the world a better place before their grandchildren arrived.

"Why business education?" asked an interview in *Washington CEO* magazine.

> As a consultant to Fortune 100 companies, Pinchot had become increasingly distressed when he kept running into people trained in business schools who held beliefs "counterproductive to the environment and fairness. When business leaders believe that their duty to their shareholders makes it 'immoral' for them to respond to their broader responsibility to society and for the environment," Pinchot says, "it is a prescription for disaster." (Winninghoff, 2004)

With that thought in mind, the Pinchots enlisted the help of Sherman Severin, PhD, the former Dean of the Business School at Marylhurst University in Portland, Oregon, and began to create the vision that became BGI. The authors of this paper joined them as the vision began to be realized—Jill, as Program Director and later Dean, in the fall of the first year, and Lorinda, as Provost, in the spring of that year. Both of the authors also serve as faculty in the program.

It's been a wild ride. From a first year enrollment of 14 MBA students to today's total enrollment of 200 (157 MBA and 43 certificates, Fall 2008). From a faculty made up exclusively of friends of the founders to a Faculty Academy of academics and practitioners drawn from around the country. From a curriculum scratched out on the back of a napkin to a fully developed program currently being evaluated for accreditation. From nothing to number one in the Net Impact student ratings of socially responsible business schools for 3 years running.

This article describes the BGI program at the beginning of its seventh year of operation, as the two of us step away from our founding roles and begin the next phase of our relationship with the program. As we've said at graduation every year, no one who has been part of the BGI experience ever really leaves the community—we simply transition into the next phase of a lifelong relationship.

RATIONALE

Before providing a further glimpse into the structure and pedagogy of the BGI academic program, we'd like to define the rationale for infusing sustainability into a business program in the first place, and provide a bit of the global context in which BGI is operating.

Business, industrial activity, and commerce are simultaneously the primary cause, and the potential solution, to many of the world's problems. Over the past 10 years, there has been a dramatic shift in business in the direction of corporate responsibility and sustainability. This awareness has been accelerated by:

- The visible effects of climate change, driving a sense of urgency
- Mounting pressures for carbon disclosure and risk management from institutional investors managing over $41 trillion in assets
- Increasing fossil fuel costs, stimulating a search for renewable alternatives
- Widespread consumer and investor expectations for sustainability reporting
- Pressure on supply chains for greater environmental and social responsibility
- Increasing regulatory pressures regarding environmental impact
- High levels of growth in LOHAS (Lifestyles of Health & Sustainability) markets

This acceleration is further fueled by the fact that sustainability is at the heart of profitability, innovation, and business development. Sustainability is frequently the source of new technologies, new markets, new business models, new products, and new services.

BGI was founded because, despite this critical imperative, few business schools were recognizing and incorporating issues and principles of corporate responsibility and sustainability into their programs or coursework. BGI was created to fill this void for students and recruiters, and to lead business education by pioneering an MBA program that fully infused environmental sustainability and social justice into conventional business education. Since BGI's founding in 2002, there has been increasing interest in these issues within mainstream business programs.

In 2005, there were only three schools in the United States (BGI, Presidio World College, and New College) offering an MBA in sustainable business or other similar variant (Weeks, 2004). By 2008, there were several more, including Green Mountain College, Dominican University-Brennan School of Business, Duquesne University (Donahoe Graduate School of Business), Marlboro College Graduate Center, St. Thomas Aquinas School, and Maharishi University of Management (Aspen Institute, 2007). Corporate responsibility is increasingly being introduced in "mainstream" business schools. Of the 114 schools surveyed in the Beyond Grey Pinstripes Report in 2007, 35 offered a special concentration or major allowing students to focus on social and environmental issues in mainstream, for-profit businesses (e.g., San Francisco State, University of North Carolina, University of Michigan). The percentage of schools requiring students to take a course dedicated to business and society issues increased from 34% in 2001 to 63% in 2007. However, few schools require that content on environmental and social sustainability be included in core courses. (Aspen Institute, 2007)

There is increasing demand for managers and employees with sustainability expertise. The majority of the 150 largest corporations now have something equivalent to a sustainability officer. According to a study conducted by the U.K.-based magazine *Ethical Corporation* and the U.S.-based consulting firm Political and Economic Link Consulting (PELC), over the past 5 years, 74% of companies have increased their investment in CSR staff, 72% have raised their corporate social responsibility (CSR) budget, and 68 percent have top executives who devote more time to CSR issues (Berman & Webb, 2003). The study reported that though 90% of CEOs said, "Sustainable development is important to their company's future," only 30% said they have the "skills, information, and personnel to meet the challenge."

These figures speak to the growing market need for sustainable business education, and the important role of BGI both in serving this need and in supporting a shift in conventional business education to incorporate environmental and social issues into the business curriculum.

THE ESSENCE OF A SUSTAINABLE MBA

At BGI we had the "luxury" of building our sustainable MBA program from scratch. Although our financial and personnel resources were anything but luxurious, we had the one thing most would-be Sustainable MBA programs did not: a blank slate on which to develop our ideas.

And, a wonderful lab for testing those ideas. Our entrepreneurial founders, strong believers in the notion that "Faster learning beats better planning," launched the program in a very unfinished (and unplanned) state. They invited the first cohort of students to join us in "co-creating" the BGI program. The two authors then spent the next 5 years "building the bicycle as we were riding it." While many of the pieces are now in place, the spirit of co-creation is alive and well at BGI, and neither of us expect that the bicycle will ever be truly finished. (And that's a good thing!)

The program that has emerged is perhaps most easily apprehended in terms of the model shown below.

PURPOSE

The mission of BGI is "to prepare students from diverse backgrounds to build enterprises that are financially successful, socially responsible, and environmentally sustainable." The vision of the school is considerably more ambitious: "To infuse environmentally and socially responsible business innovation into general business practice by transforming business education."

What is important about the mission is that all three elements of the "triple bottom line" are given equal importance. BGI is emphatically NOT a traditional MBA program with a little environmental and social

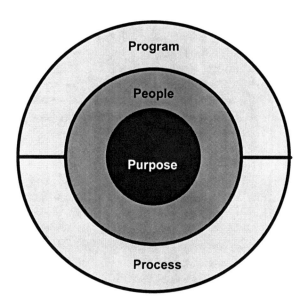

Figure 9.1.   A model of BGI.

responsibility thrown in. It is a fundamentally different approach to business education that reflects a fundamentally different approach to business—a holistic approach that we believe is far more appropriate to the resource-constrained realities—and the complex socioeconomic challengesyyyof the twenty-first century than the single bottom line capitalism of the last century.

In the conventional business model, the primary purpose of the firm is to make money for its owners. It produces public goods by providing employment, satisfying customers, honoring the law, and generating wealth that may find its way to the less fortunate through philanthropy. Sustainability—for all the lofty talk of the last few years—is still, at best, a secondary consideration. And the "business case" for sustainability is essentially an attempt to justify environmental and social actions in terms of their positive impact on the financial bottom line.

At BGI, we certainly teach the "business case," but we also attempt to go beyond it, to envision a world in which environmental and social realities—the very stuff of life—are accorded equal weight in business decisions. This is not the world we inhabit today, but it is the only path we can imagine that might actually lead to a habitable world tomorrow.

Business is the key to curbing climate change, eliminating poverty, and rebuilding community. The required transformation will require leaders with an alternative worldview and vision, the competencies to operationalize that vision, and the personal strength and support network to sustain them through challenges and setbacks. Sustainability has become a strategic issue that business leaders ignore at the peril of their organizations, not to mention their professional success. The good news is that there has been a major paradigm shift in North America since the founding of BGI. Most companies and government agencies, small and large, are clearly beginning to "get it." They are now beginning to move beyond the questions of "whether" and "why" and into the land of "how." This is precisely the question that has animated our work at BGI from the beginning.

PEOPLE

The people who show up at BGI—students, faculty, administration, staff, and volunteers—share this sense of purpose. They are an inspiring lot, perhaps best described as pragmatic idealists. Together, we have co-created this pioneering school in sustainable business.

Perhaps more than at any other business school, BGI students are a motley mix of corporate managers, aspiring entrepreneurs, dedicated non-profit staffers, and radical environmentalists, to name but a few. The range of technical expertise in the student body is always astounding, including engineers, lawyers, designers, film makers, IT experts, marketers, chefs, artists, supply chain managers, climate change experts—you get the idea. The students who gather on Bainbridge Island outside of Seattle once a month come mostly from the Pacific Northwest, but also from as far away as Chicago, New York, Texas, and Washington DC. Many BGI students already have master's degrees, and several even have PhDs in other fields. Overall, BGI students are primarily mid-career adults who seek to improve the alignment of their work with their values and are excited by the opportunity to use business to address the world's most pressing problems.

Unlike most institutions, where the faculty draws the students, BGI is a place where the students draw the faculty. We started with a mission and a set of customers who were attracted to it, and then recruited teachers who wanted to work with them. Over and over again, we hear from faculty that our students are the reason they love to teach with us. Most of our students are active agents of social change before, during and after their time with us—and most of our faculty believe that working with our students is part of their own contribution to making the world a better place.

A major strength of BGI is our unique national "Faculty Academy" structure, which has a number of important features. First, BGI's faculty model supports our programmatic goal of thoroughly integrating theory and practice. Classes are typically team taught, pairing a PhD-level academic with a seasoned business professional. The academically qualified "lead faculty" oversees curriculum design, delivery, and grading, and assumes quality assurance responsibility for the class. The professionally qualified "expert practitioner instructor" provides real world expertise and examples based on years of applied management experience in relevant fields. This applied management experience is especially important for educating business leaders in an MBA professional degree program.

Second, the Faculty Academy is made up of leading academic specialists in business sustainability from around North America, employed either part time or full time by BGI. This approach enables us to engage and benefit from the expertise of many of the continent's top academics who are integrating sustainability into traditional management fields. This structure is possible because our monthly "intensive" delivery model for the MBA program (and some certificate programs) makes traveling to BGI to deliver courses feasible. This Faculty Academy design promotes achievement of our larger vision by both enhancing our program and increasing the transfer of courses integrating sustainability back into the home institutions of Faculty Academy members.

Faculty members who teach with us regularly are invited to join the BGI Faculty Academy, which is actively involved in shaping the overall

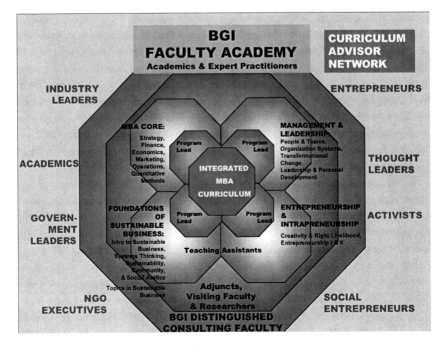

Figure 9.2.   The BGI faculty model

direction of the MBA program, as well as designing and delivering specific course content. Faculty members belong to one of four categories:

- **Distinguished Consulting Faculty,** internationally known "emeritus-level" senior faculty who teach with us occasionally and participate in overall program design, curriculum evolution, pedagogy, faculty development, and institutional advancement
- **Administrative Faculty,** members of the BGI administration who teach courses in addition to their academic program administrative responsibilities
- **Academic Faculty,** PhD-level academics who serve as lead instructors in all courses
- **Expert Practitioner Instructors,** experienced professionals with Master's degrees who bring practical business experience into the classroom

Courses are also typically assigned one or more teaching assistants (TA), primarily BGI alumnae, who provide faculty and instructional support, student coaching and support, and BGI instructional systems support.

Given the uniqueness of BGI's program and student body, the TAs play an unusually important role in maintaining and transferring BGI culture, particularly for instructors new to the system. And, the TA role provides an excellent way to keep alumnae actively engaged with the school.

At this writing, we are looking forward to adding our first Core Faculty members, whose primary role will be to help us take our curriculum to the next level of integration. At present, our curriculum is still relatively "siloed" into conventional business disciplines. All of our faculty and administration are committed to a more integrated whole, but efforts to date have been limited by the bandwidth of part-time Faculty Academy members and overworked administrators. Adding full-time Core Faculty will make a huge difference in terms of the coherence of the program, the workload for students, and the organization's commitment to a "systems approach" to understanding both problems and solutions.

PROGRAM

The BGI program is driven by a set of "MBA Program Learning Goals" developed during the 2004–05 school year by a multi-stakeholder group comprised of faculty, students, board members, renowned academics, thought leaders, corporate leaders, and diversity experts. These goals, based on our mission—"to prepare diverse leaders to build economically successful, socially responsible, and environmentally sustainable enterprises"—form the competencies expected of students graduating from our MBA program. These competencies provide a foundation for aligning coursework and developing learning assessments for all our graduates.

This wide group of internal and external stakeholders was invited to provide input based on the following stimulating questions:

> What learning goals are most important for leaders building economically successful, socially responsible, and environmentally sustainable enterprises?

> If BGI is going to change the world within 25 years, what competencies will our graduates need to have to lead this transformation?

At the institutional level, BGI aspires to:

- Provide students with the attributes, knowledge, and competencies required of leaders transforming our economic system toward sustainability;

- Equip students to achieve a satisfactory financial return for themselves and stakeholders in the very activities through which they help transform the economy;
- Create a powerful supportive network of sustainability and business experts involved in lifelong collaboration, learning, and action;
- Develop curriculum, course materials, and programs that will support the infusion of sustainability into mainstream business education;
- Make tangible contributions to the theory and practice of sustainable business through research, experimentation, and application.

At the student level, BGI graduates are expected to demonstrate the capacity to:

Core Business Functions

1. Understand and apply the core concepts of Strategy, Accounting, Finance, Marketing, Management, and Operations, and integrate them with sustainability principles for both business advantage and service to the community and nature.

Business and Sustainability

2. Articulate the underlying assumptions and global consequences of the prevailing economic system and worldview and advance alternative business models and alliances more aligned with the needs of people and planet.
3. Understand the role of business in society and the foundational concepts, principles, and practical approaches of business sustainability.
4. See opportunity in the world's major problems and see ways to use business to address these problems in ways that create value for the enterprise and the common good.

Innovation and Entrepreneurship

5. Design and build successful sustainability-driven ventures that create value for multiple stakeholders and enable all life systems (natural, individual, community) to flourish.

6. Foster breakthrough innovation throughout the value stream by applying principles of innovation and sustainability to organizational projects, processes, systems, and culture.

Leadership and Management in the Context of Change

7. Develop the self-knowledge and personal capacity to lead – ethically, effectively, and with integrity.
8. Apply systems thinking, creativity, and critical analysis to addressing problems and opportunities.
9. Leverage theory, technology, and collaboration strategies to foster learning and drive change at the individual, team, organizational, and societal level.
10. Apply cross-cultural competence to foster diversity and to work with people with different backgrounds.
11. Communicate clearly and persuasively in writing, speaking, and interpersonal relations.

The BGI program is a 60-unit MBA, which may be taken over either 2 years or 3. The entire curriculum is prescribed (that is, there are no electives) and is laid out against Four Centers of Excellence, as shown in the Table 9.1.

MBA Core

The MBA Core curriculum is spread out across the full two or three years of the program since it is not required to provide a base for later electives. Many of the course names—and all of the course syllabi—reflect BGI's focus on sustainability. Thus, for example, we don't simply teach finance and accounting, we teach "Finance and Accounting and the Triple Bottom Line." In that sequence, we cover all the basics of conventional accounting and some of the major topics in finance, while adding sections on the challenges of environmental accounting and the emerging standards for sustainability reporting. Similarly, in "Sustainable Operations," we cover green supply chains, fair labor practices, and life cycle analysis, as well as the traditional topics.

Our goal is to enable our students to go toe-to-toe with their MBA peers on basic vocabulary, concepts, and skills, while giving them the additional tools and frameworks they will need to convince their colleagues to do business differently.

Table 9.1.   The Four "Centers of Excellence" in the BGI Curriculum

MBA Core (24 Credits)	Sustainability (12 Credits)	Entrepreneurship & Intrapreneurship (9 Credits)	Management & Leadership (15 Credits)
Sustainability Integrated Into the MBA Core	Theory and Practice in This new Business Discipline	Turning Global Problems Into Business Opportunities	Building Management Systems and lEading Organizational Change Toward Sustainability
Finance, Accounting & the Triple Bottom Line I	Foundations of Sustainable Business	Creativity & Right Livelihood	Management I: People & Teams
Finance, Accounting & the Triple Bottom Line II MGT	Social Justice & Business	Entrepreneurship & Intrapreneurship I	Management II: Organizational Systems
Economics I: Neoclassical & Ecological Economics	Systems Thinking in Action	Entrepreneurship & Intrapreneurship II	Management III: Organizational Change
Economics II: Capitalism & Political Economy	Dal LaMagna Series on Responsible Capitalism		Leadership & Personal Development
Research & Quantitative Methods			
Marketing & Sales			
Sustainable Operations			
Strategy & Implementation			

Sustainability

BGI offers three required courses in this area of the curriculum. The first, "Foundations of Sustainable Business," is an overview of this emerging field, with a heavy focus on the environmental piece of the puzzle. The second, "Social Justice and Business," focuses on the people side of the equation, particularly the ever-increasing inequities between rich and poor, and how business might contribute to addressing that problem rather than exacerbating it. The third class, "Systems Thinking in Action," is a hands-on course in both systems thinking and systems modeling, two critical skills in a post-linear world. If accounting is the language of business, systems is the language of sustainability.

Entrepreneurship and Intrapreneurship

While the study of entrepreneurship is regarded as a specialty area in most MBA programs, we consider it central to bringing about the changes required to point the world in a more sustainable direction. This central role for entrepreneurship is true whether our graduates pursue their own entrepreneurial ventures, as many of them are doing, or whether they seek to effect change from within existing organizations through "intra-preneurship," a word created and popularized by one of our founders, Gifford Pinchot III.

The third course in this series, "Creativity and Right Livelihood," calls upon our students to recognize and cultivate their own creativity, as well as access the applied creativity of others. The traditional ways of thinking about business have created the problems we now face. As Einstein and others have observed, they are unlikely to be resolved by the same consciousness that created them. We believe that creativity—and training in creativity—is an essential part of preparing business leaders for an uncertain future.

Management and Leadership

In the fourth and final area of the BGI required curriculum, we require three courses in management—people and teams, organizational systems, and organizational change—and a unique six-credit sequence in leadership and personal development. Like Henry Mintzberg (2005), we believe that traditional MBA programs place excessive emphasis on technical skills at the expense of the discipline of management itself. Our goal is to rectify this by giving our change-agents-in-training an extra dose of management, with a particular focus on managing organizational change.

We also place significant emphasis on leadership and personal development, which is addressed through a one-credit course that runs throughout the two years of the program. This is a space for students to do the "inner work" that we believe is necessary to support their change efforts in the outside world. Our leadership curriculum places a premium on authenticity and bringing one's whole self to the challenges of leadership.

The matrix in Figure 9.3 gives a snapshot of the relationship between the program goals and the courses offered.

Hybrid Delivery Model

The program is delivered in a hybrid format that consists of three 4-day Intensives held once a month, combined with distance learning in between. The monthly Intensives run from mid-day Thursday to mid-day

	MBA Core							Sustainability			Entrep			Mgt/Lead	
	Finance, Accounting & Triple Bottom Line (6)	Research & Quantitative Methods (3)	Economics (6)	Research & Quantitative Methods (3)	Marketing (3)	Sustainable Operations (3)	Strategy & Strategic Management (3)	Foundations of Sustainable Business (3)	Systems Thinking in Action (3)	Social Justice and Business (3)	LaMagna Series on Responsible Capitalism (3)	Creativity and Right Livelihood (3)	Entrepreneurship and Intrapreneurship (6)	Management (9)	Leadership & Personal Development (6)
Core Business Functions															
1. Understand and apply the core concepts of Strategy, Accounting, Finance, Marketing, Management, and Operations, and integrate them with sustainability principles for both business advantage and service to the community and nature.	■	■	■	■	■	■	■	■					■	■	
Business and Sustainability															
2. Articulate the underlying assumptions and global consequences of the prevailing economic system and worldview, and advance alternative business models and alliances more aligned with the needs of people and planet.			■					■		■	■		■		
3. Understand the role of business in society and the foundational concepts, principles, and practical approaches of business sustainability.			■					■		■	■		■		
4. See opportunity in the world's major problems and see ways to use business to address these problems in ways that create value for the enterprise and the common good.			■					■		■	■		■		
Innovation and Entrepreneurship															
5. Design and build successful sustainability-driven ventures that create value for multiple stakeholders and enable all life systems (natural, individual, community) to flourish.	■	■	■	■	■	■	■	■	■	■	■	■	■	■	■
6. Foster breakthrough innovation throughout the value stream by applying principles of innovation and sustainability to organizational projects, processes, systems and culture.						■	■	■	■		■		■	■	
Leadership & Management in the Context of Change															
7. Develop the self-knowledge and personal capacity to lead – ethically, effectively, and with integrity.												■		■	■
8. Apply systems thinking, creativity, and critical analysis to addressing problems and opportunities.							■	■	■	■		■	■		
9. Leverage theory, technology, and collaboration strategies to foster learning and drive change at the individual, team, organizational, and societal level.												■		■	■
10. Apply cross-cultural competence to foster diversity and to work with people with different backgrounds.														■	■
11. Communicate clearly and persuasively in writing, speaking, and interpersonal relations.	■	■	■	■	■	■	■	■	■	■	■	■	■	■	■

Figure 9.3. A map of goals and curriculum.

Sunday and are held at IslandWood, a LEED Gold certified residential environmental education center on Bainbridge Island.

At the Intensives, instructors for each course get six hours of face-to-face time with their students. Very little of this time is spent in lectures, which we have found can be just as effectively delivered online. Instead, the time at Intensives is used for experiential exercises, discussion and debate, and project teamwork.

Online, our students work in both synchronous and asynchronous learning environments. For synchronous learning activities—such as lectures, tutorials, guest speakers, and team meetings—our students use the Elluminate Web conferencing system. For asynchronous learning activities and general course management, we use a customized environment built atop the Moodle open source platform and nicknamed The Channel. Asynchronous activities include online discussions, blogs, submission of assignments, peer and faculty review of assignments, electronic reserves, and student-constructed wikis. Both the Intensives and The Channel are used for community building and maintenance, as well as academic content delivery. Standing committees and "disappearing task forces" meet face-to-face at Intensives and continue their work online between Intensives. In addition, students have managed to commandeer both environments for pleasure, as well as business.

Theory and Practice

One of the major hallmarks of the BGI model is a thorough wedding of theory and practice. This integration is supported by our teaching model, which places teaching teams made up of a PhD-level academic with a seasoned practitioner in every class. Equally important, our course designs heavily incorporate real world experience, simulations, case studies, and exercises requiring application of concepts to finding solutions for common business challenges.

Each of the 2 years of the MBA program features a major applied project. In the first year, all students participate in a yearlong Action Learning Project (ALP) that is directly tied to their coursework in the sustainability course sequence. Companies pay to sponsor these projects and, in return, receive several hundred hours of student consulting to help them address their real world sustainability challenges. Past Action Learning Projects have included projects with a wide range of companies and organizations,

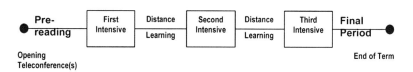

Figure 9.4.   Hybrid delivery model: A typical quarter.

including Alaska Airlines, BC Hydro, Brooks Sports, Charlottesville Community Design Center, Clif Bar, Environmental Home Center, Genie Industries, Holland America, Nature's Path, NIKE, Novex Couriers, Pangea Organics, Precor, REI, the Seattle Climate Partnership, and Teragren.

In the second year (or third year for students pursuing the 3-year option), the major project is a business plan built around the fall marketing class and a two-quarter Entrepreneurship sequence in winter and spring. Teams of students work on these projects—a number of which have gone on to become real businesses post-BGI. Examples include Eco-Fab, a firm focused on providing affordable green housing, primarily to Native Americans; FarmPower, a company turning cow manure into energy and fertilizer; and Water for Humans, a non-profit hybrid aimed at bringing clean water at affordable cost to Latin American communities.

BGI has recently added an optional set of Industry Concentration programs to the curriculum as part of its continuing efforts to combine theory and practice. Since all the coursework at BGI is prescribed, the opportunity for specialization that is typically addressed through electives is not available. As an alternative to the functional specialization offered elsewhere, BGI offers an opportunity to specialize in the issues—especially the sustainability issues—facing business in five general industry areas:

- Outdoor Industry
- Sustainable Energy Solutions
- Sustainable Food and Agriculture
- Green Building
- Sustainable Community Economic Development

To graduate with an Industry Concentration, students must complete six major projects involving that industry in the course of their regular academic studies. Typically, students earn three of their project credits through the Action Learning Project in their first year. They then complete three additional projects in the second year, working on industry-related projects in Marketing, Operations, Strategy, Entrepreneurship, or the Management sequence.

Additionally, as working adults, many of our students bring their own work problems to BGI and use their coursework to address their own real world problems. One of our students recently explained how this worked for him:

I was struck how the finance sequence last year continually gave me EXACTLY the knowledge I needed to take my business to the next level. I run an IT consulting firm. For an upcoming project, I needed to determine exactly what the fully burdened per-hour cost was for each hour of consulting labor we provide—I was going to get an accountant to run these numbers but the assignment we used gave me all the data I needed to calculate the numbers myself. When we faced an uncertain cash flow crunch a couple months out, I was able to create an Excel cash flow projection using a cash flow homework assignment to determine exactly how much cash on hand we'd have and how much credit we'd need in order to weather the dry spell in client receivables. I've used the program to rebrand our whole company from a generic IT implementation services also-ran to an eco-smart operations management consulting firm with a wide network of contract experts that we will call in for specific projects.

To add additional student exposure to real world applications of concepts, we bring outside practitioners into each weekend Intensive as Change Agents in Residence (CAIRs) as shown in Table 9.2. There are three categories of CAIRs: Entrepreneurs in Residence, Executives in Residence, and Activists in Residence. All of the individuals who act as CAIRs embody the business values that our students aspire to create in their own professional lives and all mingle freely with students throughout the weekend.

PROCESS

In many ways, THE central distinguishing feature of BGI is its Learning Community model. Our students tell us they were drawn to the school by its mission, but what keeps them coming back is the community. This is no accident. Rather, it is the result of very focused attention that begins with the student orientation experience and carries through into the alumni association.

Community building begins with a 5-day residential orientation session at Channel Rock, a 140-acre residential eco-retreat center on Cortes Island in British Columbia. This unique property, which is held in trust by BGI's founders, Gifford and Libba Pinchot, is entirely off the grid. It is largely powered by solar energy, features a solar shower, composting toilets, and a 90-year-old organic garden. The garden is maintained according to permaculture principles and supplies much of the food for the facility. Accommodations include tents, tipis, and yurts, as well as more conventional structures.

In this unique setting, students are exposed to sustainable living, as well as sustainable business, and begin building the bonds that will sustain them personally throughout their time in the program and throughout their careers. Activities include orientation sessions, lectures on permaculture and entrepreneurship, team building exercises, and inner work using the Kegan-Lahey framework (Kegan & Lahey, 2002).

Table 9.2.   BGI CAIR Program Guests

Recent CAIR Program Guests

Entrepreneurs in Residence

Alvin Duskin, Co-founder, US Windpower Corp., Chairman, FireTrade

Arran Stephens, President & Co-founder, Nature's Path Foods

Atul Desmone, Founder & President, Whole Energy Fuels Corporation

Corey Rosen, National Center for Employee Ownership

Lisa Lorimer, Former President & Majority Owner, Vermont Bread Co.

Peter Bladin, Vice President, Grameen Foundation

Robert Jeffrey, Jr. Publisher/CEO, ColorsNW Magazine

Activists in Residence

Bill Grace, Founder & ED, Center for Ethical Leadership, Founder, Deep Hope Institute

Craig Nagakawa, President, VillageReach

David Korten, Author, Great Turning, Empire to Earth Community

Kevin Danaher, Founder, Green Festivals

Sharif Abdullah, Author, Founder & Director of Commonway Institute

Van Jones, Founder & ED, Ella Baker Center for Human Rights

Winona LaDuke, White Earth Recovery Project

Executives in Residence

Ben Packard, Dir. of Environmental Affairs, Starbucks Coffee Company

Cheryl Scott, COO, Gates Family Foundation

Gene Kahn, Founder, Cascadian Farms, VP General Mills

John Frey, Dir., Corporate Environmental Strategies, Hewlett-Packard Co.

Kim Jordan, Co-founder, CEO & President, New Belgium Brewing Company

Sally Jewell, President & CEO, REI

William Morani, VP, Environmental Management Systems, Holland America Line

At Channel Rock, students are introduced to a "temperature check" group process that begins every day of every Intensive during the school year. This technique, created by noted family therapist Virgina Satir, invites participants to sit in a circle and offer comments in the following categories: Appreciations, New Information (announcements), Puzzles, Problems with Solutions, and Hopes and Dreams. This deceptively simple procedure has played an important role in building the culture of the school on a foundation of appreciation (of the good things) and shared problem solving (for less good things).

The orientation also sets the stage for co-creation, which is one of the cardinal values of BGI's Learning Community. In the beginning, co-creation was the only option: the first cohort of students who showed up explicitly agreed to help the founders create the school from scratch: the curriculum was not set, the faculty was not complete, the courses were not designed, and the organizational culture had not yet been established. The school owes a tremendous debt to its first two cohorts of students for establishing the foundation for everything that has come after.

They taught us, among other things, how to live with the chaos of life in a self-organizing system. Formal governance plays a very small role in the life of the BGI community. Instead, the school runs on the passion of individual volunteers willing to invest the energy required to make things happen. Ideas emerge, leaders emerge, followers emerge—and things get done. There are a handful of standing committees, whose leadership and agenda change from year to year: Diversity and Social Justice, Ethics, the Career Opportunities Project (COP), the Academic Improvement Committee, the Carbon Concierge. And, there are a host of Disappearing Task Forces (DTFs) that come into existence, solve a problem, and disband. Through this fluid system, we have managed commencement ceremonies, family events, orientations for new faculty members, factory tours, talent shows, business case competitions, and the student buddy system—to name just a few.

Much of this activity is anchored in Community Process Time (CPT), an evening set aside each Intensive weekend for the development and maintenance of the BGI community. In the early days when the community was small, we thrashed through all our issues sitting in a circle, all together, for as long as it took. As the community has grown, we have evolved a number of approaches to keeping the spirit of the circle alive while engaging a much larger group. We routinely uses a modified version of Open Space to surface issues that are addressed first in CPT and subsequently through a Disappearing Task Force.

BGI also has a formal governance system, which includes student and faculty representatives on the Board of Directors, the Academic Committee, search committees, and every other committee chartered by the Board. The organization strives for inclusiveness and transparency in all its dealings with stakeholders and when it has fallen short—as it inevitably has in the fast-paced, under-resourced start-up period—it has dealt with those failures as opportunities for organizational learning.

There has been much organizational learning these past 6 years. We are grateful to have been a part of that evolution and look forward to our continuing engagement with the school as we exchange our founding roles for something a bit less stressful. At this time, the Pinchots are also adjusting their founding roles for more time with the people for whom they first undertook this effort: their grandchildren.

For further information about the Bainbridge Graduate Institute, visit www.bgiedu.org.

REFERENCES

Aspen Institute Center for Business Education. (2007). *Beyond Grey in Stripes.* Retrieved July 5, 2008, from http://www.beyondgreypinstripes.org/index.cfm

Berman, J., & Webb, T. (2003). *Race to the top: Attracting and enabling global Sustainable Business.* Washington, DC: World Bank.

Kegan, R., & Lahey, L. L. (2002). *How the way we talk can change the way we work: Seven languages for transformation.* San Francisco: Jossey-Bass.

Mintzberg, H. (2005). *Managers not MBAs: A hard look at the soft practice of managing and management development*, San Francisco: Berrett-Koehler.

Weeks, A. (2004, Summer). Business education for sustainability: Training a new generation of business leaders. *Green Money Journal.* Retrieved July 19, 2009, from http://www.greenmoneyjournal.com/article.mpl?newsletterid=29&articleid=309

Winninghoff, E. (2004, May). *Breakthrough in Bainbridge, conscious choic.* Retrieved July 20, 2009, from http://www.lime.com/magazines?uri=seattle.consciouschoice.com/lime/2004/05/bainbridge0405.html

CHAPTER 10

EDUCATING FUTURE BUSINESS LEADERS IN THE STRATEGIC MANAGEMENT OF GLOBAL CHANGE OPPORTUNITIES

The Blue MBA

S. Bradley Moran, Mark M. Higgins, and Deborah E. Rosen

Climate change represents a major challenge and opportunity to a broad range of businesses and the global economy. Although "sustainability" is increasingly part of business schools' curricula, climate science has only recently begun to be formally included in management education programs. In this chapter, we describe a new MBA-MO (Master of Oceanography) dual-degree designed for students with undergraduate training in science and engineering who aim to develop management skills and prepare themselves for the opportunities and challenges of a globally sustainable world.

Annually, over 40,000, or 20%, of those who sit for the GMAT exam in the United States are students who graduated with degrees in science and engi-

Management Education for Global Sustainability, pp. 227–241
Copyright © 2009 by Information Age Publishing
All rights of reproduction in any form reserved.

neering. This potential market, coupled with the current applicants to the traditional Master of Science degree, provides a rich and diverse potential pool of students. The MBA-MO dual degree, "The Blue MBA," will be particularly beneficial to those pursuing management careers in growth markets such as renewable energy, energy efficiency, ocean technology and engineering, hazard risk management, water resources management, fisheries, and ocean and human health.

INTRODUCTION

With a greater awareness of environmental issues and energy demand, there is an increasing need for socioeconomic and environmental sustainability at the local, national, and global level. There are also mounting concerns over the relevance of traditional management theory and practice in the context of growing worldwide poverty, global warming, health care needs, and depletion of natural resources. At the same time, many of these challenges present significant business opportunities and there are clear signs of a marked increase in workforce demand in the rapidly developing green knowledge-based economy. The expansion of this new economic sector calls for a broad range of innovative and interdisciplinary educational programs that combine sound business and management skills with an in-depth understanding of climate science in the context of global socioeconomic change. In turn, there is a growing demand for leaders with skills in business and science, particularly climate-related science, to develop business models needed to manage and capitalize on global change opportunities. To address this demand, a number of business schools are beginning to offer undergraduate and MBA degrees that include coursework in climate relevant issues, such as carbon emissions management, in their portfolio of traditional management training.

This chapter presents a discussion of how universities in general, and graduate management schools in particular, need to align their educational offerings with the move toward a globally sustainable world. This discussion is followed by a detailed description of a new "Blue MBA" dual degree in business and ocean sciences that combines graduate level business training with formal education in oceanography and climate sciences. This unique program contributes to the growing focus on global sustainability and facilitates interaction between faculty and graduate students with corporate executives needing to adapt their management practices to address real-world environmental and social challenges.

ALIGNING UNIVERSITY RESEARCH AND EDUCATION OPPORTUNITIES IN SUSTAINABILITY

Universities play an important role in educating the new green knowledge-based workforce. In the context of developing new management programs in sustainability, it is instructive to consider the actions being taken at the University of Rhode Island (URI) to reduce costs, develop innovative research and education programs, and attract private investment. As the flagship state university, it is imperative that URI play a leading role in growing the green knowledge economy. Rhode Island has made some progress in developing a green economy; *Forbes* magazine recently ranked Rhode Island the 8th eighth greenest state in the nation, with the lowest per capita energy consumption and the third lowest carbon footprint of any state. Both URI's and the state's interests in growing the green economy are based squarely on the desire to find creative and profitable ways to reduce greenhouse gas emissions and energy costs and, in turn, to foster job creation and vibrant businesses.

A number of initiatives at URI are being taken to offset greenhouse gas emissions, reduce costs, and align new research and educational opportunities. An important step in this green direction came when URI signed the American College and University Presidents Climate Commitment (ACUPCC), which requires URI to take measurable steps to reduce its emissions, including a comprehensive environmental audit and analysis of URI's carbon footprint. This carbon benchmarking encourages the design and implementation of ways to improve operating efficiency and develop new curricula in sustainability. The University is also participating in a major energy performance contract that will result in an estimated 10–20% reduction in greenhouse gas emissions through upgraded electrical systems, windows, insulation, and related improvements in energy efficiency. The energy performance contract alone is guaranteed to cut millions in projected energy costs. Efforts are also being made to increase material recycling, implement Leadership in Energy and Environmental Design (LEED) certified green building practices, convert dining hall oil waste into biofuel, and develop a clean transportation policy. There are also a number of innovative green research programs, including those on offshore renewable energy, genetic modification of switch grass as a biofuel, and advances in battery technology.

As is the case for a growing number of publicly funded institutions of higher education, the green initiatives being taken at URI provide valuable lessons in ways to improve operating efficiency while reducing emissions, energy demand, and costs. Indeed, universities have much to gain by fostering the green knowledge-based economy. In addition, through creation of new interdisciplinary programs, such as the "Blue MBA," universities can produce the next generation of business leaders needed for the United States to compete globally in the green economy.

CREATING INTERDISCIPLINARY MANAGEMENT EDUCATION

While the number of Master of Business Administration (MBA) programs has grown exponentially since the late 1960s, the method of recruiting students to an MBA program has remained virtually unchanged. For the most part, universities seek to attract the best students regardless of their undergraduate degree. Although many of the elite MBA programs require a minimum of two years' work experience, the students' undergraduate areas of expertise are less important. What are relevant are undergraduate grade point averages and, more importantly, Graduate Management Admission Test (GMAT) scores.

The content covered in MBA programs throughout the world is very similar and includes courses in economics, accounting, marketing, finance, strategy, and organizational behavior. The primary difference between MBA programs is in the depth and the perspective from which these topics are covered. For institutions that offer a one-year program, the depth of topical coverage is limited. Also, unlike two-year programs where a student can delve into more than one area, students are limited to at most one area (e.g., finance) in which they can pursue additional coursework. Students enrolled in two-year MBA programs typically pursue additional courses in one or more specialized areas, thereby providing the student with greater depth in multiple areas of business. In both of these types of programs, the material is taught from the perspective that the student will be hired in an entry-level management position. While various management issues and strategies are discussed, it is conveyed from the perspective that the student will be carrying out, though not designing, higher-level corporate strategy.

In addition to the format of the program and the opportunities for in-depth study, many business schools have embraced corporate social responsibility and sustainability as underlying themes within their MBA programs. Evidence suggests that including these themes has been carried out with varying degrees of success. On one end of the spectrum, there are the programs that are highly ranked by the Aspen Institute Center for Business Education which publishes "Beyond Grey Pinstripes," a ranking of MBA programs focusing on the degree to which an MBA program integrates social and environmental stewardship in the curriculum (Aspen Institute, 2007-2008). From this research, it is clear that some schools are doing a better job than others in their efforts to integrate corporate profitability and social value. Like all green initiatives, a certain amount of "green washing" is taking place (Hart, 2008). Many schools do not really integrate sustainability into their curriculum through existing courses or through specific sustainability electives. The sustainability initiatives merely appear as add-ons to standard course content. Even when a school does a good job of integrating sustainability and environmental stewardship into its curriculum, it is the strategy elements that are the focus rather than the science behind these topics (e.g., Bridges & Wilhelm, 2008).

GRADUATE MANAGEMENT EDUCATION AND OCEAN SCIENCES: THE BLUE MBA

As part of a national and international trend toward integrating sustainability with management education, a number of business schools are beginning to offer undergraduate and MBA degrees that include course work in climate relevant issues in their traditional management curricula. These new degree offerings range from broadly defined training in corporate social responsibility to more climate-specific topics, such as carbon emissions management, carbon markets and trading, and green supply chain management.

In a further evolution of green business school programs, The University of Rhode Island recently developed a new Master of Business Administration-Master of Oceanography (MBA-MO) dual degree specializing in ocean and climate science and technology. Marketed as the "Blue MBA," students began formally enrolling in this degree in Fall 2008. By combining the existing strengths of the College of Business Administration with the world-class reputation of the Graduate School of Oceanography, this business-science graduate degree provides a unique educational opportunity for students interested in the application of strategic management, leadership, and science skills to important real-world problems.

The URI MBA-MO recognizes that the development of business leaders with the knowledge to solve environmentally based problems requires immersing students, not only in the business and social aspects of environmental stewardship, but also in the science of environmental sustainability. MBA programs that focus on global social issues or sustainability are designed for all students who have an interest in learning about the social, environmental, and economic perspectives for a business. URI's new MBA-MO dual-degree is different from traditional MBA programs because it targets a particular student applicant pool, one that is well versed in science or has a strong aptitude for science. Importantly, it requires additional science courses, while at the same time structuring the business courses with examples that draw on environmental issues (e.g., quantifying carbon emissions, trading carbon credits). Most successful sustainable "green" MBA programs produce students who have a business understanding of how corporate social responsibility or sustainability issues will affect corporations. With the MBA-MO "Blue MBA" dual degree, not only will students have a business understanding of how environmental issues affect corporations, they will also have the scientific background to address these issues. This program is unique in that it will produce students who can work with CEO's as the CENO (Chief Environmental Officer) and also function as the CEO of a corporation that provides services or creates products that provide solutions to environmental problems.

The MBA-MO is a strategic graduate degree in the sense that it benefits from combining the resources of having both a business college and a graduate oceanography school within the same university. In particular, the College of Business Administration (CBA) has been educating future business and government leaders for over 80 years and is fully accredited by the Association to Advance Collegiate Schools of Business (AACSB). The major accrediting agency for programs in business administration and accounting, AACSB accreditation is highly sought after by universities and has been achieved by fewer than 15% of management education institutions. The Graduate School of Oceanography is one of the largest and most widely known graduate schools of oceanography in the United States and is the cornerstone of an array of marine programs at The University of Rhode Island. In 1989, the Graduate School of Oceanography was named a National Oceanic and Atmospheric Administration (NOAA) Center of Excellence in coastal marine studies. The National Research Council has ranked the Graduate School of Oceanography's PhD program one of the best in the country and fifth among oceanographic institutions. Thus, the formal academic ties between these two schools within the University provides for an efficient merger of mutual interests in developing a program that combines management and business skills with ocean and climate science.

Defined broadly, the goal of the new MBA-MO degree is to educate future leaders in global change opportunities. It is structured around a central theme: the business of climate-driven global change. There is now overwhelming evidence that global warming is a direct result of man's activities over the past century, particularly through combustion of fossil fuels. These activities have caused marked increases in atmospheric CO_2 and other radioactively important gases. As noted by Jeffrey Immelt, CEO of the General Electric Corporation, we are living in a carbon-constrained world and businesses need to adapt to this global scale change. It has become increasingly clear that strategic management of the risk associated with climate change represents a substantial challenge to a broad range of businesses and the global economy. In turn, there is a rapidly growing opportunity for businesses that focus on the many and varied aspects of global climate change. These opportunities are increasing the demand for individuals with both the business and science skills necessary to manage and capitalize on the expanding green economy that has grown as a result of the mounting awareness of global change.

The Blue MBA is designed to train future business leaders to manage sustainability-driven divisions of major corporations, new green businesses, and existing green businesses as they adapt to climate change. As discussed below, these businesses include ones involved in energy, energy efficiency, ocean technology and engineering, hazard risk management, water resources management, fisheries, carbon emissions management, and ocean and human health.

Market Analysis

The MBA-MO degree was developed with the idea that future corporate leadership will require and benefit from individuals that have expertise in science and engineering related to global climate change. Building on that idea, this dual degree is targeted primarily at students with an undergraduate training in science or engineering because such coursework provides the necessary foundation of knowledge to succeed in ocean sciences courses as well as graduate business courses. It was realized at the outset that few undergraduate students with a traditional business degree would have sufficient preparation in science and mathematics to complete the rigorous course curriculum of the Master of Oceanography.

Because of the non-traditional academic background of students needed for the MBA-MO dual degree, namely science and engineering students with an interest in ocean and climate science, we conducted a market analysis of the potential applicant pool that would be required to ensure a viable program. The population of science and engineering students that might be interested in broadening their skills to include management education was estimated using GMAT exam data recorded over a 5-year period prior to the initiation of this dual degree. As indicated in Figure 10.1, approximately 40,000 individuals taking the GMAT per year are science and engineering majors, equivalent to roughly 20% of the total GMAT exams taken on an annual basis.

By comparison, a typical incoming class for the regular full-time MBA degree at URI is 20–25 students, and 10–15 students per year typically enroll in the MS and PhD programs in oceanography. Based on these GMAT exam data, and taking into consideration that there are presently

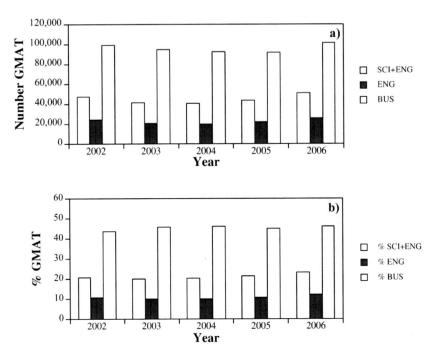

Figure 10.1.   The number (a) and percentage (b) of General Management Aptitude Test (GMAT) exams taken by science, engineering, and business majors for the period 2002–2006. These data indicate the potential market of science and engineering majors for the MBA-MO dual degree. Data from the Graduate Management Admission Council.

very few MBA degrees in ocean and climate science (discussed below), there was indeed good reason to predict a strong applicant pool for the MBA-MO degree.

The initial goal was to grow the MBA-MO to recruit 5–10 students per year. If this recruiting goal was to be successful, it would represent a significant though manageable fraction of the incoming class for each school. In fact, before this degree was officially offered or formally advertised, there were numerous inquiries from students as well as from several major corporations based on two press releases describing the degree. This strong initial interest benefited from the timing of this dual degree with the wide spread interest in sustainability and concerns over global warming.

While a number of business schools offer broadly defined green or sustainability MBAs, only a few degrees presently offered in the world share similarities with the MBA-MO. In September 2008 the University of California's Scripps Institute of Oceanography began offering a joint PhD in

Oceanography with a formal MBA from the Rady School of Management. Because this degree is offered only as a PhD-MBA dual degree, students who take it will require considerably longer to complete the degree (most likely 5-7 years) than the 16 month MBA-MO at URI. In this regard, the Scripps-Rady PhD-MBA degree is intended to graduate doctoral-level research scientists with formal management training.

In the United Kingdom, there are two new graduate degrees that share similarities with the MBA-MO. Both of these are focused on carbon management and hence are inherently based on global warming, though they lack graduate-level courses in ocean sciences. Beginning in January 2008, the Norwich Business School started offering an MBA in Strategic Carbon Management. This 12-month specialty MBA has a curriculum that is focused on pairing traditional management training with a curriculum that includes economic, business, social, and legal aspects of carbon, including courses on carbon finance, trading, management, and entrepreneurship. In addition, the School of Geosciences and the Business School of the University of Edinburgh offer a new 12-month Master in Science in Carbon Management joint-degree. This graduate degree is designed for economics, business, social, and physical science undergraduates, though it does not provide students with the MBA degree.

Program Development, Structure, and Curriculum

A necessary first step in developing this dual degree was to gain the interest and support of the Deans and faculty in the College of Business Administration and the Graduate School of Oceanography. Initial meetings with the Business and Oceanography Schools led to an Executive Summary that was met with unanimous approval from faculty and senior University administrators. The next steps in the development of the program were to document the structure of the new dual degree program, seek the necessary administrative approvals, and develop a marketing and recruitment strategy.

Taking into consideration the University's resources, the most efficient starting point for the new degree curriculum was with science and engineering majors able to meet the individual requirements of the existing MBA and the non-thesis Master of Oceanography degree (MO). Such students would be required to enroll in: (1) MBA courses that best meet the needs of the new dual degree program; (2) ocean science courses required for the MO; (3) joint courses from other departments that meet the requirements of the MBA and MO, including courses in economics and natural resource economics. This strategy efficiently leverages the existing courses offered by the business and oceanography schools and serves as the foundation to meet the new dual degree requirements.

The result is a 60-credit full-time dual degree that can be completed in 16 months (three semesters plus one summer). The summer includes six credit hours of coursework (i.e., two courses) and a six-credit-hour full-time internship. The two courses are taken online (i.e., distance learning) to avoid any conflicts with the full-time internship. The MBA-MO curriculum is outlined by semester in Table 10.1 and a description of the individual courses is listed in the Appendix. The business courses include organizational behavior, marketing, finance, accounting, and supply chain management. The oceanography course work includes all of the main disciplines (biological, chemical, geological, and physical oceanography) as well as participation in the student seminar in the first year. Additional courses include managerial economics and natural resource economics.

Corporate Advisement and Involvement

Developing relationships with major corporations and business and science leaders, including several that sit on the URI College of Business Advisory Council, is an essential part of assessing the needs of the business world in the University's effort to train future business-science leaders. Inviting such interaction provided invaluable input and advisement regarding the MBA-MO and was deemed necessary to the success and continuation of this new graduate program. A formal presentation of the Blue MBA to the members of the Business Advisory Council brought discussion on relevant topics to consider in the curriculum, including: corporate climate risk assessment and management; carbon trading, credits, and policy; carbon sequestration; renewable energy and energy efficiency; climate-related hazards and risk prediction; national security and climate change; water resource management; fisheries; and ocean and human

Table 10.1   MBA-MO Curriculum by Semester. Couse Descriptions Listed in Appendix. Credit number in Parentheses (60 Total Credits)

Fall I	Spring I	Summer	Fall II
MBA 502 (3)	MBA 505 (3)	MBA 510 (3) (online)	MBA 565 (3)
MBA 503(3)	MBA 504 (3)	MBA 550 (3) (online)	MBA 555 (3)
MBA 530 (3)	OCG 540 (3)	MBA Internship/Directed	OCG 561 (4)
OCG 501(3)	OCG 521 (3)	Study (3)	OCG XXX (3)
OCG 695 (1)	OCG 695 (1)	OCG Internship/Directed	OCG YYY (3)
ECN 590 (3)	MBA 560 (3)	Study (3)	

health. Discussion with senior executives from several major corporations (e.g., IBM, GE, and ICF International) and smaller businesses continues as they engage the University to learn more about this new degree. Business and science leaders will help shape this new program during the initial stages of development through guest lectures and meetings at URI.

An important goal of this aspect of the program's development is to develop more structured interactions between businesses and the University, including the development of new MBA-MO student internships and the creation of an environment that fosters new funding opportunities to support students and research activities. In this regard, the University's new Research Foundation [operated as a 501(c)(3)] will be an important aspect of discussions between URI and business leaders.

Advantages and Limitations of the Blue MBA

There are a number of positive aspects of the MBA-MO dual degree. First, by leveraging the existing strengths of the College of Business Administration and the Graduate School of Oceanography, the MBA-MO dual degree provides a timely opportunity to educate science and engineering majors to be future leaders of businesses as they adapt to global change opportunities. No other U.S. higher-level education institution offers such a unique and innovative graduate business-science degree. Furthermore, this dual degree is specifically designed to provide individuals with the science and business skills to meet global change opportunities that will benefit a more sustainable world.

A further benefit is the increased enrollment in management courses by science and engineering students that would not typically register in this discipline. Unlike the traditional model of external grant supported students pursuing the Master of Science in Oceanography, the MBA-MO dual degree students pay tuition and thereby provide a new source of revenue to the institution. The MBA-MO is more than just a "niche" business-science MBA program in that students will graduate with expertise in both science and business gained through dual degree course requirements. In addition, the dual degree format leverages the strengths and existing resources of the College of Business and the School of Oceanography. It does so, in particular, by fostering faculty interaction with businesses involved in ocean science and technology in a broad context that enhances external funding opportunities. The dual degree also leads to increased interaction between faculty and students in business and ocean sciences whose buildings are located on different campuses at the University. Finally, the MBA-MO provides for interaction with a wide range of businesses through the URI Research Park and provides infrastructure for and proximity to corporate incubators.

One of the limitations of the dual degree format of the MBA-MO is the University's individual credit requirement for the MBA and MO degrees. While there is provision for a 20% credit reduction by combining each degree into a dual degree format, the total number of credits and, perhaps more importantly, the somewhat restrictive nature of the MO curriculum makes for a demanding degree. At the same time, the regular full-time MBA program is demanding in itself at 15 credits per semester, which is not significantly different than the credit load of the MBA-MO (Table 10.1). The advantage of using the dual degree format is that both the MBA and MO were already approved by the University, which greatly simplified and accelerated the rate at which this unique degree could be fully approved by the University as a new offering. The alternative approach would be to define a truly new degree, based on existing and new courses. An advantage of such an approach would be fewer required credits and more flexibility for the student in designing a course curriculum. While this alternative approach would have required more faculty involvement and calendar time to develop new course offerings in its early stages, these investments will occur later as the program evolves and demand for specific course materials and business-science expertise changes in the future.

CONCLUDING REMARKS

The business community will likely bear the brunt of the challenge to find ways to reduce the world's greenhouse gas emissions, yet few individuals have the necessary training in both business and climate science to lead the way. The new Blue MBA business-science dual degree will educate students in the application of strategic management, leadership, and ocean and climate sciences to important real-world problems. This degree is designed to provide tomorrow's leaders in science with the knowledge and skills to develop business models to ensure an environmentally sustainable world for future generations. The degree is intended for students with undergraduate training in pure science, environmental science, or engineering who want to develop management skills and diversify their career opportunities. The degree will be particularly beneficial to those seeking management careers in industries such as renewable energy, energy efficiency, ocean technology and engineering, hazard risk management, water resources management, fisheries, and ocean and human health. As global climate change accelerates and the business community responds, there will be an increasing demand for graduates who can claim a rigorous background in ocean and climate science while also having the benefits of an MBA. The MBA-MO offers an outstanding chance for students to take advantage of this challenge.

ACKNOWLEDGMENTS

We thank Lisa Lancellotta for technical assistance and Susan Gomes for editorial assistance. This work was supported in part by funding from the National Science Foundation.

APPENDIX

Course Descriptions (Credit Number in Parentheses)

MBA 502 Organizational Behavior (3): Examination of the theory, research, and practice of organizational behavior in work settings, focusing on individual differences, communications, group dynamics, motivation, and leadership in the workplace.

MBA 503 Financial Accounting (3): Basic accounting principles, accounting systems design, and financial reporting issues. Focusing on financial statement analysis techniques necessary to accurately assess a company's financial position and results of operations.

MBA 504 Financial Management (3): Functions and responsibilities of financial managers. Examination of financial statement analysis, cost of capital, capital structure, valuation, markets, capital budgeting, working capital, mergers, bankruptcy, multinational finance.

MBA 505 Managerial Marketing (3): Analysis of marketing problems and determination of marketing policies in product development, promotion, pricing, channel selection, legal aspects.

MBA 510 Managerial Accounting (3): Determination of accounting information for the purposes of decision making, control, and evaluation with emphasis on decision models using accounting information.

MBA 530 Legal Environment of Business (3): Substantive and procedural rules of law in the civil and administrative law field with emphasis on business, regulation, societal, and ethical issues.

MBA 550 Managing with Information Resources (3): Concepts of information technologies and systems as they relate to the information-age organization. Major focus is on how the various information resources can be managed to facilitate organizational effectiveness. Topics include information and communication technologies, decision support and information systems, technology-enabled process re-engineering, and information architecture.

MBA 555 Managerial Economics (3): The applications of economic theory and methodology to business problems.

MBA 560 Operations and Supply Chain Management (3): Management of manufacturing and service operations. Topics include flow processes, inventories, scheduling, capacity, and operations strategy.

MBA 565 Strategic Management (3): Case studies of management problems and evaluation of alternative solutions by integrating functional areas of business. Discussion of ethical, social, and regulatory environments in domestic and multinational firms.

OCG 501 Physical Oceanography (3): Physical properties of seawater, heat budget, distribution of variables, dynamics, water masses and general circulation, waves and tides.

OCG 521 Chemical Oceanography (3): Processes regulating the composition of seawater and the distribution of chemical species. The interaction of marine chemistry with the ocean floor, atmosphere, and marine organisms.

OCG 540 Geological Oceanography (3): Origin and evolution of the ocean basin and its margin: morphology, structure, plate tectonics, volcanism, geochemistry, stratigraphy, sedimentation, and paleoceanography.

OCG 561 Biological Oceanography (4): Dynamics of marine ecosystems; patterns of production and distribution of plankton, benthos, and nekton in relationship to their environment.

OCG 695 Seminar in Oceanography (1): Seminar on problems and current research in oceanography.

OCG XXX and YYY (3 each): Six credits in oceanography or other science departments.

ECN 590 Principles of Economics (3): Survey of micro- and macroeconomic theory.

REFERENCES

Aspen Institute, (2007–2008). *Beyond grey pinstripes.* Retrieved September 23, 2008, from http://www.beyondgreypinstripes.org/about/index.cfm

Bridges, C. M., & Wilhelm, W. B. (2008). Going beyond green: The "why and how" of integrating sustainability into the marketing curriculum. *Journal of Marketing Education, 30*(1), 33–46.

Hart, S. (2008, October). Sustainability must be integral to schools' DNA. *Financial Times, 13,* 15.

CHAPTER 11

THE CONTRIBUTION OF FRENCH BUSINESS AND MANAGEMENT EDUCATION TO THE DEVELOPMENT OF KEY SKILLS IN SUSTAINABLE DEVELOPMENT

Vera Ivanaj and John R. McIntyre

Over the past 5 years, French business and management education system has become deeply involved in the development of training courses for sustainable development. These courses are mainly offered at graduate level through the creation of numerous professional master's degrees. Training courses which integrate real-life company problems are also accessible for executives and can reach a large range of learner profiles: engineers, legal advisors, economists, human resources managers, chemists, architects, and so forth. The aim of these courses has been to prepare participants and researchers to cope with national and international sustainable development issues using a broad-gauged multidisciplinary approach. Lecturers are both professionals and academics and offer a wide range of active learning methods including debates and case studies. The full range of subjects relat-

Management Education for Global Sustainability, pp. 243–263

ing to global sustainability is covered in these newly developed courses including economic, environmental, societal and ethical questions.

This chapter presents an overview of the contribution of the French higher education system to the development of key managerial skills in the management of sustainable development. It buttresses its finding on an analysis of training programs at the master's degree level. Emphasis is placed on direct actions undertaken by universities such as the professionalization of programs, increasing both flexibility and attractiveness of teaching such courses, and forging deeper links with important figures and interest groups in the economic domain.

INTRODUCTION

Today "sustainable development" (SD) management has become an essential subject for both public and private actors in a globalized world economy. Companies, national and international organizations, schools, universities, and environmental and human rights associations are all looking for managers able to deal with the environmental, economic, and societal stakes linked to SD. The capacity to make decisions that enhance the overall long-term performance of a company has thus become an indispensable managerial skill for tomorrow. Present and future generations of managers must be able to make strategic choices that enable a company's products and methods of production and distribution to evolve in harmony with the principles, findings, and practices of SD. They must be able to identify the role played by economic, environmental, and societal variables such as economic profitability, competition, open markets, public policies, legal standards and constraints in the decision making process, how societal values, national cultures, and economic systems define the operational constraints and resulting choices. These managers are now responsible for helping their organizations find lasting solutions responsive to essential questions such as the intensity of exploitation of natural resources, how far the impact of technological solutions has spread, shareholders' interests, risks for future generations.

In this context, higher education's role in business management is emerging as a central component of a sustainable environment. As national and international strategies evolve and questions of implementation are raised, universities and management schools must ask themselves how they can interface with this process both through institutional involvement in SD and through training of students and managers in fast-changing SD skills. This responsibility is accentuated by the expressed needs of the corporate world for capable managerially trained personnel and relevant educational offerings in sustainability (Wheeler, Dezso Horvath, & Victor, 1999).

Over the last few years, French higher education has become heavily involved in the process of training in SD because of the impetus given by government policy and the growing demand for SD training expressed by organizations, corporate boards, shareholders and corporate managers. Many new SD training courses have been set up in close collaboration with local, national, and occasionally international partners. These courses have been developed around existing core of management courses by adding modules, cases, interactive material, speaker series, etc. to sensitize students to SD issues. In addition, many dedicated and degree-granting educational programs have been set up both in engineering and in business and management schools.

This chapter pays particular attention to newly emerging educational and training courses in SD. It reviews the manner in which training at the master's degree level in SD is growing and the overall trends emerging. To do so, the chapter first elaborates on the political and institutional context in France which gave rise to the rapid emergence of "Education for Sustainable Development" (ESD) in higher education in general. The chapter then analyzes how educational courses at the master's degree level in business and management are developing in the field of SD.

EDUCATION IN SUSTAINABLE DEVELOPMENT IN THE FRENCH HIGHER EDUCATIONAL SYSTEM

Since the official introduction of the concept of SD in the Brundtland Report, *Our Common Future* (World Commission on Environment and Development, 1987), it has spread throughout the world, becoming a matter of great political and socioeconomic importance. Agenda 21, which was adopted in 1992 in Rio de Janeiro at the "United Nations Conference on Environment and Development," stressed the importance of education in implementing SD principles, notably through entrenching respectful values and attitudes to the environment and to society as a whole. Since 1992, a consensus on the crucial role of ESD has been maintained at all United Nations conferences.

The United Nations Economic Commission for Europe defines ESD as follows:

> Education for sustainable development develops and strengthens the capacity of individuals, groups, communities, organizations and countries to make judgments and choices in favor of sustainable development. It can promote a shift in people's mindsets and in so doing enable them to make our world safer, healthier and more prosperous, thereby improving the quality of life. Education for sustainable development can provide critical reflection and greater awareness and empowerment so that new visions and

concepts can be explored and new methods and tools developed. (United
Nations Economic Commission for Europe, 2005, p. 1)

The Johannesburg Summit (World Summit on Sustainable Development,
2002) reaffirmed the objectives of ESD by proposing the idea of a
"Decade of Education for Sustainable Development." At the UN General
Assembly in December 2002, this concept was defined as having the overall aim of integrating SD principles, values, and practices into all areas of
education and apprenticeship (United Nations Educational, Scientific
and Cultural Organization, 2004).

It is in this international political context that the French government
and its national educational authorities have become involved in the elaboration and implementation of an overall ESD policy. This strategy
addresses all spheres of education in France, primary, secondary, and
higher education. The following section explains how this national gov-
ernment-inspired strategy has driven educational initiatives in the field of
SD throughout France's higher education system.

THE FRENCH POLITICAL CONTEXT FOR SD IN
THE HIGHER EDUCATION SYSTEM

ESD was introduced relatively recently into the French educational system. Its origins can be found in the 1970s in what was called "Education
Relative à l'Environnement" (Education related to the environment),
Tremblay, 2007). This environmental educational policy continued until
2003 with a study of ecosystems laying out theoretical and pedagogical
approaches (De Robin, 2005). The major political commitments made by
the United Nations influenced the French government in concluding that
education for SD in France needed to be transformed completely. The
French government thus adopted a "National Strategy for SD" in June
2003 (Comité interministériel pour le SD, 2003) which led the French
National Education Ministry (*Ministère de l'Education Nationale*) to commit
to a wide-scale movement called "environmental education for SD." This
movement began with an experimental initiative involving 10 "acade-
mies" (regional education authorities) made up of 84 teaching teams in
40 primary schools, 22 "*collèges*" (middle schools) and 22 secondary
schools in the fields of general, technical and professional education
(Ministère de l'Education Nationale, 2003). The aim of this experimental
initiative was to analyze the pedagogical practices and content used by
teachers and to discover emerging training gaps. This work led to a
framework circular in July 2004 whose aim was for ESD to be taught to all
pupils during their school years (Ministère de l'Education Nationale,

2004). The 2004 circular was followed up in February 2007 by a new 3-year plan (2007–2010) for "environmental education in favor of SD" (De Robien, 2007). The objectives of this plan were threefold:

1. for ESD to be more widely included in teaching courses;
2. to multiply overall ESD initiatives in establishments and schools;
3. to train teachers and other staff working in education (Ministère de l'Education Nationale, 2007).

Those National Education Ministry's political commitments and initiatives have the unequivocal effect of promoting the development of ESD in French primary and secondary education. The question of ESD in higher education was included in the debate surrounding those initiatives but was not the object of a specific policy. However, following the "Grenelle de l'Environnement" (Environmental Forum) organized by the Ecology, Energy, Sustainable Development and Territorial Development Ministry (*Ministère de l'Ecologie, de l'Energie, du Développement Durable et de l'Aménagement du Territoire*) in 2007, an important political initiative underlined the National Education Ministry's will to extend its policy support to ESD throughout the whole of the French education system. This initiative created an interministerial working group on ESD in December 2007 (Darcos, 2007). The composition of the working group was intentionally rich and varied, with members coming from the main political, economic, and social spheres such as education, nongovernmental organizations (NGOs), the State, employees, employers, and others involved in the issue of ESD (Groupe de travail Education au Développement Durable, 2008a, 2008b). The group's mission was to study the real questions faced by those working in ESD and to use that understanding to propose initiatives and a strategy for the future in primary, secondary and higher education along with general, technological, and professional basic training. It also examined the questions of continuous training and how to train trainers. There were two main axes of analysis: pedagogical approach and training (Groupe de travail Education au Développement Durable, 2008b).

This working group formulated a number of proposals aimed at helping the National Education Ministry integrate and generalize ESD teaching in close working collaboration with appropriate partners. On the pedagogical level, the working group recommended that ESD should not be considered as a discipline but as a dimension of teaching which must be integrated "into the heart of all disciplines" by adopting a "plural" or interdisciplinary pedagogical process in close collaboration with partners. It was to be "orientated toward action" and should be based on an "empirical and sensitive approach" (Groupe de travail Education au Développement Durable, 2008b, pp. 6–7).

In terms of training, the group insisted on the necessity to train not only those working in education (teaching staff, administrative, and management personnel etc.) but also others concerned with the subject, such as companies, local authorities, public establishments, administrative organizations, and so forth, ESD "must become part of apprenticeships in each professional sector and do this with direct links to companies and regional authorities both in basic and continuous training" (Groupe de travail Education au Développement Durable, 2008b, pp. 6–7). The working group's recommendations also dealt with the necessity to set up support systems for ESD initiatives:

1. "The creation of university chairs linked to regional problematic.
2. The sensitization and training of public and private decision-makers.
3. The training of experts on fields linked to SD, like the environment and health.
4. Training trainers in research into sciences of applied education in ESD.
5. Setting up an integrated network of pedagogical resource centers.
6. Developing evaluation methods (a well-adapted measuring system, indicators, reference systems).
7. The promotion of professions linked to the environment and SD and training in the key professions" (Groupe de travail Education au Développement Durable, 2008b, pp. 6–7).

This governmental context led the main higher education authorities in France to adopt SD charters supporting ESD teaching. The "Conférence des Grandes Ecoles" (Association of Graduate Elite Schools) adopted an SD Charter in 2003 (Conférence des Grandes Ecoles, 2003). This association regroups 121 elite engineering and management schools which teach students after their baccalauréat (national high school diploma) on a 5-year program leading to a major national degree. The charter recommends that the institutions adopt a strategy favoring SD. It suggests they evolve their own charters and action plans and asks them to take part in implementing the stated SD ambitions of the charter. In doing so, they are urged to follow a number of concepts:

1. developing and adapting missions (life-long training, research, development and transfer of knowledge, international cooperation programs);
2. following best training and research practices that lead to a cross-disciplinary discipline based on partnerships;

3. forging relationships with the stakeholders (former students, companies);
4. influencing others and spreading concepts as responsible stakeholders within society, particularly regarding cooperation initiatives.

In a similar vein, the "Association of University Presidents" (*Conférence des Présidents d'Université*) plays a major role in the public debate on higher education and research in France. The Association signed a charter to create an "Alliance of French Universities which support SD" (Conférence des Présidents d'Université, 2008). This association is composed of 82 universities, 3 technological universities, 3 National Polytechnic Institutes, 4 Ecoles Normales Supérieures (Elite Graduate Schools), 3 National Institutes of Applied Sciences and 8 "Grands Etablissements" or Elite/Graduate Establishments. The member institutions committed to offer "all their users (students teacher-researchers, researchers, teachers, administrative and technical staff) training modules aimed at sensitizing them to the principles of SD." To achieve this goal, the members agree to include "in the curriculum of each educational program, a cross-disciplinary training module adapted to implementing SD in the field of study and the professions students aim to work in" and to propose "courses or pedagogical projects to students which are linked to implementing SD in the establishment concerned."

AN OVERVIEW OF UNIVERSITY COURSES IN SD

French higher education's political and institutional commitment to ESD has led to a considerable level of development in training courses in the field recently. The "National Office of Information on Teaching and Professions" (*Office National d'Information Sur les Enseignements et les Professions*, ONISEP, 2008) study of educational courses at the master's level provides an insight into and overview of ESD in French higher education.

"Onisep" is a public establishment under the umbrella of the National Education Ministry. It is tasked with devising and distributing information on educational opportunities and career paths to students, parents, and teaching teams. The search keyword "SD" in Onisep's online database brought up 96 courses taught to post-baccalauréat students in France. Most of these courses (50) are at the "professional master's" level. Next are 33 "research master's" courses. Six courses are available under the title of "specialized master's" and seven are professional degree courses.

An analysis of Onisep's data shows the areas of study of these 96 SD courses. Some of the courses can be classified into more than one field.

Table 11.1.   Disciplinary Fields Addressing Issues of SD

Field of Activity	Number of Courses Concerned	Field of Activity	Number of Courses Concerned
Corporate management	9	Human resources	1
Farming	9	Geography	7
Food industry	3	Property	1
Decision support systems	5	Information and communication	2
Town and country planning	24	Philosophy	1
Landscaping	1	Hygiene	1
Automatisms	1	Research	1
Building studies—finishing work	1	Health	1
Building studies—public utilities	1	Earth sciences	2
Biology	2	Economic sciences	20
Chemistry	3	Political sciences	11
Law	8	Social sciences	2
Environmental law	3	Safety and accident prevention	3
Electronics	1	Tourism	1
Energy	8	Transport	1
Environment	81	Social work	7
Production	5		

Source: Table 11.1 compiled from data from the Onisep Web site (2008).

The majority of the courses (81 out of 96) are in the environmental field. This concentration is not surprising given that the environmental dimension of SD has quickly attracted the attention of world political and socioeconomic decision makers. As Barthel and Ivanaj (2007) point out, companies have tended to restrict the conceptualization of SD just to environmental concerns. Companies first oriented themselves toward environmental risk management programs, the implementation of an Environmental Management System (EMS), adopting quality standards such as ISO 14001, and so forth. This emphasis led to environmental management courses flourishing in French universities for at least twenty years (Tremblay, 2007). A deeper analysis of the fields of study and course descriptions of master's degree courses in environmental studies indicate that the courses available cover a multitude of disciplines ranging from the sciences to economics and social studies. The disciplines concerned include political science, economics and management studies, technological sciences, social sciences, literature, languages and the arts, law, health, and urbanism.

After the environment, the second most represented field of study is economics and management, with a total of 29 courses (20 in economics and 9 in corporate management). Economics-oriented courses cover SD questions through macro and micro-economic analyses in very specific geographic contexts: national, European, international and rural economies, etc. Courses in corporate management tend to cover strategic and operational matters in the management of organizations, with a stress on the concept of companies' social responsibility. The relatively important position of economics and management courses suggests that the economic dimension of SD is becoming increasingly well integrated into university training programs, with an increasingly closer link to environmental concerns. These courses are analyzed in more depth in the second part of this chapter.

Twenty-four SD university courses address town and country planning. These courses are mainly in the fields of human and social sciences and deal essentially with the third dimension of SD: the social and societal dimension. The course names that crop up the most are town planning and regional development, with an accent on territorial systems.

The SD emphases of the courses in some of the remaining disciplinary fields in Table 11.1 are as follows:

1. Eleven political science courses underlining international economic policies and local and national public action programs;
2. Nine agriculture courses with an emphasis on agricultural sustainable development;
3. Eight energy courses covering the question of new and renewable energy sources;
4. Eight law courses include a focus on environmental law;
5. Seven social work courses dealing with the question of SD in developing and/or "transition" countries;
6. Seven geography courses covering the question of emerging territories.

The remaining courses deal with SD questions in relation to specialist fields such as chemistry, biology, farming and the food industry, health, transport, and tourism. These courses are a contribution to more specialized education linked to the exact nature of the professions and sectors of activity concerned.

HIGHER EDUCATION IN BUSINESS AND MANAGEMENT: A KEY PART OF SD EDUCATION

The preceding overview of ESD described the political and institutional context in which a large number of university courses have developed in all disciplines. Business and management take up a considerable part of the total courses available, around a third in fact. The following paragraphs are devoted to the contents of the courses, the pedagogical methods that are used, the teaching staff involved, the system for evaluating the courses, and the careers open to students. However first, the business and management education system in France will be looked at in more detail.

A Short Reminder of How Higher Education in Management is Organized in France

The place occupied by the French business management higher education system and the system's specific features are closely linked to the history of management sciences in France. This disciplinary field is a relatively young one compared to other human and social sciences disciplines such as economics and law (Malherbe, 2006). Although the first "Grandes Ecoles" in management were founded in the nineteenth century, management sciences became an institutionalized part of the education system only toward the end of the 1960s with the creation of an expert subcommittee by the Universities Consultative Committee in 1969. The establishment of the National Foundation for Teaching Company Management ("*Fondation Nationale pour l'Enseignement de la Gestion des Entreprises*"—FENGE) in 1968 was the reflection of the state's strong political commitment to the development of higher education in management in France. The FENGE was set up to develop a more coherent system of management education and has contributed a great deal to the institutionalization of management sciences particularly through the creation of specific diploma-based courses such as the master's degree and doctorate program in management sciences. This institutionalization of management studies has led to courses in business management acquiring a greater visibility in society. Currently, management courses train around 17% of students in basic programs and about 13% of interns in continuing education training (Durant & Dameron, 2005).

Today, the term "management sciences teaching and research establishment" covers "all French public and private establishments which permit students to obtain a management diploma" (Durant & Dameron, 2005, p. 6). The main players in the field of higher education in management in France can be divided into three categories:

1.   Graduate Elite Schools (Grandes Ecoles) in business,
2.   Universities and
3.   other schools and newer establishments.

The Graduate Elite Business Schools are those higher education establishments recognized as such by the Association of Graduate Schools ("*Conférence des Grandes Ecoles*"). These schools are pedagogically and financially autonomous and recruit their students through a national competition which allows them to be highly selective. Their degrees are recognized by the French National Education Ministry and their courses give high-level professional training in various activity sectors, ranging from commerce to manufacturing and service industries. The management courses run by these business schools account for a large part of the business courses available in France, teaching 30% of students in higher education and 17% of post-graduate students (Durant & Dameron, 2005, p. 12). Unlike French universities, these business schools are not State-financed and are funded mainly by:

1.   support from the Chambers of Commerce and Industry if they are "écoles consulaires" (public sector schools linked to Chambers of Commerce),
2.   teaching fees (around 7,000 euros per year per student) and the marketing of executive training courses,
3.   financial support from companies via the French apprenticeship tax ("taxe d'apprentissage"), or other measures like donations, research chairs, foundations, and so forth (Durant & Dameron, 2005, p. 13).

Management education offered by French universities covers the full range of courses in the field but, unlike business schools, the cost of the courses is much lower. Courses are organized in three different frameworks:

1.   in a specific teaching department of a University or Training and Research Unit (*Unité de Formation et de Recherche, UFR*),
2.   in an institute such as a "Business Administration Institute" ("*Institut d'Administration des Entreprises*," IAE) which has a certain degree of autonomy although still part of a university,

3. in courses other than management itself, such as economics, engineering science, etc. through specific curricula in management (Durant & Dameron, 2005, p. 13).

Finally the business schools and universities' courses are now in competition with a number of newer establishments in the field, like company-run management institutes, private business schools, and others working in the field of private training, such as consultants.

Business Courses in the Field of SD

The higher education system in management in general, including universities teaching management sciences and business and management schools, has strongly committed to the development of SD courses. An analysis on the ONISEP database of master's level courses shows there are 30 SD courses available to students. Table 11.2 displays the range of courses. Most of these master's level courses (17 out of 30) are "professional master's" courses (PM) aimed at training future company management staff for their future jobs linked to SD. These courses are mainly organized by universities that also offer "research master's" courses (RM). Six of the thirty programs are devoted to preparing students for positions in management science research. Finally, there are seven "specialist master's" course options (SM) run by business schools. Some of these establishments have made SD courses a priority initiative, offering more than one master's programs in different specialized fields. This is the case of the Nantes Business Administration Institute (*Nantes University*) which runs four specialized courses:

1. SD in the food industries,
2. European and international economic development,
3. Local development and employment economics,
4. SD Economics.

University of Nantes courses are run under a common title for four different disciplines belonging to the wider field of "human and social sciences": legal sciences, political science, economic sciences and management sciences. The University of Versailles Saint-Quentin-en-Yvelines (Human and Social Sciences UFR) runs two master's level courses focusing particularly on the field of SD engineering in disciplines that are less directly related to SD, such as environmental and territorial sciences.

The contents of the courses in Table 11.2 are analyzed next to provide a better understanding of their contribution to training future business and management staff in the field of SD. Training subjects and course content, pedagogical methods, student evaluation methods, selection of students, and career opportunities are discussed.

Table 11.2.   Master's Degree Classes in Management-Related Fields Offered in France's Graduate Schools

Spéciality SUBJECT OF THE Master's Program	Establishment
Sustainable agricultural development: international economics and food safety—PM*	University of Paris-South 11 Law economics and management UFR—Jean Monnet Faculty
Sustainable agricultural development: international economics and food safety—RM	University of Paris-South 11 Law economics and management UFR—Jean Monnet Faculty
SD in the food industries—PM	University of Nantes Nantes Business Administration Institute—IAE
SD in developing and transition countries—PM	University of Clermont-Ferrand I Economic and Management Sciences UFR
European and International Economic Development—PM	University of Nantes Nantes Business Administration Institute—IAE
Environmental and SD law and management—PM	University of Montpellier I Law and social sciences UFR
SD, environmental and energy economics—RM**	University of Paris 10 Nanterre Economic sciences, management, mathematics and computing UFR
SD Economics—RM	University of Nantes Nantes Business Administration Institute—IAE
Local development and employment Economics—RM	University of Nantes Nantes Business Administration Institute—IAE
Environmental and SD economics and management—PM	University Littoral—Côte d'Opale—ULCO Lamartine University Center
Environmental and SD economics and managemen—PM	University of Lille 3 Mathematics, economics and social sciences UFR

Table continues on next page.

Table 11.2.   Continued

Spéciality SUBJECT OF THE Master's Program	*Establishment*
SD Economics and Management—RM	University of Montpellier I Economic sciences UFR
Geographical environmental economics—RM	University of Corsica Law, social economic and management sciences UFR
Evaluation, perspectives and SD—PM	University of Reims Economic and management sciences UFR
Quality Management and SD—PM	International Management Institute, organization department
SD management and climate change—SM	Graduate business school group of Toulouse, ESC program
Territorial development engineering—PM	University of Corsica Law, social economic and management sciences UFR
Company social responsibility Management—PM	University of Paris XII Economic and management sciences UFR (and IAE Gustave Eiffel)
Human resources management and company social responsibility—PM	University of Paris 1 Panthéon-Sorbonne UFR 13 Business Administration Institute
Management of SD—SM	HEC Groupe – Graduate schools program
Sustainable Management—PM	Sup de Co Group La Rochelle (ESC Program)
Sustainable Management—PM	University of Poitiers UFR Business Administration Institute IAE
Ecological Management and SD—SM***	Research and Commercial Institute – Lyon
Operational management and sustainable performance—SM	Graduate Business Institute
Quality management, human resources option—SM	BEM Bordeaux Management School - ESC Bordeaux program
Strategic SD Management—SM	CERAM Business School, ESC program
Mediation of environmental knowledge: SD partnerships—PM	University of Versailles Saint-Quentin-en-Yvelines Human and Social Sciences UFR
SD Strategy—SM	Sup de Co Group, La Rochelle (Program ESC)
SD Strategies , company social responsibility - PM	University of Versailles Saint-Quentin-en-Yvelines Human and Social Sciences UFR

Sustainable Tourism—PM	University of Corsica Law, social economic and management sciences UFR
*PM : Professional Master's **RM : Research Master's ***SM : Specialized Master's	*UFR : Training and Research Unit (Unité de Formation et de Recherche,)

Training Subjects and Course Content

An analysis of the master's level courses reveals two main recurrent subject areas: SD management and SD economics. SD management courses concentrate on teaching skills and knowledge by focusing on strategy-based SD questions. This is notably the case of the "SD Strategy" master's degree at the Sup de Co Group in La Rochelle. The course objective is to train high-level management staff working on global strategy and policies for large companies. It does so by concentrating on the methods and techniques required to build and improve environmental performance measuring tools. Similarly, the CERAM Business School program defines the pedagogical objective of its "Strategic SD Management" master's diploma as the training of students to acquire requisite knowledge of the SD emerging field and its best strategic and operational management tools. The content of this degree-granting course is rich and covers diverse themes such as "SD and strategy," "the environment," "human and social interaction in a company," "company finance and management", and "management of stakeholders."

The other SD management courses such as Groupe HEC's "SD management" programs tend to be more general in their approach to SD management and to cover of the full range of company activity (marketing, sales, accounting, communication, finance, human resources, etc.). There are also master's courses on a less general theme like, for example, the operational management and sustainable performance degree-seeking program run by the Graduate Business Institute; the quality management in human resources option at BEM Bordeaux Management School and the IAE in Paris (University of Paris 1, Panthéon-Sorbone); or the global quality management course run by the International Management Institute. These courses differ because of their skill-based modules which allow students to garner deeper knowledge in specialist fields.

Concerning the topics covered in the "SD economics" courses, the second major theme of SD courses, deals with:

1. Economic analysis, decision making and evaluation (e.g., the "Evaluation, perspectives and SD" Professional Master's run by the University of Reims).

2. European and International Economic Development (e.g., European and International Economic Development at the Nantes Business Administration Institute).

3. Local development and employment (e.g., the professional master's course in "Local development and employment" at the Nantes Business Administration Institute, University of Nantes).

4. SD in developing and transition economies (e.g., Professional Master's in "SD in developing and transition countries at the University of Clermont-Ferrand I, Economic and Management Sciences UFR).

Pedagogical Methods

In the professional and specialized master's programs, the teaching methods used tend to emphasize the concrete, practical side of training. The objective is to make the teaching as close as possible to students' later professional life, teaching skills that can be used directly in the corporate environment. To achieve this objective, most of the SD courses are organized in the following format—a 6–8 month course of lessons followed by a 3–6 month company internship. Some courses are based more on the "apprenticeship" format. This apprenticeship emphasis is the case for the "SD Strategies and company social responsibility" Professional Master's program taught at the University of Versailles Saint-Quentin-en-Yvelines and the "Human resources management and company social responsibility" Professional Master's program taught at the Paris Business Administration Institute (*University of Paris 1 Panthéon-Sorbonne*). These dual education degree-seeking programs mix apprenticeships in a company with technical education at a school, thus allowing students to occupy a position in the field of SD straight away. The apprentice enrolls at the university and also signs an apprenticeship or "co-op" contract with a company, thus obtaining employee status to be paid a wage.

Teaching methods in this field concentrate on the importance of a strong link between the practical and the theoretical by employing interactive pedagogical methods. Case studies, group practical projects, situational training, lessons from professional company personnel, organized events with high research and innovation content, study trips, and so forth are all part of the pedagogical teaching methods used in most of these SD courses. For example, in the Graduate Business Institute's

"Operational Management and Sustainable Performance" Master, about 50% of the teaching is based on situational training in practical contexts. In its "SD Strategy" course, the La Rochelle Sup de Co Group uses an interesting pedagogical formula known as "field missions." In these assignments, students work in groups of two or three on a project corresponding to a specific company requirement for 2 days a week over a 3-month period. This kind of apprenticeship or co-operative education method, using the project format, is also used in the "Company Social Responsibility Management" course run by the University of Paris XII (IAE Gustave Eiffel) where it is titled a "collective project". Students work in pairs on problem-focused projects chosen by organizations that are highly involved in the fields of SD (e.g., companies, consultants, rating agencies, unions, NGOs, etc.) They work on the project one day per week throughout the program. The students write a report on their collective project and present it to their fellow students.

To anchor courses in the practical realities of company life, teaching is carried out by a balanced mix of full-time professors, company professionals, and SD specialists. Company personnel are often experts on certain specialized problems such as environmental law, safety, ecological industrial design, risk management, waste management, and so forth.

Student Evaluation

The methods used to evaluate students' work on theoretical and practical work tend to rely more heavily on collective or individual projects and continuous evaluation than on more traditional methods like examinations. Evaluation of students' knowledge and skills linked to solving SD problems faced by companies is important for their grades. To guarantee an effective link between the theoretical knowledge students are taught and how it can be immediately transferred into the practical world is a critical component of student. They write a "professional thesis" which consists in a theoretical and empirical study of a subject which comes directly from the field and is linked with the job performed during the internship. Students are given close pedagogical support, benefiting from a double tutorship system. First, they have a company "mentor," usually the student's supervisor during the internship, whose role is to help the student work on collecting and analyzing data while making sure the work is useful for the company where the student works. The student also has a pedagogical tutor, a teacher from the school or university running the master's program. This tutor's role is to help the student choose a study theme linked to the SD questions worked with during the internship. The tutor also makes sure the student respects the quality standards expected in the course. The thesis topics in these courses are highly varied and are linked to very real questions for companies in the field of SD management. The topics range from solving problems posed by CO_2 pollution to socially responsible investments to fair trade and so on. Students write a thesis which they present to an examination panel which very often consists of a full-time professor and a company professional.

How Students are Selected

These SD masters degrees are available in full-time and continuing education format and are open to students and professionals with varied profiles. Their profiles show a wide range of academic backgrounds, such as engineering in different subfields, business law, economists, literature, politics, and so forth. Interdisciplinary and cross-disciplinary learning methods are essential in these degree programs. Certain master's programs require students to have professional experience for admission. For example, students applying to the "SD management" program run by the HEC in Paris need at least 3 years of professional experience in a field. The only exceptions to this rule are for students with an exceptional academic record and particularly relevant and interesting career objectives.

The student selection process for these SD masters varies from one school to another. In general, there are two stages to the selection of students. The first stage consists of the evaluation of the student's application file and/or sometimes management aptitude tests (e.g., TAGE-MAGE) and language tests (e.g., TOEFL, TOEIC). Candidates chosen from the first stage of selection are interviewed by a selection panel made of up both professors and company professionals. In this second stage, candidates' motivation is assessed as well as their own career objectives.

Career Opportunities

Career opportunities for students completing their course work in SD are quite varied. Company positions occupied by graduates of the programs described include: SD strategic manager, environmental, hygiene and safety manager, SD projects manager, ethical fund manager, SD auditor, eco-conception specialist, risk manager, compliance officer, ethical supervisor, economic intelligence expert, and company SD advisor.

Students coming from the research master's track tend to opt for careers like teacher-researcher and often move on toward doctoral studies based on a specific SD subject.

CONCLUSION

This chapter has presented the recent commitment to ESD in French higher education in the field of management. Important commitments to ESD by national and international political authorities paved the way for the growth of higher education courses covering the economic, environmental, and social aspects of SD. Business management establishments account for a significant part of the courses available at the master's level. These establishments are in both the public and private sectors. They offer SD courses involving a wide range of training to professional-level students and professionals. Training themes for most of these courses focus on strategic and operational SD management questions and economic matters in the field of SD. These courses teach know-how and skills which correspond to the growing needs of public and private organizations in the field. Teaching methods concentrate on a pragmatic approach to education with an emphasis on direct links with practical problems faced by companies. The teaching staff of these courses is increasingly varied and often involves SD professionals themselves. These training courses offer interesting opportunities for careers in key organizational posts linked to the environmental, economic, and ethical aspects of SD. Thus, France, as a European Union member country, has cut a unique and determined path in sustainable development higher education, focusing substantial governmental resources to that effect.

REFERENCES

Barthel, P., & Ivanaj, V. (2007, Special Issue). Is sustainable development in multinational enterprises a marketing issue? *The Multinational Business Review, 15,* 67–89.

Comité interministériel pour le développement durable. (2003). Stratégie Nationale du Développement Durable (SNDD). Ministère de l'Ecologie, de l'Energie, du Développement Durable et de l'Aménagement du Territoire. Retrieved September 30, 2008 from http://www.ecologie.gouv.fr/IMG/pdf/sndd-2.pdf

Conférence des Grandes Ecoles. (2003). *Charte de la conférence des grandes écoles pour le développement durable.* Retrieved September 30, 2008 from http://www.cge.asso.fr/presse/congres/Charte_DD_CGE_mai-2003.pdf

Conférence des Présidents d'Université. (2008). *Charte pour une « Alliance des universités françaises en faveur du développement durable ».* Retrieved September 30, 2008, from http://www.cpu.fr/fileadmin/fichiers/actu/Charte_DD_3_juillet_2008.pdf

Darcos, X. (2007). *Communiqué de presse sur le lancement du groupe de travail sur l'éducation au développement durable.* Retrieved September 30, 2008 from http://

www.education.gouv.fr/cid20635/lancement-du-groupe
-de-travail

De Robin, G. (2005). *Discours d'installation du comité national français de la décennie pour l'éducation en vue du développement durable.* Retrieved September 30, 2008 from http://www.education.gouv.fr/cid753/installation-du-comité-national...

De Robin, G. (2007). *Discours lors du séminaire villes et développement durables.* Retrieved September 30, 2008 from http://www.education.gouv.fr/cid4646/le-developpement-durable- a...

Durant, T., & Dameron, S. (2005). *Prospective 2015 des Etablissements de Gestion: Cinq scénarios pour agir. Etude Réalisée pour la Fondation Nationale pour l'Enseignement de la Gestion des Entreprises, Février 2005.* Retrieved September 30, 2008, from http://www.strategie-aims.com/angers05/TR/Prospective2015%20rapport%20VF%20210205.pdf

Groupe de travail Education au Développement Durable. (2008a). *Document d'orientation préliminaire. Ministère de l'Education Nationale.* Retrieved September 30, 2008 from http://media.education.gouv.fr/file/1501_developpement_durable/13/5/document_orientation_preliminaire_22135.pdf

Groupe de travail Education au Développement Durable (2008b). *Rapport du groupe de travail interministériel sur l'éducation au développement durable.* Ministère de l'Education Nationale. Retrieved September 30, 2008, from http://media.education.gouv.fr/file/2008/27/0/Strategie_pour_l_EDD_23270.pdf

Malherbe, D. (2006). *Initiation aux sciences de gestion : histoire, actualité, métiers et formations.* Parsis, France: Vuibert.

Ministère de l'Ecologie, de l'Energie, du Développement Durable et de l'Aménagement du Territoire. (2007). *Lancement du Grenelle Environnement. Dossier de presse du 6 juillet 2007.* Retrieved September 30, 2008 from http://www.legrenelle-environnement.gouv.fr/grenelle-environnement/IMG/pdf/Dossier_de_presse_grenelle.pdf.

Ministère de l'Education Nationale. (2003). *Éducation à l'environnement pour un développement durable* (E.E.D.D.) Retrieved September 30, 2008 from http://www.education.gouv.fr/cid205/education-a-l-environnement-pour-un-developpement-durable-e.d.d.html

Ministère de l'Education Nationale. (2004). *Instructions pédagogiques: Généralisation d'une éducation à l'environnement pour un développement durable(EEDD)—rentrée 2004.* Bulletin officiel n°28 du 15 juillet 2004—sommaire. Retrieved September 30, 2008, from http://www.education.gouv.fr/bo/2004/28/MENE0400752C.htm

Ministère de l'Education Nationale. (2007). *Education au développement durable : Seconde phase de généralisation de l'éducation au développement durable (EDD). Bulletin officiel n°14 du 5 avril 2007 - sommaire.* Retrieved September 30, 2008, from http://www.education.gouv.fr/bo/2007/14/MENE0700821C.htm.

Office national d'information sur les enseignements et les professions (Onicep). (2008). Retrieved September 30, 2008, from http://www.onisep.fr/.

Tremblay, P. (2007). L'éducation au développement durable (EDD). In L'école et la ville – Commission communautaire française (Ed.), *Education au développement durable: Quelques pistes de réflexion et d'action* (pp. 54–61). Patrick Debouverie, Bruxelles, Belgium. Retrieved September 30, 2008, from http://www.cocof.irisnet.be/site/fr/parasco/Files/EV2.pdf.

United Nations Economic Commission for Europe. (2005). *UNECE Strategy for Education for Sustainable Development.* Retrieved September 30, 2008 from http://www.unece.org/env/documents/2005/cep/ac.13/cep.ac.13.2005.3.rev.1.e.pdf.

United Nations Educational, Scientific and Cultural Organization (2004). *United Nations Decade of Education for Sustainable Development 2005–2014.* Draft International Implementation Scheme. Paris, France: UNESCO.

Wheeler, D., Horvath Dezso, D. H., & Victor, P. (1999). Graduate learning for business and sustainability. *Journal of Business Administration and Policy Analysis, 27–29,* 123–144.

World Commission on Environment and Development. (1987). *Our common future.* Oxford, England: Oxford University Press.

World Summit on Sustainable Development (2002). *Plan of implementation of the World Summit on Sustainable Development.* New York: United Nations.

CHAPTER 12

UNDERGRADUATE MANAGEMENT EDUCATION FOR SUSTAINABILITY

A Perspective From the Liberal Arts

Kirk R. Karwan, Robert L. Underwood, and Thomas I. Smythe

Furman University, a national liberal arts institution founded in 1826, first incorporated the concept of sustainability into the University's strategic mission as an overarching goal in 2004. Furman is pursuing its desire to become a national leader among liberal arts colleges in sustainability education and operation via university practices, curricula development, scientific research, public policy analysis, and community awareness. Specific initiatives have included the University's designation of a "Year of the Environment," the hiring of a full-time Director of Sustainability and Environmental Education, the development of an Environmental Studies concentration, the formation of an on-campus sustainable living community, environmentally-friendly landscaping and maintenance practices, the adoption of green building practices in all academic and residential facilities, and substantial efforts to increase faculty and student research addressing sustainability across disciplines.

The activities of the Business and Accounting Department parallel the sustainability initiatives of the greater university. Each of these activities is

Management Education for Global Sustainability, pp. 265–281

265

captured and highlighted in the department's curricula through planned activities and other interactions with faculty and students (from across the liberal arts) who are engaged in questions related to environmental steward-ship and social responsibility. This chapter details the Furman approach to the integration of sustainability concepts, management theories and prac-tices, and concepts from various liberal arts disciplines (e.g., history, philos-ophy, psychology, political science, and the sciences). Although this integrative framework capitalizes on the unique strengths of a liberal arts and smaller university, this approach may be equally applicable across all University environments. The chapter begins with an overview of Furman University's commitment to sustainability, followed by an examination of the integration of sustainability initiatives between the University and the Department of Business and Accounting. An in-depth look at the specific sustainability curricular and co-curricular programs of the Department of Business and Accounting is provided, and the chapter concludes with com-ments about the broad applicability of the Furman approach.

FURMAN'S COMMITMENT TO SUSTAINABILITY

The liberal arts environment affords a unique opportunity for educating future managers in the sustainability paradigm. Blaich, Bost, Chan, and Lyncy (2004) contrast the basic objective of liberal arts institutions with the objections of universities not steeped in the "liberal tradition." They note that liberal arts entities seek to establish an ethos and tradition that focuses more on the development of intellectual arts than on vocational or professional skills (Petkus, 2007). Winter, McClelland, and Stewart (1981) summarize the common goals of a liberal arts curriculum as the development and enhancement of the following abilities: critical think-ing; formation of abstract concepts; analytical skills; independent think-ing; appreciation of cultural experiences; leadership ability; the demonstration of mature and social judgment; and oral and written com-munication skills.

Most importantly, the liberal arts environment typically affords a broad curricular path to achieve these outcomes, including efforts designed to integrate learning across disciplines and enhance interaction between stu-dents and professors in and out of the classroom (Blaich et al., 2004; Pet-kus, 2007). This description is most certainly appropriate for Furman University, where opportunities for integration and interaction are facili-tated by a small student population (approximately 2,600 students) and general education requirements that transcend academic discipline, phi-losophy, and pedagogy. The general education courses offer all students a great breadth in curriculum, including a pair of first year seminars designed to foster careful thought and intense discussion; core requirements in body and mind, empirical studies, foreign language, human cultures, mathematical and formal reasoning, and ultimate questions; and global awareness offerings focusing on humans and their natural environment and world cultures (Furman University Catalog, 2008).

Since the initial incorporation of sustainability into the University's strategic mission, Furman has continued to grow in its commitment and desire to integrate the sustainability paradigm within all dimensions of university life. While not a comprehensive accounting of the University's commitment and strategy, the following overview presents a clear picture of much of it.

Governance and Administration

Furman president, Dr. David Shi, has been an instrumental force in the development of the American College and University Presidents Climate Commitment (ACUPCC). The mission of the ACUPCC is to gain commitments from Universities nationwide to neutralize greenhouse gas emissions and to accelerate educational and research efforts dedicated to assisting society in stabilizing the earth's climate (ACUPCC Web site). Dr. Shi is a charter signatory of ACUPCC and a current member of the ACUPCC steering committee.

In 2007, Furman formed a Sustainability Planning Group, composed of faculty, staff, administrators, and students, to develop a master plan to meet the expectations set forth by ACUPCC and chart a path for Furman to achieve carbon neutrality. After 1 year focusing primarily on the assessment of the university's carbon footprint and environmental impact, this group was reconstituted as the Sustainability Planning Council (SPC) to promote more rapid movement on holistic and meaningful sustainability initiatives on campus. The committee structure is now more "organic," with small task forces rapidly constituted and disbanded in an effort to support the Council's goals of moving the university forward in terms of facility, curricular, co-curricular, and awareness issues. See Figure 1.

In the summer of 2008, Furman hired Dr. Angela Halfacre, PhD, Political Science, as Director of Sustainability and Environmental Education to lead sustainability initiatives and coordinate the newly constructed Campus Sustainability Center. The creation of this office illustrates a tangible commitment to sustainability. The office is a central point of contact to energize and facilitate discussions, studies, and initiatives throughout the university. Dr. Halfacre is now also one of the co-chairs of the SPC and has taken on the key role of stimulating the university's sense of urgency in making headway toward its ACUPCC and related commitments.

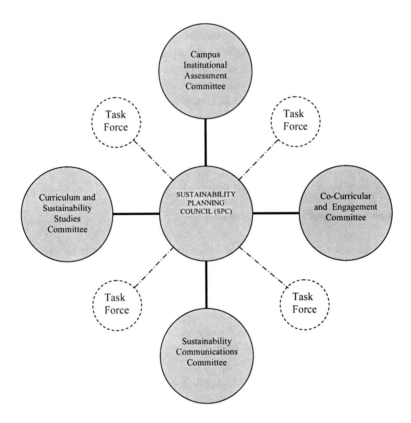

Figure 12.1.   Sustainability Master Planning Council—Organic Model.

Since 1997, Furman has worked extensively with the Associated Colleges of the South's Environmental Initiative (ACSEI). Utilizing student interns and Faculty Fellows, Furman has contributed on a regular basis by hosting and attending workshops and conferences supporting ACSEI alliances.

Operations

On June 14, 2008, the first environmentally sustainable Southern Living Showcase Home (The Cliffs Cottage) opened on the Furman University campus for public tour. The Cliffs Cottage is a cooperative effort between Southern Progress, Inc. (Southern Living Magazine), Furman University, the Cliffs Communities, Duke Energy, and Bank of America.

The Cliffs Cottage is designed as a model for sustainable home design and construction. Cutting edge features of the home include photovoltaic and solar thermal systems, a geothermal ground source heat pump, rainwater collection for irrigation, sustainable flooring and insulation methods, low VOC paints, and an organic vegetable garden. The home will serve for 1 year as a showcase attraction for builders and consumers interested in sustainable design; thereafter, the University will retrofit the home to serve as the office for the University's Center for Sustainability.

Among academic institutions in South Carolina, Furman University has taken a leadership role in sustainable energy-efficient design and with LEED practices for new construction and building renovations on campus. In 2003, Furman's Hipp Hall became the first LEED certified building on a university campus in South Carolina. Recently, the University's James B. Duke Library earned Gold LEED certification. It also received the 2006 Sustainable Design Award from the Carolinas Chapter of the International Interior Designers Association following a renovation and expansion completed in 2004. Completed in October 2008, the $63 million Charles H. Townes Center for Science was designed to be a "living building and laboratory" featuring solar thermal panels, rainwater collection, and a solar aquatic treatment facility. The University's trustee policy requires all new and renovated buildings to meet LEED construction standards, and the University leads the state of South Carolina in the number of LEED-certified buildings.

The development and expansion of the University's Eco-Cottages also directly impacts Furman students by involving them in the operational aspects of sustainable living. The Eco-Cottages are eco-friendly on-campus housing units that feature solar tubes and geothermal systems. They housed 28 students for the 2008–2009 academic year. Originally referred to as the Village Green and now part of a larger Eco Village, the cottages clearly illustrate and promote a model of environmental residential responsibility.

Additional operational examples of sustainability at Furman include: the restoration of the campus lake to a more natural, healthy environment; increased sourcing of food products from local farmers by University Dining Hall services, and a campus-wide energy conservation program incorporating all University buildings and computing and information services.

Curriculum and Research

Beginning with the fall 2008 semester, all Furman students were required to take two courses in the area of "Global Awareness," one of which will focus on the relationship between "Humans and the Natural Environment." This class marks an important step in the evolution of Furman's curriculum in terms of sustainability. With this requirement, Furman recognizes three major principles:

- Human cultures exist and evolve within an environmental context;
- Students' understanding of how the world operates as an environmental system supporting life is critical to human development;
- Environmental issues have a moral dimension that require students to evaluate how human behaviors and patterns of resource use and waste production directly and indirectly affect the people and organisms on the planet.

Thirty-four courses were offered in the environmental studies major/concentration in 2007–2008, and nine departments in the natural sciences, social sciences, and humanities now contribute to a Concentration in Environmental Studies. The Chemistry department has added a certified track in Environmental Chemistry, as well as new courses to the curriculum such as Environmental Ethics.

Environmental research by faculty and students is growing rapidly. The River Basins Research Initiative, a project piloted by the Earth and Environmental Sciences Department, is supported by nearly $2 million in grants from the Associated Colleges of the South, the Environmental Protection Agency, NASA, the National Science Foundation, the Rockefeller Brothers Foundation, the Saluda-Reedy Watershed consortium, and the South Carolina Department of Health and Environmental Control (DHEC). Beginning in 1997, this research program has involved as many as eleven faculty from seven departments across the University. Over 140 students have conducted research on the effect of land use on water quality in major upstate river systems. This project is the largest single research initiative in Furman's history, providing undergraduate students with an unparalleled interdisciplinary research experience in the environmental aspects of sustainability.

Additional curriculum and research examples include the development of student environmental fellowships, a formal research partnership with The Nature Conservancy, and a $100,000 Bank of America gift to establish an Environmental Fellows program.

Campus Culture

Creating a student culture and expectation of sustainable-related interests and behaviors is a critical dimension of Furman's sustainability strategy. The organic garden associated with the Cliffs Cottage illustrates one such student led activity. Managed by students and the sustainability coordinator, the garden is an outdoor classroom where students, faculty, and staff learn about small-scale food production, sustainable agriculture, and food systems.

The Environmental Community of Students (ECOS) residential living program recently completed a successful second year of operation. Students who have expressed strong interest in the environment live together in a residential dorm and perform three hours of environmental community service each week. Additionally, students have the opportunity to sign Eco-Pledge and Senior Green Graduation Pledges wherein they agree to lead a green lifestyle while on campus and beyond graduation. Students who sign the pledge receive monthly green tips via e-mail.

Additional examples of sustainability initiatives becoming part of campus culture include: the Kill A Watt challenge, an energy saving competition among upper class dorms; the completion of an online student "Green Guide to Sustainable Living;" the sale of reusable organic cotton grocery bags to faculty, staff, and students; an educational food waste program; and an extremely active student organization known as the Environmental Action Group (EAG).

Community Outreach

Furman collaborates on sustainability issues with community stakeholders in multiple ways. A grassroots effort to convert the abandoned "Swamp Rabbit" rail line in Greenville, South Carolina into a trail for hikers, runners, and cyclists is one such example. With nearly 2 miles running through the Furman campus, the 13-mile railroad line extends from downtown Greenville to Traveler's Rest, South Carolina. Additionally, Furman is a project partner in the Saluda-Reedy Watershed Consortium, a group of organizations and individuals concerned with the impact of development and changing land use on waterways and lakes in the Saluda-Reedy River basin. Finally, Furman University President David Shi is chair of Greenville's Vision 2025, a visionary process designed to create a sustainable Greenville by the year 2025, when the city's population is estimated to reach 1.3 million.

LINKS BETWEEN THE UNIVERSITY AND THE DEPARTMENT OF BUSINESS AND ACCOUNTING

The discussion above highlighted Furman's broad strategic commitment to sustainability and the significant operational steps the University has taken to demonstrate that commitment. The remainder of this chapter focuses on how, without a stand-alone business or management school, a liberal arts institution can provide a rich environment for students and faculty to study and synthesize management theories and the practical sustainability issues confronting today's corporations.

Almost all undergraduate liberal arts institutions that teach business or management classes do so through their economics departments. Furman is one of a handful of liberal arts colleges and universities that houses a separate academic unit for business or management. Formally separated from the Economics Department in 2004, the Business and Accounting Department (BAC) offers two distinct Bachelor of Arts degrees, one in business administration and one in accounting. The department is a member of AACSB-International and BAC faculty attend and monitor programs promoted by this and other accrediting organizations.

One of the advantages of the BAC at Furman relative to business schools, and especially those accredited by AACSB, is flexibility. Although almost all faculty members in the department have previously taught at well-known, accredited business schools, the department subscribes to the philosophy of liberal education and actively encourages students to integrate ideas from the humanities, sciences, history, social sciences, and other disciplines into classroom discussions and analysis of business situations. Equally important, BAC faculty seek to reciprocate by demonstrating, where appropriate, how ideas in business and accounting are relevant to a liberal education, especially with regard to critical thinking and innovation. In so doing, BAC faculty are not as rigorously bound by management discipline to impart certain amounts or types of material, but instead have the freedom to expound and focus on topics of long-lasting relevance such as sustainability, globalization, and so forth. This flexibility has enabled BAC to move rapidly in bringing the university's strategic sustainability initiative into department goals and activities and to be active participants in university-wide sustainability initiatives.

The department's role in sustainability initiatives evolved from the university's strategic planning efforts during the 2003-2004 academic year when sustainability (specifically, environmental issues related to sustainability) became a core component of the university's long-term strategy. As part of the strategic planning review process, a sub-group of the university's Strategic Planning Committee was formed specifically to address sustainability as a core strategic goal for the university. The sub-group's composition represented a broad array of university constituencies, many of which would be expected: facilities services, academic departments relating specifically to environmental sustainability, purchasing, and others. However, the sub-group members also included a faculty representative from BAC. The representation of BAC on the sub-group began a pattern of inclusion that continues today in the university's sustainability initiatives.

Inclusion in the sustainability sub-group was the first time a business faculty member had been part of discussions related to the university's sustainability efforts. Initially, the reason for including a BAC member on the committee was to bring a sense of financial pragmatism and fiduciary understanding to the group as it addressed financial costs and benefits associated with sustainability programs. As the group worked throughout the 2003-2004 academic year, other group members and the BAC faculty representative began to appreciate what each brought to the discussions, with the end result being a better product for the sub-group and the beginnings of the sustainability concept's absorption into BAC's departmental planning.

Since the 2003–2004 academic year, BAC has been a regular partner in university-wide sustainability initiatives. For a number of years, Furman has developed annual themes around which to center university activities for the academic year. The 2006–2007 academic year theme was the Year of the Environment. Activities from seminars to highlighted research to outside speakers focused on environmental and sustainability issues and their significance in liberal education. On the surface, it might seem unusual for a member of BAC to be a part of the organizing committee for the year's theme, but one was included. In fact, this faculty member launched the start of the year and introduced its theme to the local community by writing an editorial in the local newspaper. Many of the activities sponsored by the organizing committee were intended to engage the broader community and the editorial provided a kick-off for the year's events. Additionally, the department's representation on the organizing committee provided an impetus for the department to broaden its initiatives in this area. One area where this goal has been realized is the inclusion of speakers in the BAC department's Executive Lecture Series to address issues of sustainability.

During the 2007–2008 academic year, the department's involvement with the university's sustainability initiatives continued to grow. At the university level, as noted earlier, Dr. Shi appointed a Sustainability Planning Group (SPG) whose mission was to "chart a path for Furman to achieve carbon neutrality." As with the organizing committee for the Year of the Environment and the Sustainability sub-group of the Strategic Planning Committee, a member of BAC was included on this committee, and a second BAC member was added to the group when it was reconstituted as the SPC. One of the contributions of these faculty members involved raising and exploring the question of how "sustainability" should be defined. Until

2007, Furman had largely used the terms sustainability and environment interchangeably. With the encouragement of BAC's representatives, an enhanced definition is beginning to emerge that more closely resembles the *triple bottom line* familiar to many business organizations.

Another effort, with which the department was intimately involved, arose at the university level during the 2007–2008 year. The university has ties with a local developer of high end residential communities who also has an ecological resort in southern Chile. The resort is located in an area where the population is largely rural poor, employed in fishing and agriculture, and with limited sources of income. A large amount of the area's land is being cleared for farming and the fishing techniques are leading to a reduction in the quantity and average size of the predominant product, abalone. The university and the developer sponsored a trip to the region where approximately 15 faculty representatives from Furman met with members of the local community, political representatives at the local and national levels, and members of the scientific community to explore the possibilities of helping the region develop in a more sustainable manner. Two of the Furman team members were from BAC and another from the university's economics department. As illustrated by these latter efforts, the university has recognized the important role that BAC has in furthering the university's strategic goal of sustainability, more broadly defined to involve both environmental issues and social responsibility initiatives.

One last effort by the department, in place now for 5 years, and only now being seen as part of the social justice aspect of the university's sustainability efforts, is its involvement with the Volunteer Income Tax Assistance (VITA) program. This nationwide effort, is sponsored by the IRS and administered in Greenville, South Carolina by a member of the BAC's accounting faculty. The program provides free tax preparation and electronic filing for low-income members of the local community, and is staffed by volunteers, many of which are students from BAC. In 2008, the program assisted over 600 low-income local residents.

In summary, the Department of Business and Accounting at Furman has become an integral part of the university's sustainability efforts primarily through its representation on university level committees that address sustainability. Significantly, the broader university community has begun to appreciate how its academic management component is having a positive impact on these initiatives, in both the practical implementation stages and in helping to broaden the definition of sustainability on campus in ways that allow an increasing number of faculty, students, and departments to become involved.

DEPARTMENTAL AND PROGRAMMATIC INITIATIVES

While universities across the country report the presence of active stu-dent-led environmental organizations, they have simultaneously observed a lack of awareness of sustainability issues and even a resistance to sustain-ability concepts from the general student population. This "paradox" was most recently evidenced in sessions at the 2008 AASHE (Association for the Advancement of Sustainability in Higher Education) meeting in Raleigh, North Carolina. Furman is no exception; a large number of its students' lives have been relatively unaffected by the economic, political, and social realities linked to sustainability issues, and many of those stu-dents evidence very little awareness of those issues.

As a result, and despite involvement of individual student and faculty with the array of campus activities related to sustainability, the primary role of Furman's Business and Accounting department in this arena has been in the development of pedagogy and engagement mechanisms that bring awareness to students. The fact that faculty across the business disci-plines have embraced the sustainability paradigm is quickly diffusing any built-in cynicism that business, accounting, and other students have had about sustainability. In fact, when faculty talk about the need for today's organizations to ask questions about new "business models" that explicitly and realistically define the role of the corporation in terms of economy, environment, and social responsibility, our experience shows that students tend to sense that they will play an important role in defining these mod-els of the future.

Using an "organic" model akin to that of the Sustainability Planning Council (Figure 12.1), the department has developed an approach to infuse sustainability concepts throughout the curriculum, in engaged learning activities, and into our everyday thinking. This approach is rep-resented schematically in Figure 12.2.

Like other groups before us, in developing our approach we were first confronted with the need to reach some consensus on the definition of the term sustainability. Although Furman University, as detailed above, had taken a tack that initially defined this strategic objective primarily in terms of the environment, we opted in Business and Accounting to pro-mote a definition that more-broadly recognizes the "triple bottom line." Our rationale was fairly straightforward: at this point in time, it is appar-ent that leading business organizations and think tanks are taking a broad perspective, which recognizes societal obligations in terms of environ-mental stewardship, social justice, and corporate social responsibility. We cite, for example, the very powerful and compelling discussions in Hart (2007) and Grayson et al. (2008).

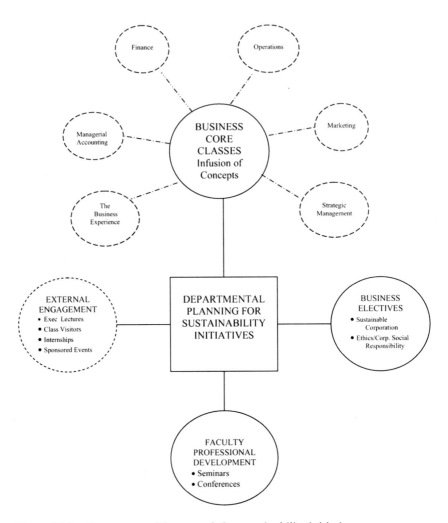

Figure 12.2.   Departmental framework for sustainability initiatives.

As shown in Figure 12.2, BAC's approach has been to develop specialty or focused business classes to address both the environmental and social aspects of the triple bottom line and to simultaneously encourage the inclusion of aspects from both into core classes taught by departmental faculty (i.e., finance, managerial accounting, marketing, operations, and strategic management). In terms of "focused" coursework, the department is now teaching classes entitled "The Sustainable Corporation" and "Ethics and Corporate Social Responsibility."

The first of these topical courses presents the "business case" for an organization to consider environmental and social goals along with their financial objectives, and in doing so to place primary focus on environmental issues. Students read "classic" eco-business books such as Hawken, Lovins, and Lovins' *Natural Capitalism* (2008) and industrialist Ray Anderson's *Mid-Course Correction* (1998), as well as more recent writings by management professors (e.g., Stuart Hart's *Capitalism at the Crossroads: Aligning Business, Earth, and Humanity*, 2007). The intent of the course is to have students wrestle with the question of whether or not a "refined" version of capitalism is possible, and whether or not (and how) business organizations can actually sustain themselves using a triple bottom line.

In the second course, students first engage ethical issues and develop frameworks for ethical thinking, and then study texts and cases written by management academicians, for example, Hartman and DesJardins' *Business Ethics: Decision Making for Personal Integrity and Social Responsibility* (2008). The intent of this course is to have participants grapple with the growing sentiment that corporations should (or will be mandated to) have explicitly stated social goals.

In true liberal arts fashion, these two elective classes have been designed so that they are open to university students with a minimum of prerequisites. As a result, classrooms are populated with students representing a broad array of majors, promoting an interesting breadth of perspectives that are so important to a meaningful discussion of sustainability.

Figure 12.2 also highlights how the basic core curriculum is being modified by conscious incorporation of relevant sustainability concepts into each of the business discipline-based courses. Although the precise level of material is left up to individual faculty members, Furman business and accounting professors have embraced the opportunity to highlight relevant materials from current textbooks and to complement these with readings and projects that raise triple bottom line issues. For example, in the core marketing management class, the professor requires a "strategic analysis group project," in which each team has the task of developing a "green" product for a current publicly held firm. Examples of these "potential green products" include: Coleman developing coolers that utilize solar power; Gerber developing an organic line of children's snack food; Hewlett Packard creating a solar-powered laptop; Levi's manufacturing jeans from bamboo; and Mercury Marine building hybrid boat engines.

Figure 12.2 also depicts one other component of the core curriculum, a capstone "Business Experience" that is being finalized and will require students to incorporate sustainability into a strategic planning exercise and/or new product development plan from concept development to product recapture. In this course, students will again work with an existing firm, and be responsible to a board of directors representing a local or regional corporation.

While the university has recently introduced Freshman Seminars into the core curriculum and encouraged each department on campus to develop these, Business and Accounting is developing its new offerings to focus on the sustainability paradigm. Although freshmen are often ill-equipped to discuss complex business cases, interesting seminars dealing with the Ecology of Business, Ethics and Management Responsibility, and Global Sustainable Business are being considered.

The Department's approach to sustainability engages the larger community in other ways. Classroom activities are enhanced through student and faculty engagement with business leaders and organizations. Major firms such as BMW, Caterpillar, Interface, and Milliken have visited Furman regularly to share their expertise and practices concerning global sustainability. The Furman Executive Lecture Series, although not entirely focused on these issues, sponsors one or two corporate speakers each year to address triple bottom line questions. For example, the series recently hosted the global sustainability director from one Fortune 50 company and the former CEO of another. The former CEO has now moved on to direct a foundation devoted to social and community issues. While also delivering public addresses, visitors are encouraged to spend most of their day(s) on campus, engaging smaller student groups in discussion of a variety of management topics.

An important part of the Furman experience is the management internship. Students are encouraged to enhance their résumés and learning with "significant" work experiences, paid or unpaid, while they are completing their university requirements. The department offers academic credit for many of these with a faculty member monitoring the experience and supplementing learning with a customized set of readings related to the specific internship. Working with the university's Director of Internships, BAC is placing an increasing number of business and accounting students in positions that allow them to apply concepts or learn more about corporate sustainability. Two recent assignments were particularly interesting. One business student, working as an intern for a global public relations firm in Europe, was invited to be part of the firm's team to develop a strategic plan for a large client *specifically* because she had working knowledge of the sustainability paradigm from her Furman training. In another case, a student intern with knowledge of business sustainability issues was instrumental in writing the first sustainability strategic plan for the subsidiary of a well-known and influential corporation.

The department is also proactively making an effort to organize or co-sponsor special organizations and events that relate to environmental and social issues. As mentioned earlier, one departmental faculty member directs the Volunteers for Income Tax Assistance (VITA) program. Another effort is being contemplated to promote student awareness of micro-lending practices and practicalities, with a May Experience (3-week) course revolving around these issues. The Furman Entrepreneurs (a student organization founded and directed by business and accounting students) recently sponsored an elevator pitch contest where all university students were invited to make presentations on how students could best contribute to energy savings initiatives on campus. A panel of judges that included the university's provost, the director of sustainability, and the founder of a regional alternative energy company served as the judges. Cash awards were made for the best ideas.

Although student awareness and engagement is currently BAC's primary goal, faculty involvement and buy-in is paramount in achieving that goal. Faculty members are encouraged to attend conferences that deal with sustainability issues, both within their specific fields and across disciplinary lines. One faculty member recently delivered a presentation about environmental accounting issues at a conference attended by some of the world's academic leaders in accounting. Others have attended both AACSB and AASHE meetings to learn about other universities' approaches, successes, and failures.

OBSERVATIONS AND CONCLUSIONS

With its emphasis on sustainability, Furman's approach to liberal arts-based management education at the undergraduate level may be unique. It is necessarily more broad-based than the sustainability education provided by most business schools. Although our basic curriculum is quite similar to that at any AACSB institution (i.e., with requirements in economics, statistics, accounting, marketing, operations, finance, and strategic management), our focus on broader issues ensures that students are trained in the "liberal tradition." Given the university's strategic goals of "advancing environmental sustainability" and "serving the greater community," it is natural for almost all university programs and initiatives to be oriented toward the development of well-rounded graduates with both depth and breadth of judgment.

On the other hand, the integrated approach described in this paper is readily replicable. Other than the will to do so, there is nothing preventing other liberal arts and/or business schools from moving down the same path. Although it is too early to make this statement in a definitive fashion, it is our opinion that the AACSB may need to take a lead in ensuring that sustainability issues are infused more broadly in management programs. The organization has already sponsored conferences on the issues, but may need to find a more aggressive mechanism as business schools confront the problems of implementation.

BAC's approach in this arena is similar to the approach most business schools followed as they infused international issues into management programs. Most proactive schools that have developed a strong international focus have done so by first developing specialty classes and/or majors. Then they infused concepts throughout the broader management curricula and expanded experiential activities for students (e.g., foreign study and internship/career opportunities). Textbooks in all management disciplines now introduce international and global issues in the first chapter. The same is likely to occur for sustainability topics in an even shorter period of time, making it easier for schools to ensure awareness and stimulate conversation among students and faculty.

Perhaps the most important advice we can offer from our experiences at Furman is that a purposeful approach to sustainability needs to be both integrative and cooperative. At this point, there is still too much opportunity for ignorance, skepticism, and inertia on the part of both faculty and students to impede curricular, co-curricular, and idea development (research) in sustainability. Efforts to educate both faculty and students are required, but the best approach is to involve all willing participants in a comprehensive and cooperative (rather than coercive) fashion. Business leaders, often accused of creating environmental and social problems, point out that they have never met one of their own who really wanted to poison the environment or do harm to neighbors or fellow citizens. Students and faculty members can generally say the same about their own peers. The problem, at this point, is that we are all still learning about the issues, opportunities, and realities. Like business leaders, students and faculty are most effective when they develop their own thinking, approaches, and solutions to the very real issues presented by the sustainability paradigm.

REFERENCES

Anderson, R. (1998). *Mid-course correction*. Atlanta, GA: Peregrinzilla Press.
Blaich, C., Bost, A., Chan, E., & Lynch, R. (2004). *Defining liberal arts education*, Center of Inquiry in the Liberal Arts. Crawfordsville, IN: Wabash College. Retrieved May 19, 2009, from http://www.liberalarts.wabash.edu
Furman University Catalog. (2008). Greenville, SC: Vol. LV/No. 1
Grayson, D., Lemon, M., Slaughter, S., Rodriquez, M., Jin, Z., & Tay, S. (2008). *A new mindset for corporate sustainability* (White Paper). British Telecommunications PLC and Cisco Systems. Retrieved May 19, 2009, http://www.biggerthinking.com

Hart, S. (2007). *Capitalism at the crossroads: Aligning business, earth and humanity* (2nd ed.). Upper Saddle River, NJ: Wharton School,

Hartman L., & DesJardin, J. (2008). *Business ethics: Decision making for personal integrity and social responsibility.* Boston: McGraw Hill.

Hawken P., Lovins, A., & Lovins, L. (2008). *Natural capitalism.* Snowmass, CO: Rocky Mountain Institute.

Petkus, E. (2007). Enhancing the relevance and value of marketing curriculum outcomes to a liberal arts education. *Journal of Marketing Education, 29*(1), 39–51.

Winter, D., McClelland, D., & Stewart, A. (1981). *A new case for the liberal arts.* San Francisco: Jossey-Bass.

PART III

INSTITUTIONAL AND PROGRAM LEVEL INNOVATIONS IN MANAGEMENT EDUCATION FOR GLOBAL SUSTAINABILITY

CHAPTER 13

INVESTING IN
A SUSTAINABLE FUTURE

Mark White and Edeltraud Günther

This chapter illustrates one approach to teaching sustainability in business schools by describing the rationale and structure used to develop and deliver our course, "Investing in a Sustainable Future," a cross-disciplinary, cross-cultural and collaborative learning experience providing participants the opportunity to identify, evaluate and apply innovative business-based solutions to environmental and social problems. In this course, upper-level students from the United States and Germany learn about the many challenges associated with the transition to a sustainable society, and work together in multidisciplinary teams to analyze real-world investment projects meeting rigorous standards for sustainability, strategic fit, financial performance, and business practicality.

This capstone class provides participants with the opportunity to integrate and apply knowledge acquired in their earlier coursework and work experiences towards the solution of an important real-world problem, i.e., the creation of value within the dynamic of increasing resource demand and decreasing resource availability. The deliberate use of an integrated and active learning pedagogy, coupled with a real-world sustainable investment project, provides a unique opportunity for students to learn more about ways of mitigating humanity's impact on the planet. Instructors wishing to

Management Education for Global Sustainability, pp. 285–304
Copyright © 2009 by Information Age Publishing
All rights of reproduction in any form reserved.

offer similar courses should find the experiences, assignments, and exercises described in this chapter helpful in designing their own curricula.

INTRODUCTION

"Has anyone ever seen one of these before?," the instructor asks, as a picture of an unfamiliar installation appears on the screen (Figure 13.1).

"It's a marine turbine," he continues, "a promising technology for generating electricity from the movement of ocean currents. We'd like you to quickly form groups of three or four persons and discuss the following questions:

1.   What do you think about this technology's potential for creating a sustainable future?

Source: Marine Current Turbines Limited (www.marineturbines.com). Reproduced with permission.

Figure 13.1.   Marine Current Turbine.

2. What questions or issues would you like to have answered before making a recommendation to implement such an installation off the Virginia coast?"

These are the first words students hear in our course, "Investing in a Sustainable Future," a collaborative, cross-disciplinary, cross-cultural course emphasizing experiential learning and business problem-solving. After 10 minutes have passed, we ask the groups to share their thoughts with the larger class, writing them on the board as they're offered. The following responses are typical of those we've received to these questions.

(a) What impact do these turbines have on marine life? Will fish get chopped up into sushi as they swim through the blades? Do they exert any harmful effects on the sea floor?
(b) What happens during a storm? Can they withstand high winds?
(c) How does one service a marine turbine? Will any harmful substances be released into the surrounding waters?
(d) How far offshore will the turbines be? How is the electricity transmitted back to the land? It seems like it would take a really long extension cord!
(e) Who would own and install them? Are we talking about a private company, or the government?
(f) How much does a turbine cost? How much energy is it expected to generate? How many years will it be before an investor recoups his money?
(g) Does the amount of energy a turbine will generate during its lifetime offset the energy used in its construction? From a life cycle point of view, is this project energy-positive? By how much?
(h) How do marine turbines compare with other forms of alternative energy, e.g., tidal power? How far away is it practical to transmit the electricity? What's the service area?
(i) Won't a series of these marine turbines interfere with shipping? What happens if a boat runs into one? What about submarines?
(j) Who owns the land underneath the turbines?

After each group has offered its contributions, we note how their concerns seem to fall into four main categories—(1) *Sustainability* concerns (a, c, g, h), (2) *Strategic* concerns (e, h), (3) *Financial* concerns (f, h) and (4) *Practical* concerns (b, d, h, i)—and then observe that these are the *exact* issues we'll be dealing with in the course! In fact, as will be described later in this paper, these four concerns form a set of ordered criteria against which one might evaluate investment projects appropriate for a sustainable future—the title of the course!

By posing a set of questions and soliciting feedback about this intriguing and novel technology, we have been able to immediately engage students in the process of *thinking about the future*—the sole characteristic that distinguishes us from animals, according to psychologist Dan Gilbert (2006). The fact that the decision framework we'll be using arises out of their own contributions provides an immediate sense of ownership and understanding, which we're able to exploit as we move through the course.

"Investing in a Sustainable Future" was designed as a capstone class for upper-level students from multiple disciplines. Recent enrollments have included students from business, engineering, architecture, urban planning, environmental sciences, and the humanities. We assume participants have already acquired substantial formal training in their respective fields of study and are eager to apply this knowledge to the problems of sustainability. Our objectives are (1) to communicate structures for examining the challenges associated with achieving a sustainable society, (2) to equip students with tools necessary for making wise decisions, and (3) to provide a forum for application and experimentation. The overall course structure—"Identify—Evaluate—Apply"—mimics these goals while providing a handy framework for future problem solving.

STUDENT-CENTERED LEARNING

In designing this course, which emphasizes hands-on, experiential learning, we were heavily influenced by Postman and Weingartner's (1969) classic text, *Teaching as a Subversive Activity* and Dee Fink's (2003) *Creating Significant Learning Experiences*. Both of these books advocate a student-centered form of education known as the *inquiry method*, which we find particularly compelling for the teaching of sustainability.

Among other things, Postman and Weingartner suggest that *good* learners

- are self-confident with respect to their learning ability
- take pleasure in solving problems
- have a keen sense of relevance
- rely on their own judgment over that of other people or society
- have respect for facts, and are able to distinguish between facts and opinion
- do not need final answers to all questions, but take comfort in not knowing an answer to a difficult question, rather than settling for a simplistic answer

Although most educators would agree with this list of characteristics, *Teaching as a Subversive Activity* antagonized more than a few persons in the educational community when it was first published by arguing for the abolition of most textbooks; the dissolution of all subjects and course requirements; required cross-disciplinary teaching, and a prohibition on teachers "asking any questions they already know the answer to." Postman and Weingartner (1969) exhorted their readers to focus on the teaching *process* rather than the teaching *product* (predetermined curriculum and test scores). According to the authors, a good teacher

- rarely tells students what he/she thinks
- poses a problem for students
- allows lessons to develop from the responses of students, and not from a predefined "logical" structure
- generally does not accept a single statement as an answer to a question
- encourages student-student interaction vs. student-teacher interaction
- •rarely summarizes the positions taken by students, recognizing that the act of summary or closure tends to have the effect of ending further thought

Today more than ever, we believe it is necessary to emphasize course design over course content. Partly as a result of U.S. educational policies emphasizing achievement on standardized tests and exams, many students arrive at a university master's of rote learning, but woefully lacking in higher-order reasoning skills. Further, the advent of the Internet and the concomitant explosion in information availability calls into question the very meaning of foundational knowledge. The noted English literary critic, Samuel Johnson, once remarked, "Knowledge is of two kinds. We know a subject ourselves, or we know where we can find information upon it." Why memorize facts and figures when they're just a Google away? Finally, for whatever reason—perhaps because of so much time spent socializing, watching television, playing video games, e-mailing, IM-ing, text-messaging, and so forth—there appears to be a fundamental change in the way current students are responding to traditional classroom experiences, as exemplified by Figure 13.2 (next page).

If Figure 13.2 is an accurate reflection of how well students retain information under different learning circumstances, then clearly, our teaching techniques need to change. Professors can no longer afford to be "the sage on the stage" if they wish their students to understand and remember course material—much less actually apply their new knowledge!

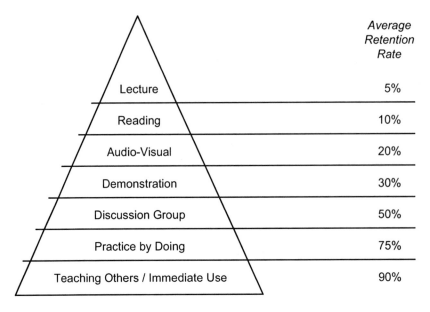

	Average Retention Rate
Lecture	5%
Reading	10%
Audio-Visual	20%
Demonstration	30%
Discussion Group	50%
Practice by Doing	75%
Teaching Others / Immediate Use	90%

Source: National Training Laboratories, Bethel, ME. www.ntl.org, as cited in Farley, Erickson and Daly, *Ecological Economics: A Workbook for Problem Based Learning* (Farley et al., 2005). Reproduced with permission.

Figure 13.2.   Retention rates for different learning media.

Therefore, we designed our course to be as experiential as possible. In doing so, we actively addressed and incorporated the six different kinds of learning in *Creating Significant Learning Experiences* (Fink, 2003).

SIGNIFICANT LEARNING

Building on the insights of Bloom (1956), Postman and Weingartner (1969), and many other modern pedagogical scholars, Dee Fink (2003), a professor and instructional consultant at the University of Oklahoma, proposed a taxonomy of significant learning (Figure 13.3).

Foundational knowledge, or "understand and remember" knowledge, provides the basic understanding necessary for other kinds of learning. *Application*—skill development, along with critical, creative, and practical thinking—allows other kinds of learning to become useful. *Integration* occurs when students see and understand connections between different ideas. It provides learners with a new kind of intellectual power. The *human dimension* of learning refers to better knowledge about oneself and

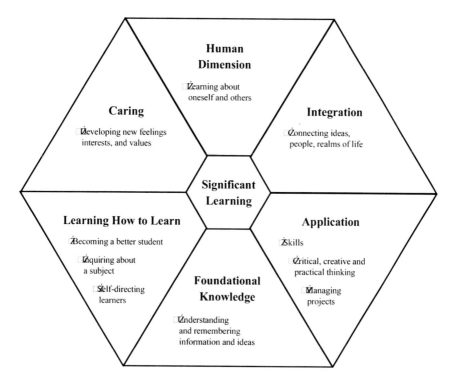

Adapted from Fink, *Creating Significant Learning Experiences* (2003). Reproduced with permission.

Figure 13.3.   A taxonomy of significant learning.

others, allowing for improved personal interactions. *Caring* is reflected in the development of new feelings, interests or values. Fink notes that when we care about something, we gain energy for learning more about it and making it a part of our lives. Finally, many of us wish our students would become life-long learners. To do so, it is important to provide opportunities for them to *learn how to learn*, that is, to become more self-directed and effective learners.

Fink (2003) defines learning in terms of change. *Significant learning* requires that there be some kind of enduring change in the learner's life. Further, the six categories of significant learning shown in Figure 13.3 *reinforce one another* to bring about lasting change in student abilities and attitudes. He notes,

each kind of learning is related to the other kinds of learning and ... achieving any one kind of learning simultaneously enhances the possibility of achieving the other kinds of learning as well. This interrelation matters to teachers because it means the various kinds of learning are synergistic. And this in turn means that teaching is no longer a zero-sum game. That is, teachers don't automatically have to give up one kind of learning to achieve another. Instead, when a teacher finds a way to help students achieve one kind of learning, this can in fact enhance, not decrease, student achievement in the other kinds of learning. (p. 32)

Building on this notion of synergistic learning, and with an intuitive sense of systems dynamics, Fink argues that of the four major components of teaching—knowledge of subject matter, teacher-student interactions, course management, and course design, the latter has the greatest potential for effecting significant learning. The majority of his book, which we enthusiastically recommend to readers of this chapter, describes how to design an effective, learning-centered course by integrating learning goals with teaching/learning activities and feedback/ assessment practices. We have taught this course several times, and it is apparent to us that this approach has resulted in substantially greater student engagement with the material, and, we believe, greater learning overall.

SAMPLE CLASSROOM EXERCISES

In preparing our course, we have experimented with a wide variety of hands-on learning techniques including classroom games, economics simulations, case studies, role plays, student debates, poster sessions, book reports, guest speakers, field trips, reflective essays, consumption journals, etc. A generous gift from the Procter & Gamble Foundation has allowed us to explore a much broader selection of pedagogical ideas and activities than would otherwise have been the case. For example, although we now offer simultaneous sections of the course in our respective universities using IP-based videoconferencing technology, the grant made it possible for us to team-teach the course's first offering together in the same geographic location.

In the spirit of assisting faculty developing their own experiential learning-based curriculum for teaching sustainability, we offer descriptions of four exercises and a set of classroom demonstrations which we have used with success in our classes. The course's ultimate work product —the Sustainable Investment Project (SIP)—is described in the final section of this chapter.

Sustainable University Calendar

A recurring theme in our course, and many others dealing with the topic of sustainability, is that we are essentially living in a full world. We frequently find ourselves drawing a rudimentary "funnel graph" from *The Natural Step* on the board, with an upward-sloping line representing the growth in consumption and resource demand by the world's teeming billions, and a downward-sloping line depicting diminishing supplies of natural resources and the ability to absorb wastes (The Natural Step, n.d.). As time passes, the two lines approach one another to create a funnel shape, indicating a diminishing margin for action.

A key objective of our early class meetings was to raise awareness regarding the many challenges facing humanity and the planet, but we were loathe to lecture on these topics (as doing so could easily last the remainder of the course!). Rather, we assigned a few seminal readings, including a summary of the Millennium Ecosystem Assessment (2005) and then asked students to create a poster for a "Sustainable University Calendar," informing members of the academic community about these issues, and ways in which they might change their own personal behaviors to live more lightly on the planet. We displayed the results on the classroom's walls at our next meeting and asked participants to walk around and examine the posters, and to indicate the best three submissions for inclusion in the hypothetical calendar using Post-It notes. After they all made their selections, we tallied the votes and then had a discussion about why certain posters were selected and others were not, along with suggestions for topics we thought had been overlooked. The exercise was a tremendous success—students were exposed to a tremendous number of sustainability-related topics (water use, soil erosion, income disparity, global warming, etc.) in a relatively short time and were quite proud to explain their concerns and work to their peers. In our highly-competitive academic environment, the fact that the posters were of varying quality also proved beneficial in establishing high standards toward which the majority of students worked during the rest of the course.

Food for Thought

To highlight the problem of limited resources and the unequal distribution of world populations and consumption, we used an exercise developed by Population Connection (2004), "Food for Thought." In this exercise, which requires some prior preparation, we used yarn to establish proportionately-sized circles on the classroom floor corresponding to the world's five major inhabited land masses—Africa, Asia, Europe, North America, and Latin America. Students were then divided into groups and asked to sit in one of the circles in proportion to the relative populations of these land area. In our class, this meant one person sitting alone in North America while fifteen others crowded into the not-very-much-larger circle corresponding to Asia. After all students were situated in their circles, we introduced various global demographic, health, and geographic statistics and asked "ambassadors" from each region to share previously-prepared information regarding conditions in their respective locales.

We facilitated three rounds of this sort of sharing, and then concluded the exercise in a very graphic way by distributing plastic bags containing chocolate, candies, and matches proportionate to each of region's respective per-capita incomes and energy use. Africa, which had three people in its circle, received two candies and three matches. Asia received six candies and six matches to divvy up among its fifteen residents. Continuing around the room in this fashion, we ended up at North America, whose sole inhabitant received a bag bulging with 99 candies and 60 matches! A heated, albeit thoughtful discussion followed with students arguing (still from their positions on the floor!) back and forth about likely future scenarios arising from their shared experiences. Poverty, humanitarian aid, development, health care, education, immigration, justice, entitlement—all the big issues—were discussed in a frank and open manner.

The atypical seating arrangements, deliberate use of alternative voices, and generally relaxed conversation combined to create a powerful learning experience about relative disparities in income, health, land use, education, and consumption across the world that we believe will never be forgotten. We doubt that a single person will remember the exact infant mortality figures for Africa, but that wasn't the point of the exercise. Reams of specific information are readily available on the Internet and in dozens of government and UN-sponsored publications. What will remain with all of us, we believe, is the memory of fifteen students crowded into a too-small circle with only six small candies to share among them, while one "fat cat" in an expansive North American space gobbled down handfuls of the treats. (This situation did not actually happen—the young woman in North America did not *really* consume all 99 candies in the 15 minutes left at the end of class. But neither did she pass around the bag for all to share, as one might have hoped. Rather, a student in Africa asked for, and received, some candies, while a few students from Asia indicated their intention to move to the North American circle and share in the bounty.)

The Systems Game

This exercise, described in Macy and Brown (1998) has worked well for us in a variety of situations. It provides students with an "up-close-and-personal" experience with the dynamic nature of open systems, highlighting their ability to self-organize. To play this game, we go outside and ask participants to gather in a circle. We then instruct each student to select two other people in the group, and *without indicating those choices*, to begin moving in such a fashion as to keep an equal distance between himself or herself and each of these two people.

What follows is a rather hectic moving-about, accompanied by much laughter, as each individual attempts to accomplish his or her goals. The process continues in fits and starts until, eventually, equilibrium is reached and all are settled. For a while, especially with a big group, it seems as though this point will never be reached, but it always is. We then quickly debrief the exercise, asking students what they've observed and what they've learned. They almost always identify key elements of systems thinking, for example, complexity, positive and negative feedback, delays, and self-regulation. We observe that the system eventually comes into balance, without the need for an external coordinator, and ask what it is about the system that allowed it to come into balance. They recognize that the key is to focus less on one's own actions and more on the actions of others. We close by remarking on similarities between the game's solution and what is needed to harmonize the ecological, economic, and social aspects of sustainability. It will be a difficult process, with many possible solutions, but ultimately, the system does achieve stability. This result, which we allude to again and again, serves as an encouraging reminder as we move through the course.

Vampire Power Exercise

Another set of exercises which have worked well for us are those that ask students to measure their personal impact on the planet. They calculate their ecological footprint using both simple and complex calculators (Redefining Progress, 2008), identify the major countries responsible for the manufacture of their clothing, tally their energy and water use for a week, and compute the amount of power drawn by appliances in their rooms, both during use and while in standby mode. This latter situation, colorfully known as "vampire power", has come under criticism as an unnecessary and inefficient use of energy (Lamb, 2008).

Essentially, we provided students with a worksheet asking them to identify all of the electrical appliances currently in use in their dorm or apartment rooms. For most students, this was around three to twenty appliances. Then, we required them to compute the amount of energy used by these appliances, using a table and calculations similar to those shown in Table 13.1.

This assignment offered just enough mathematical challenge to make it interesting for most students. They learned that there is no standard way of reporting energy usage (at least in the United States). Some appliances note the amount of power (watts), while others indicated the amount of current (amps) needed. In the latter instance, we asked them to use Ohm's Law ($V = IR$, where V = voltage in volts, I = current in amperes, and R = resistance in ohms) to arrive at a consistent measure of energy use (in kWh).

The results were enlightening. Not only did students get "hands-on" experience with the details of energy auditing, but they also identified opportunities for personal savings! For example, some students found their color televisions drew more energy during standby mode than while they were actually watching them! (Although energy draw is obviously much higher during actual use, these students watched their TVs very few hours per day). This exercise, and other similar measurement assign-

Table 13.1.   Calculating Energy Use

Appliance	Watts	Hours Per Day	Days Per Month	kWh Per Month	Monthly Cost
Clock Radio (16W)	16	24	30	11.52	$ .87
TrueAir Fan (.2A)	22	24	30	15.84	1.20
Lava Lamp (40W)	40	4	10	1.60	.12
Dehumidifier (5.9A)	649	24	30	467.28	35.42

ex) Mr. White's dehumidifier draws 5.9 A of current. 5.9 A x 110 V = 649 watts. Electricity costs $.0758 per kWh in Charlottesville, for a monthly expense of $35.42.

The task becomes more complicated when we consider appliances with phantom or vampire loads. The best way to measure vampire power draws is with a meter, but since most of us don't have them handy, we're going to use estimates from others who've worked in this area. Consider the case of Mrs. White's coffeemaker: It draws 1025W (!) in use and 10W in standby mode (it's one of those fancy ones that starts brewing coffee before you get up in the morning).

Operating Costs

1025W x .75 hrs/day x 30 days/month = 23.06 kWh/month ... $1.75 operating costs

Vampire Power Costs

10W x 23.25 hrs/day x 30 days/month = 6.97 kWh/month ... $0.53 vampire power costs

The vampire power costs of this machine are almost 25% of the TOTAL costs!

ments, is a great example of integrating the foundational knowledge, application, and caring components of Fink's taxonomy of significant learning.

Object Lessons

We've used a number of classroom demonstrations and object lessons to introduce and reinforce concepts in students' minds. We have found that, especially in a cross-disciplinary course such as this one, it is important to use as many "hooks" as possible to engage participants with widely differing backgrounds.

The Ecosphere

One of us owns an EcoSphere®, a sealed glass globe containing seawater, algae, and brine shrimp (Ecosphere Associates, 2006). This self-sustaining ecosystem is a useful visual illustration metaphor for "Spacehip Earth," highlighting the fact that we exist on a planet with finite resources, finite sinks for waste, and with solar energy as our sole external input. In an EcoSphere, energy from the sun enables the algae to synthesize food and oxygen from carbon dioxide and inorganic nutrients. The shrimp eat the algae, respiring carbon dioxide and excreting organic wastes, which feed bacteria. The bacteria break down these wastes into inorganic nutrients that combine with carbon dioxide to provide the building blocks for renewed photosynthesis by the algae. In an EcoSphere, as on the Earth, there is no "away"—everything must go somewhere. Students are fascinated to learn that the oldest EcoSpheres are now 10+ years old, and speculate on what it would take to maintain such balance in our own ecosystems.

Beanie Baby Extinction

Many undergraduate students participated in the Beanie Baby craze of 1995–99, and thus were perhaps intrigued to see a row of them lined up next to one another on a table at the front when they entered class. They were certainly a little surprised when one instructor, twenty minutes into the class, pushed one of stuffed animals off the table and it fell, "Plop!" on the floor. Twenty minutes later, he pushed another one off. And then another, twenty minutes after that. After the break, as part of his opening remarks, the instructor explained what had happened since they had entered class that day. According to some scientists, a species goes extinct every twenty minutes. In the hour they'd spent together in class, three species had disappeared, never to return. "Good-bye, beautiful parrot," he remarked, "good-bye strangely-colored lizard; good-bye rare white tiger—we'll miss you." Of course, the disappearing species were unlikely to be the charismatic megafauna personified by the Ty Company, but the point had been made. We're losing species, and at a disappointingly rapid rate!

Paul and Anne Ehrlich (1981), in their book, *Extinction*, recount an anecdote about an airplane wing and rivets. For safety reasons, airplanes are generally over-engineered, with more rivets than necessary holding the aluminum wings and fuselage together. In other words, there's a certain amount of redundancy in design, and it's possible to pop off some rivets and the plane will still fly. However, at some point, you'll remove a critical rivet, and the plane will crash. Ehrlich likens this scenario to our current extinction crisis—we're losing a species here, a species there – but we don't know which one will bring down the whole ecosystem.

Lessons From the Möbius Strip

Toward the end of the semester, we use a mathematical curiousity to reiterate some of the lessons we hope have been imparted during our time together. It's called a Möbius strip, after Augustus Möbius, who described the figure in the mid-1800s. It's an interesting object, and we invite students to create one and explore its properties along with us. We pass out strips of paper, glue and scissors, then ask students to create the strip by taking the paper, making a loop with a single twist, and then gluing the ends together, as illustrated in Figure 13.4 (see p. 299).

The strip has a number of interesting characteristics. For example, we ask students to take a pencil and begin drawing a line down the center of one side of the strip. How many sides does the Möbius strip have? Most are surprised to discover that there's only one side – that's one of the key elements of a Möbius strip—it's an unusual, one-sided surface. We find it a useful metaphor for the issues we've been working with in the class. Really, everything *is* connected to everything else, and in fact, Mathis Wackernagel, co-creator of the ecological footprint notes, "The two-word definition of sustainability is 'one planet' " (Sheltair Group, 2009). This is the first lesson of the Möbius strip—we live on one planet, and share one future.

We then ask students to take the pair of scissors and to cut the Möbius strip along the lines they have drawn. What happens? This result also generally comes as a surprise—the loop doubles in size. We use this activity to motivate the second lesson of the Möbius strip: with a bit of cleverness, it ought to be possible to achieve substantially greater human well-being with the same amount of resources. The trick is finding (and justifying and

Figure 13.4.   The Möbius Strip.

defending) a clever solution to the challenges we're facing. (This is what we hope our students are doing with their projects during the course!).

Finally, we ask students to cut their strips down the middle once more. If done correctly, they end up with two rings—with a twist. This is pretty interesting, too, as few people really expect it to happen. Metaphorically, one might think of this situation as illustrative of the *interconnections* between peoples on the planet—between individuals, governments, and communities. We all get by with a little help from our friends, and in fact, it's likely that this very characteristic—our social nature—will ultimately prove most helpful in achieving a sustainable society.

We sum up this exercise by reiterating the three lessons of the Möbius strip—that everything's connected to everything else, that cleverness can increase resource productivity, and that ultimately, it's our human connections that will save us. Finally, we note that the near-ubiquitous recycling symbol is really just a squashed Möbius strip (Figure 13.5, see p. 300).

SUSTAINABLE INVESTMENT PROJECT

The sustainable investment project (SIP) is the course's capstone experience, offering participants the opportunity to integrate, analyze and

Figure 13.5.   The Möbius Strip as recycling symbol.

apply the concepts, frameworks, and strategies developed throughout the semester. Working collaboratively in cross-disciplinary teams, students develop proposals to resolve real-world business and social problems in a manner consistent with the attainment of a sustainable future. Past projects have included the development and installation of ceramic water filters in an African village, an exploration of viable methods for the disposal of glass wastes on a Caribbean island, the use of green roofs, and office building retrofits resulting in environmental and productivity gains. Worth almost forty percent of the grade, the SIP quickly becomes the course's focus after the major themes have been laid out.

We kept the three key elements of experiential learning—real-world situations, collaborative problem-solving, and public presentation of results—firmly in mind when designing guidelines for the SIP (Joplin, 1995; Kolb, 1984). We also developed an ordered set of four investment criteria against which projects were to be evaluated. Briefly, we expected students to evaluate their proposals for *sustainability*, using one or more of the frameworks discussed in class, e.g., ecological footprint, The Natural Step, triple bottom line, cradle-to-cradle, life cycle analysis, etc. Second, project proposals had to be assessed for *strategic fit* within the organizations expected to implement them. Porter's (1980) "five forces" analysis,

SWOT analysis, and Reinhardt's (2000) five classes of environmental business strategies were helpful tools in ensuring this hurdle was vaulted. Standard investment appraisal techniques, for example, net present value, economic value added, and payback period were used to ensure projects were *financially viable*. Finally, we asked students to comment upon the *practical hurdles* (Günther & Scheibe, 2005) needed to be overcome before the actual implementation of their recommendations.

In some instances, students prepared field-based sustainable investment case studies for use in future classes, rather than proposing and presenting an investment decision themselves. We provided these groups with additional training and materials (Leenders, Mauffette-Leenders, & Erskine, 2000).

The sustainable investment project has taken several different forms, depending on the amount of time available for cross-cultural collaboration. In our inaugural offering, with just domestic students, the project proceeded in three phases, each associated with specific deliverable ("milestones"). The first milestone, *Project Identification*, was due three weeks into class, after students had been exposed to basic foundational knowledge and had had time to bond with one another and to identify a promising sustainability challenge. The instructors provided swift feedback to ensure students were on the right track and that the projects they had selected were manageable within the timeframe of the course. The second milestone, *Sustainability and Strategic Evaluation*, due about eight weeks into the class, also provided a vehicle to monitor student progress and to offer feedback on the first two key hurdles. By this time effective groups were well on their way to completion of the project. (Because our students were all upper-level with significant experience working in teams, we did not provide any formal support for together, and in fact, there was relatively little friction between group members. We can imagine, however, that a different situation might call for additional facilitation of the "forming—storming—norming—performing" process of group dynamics).

The last milestone, *Final Report and Presentation*, entailed the delivery of a 15–20 page report and attendant presentation to the class and invited outside guests. This is perhaps where the multidisciplinary elements of the class shone the brightest. Engineering students developed detailed diagrams of their proposed innovations, students from the architecture school created gorgeous posters and slides, and the business students gave incisive presentations with compelling financial justifications for their arguments. We do not believe the results would have been anywhere near as impressive had the course been confined to students from a single discipline.

In subsequent semesters, when working with students from both the United States and Germany, the sustainable investment project morphed into a less "hands-on" experience, owing to the physical and temporal distances between the two sets of students. We encouraged participants to select projects which both cultures could relate to, while still maintaining the four-part nature of the analysis. The results were somewhat more generic, dealing with geothermal power plants, electricity generation from methane, biodiesel production and SkySails—an innovative proposal involving the use of large sails to propel commercial shipping vessels. The availability of detailed financial information was a key element circumscribing the universe of potential projects in these instances. Nonetheless, participants on both sides of the ocean indicated it was a valuable learning experience. They especially appreciated the different points of view held by team members from the different countries.

GOING FORWARD

Experiential learning is a proven pedagogy for teaching students not only to know, but to act. The methods for teaching sustainability described in this chapter are based on sound pedagogy and will hopefully prove useful for others interested in enhancing student learning about these issues. We have offered this course jointly and simultaneously at both the undergraduate and graduate level at our respective universities in the United States and Germany. The creation of interdiscliplinary, intercultural teams adds an exciting element to the Sustainable Investment Project as students from different backgrounds and experiences strive to develop appropriate solutions to what are essentially global problems.

Finally, it's important to note that recent years have seen the development of many courses related to sustainability and that there are a number of useful resources for instructors wishing to improve their pedagogies. With respect to experientially-based teaching strategies for sustainability in business schools, we recommend, in addition to other chapters in this text, Galea (2004, 2007), Farley, Erickson, and Daly (2005), Wankel and deFelippi (2006), and Shrivastava, Allen, and Hiller (2008).

ACKNOWLEDGMENTS

We would like to acknowledge University of Virginia and Technische Universität Dresden professors and administrators Milton Adams, Mike Atchison, Tim Garson, Tom Jones, Andrea Larson, George Overstreet, and Carl Zeithaml for their encouragement and support of our efforts to integrate sustainability concerns throughout the UVA curriculum. We are grateful to our students, who have blessed us with our own "experiential learning" activity and helped us to think through the nuances of course design. Most importantly, we thank the Procter and Gamble Foundation for its vision and financial generosity enabling the development and delivery of this innovative course.

REFERENCES

Bloom, B. S. (Ed.). (1956). *Taxonomy of educational objectives. The classification of educational goals, Handbook 1: Cognitive domain*. New York: McKay.

Ecosphere Associates. (2006). *How ecospheres work*. http://www.eco-sphere.com/care_manual.htm. Retrieved May 16, 2009.

Ehrlich, P. R., & Ehrlich, A. H. (1981). *Extinction*. New York: Random House.

Farley, J., Erickson, J. D., & Daly, H. E. (2005). *Ecological economics: A workbook for problem-based learning*. Washington: Island Press.

Fink, L. D. (2003). *Creating significant learning experiences*. San Francisco: Jossey-Bass.

Galea, C. (Ed.). (2004). *Teaching business sustainability*: *From theory to practice* (Vol. 1). Sheffield, UK: Greenleaf.

Galea, C. (Ed.). (2007). *Teaching business sustainability*: Cases, simulations and experiential approaches (Vol. 2). Sheffield, UK: Greenleaf.

Gilbert, D. (2006). *Stumbling on happiness*. New York: Knopf.

Günther, E., & Scheibe, L. (2005). The hurdles analysis as an instrument for improving environmental value chain management. *Progress in Industrial Ecology, 2*(1), 107–131.

Joplin, L. (1995). On defining experiential education. In K. Warren, M. Sakoffs, & J. S. Hunt (Eds.), *The theory of experiential education* (pp. 17–19). Dubuque: Kendall/Hunt.

Kolb, D. A. (1984). *Experiential learning: Experience as the source of learning and development*. Englewood Cliffs: Prentice-Hall.

Lamb, R. (2008). *How vampire power works*. Retrieved May 16, 2009, from http://electronics.howstuffworks.com/gadgets/other-gadgets/vampire-power.htm.

Leenders, M. R., Mauffette-Leenders, L. A., & Erskine, J. A. (2000). *Writing cases* (4th ed.). London, Ontario: Ivey Business School.

Macy, J., & Brown, M. (1998). *Coming back to life*. Gabriola Island, BC: New Society.

Millennium Ecosystem Assessment. (2005). *Ecosystems and human well-being: Synthesis report*. Washington, DC: Island Press.

The Natural Step. (n.d.) The funnel. Retrieved May 25, 2009, from http://www.naturalstep.org/en/the-funnel

Population Connection. (2004). *Food for thought*. Retrieved May 16, 2009, from www.populationeducation.org

Porter, M. (1980). *Competitive strategy: Techniques for analysing industries and competitors*. New York: Free Press.

Postman, N., & Weingartner, C. (1969). *Teaching as a subversive activity*. New York: Dell Publishing.

Redefining Progress. (2008). *How big is your ecological footprint?* Retrieved May 16, 2009, from http://www.myfootprint.org/en/

Reinhardt, F. (2000). *Down to earth: Applying business principles to environmental management*. Boston: Harvard Business School Press.

Sheltair Group. (2009). *About us.*Retrieved May 16, 2009, from http://www .sheltair.com/content/ABOUT_US/7

Shrivastava, P., Allen, D. E., & Hiller, T. B. (2008). Designing undergraduate education on "Managing for Sustainability." In C. Wankel & J. A. F. Stoner (Eds.), *Innovative approaches to global sustainability*. (pp. 159–173). New York: Palgrave Macmillan.

Wankel, C., & DeFillippi, R. (Eds.). (2006). *Educating managers through real world projects*. Greenwich, CT: Information Age.

CHAPTER 14

THE SUSTAINABILITY BUSINESS CASE

Educating MBAs in Sustainability

Wendy Stubbs and Ed Lockhart

There is a critical need for increased education on sustainability in the business curriculum to enable future business leaders to understand and respond to social and environmental risks and opportunities, and to help them create environmentally and socially sustainable organizations. This chapter describes the business case approach to teaching sustainability to MBA students at Monash University. This approach uses language and tools already familiar to management students to integrate sustainability into their business practices. The first part of the unit expands students' knowledge of sustainability by discussing the environmental, social, and economic issues of "business-as-usual." It presents a sustainability framework to help the students critique and reconcile different sustainability perspectives. The second part of the unit uses a SPIR (Situation-Problem-Implication-Response) tool to help students develop skills for analyzing the sustainability impacts of business and for developing strategic responses to address these impacts. Guest speakers from various industries supplement this learning by presenting real-world approaches to creating sustainable organizations. Finally, postulating that organizational change is predicated on

Management Education for Global Sustainability, pp. 305–325

personal change, an "inspirational life coach" asks students to reflect on their own attitudes and challenges them to think about how they will—or will not—personalize sustainability in their careers or lives.

INTRODUCTION

The many reports of environmental devastation and global warming suggest that sustainability is an increasingly critical issue for business leaders. In its report *One Planet Many People: Atlas of our Changing Environment*, the United Nations Environment Programme (UNEP, 2005) describes the degradation brought about by continued unsustainable economic development and business practices. Half the world's wetlands have already been lost. Logging and land use conversion have reduced forest cover by at least 20%, and possibly by as much as 50%. Nearly 70% of the world's major marine fish stocks are either over-fished or being fished at the biological limit. Over the last 50 years, soil degradation has affected two-thirds of the world's agricultural land. Each year about 25 billion metric tons of fertile topsoil is lost globally. Each year about 27,000 species disappear from the planet—approximately one every 20 minutes. Dams and engineering works have fragmented 60% of the world's large river systems. These projects impede water flow so severely that the time it takes for a drop of water to reach the sea has tripled. This profoundly alters the amount and location of water available for both human uses and for sustaining aquatic ecosystems (World Resources Institute [WRI], 2000). Human activities are significantly altering the basic chemical cycles upon which all ecosystems depend.

The Intergovernmental Panel on Climate Change (IPCC, 2007b) predicts that global average surface temperature will increase between 1.4 and 5.8 degrees Celsius from 1990 to 2100. Emissions are projected to increase by up to 90% by 2030, and if they continue to rise, surface temperature will rise by up to five degrees by 2050. While the scale of the impacts of global warming and the resulting climate change is uncertain, the IPCC expects the increase in surface temperature to create increased risk of extinction of some vulnerable species, and predicts that almost one third of the world's species will face extinction if greenhouse gases continue to rise. Climate change will exacerbate water shortages in many water-scarce areas of the world. Twenty percent of the world's population will face a great risk of drought. Sea-level rise and storm surges will endanger small islands and low-lying coastal areas leading to increasing displacement of people.

These issues will increasingly impact business and other organizations' ability to conduct their operations. For example, UNEP's Climate Change Working Group (UNEP, 2007) predicts that the scale of losses from extreme weather events could reach U.S.$1 trillion in a single year by 2040. The OECD (Nicholls et al., 2008) estimates that a mean sea level rise of 0.5 meters by 2070 will have a financial impact of U.S.$35 trillion.

It is important that business schools prepare students (future business leaders) to be able to respond to these issues and manage the associated environmental and social risks. However, understanding and managing environmental and social issues require a particular set of skills and insights (Roome, 2005). Rands (1993, 2007) argues that teaching students about sustainability must occur on three dimensions: knowledge, skills, and attitudes.

This chapter describes how corporate sustainability is taught to MBA students at Monash University in Melbourne, Australia. It first provides the context for a "Corporate Sustainability: The Business Case" (CSTBC) unit by reviewing different approaches to teaching sustainability to business students. It then provides some background information on the MBA program and the sustainability unit. It discusses the major components of the unit and how the tools and frameworks employed expand the students' knowledge about sustainability, help them develop skills for incorporating sustainable business practices into their organizations, and encourage them to reflect on their own attitudes to personalize sustainability in their own careers or lives. Finally, the chapter provides some concluding remarks on the future of corporate sustainability education within the business faculty at Monash University.

SUSTAINABILITY AND BUSINESS MANAGEMENT EDUCATION

Rands (1993, 2007) developed a Principle-Attribute Matrix for Management Environmental Education that applies the three attributes—knowledge, skills, and attitudes—to three guiding principles: sustainable development, organizational responsibility (all organizations have a responsibility to contribute to sustainable development), and personal responsibility (individuals have a responsibility to contribute to sustainable development by working toward achieving personal and organizational sustainability). In concert with this approach, Shephard (2008, p. 90) suggests that sustainability education seeks three primary outcomes: graduates should know about sustainability issues, they should have the skills to act sustainably if they wish to, and they should have the personal and emotional attributes that would lead them to behave sustainably.

With respect to the knowledge dimension, students need a basic understanding of what sustainability is and the environmental, social, and economic "pillars" of sustainability. However, there is no consensus in the literature on the meanings of sustainability or sustainable development, and multiple conflicting perspectives of sustainability (such as the deep green, ecological modernist, and economic rationalist views) cannot be reconciled in terms of each other (Robinson, 2004). Students require an understanding of the different approaches to sustainability to help them understand different stakeholders' perspectives (such as business, government, and environmental NGOs). The most cited definition of sustainability comes from the World Commission on Environment and Development (WCED) report (1987, p. 43), often referred to as the Brundtland report:

> Sustainable development is development that meets the needs of the present without compromising the ability of future generations to meet their own needs...The concept of sustainable development does imply limits—not absolute limits, but limitations imposed by the present state of technology and social organization on environmental resources, and by the ability of the biosphere to absorb the effects of human activities...Even the narrow notion of physical sustainability implies a concern for social equity between generations, a concern that must logically be extended to equity within each generation.

The Brundtland definition touches on a number of key sustainability principles which have since been embodied in a range of national and international agreements (Harding, 1996, 1998). These include:

1. Intergenerational Equity: Equity between generations.
2. Intragenerational Equity: Equity within a single generation.
3. Precautionary Principle: Uncertainty should not be used as an excuse for inaction.
4. Conservation of Biological Diversity: The variety of all life, their genes, and their ecosystems.
5. Internalization of Environmental Costs: Include the interest of those not in the market place so that adverse impacts on these people are included in market prices and costs.

A basic understanding of sustainability concepts needs to be supplemented by knowledge of the environmental, social, and economic problems of "business-as-usual" (and the interaction between the three). Knowledge of sustainability helps students understand how environmental, social, and economic outcomes can be achieved (Rands, 1993). To enable this understanding to occur, Rands (p. 30) argues that students must engage in four critical activities: "environmental problem recognition, problem analysis, development of proposals to lessen environmental impacts, and implementation of these proposals." To aid this process, he recommends that guest speakers who are "articulate advocates of sustainability" (p. 30) provide students with visions of sustainable societies and companies.

Skills required for bringing sustainability to organizations include: problem identification and anticipation; analysis of implications and impacts of problems; communicating and selling sustainability to management; stakeholder analysis and interaction; and facilitating organizational change for sustainable outcomes (Rands, 2007). Students require tools (Cervantes, 2007) to help them apply these skills.

Shephard (p. 88) proposes that "the essence of education for sustainability is a quest for affective outcomes" (p. 88). Affective learning relates to values, attitudes, and behaviors, and involves the learner emotionally, in contrast to cognitive learning which relates more to acquiring knowledge and skills. Kearins and Springett (2003) argue that sustainable development calls for radical change. They respond to this challenge by using critical theory to inform their teaching of sustainability. Aligned with Shephard's work, their approach entails self-reflection (thinking through both personal and broader societal values), social action/engagement (asking students to think through ways they could act more sustainably), and critique (exploring alternatives to business-as-usual).

Rands's (1993, 2007) third dimension of education for sustainability supports these views. His third dimension, *Attitudes*, is affective learning. This dimension entails: providing students with experiences that cause them to reflect on their environmental and social attitudes, and instilling "scripts suggesting that the appropriate response to environmental performance problems is taking personal action to attempt to bring about organizational change. Course assignments can be developed which give the students such experience" (Rands, 1993, p. 39). Rands emphasizes that educators should use means that are open and non-manipulative and make it clear that failure to adopt pro-sustainability attitudes will not negatively affect students' grades. Activities for affective learning include: discussion, open debate, peer involvement, role playing, problem-based learning, engaging with role models, simulations, games, group analysis of case studies, expert engagement, perspective sharing via reflection, and use of multimedia to trigger responses (Shephard, 2008).

Svanström and colleagues (2008) attempted to summarize the different learning outcomes for sustainable development in higher education across countries and cultures. The four key learning outcomes they describe reinforce the approaches taken by the scholars mentioned in the preceding paragraphs: systemic or holistic thinking (recognizing the interconnectedness of environmental, social, and economic issues); integrating different perspectives; developing skills such as "problem-solving, critical thinking, creative thinking, self-learning, and skills related to communication, teamwork, and becoming an effective change agent to shift policies, practices, and societal norms" (p. 342), and an integrated approach to knowledge, attitudes, skills, awareness, and values.

CORPORATE SUSTAINABILITY: THE BUSINESS CASE

The Monash MBA was first offered in 1968. In 2007 it was the only Australian MBA program ranked in the world's top 50 in the Economist Intelligence Unit's ranking survey and it was placed second in the world in the category "personal development and educational experience." It is accredited with EQUIS (the European Quality Improvement System) and AMBA (the Association of MBAs).

The CSTBC unit was first introduced into the Monash MBA program in the mid- 1990's. It was developed by the School of Geography and Environmental Science (SGES) and is still taught by SGES lecturers. For nearly all of the students, it is their first introduction to sustainability coursework. Sustainability is currently not integrated into the MBA core units, although one or two MBA lecturers discuss sustainability concepts in their units.

The CSTBC unit is currently offered as a summer intensive elective, over a 5-week period (4 Saturdays and 3 Wednesday afternoons), with a 1-week break after the second week. The break was introduced at the suggestion of past students who felt they needed more time to assimilate the concepts. The unit is co-taught by two lecturers who also teach corporate sustainability units in the Master of Corporate Environmental and Sustainability Management (MCESM) program offered by SGES. The aim of the unit is to prepare business students to respond to emerging sustainability threats and opportunities. The learning outcomes for the students of the CSTBC unit are:

1. Demonstrate an understanding of what constitutes sustainability;
2. Determine where and how sustainability impacts business risks and opportunities;
3. Formulate basic strategies to respond to these risks and opportunities; and
4. Reflect on how sustainability will impact the student's career and future direction.

The CSTBC unit consists of three parts. The first part seeks to develop an understanding of the sustainability problems from an environmental, social, and economic perspective (the three pillars of sustainability). This is an important aspect as different businesses within different industries will have different levels of exposure to different sustainability issues. This part of the unit consists of a series of assigned readings, lectures, videos, audio, and discussion forums outlining the three dimensions of sustainability, followed by industry case studies and guest speakers to explore and reinforce the key concepts. Part 1 is aligned with Shephard's (2008) first primary outcome of sustainability education and Rands's (1993, 2007) attribute of "knowledge," engaging in the four critical activities discussed by him. The guest speakers are "articulate advocates of sustainability" (Rands, 1993, p. 30).

Part 2 of the CSTBC unit, an interactive workshop, is focused on "skills," aligning itself with Rands's (1993, 2007) attribute of "skills" and Shephard's (2008) second primary outcome of sustainability education—skills to act sustainably. The aim of the workshop is for students to understand where and how sustainability issues impact two industries (using a service-based company and a product manufacturing company) and how to formulate basic strategic responses to these impacts. This part seeks to teach students how to undertake an analysis of the material risks and benefits that sustainability implies for a business, with executive management as the principal target audience for this analysis. There are many cases that can be made for sustainability, such as social, moral, ethical, and environmental. While not ignoring these positions, the emphasis of this part of the unit is on the business case: the financial bottom line, which can be either enhanced or undermined through such factors as reputation, brand equity, innovation, productivity, risk profile, access to capital, license to operate, and ability to attract and retain talent. Consequently, part 2 is primarily *applied*, designed to address the following scenario:

> It's 8:00 A.M., and the Chief Executive Officer (CEO) has just phoned you to request a briefing paper for the next Board meeting. The CEO has been informed that in response to an institutional investor, the Board is concerned about the company's exposure to sustainability issues. Fundamental questions are being raised about whether the company can continue to generate economic capital without compromising social capital or natural capital. Specifically, the CEO wants you to identify the sustainability issues facing the business, identify the financially material implications arising from these issues, and then suggest a strategic response.

In the third part of the unit, an inspirational life coach challenges students to reflect on their own attitudes, values, behaviors, and career and life direction. This part aims to integrate Rands's attribute of "attitudes" and Shephard's affective learning approach.

Table 14.1 summarizes the topics covered in Parts 1, 2, and 3. Because industry speakers are scheduled for Wednesday afternoons (during business hours), the contents of Part 2 are interspersed throughout the unit.

PART 1: SUSTAINABILITY AND THE THREE PILLARS

After first presenting sustainability's different definitions and underlying principles, the impact of human and business activity on the natural environment is discussed. This discussion includes the impacts on the environment of population growth, increasing consumption, and the use of fossil-fuel-based technologies (Holden & Ehrlich, 1974), as well as discussions on global warming and the findings of the Intergovernmental Panel on Climate Change (IPCC, 2007a). The video *What's Up With the Weather?* is screened. The video details "the catastrophic results that some scientists predict if global warming continues" (WGBH International, 2001).

The social aspects of sustainability are then discussed, including the concepts of social equity and justice (inter- and intragenerational equity), social capital and human capital, community development, and corporate social responsibility. The Miniature Earth (Sustainability Institute & Meadows, 2001) 3-minute video is also played as part of the discussion. The video touches on issues of poverty and social inequities (wealth, health, education, consumption, and access to resources). In previous years, Arundhati Roy's (2004) 35 minute acceptance speech for the 2004 Sydney Peace Prize was used. In her speech, she discusses social sustainability issues such as justice, equity, human rights, free markets, poverty, the separation of social decisions and business/market decisions, and profits without principles.

The economic pillar of sustainability is presented with particular reference to the neoclassical economic underpinnings of business-as-usual (the "technocentric" worldview) and the free-market assumptions that are in conflict with the concept of sustainability, such as: the absence of externalities (markets do not capture all the costs or impacts of activities such as pollution, global warming, erosion, or depletion of natural resources); failing to value ecosystem services and natural resources, and therefore considering them to be "free"; discounting the future (which encourages short-term consumption of natural resources); and assuming the infinite substitutability of man-made capital for natural capital. The potential economic costs of climate change (Garnault, 2008; Stern, 2006) and their impacts on business are also discussed.

**Table 14.1.   Corporate Sustainability:
The Business Case Sample Unit Outline**

Day	Topic
PART 1—KNOWLEDGE	
Day 1 Saturday 9.00 A.M. to 5.00 P.M.	• Introduction • Problem: Environment • Problem: Social • Problem: Economics • The Natural Step & Natural Capitalism • Consolidation
Day 2 Wednesday 2.00 P.M. to 6.00 P.M.	• 1-hour Test • Guest Speaker: • CEO, Interface Asia Pacific • SPIR Model: Situation, Problem, Implication, Resolution
PART 2—SKILLS	
Day 3 Saturday 9.00 A.M. to 5.00 P.M.	• Recap & Discuss • Situation—Manufacturing • Problem—Manufacturing • Implication—Manufacturing • Stakeholder Models
Day 4 Wednesday 2.00 P.M. to 6.00 P.M.	• Guest Speaker: • Head of Sustainability, Institutional & Corporate, ANZ Bank • Guest Speaker: • General Manager, Corporate Communications & Government Affairs, Origin Energy
1 week break	• Reflect on what has been learnt to date
Day 5 Saturday 9.00 A.M. to 5.00 P.M.	• Recap & Discuss • Situation—Banking • Problem—Banking • Implication—Banking • Strategy Development
PART 3—ATTITUDES	
Day 6 Wednesday 2.00 P.M. to 6.00 P.M.	• Guest Speaker: • General Manager, Corporate Affairs, Bendigo Bank • Guest Speaker: • CEO, Inspirational Coaching
PART 2—SKILLS	
Day 7 Saturday 9.00 A.M. to 5.00 P.M.	• Student group assignment presentations • Case study—Steel industry company • Resolution—Manufacturing • Resolution—Banking • Wrap-up

Two alternative views to the technocentric worldview are then presented: deep green (ecocentric) and ecological modernization (sustaincentric) (Gladwin, Kennelly, & Krause, 1995). The lecturers describe the characteristics of organizations within each worldview. The aim of this sustainability framework (Stubbs & Cocklin, 2008) is to stimulate and broaden business students' interest in sustainability (Cordano, Ellis, & Scherer, 2003; Kearins & Springett, 2003; Rusinko, 2005; Springett, 2005) and shift their thinking beyond the prevailing neoclassical paradigm. This framework is used throughout the unit to examine different approaches that business can take to sustainability issues and, in particular, to analyze the different approaches of the guest speakers' organizations.

After in-depth discussions about the problem, two alternative approaches are presented to the class to finish day one on a more positive note: The Natural Step (TNS) (Robèrt, 1997) and natural capitalism (Hawken, Lovins, & Lovins, 1999; Lovins, Lovins, & Hawken, 1999). Table 14.2 summarizes the concepts discussed in class.

Day one covers a significant amount of material that is essential for the students to understand to participate in the workshops in Part 2. To complete Part 1, a 1-hour exam is held at the beginning of day 2. The aim of the exam is to embed the concepts and reinforce the knowledge gained on day one in preparation for Part 2. This exam is followed by a guest speaker and a session introducing the students to the SPIR (Situation, Problem, Implications, Resolution) tool, which is used throughout Part 2.

Table 14.2. Concepts and principles of The Natural Step (TNS) and Natural Capitalism

Four Systems Conditions of TNS	Four Principles of Natural Capitalism
In a sustainable society, nature is not subject to systematically increasing concentrations of substances extracted from the Earth's crust	Radically increase the productivity of natural resources.
In a sustainable society, nature is not subject to systematically increasing concentrations of substances produced by society.	Adopt closed-loop production systems that yield no waste or toxicity (waste=food).
In a sustainable society, nature is not subject to systematically increasing degradation by physical means.	A fundamental change of business model —from one of selling products to one of delivering services.
In a sustainable society, human needs are met worldwide.	Reinvest in natural capital to restore, sustain, and expand the planet's ecosystem.

PART 2: INTERACTIVE CASE STUDIES USING A SPIR TOOL

The aim of Part 2 is to use the SPIR tool to analyze the sustainability impacts of a business and then develop strategic responses to the major sustainability issues. The SPIR tool is adapted from the SPIN (Situation, Problem, Implication, Need-payoff) selling technique (Rackham, 1996) and is grounded in a risk assessment approach. This approach helps students build the business case for sustainability, using language familiar to senior management and MBA students. It also helps them to communicate and sell sustainability to management (Rands, 2007). The risk approach augments the strategic management tools that are offered in other MBA units. According to Gosling and Mintzberg (2004), education must be provided within the context of students' practical experience, acknowledging what they will confront when they return to their organizations and attempt to apply their new knowledge and skills. For this reason, the focus of this unit is primarily *applied*: "How will the organization respond to sustainability risks and opportunities? How will I respond?" This approach recognizes that different organizations across different sectors will have different levels of exposure to different sustainability issues. While there will be generic sector or industry-based issues, the approach focuses on the competitive positioning implications of any business response to sustainability.

SPIR involves an "inside-out" perspective where students examine the social and environmental impacts of the firm's value chain activities (Porter & Kramer, 2006). Standard risk analysis is then used to determine which issues are financially material to the company. Finally, a response is developed to address these issues.

During the second part of the unit, SPIR is applied to two industry sectors: service-based (a bank) and manufacturing (a motor vehicle manufacturer). In small groups, students undertake an analysis of these two sectors and present their findings to the class. A class discussion follows each break-out session.

Situation

The situational analysis involves asking factual questions about how a particular business generates financial value. The object is for students to understand precisely how the firm generates economic value. In the SPIR lecture, a value chain analysis (VCA), life cycle assessment (LCA), and a simpler input-process-output (IPO) approach are presented, and the students can choose which approach to apply. An important distinction is made between describing the firm in terms of size, profitability, or the markets in which it operates from describing *how* it makes money. Specifically, students are directed to examine what inputs, such as energy, materials used, labor, and capital, are used to make the firm's products, and what processes are employed in transforming these inputs into products (in other words, how the products are made). Finally, students are asked to consider the outputs of this process. Apart from the products themselves, what other by-products such as heat or waste have resulted? Figure 14.1 illustrates the output of a situation analysis for car manufacturing.

Problem

The second stage of the SPIR process examines the sustainability issues arising from the situational analysis. Specifically, it asks the students to identify the direct and indirect environmental and social problems arising from the IPO, LCA, or VCA. It is during this stage that students begin to understand the different stakeholder perspectives (such as customers, employees, suppliers, local communities, unions, governments, and NGOs) on what constitutes an environmental or social problem. In this context, students are encouraged to seek a wider stakeholder view of the firm. Rands (2007) identified stakeholder analysis as a skill required by

Situation: Car Manufacturing

Input	Process	Output
• engines	• assembly	• cars
+Windscreens	•Operations: marketing,	•Spare parts
•Doors, windows	sales, planning, design,	•Waste
•Fittings	prod dev, testing,	+Hard (metal,
•Steel	distribution/export	plastics, glass)
•Plastic	•Painting, spraying	•Liquid
•Wiring	•Manufacturing	•Emissions (VOC,
•LPG	•Quality control	GHG)
•Timber	•OH&S procedures	•Recyclable/non-recyc
•Glass	•Managing, organising	•Safe workplace
•Energy	•Community consultation	
•Leather		
+Iron ore		•Accidents
•Silica		•Road congestion
•PE		•Deaths/injury
•Trees		•Road wear & tear
•Oxygen		•Social interaction, social
•Toxic inputs (paints)		capital
•R&D		•Wages, jobs
•Labour		
•Capital		
•Transport/logistics		

Figure 14.1.   Situation analysis for car manufacturing.

students. A stakeholder lecture is presented at this stage to facilitate the students' learning. Figure 14.2 outlines sample problems identified by students for car manufacturing.

Implications

Having understood how a firm makes its money and the sustainability problems associated with doing so, students are then asked to analyze the financial impact of these problems on the firm. A risk assessment framework (Standards Australia International Ltd. and Standards New Zealand, 2004) is used to identify the most financially material impacts. The risk assessment approach is familiar to MBA students and it helps them build a business case for sustainability to present to executive management.

Risk is measured in terms of the likelihood of an event occurring and the consequences (scale or magnitude of impacts). Consequences are scored on a 1–to–5–Likert scale, with "negligible" being a score of 1 and "catastrophic" a score of 5. Similarly, the likelihood of an issue occurring is scored on a 1-to-5 scale, with "a remote chance of it occurring" being a score of 1 and "a high chance of it occurring" being a score of 5. Students allocate a likelihood score and a financial consequence score to each sustainability problem.

Problem: Car Manufacturing

	Input	Process	Output
Environment			
Direct	Spills & leakages (oils, lubricants, paints) Packaging Emissions	Emissions Energy consumption Waste streams	Car emissions Packaging
Indirect	Depletion of natural resources Oil Rubber plantations	Impact on other species located near plants: displaced by plants Waste from people working in plants	Noise pollution Deaths/injuries from accidents Cleaning of cars Advertising billboards Destruction of environment Use of cars rather than public transport
Social			
Direct	Employment layoffs & hiring Squeezing suppliers/OEM contracts Asbestos in brake pads	Employment OH&S	Employment lay-offs Grand Prix noise pollution Increased consumerism Obsession not need
Indirect	Pollution – health issues Utilisation of resources Loss of environment for recreation & other uses Employee satisfaction & morale Work-life balance	Workcover costs Family breakdowns from over-work - impact of shift work Dilute human capital Labour displacement Dependence of one-industry communities	Dilution of social capital Obesity, health issues Road rage (stress) Burden of on-costs: insurance, registration Compliance with legislation Loss of self-esteem Accidents (impact on family etc) Loss of productive time and social interaction (traffic congestion)

Figure 14.2.   Problem analysis for car manufacturing.

The outcome is a matrix of issues designed to generate response prior-ities. Figure 14.3 outlines some examples of implications that students generated for car manufacturing. In this case, considerable debate emerged amongst students regarding the potential financial consequence of growing traffic congestion. Rather than make an arbitrary decision, stu-dents decided to flag the issue as having a potential continuum of conse-quences that required monitoring before a final decision could be made.

Resolution

The final stage of the SPIR process requires students to develop a stra-tegic response to the sustainability implications. In the case of the car manufacturing example, three implications emerged as having high financial materiality to the business: CO_2 emissions from cars (and the threat of carbon taxes or an emissions trading scheme in the foreseeable future); traffic congestion; and the internalization of environmental costs associated with steel production. To help students formulate a strategic response, a lecture covering strategic choice, strategic implementation, and strategic evaluation is presented.

The area of strategic choice asks students to consider three questions, drawing on the work of Courtney (2001):

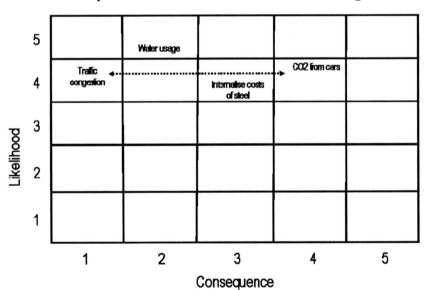

Figure 14.3.   Implications analysis for car manufacturing.

1. Shape or Adapt: under what circumstances is it better for a business to shape an industry or to adapt to industry changes over time?

2. Focus or Diversify: under what circumstances is it better for a business to craft more focused strategies across a range of possible futures or to craft more diverse strategies across that same range of futures?

3. Now or Later: under what circumstances is it better for a business to make immediate full-scale commitments or to postpone major commitments over time?

The primary objective behind the use of these questions is to motivate students to think of both incremental change solutions, such as eco-efficiency, and more radical (transformational) change (Kearins & Spring-ett, 2003), such as that proposed by natural capitalism (Hawken, Lovins, & Lovins, 1999; Lovins, Lovins, & Hawken, 1999): implementing closed loop systems (or biomimicry); radical resource efficiency (a ten-fold increase in resource productivity); or moving toward a service-and-flow business model which emphasizes selling the functionality of the product rather than the form of the product. Figure 14.4 summarizes some examples of strategic choices identified by students for car manufacturing.

1. Strategic Choice

	Shape Adapt?	Focus Diversify?	Now Later?
CO2 Car Emissions	Adapt: smaller cars; hybrid; Lego component cars Shape: urban planning		
Congestion	Shape: A young fleet permit system (equity issues Reduce volume of cars Adapt: Car sharing/leasing programs		
Steel costs internalized	Adapt: substitution of materials Shape: lease not own (service model) Total recycling of components; Lego components		

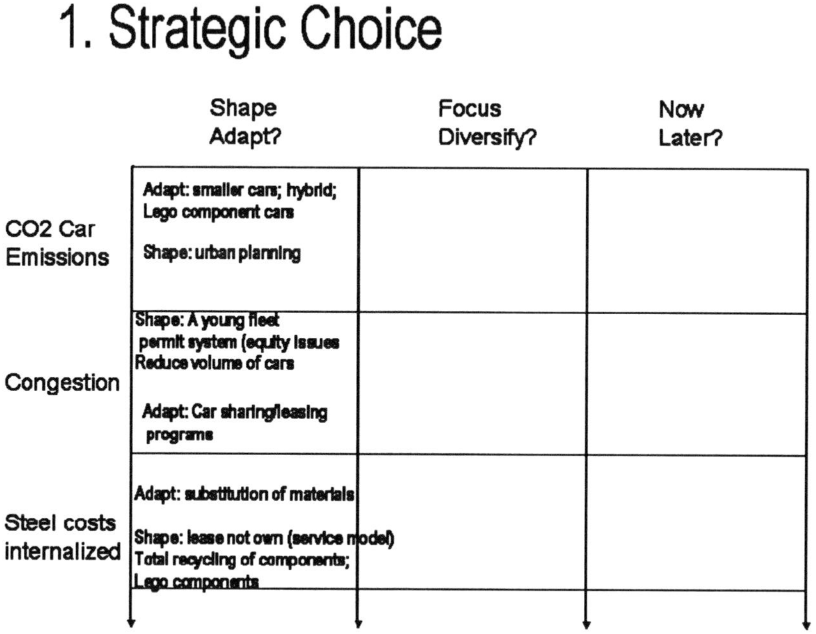

Figure 14.4.   Strategic choice analysis for car manufacturing.

Subtle questioning of the assumption-base upon which the business-as-usual paradigm is founded lies at the heart of this session on strategic choice. What would business look like if, instead of thinking of Earth as a resource base for humans to exploit, we thought of it as a life support system?

To appreciate fully the interrelated complexities of implementing a strategy, particularly if it is a *shaping* strategy, the students are asked to consider how the choice will impact the organization. This analysis is guided by the McKinsey 7S model (Waterman, Peters, & Phillips, 1980): super-ordinate goals (core values, guiding concepts, aspirations); strategy (corporate, business unit, and operational); structure; systems (formal and informal procedures); style (culture and leadership); staff levels and capabilities (developing people); and skills and competencies. The 7S framework is projected across a range of time horizons to augment the learning from Courtney (2001) regarding the timing of a full-scale commitment to a new strategic agenda. Figure 14.5 is used as a template to guide students through these interrelated complexities.

The strategic evaluation component asks students to consider how the strategic responses will be evaluated and monitored. The lecturers discuss various sustainability key performance indicators drawing on a balanced

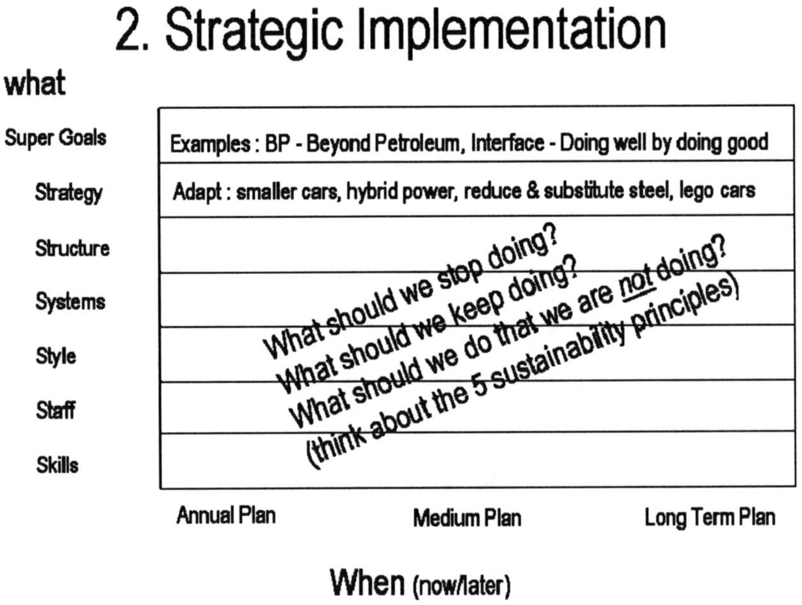

Figure 14.5.   Strategic implementation analysis.

scorecard approach (Kaplan & Norton, 1996) that incorporates sustainability (Epstein & Wisner, 2001; Figge Hahn, Schaltegger, & Wagner, 2002) and frameworks such as the Global Reporting Initiative (2006).

To complete Part 2, a 4,500-word group assignment asks students to undertake a sustainability assessment for a "real life" business using the SPIR model outlined in previous sections. This assignment simulates the situation of the CEO asking what the business should be doing to address sustainability issues. The groups provide a progress report to the Board on day seven of the unit, covering the *situation, problem,* and *implications* (see Table 14.3 for a summary of the assessment). The final report includes the full SPIR analysis.

PART 3: PERSONALIZING SUSTAINABILITY

In the final part of the unit, the CEO of the organization Inspirational Coaching addresses Rands's (2007) third dimension of sustainability education, *Attitudes*, through a series of exercises "that have the power to change how people are living" (Tighe, 2008). In the quest for affective outcomes (Shephard, 2008), this part of the unit encourages students to examine their own attitudes, values, and behaviors, and reflect on their career and life goals. The CEO invites the students to live with courage and work with passion. The session aims to create new ways of thinking through a questioning approach: "When new ways of thinking are created, new possibilities, options, and strategies become apparent" (Tighe, 2008).

At the completion of the unit, the students are asked to submit a 1,200-word essay to examine and assess how sustainability will impact their chosen career path. The lecturers make it clear that there are no "right" or "wrong" answers. If the students do not perceive that sustainability will influence their careers, then they are asked to explain why they think this is

Table 14.3.   Assessment Summary

Assessment Task	Value	Objective
In class test, 1 hour	15%	Comprehend key sustainability concepts.
Group Presentation & Group Company Project	10% 40%	Develop the skills necessary to undertake a sustainability assessment for a "real life" business.
Individual essay	25%	Personalize sustainability via your desired career path.
Participation	10%	Share your knowledge and experience.

the case. They are assessed on their ability to provide a plausible, coherent, and informed appraisal. The guidelines provided for the essay are:

1. Outline your *intended* career path for the next 3 to 5 years.

   - What industry, what profession, what role?
   - Why do you want this career? Think about means versus ends.
   (It is recognized that you may not be certain about your intended career path. However, you may elaborate a desired career path for the purposes of this assignment).

2. Identify the key sustainability issues and their implications for that chosen career.

   - What are the sustainability issues?
   - How will they impact your career—opportunities, threats?

3. How will you respond?

   - What is your strategy?
   - How will you implement your strategy?

CONCLUSION

This chapter outlined an approach to teaching sustainability to MBA students that aims to provide practical tools and frameworks for implementing sustainability in organizations as well as achieving affective outcomes. The business case approach using the SPIR tool is a pragmatic way to get MBA students to embrace sustainability, while also shifting their perspective beyond the economic rationalist (technocentric) paradigm. While the feedback from the students has been very positive over the 10-plus years it has been offered, it is not a core unit in the MBA program. This fact means that most Monash MBA students are graduating without understanding the serious risks associated with environmental and social issues such as climate change, "the greatest and widest-ranging market failure ever seen" (Stern, 2006, p. i). To move the sustainability agenda forward, sustainability concepts must be integrated into the core units of the MBA program in addition to offering a core unit on sustainability principles and tools.

More progress is occurring in a wider university context. In 2007, Monash University joined 375 universities from around the world to sign the Talloires Declaration (Association of University Leaders for a Sustainable Future (ULSF, 1990). The Declaration includes a Ten Point Action Plan for integrating sustainability and environmental responsibility into all aspects of the university's operations, teaching, research, and community engagement. Monash University is in the very early stages of integrating a "balanced coverage" of sustainability issues in the overall business management curriculum. Integrating this balanced approach will supplement the postgraduate program in corporate sustainability—Master of Corporate Environmental and Sustainability Management (MCESM)—offered by SGES since 2000 and the MBA/MCESM double-degree launched in 2007.

ACKNOWLEDGMENTS

The authors gratefully acknowledge the contributions of Mrs. Jo Strahan who co-developed the SPIR approach referred to in this chapter and Dr. James Moulder who provided guidance on teaching an intensive unit.

REFERENCES

Association of University Leaders for a Sustainable Future. (1990). *Talloires Declaration*. Retrieved September 11, 2008, from http://www.ulsf.org/talloires_declaration.html

Cervantes, G. (2007). A methodology for teaching industrial ecology. *International Journal of Sustainability in Higher Education, 8*(2), 131–141.

Cordano, M., Ellis, K. M., & Scherer, R. F. (2003). Natural capitalists: Increasing business students' environmental sensitivity. *Journal of Management Education, 27*(2), 144–157.

Courtney, H. (2001). *20/20 foresight: Crafting strategy in an uncertain world*, Boston: Harvard Business School Press.

Epstein, M. J., & Wisner, P. S. (2001). Using a balanced scorecard to implement sustainability. *Environmental Quality Management, 11*(2), 1–10.

Figge, F., Hahn, T., Schaltegger, S., & Wagner, M. (2002). The sustainability balanced scorecard: Linking sustainability management to business strategy. *Business Strategy and the Environment, 11*(5), 269–283.

Garnault, R. (2008). *Garnault climate change review draft report June 2008*. Canberra: Attorney-General's Department.

Gladwin, T. N., Kennelly, J. J., & Krause, T.-S. (1995). Shifting paradigms for sustainable development: Implications for management theory and research. *Academy of Management Review, 20*(4), 874–907.

Global reporting initiative. (2006). Sustainability reporting G3 guidelines. Retrieved September 11, 2008, from http://www.globalreporting.org/ReportingFramework/G3Guidelines/

Gosling, J., & Mintzberg, H. (2004). The education of practicing managers. *MIT Sloan Management Review, 45*(4), 19–22.

Harding, R. (1996). *Sustainability: Principles to practice. Outcomes* (pp. 13-18). Fenner Conference on the Envrionment 1994. Canberra: Department of the Environment, Sport and Territories.

Harding, R. (1998). *Environmental decision-making: The roles of scientists, engineers and the public*. Leichhardt, NSW: Federation Press.

Hawken, P., Lovins, A. B., & Lovins, L. H. (1999). *Natural capitalism: The next industrial revolution*, London: Earthscan.

Holden, J. P., & Ehrlich, P. R. (1974). Human population and the global environment. *American Scientist, 62*, 282–292.

Intergovernmental Panel on Climate Change. (2007a). *Climate change 2007: Synthesis report. Contribution of working groups I, II and III to the fourth assessment report of the Intergovernmental Panel on Climate Change* (Working Group IV Report). Geneva, Switzerland: Author.

Intergovernmental Panel on Climate Change. (2007b). *Climate change 2007: The synthesis report summary for policymakers* (Working Group IV Report). Valencia: Author.

Kaplan, R. S., & Norton, D. P. (1996). *The balanced scorecard: Translating strategy into action*. Boston: Harvard Business School Press.

Kearins, K., & Springett, D. (2003). Educating for sustainability: Developing critical skills. *Journal of Management Education, 27*(2), 188–204.

Lovins, A. B., Lovins, L. H., & Hawken, P. (1999). A road map for natural capitalism. *Harvard Business Review, 77*(3), 145–158.

Nicholls, R. J., Hanson, S., Herweijer, C., Patmore, N., Hallegatte, S., Corfee-Morlot, J., et al. (2008). *Ranking port cities with high exposure and vulnerability to climate extremes: Exposure estimates* (OECD Environment Working Papers, No. 1). Paris: OECD.

Porter, M. E., & Kramer, M. R. (2006). Strategy and society: The link between competitive advantage and corporate social responsibility. *Harvard Business Review, 84*(12), 78–92.

Rackham, N. (1996). *The SPIN selling fieldbook*, New York: McGraw-Hill.

Rands, G. P. (1993). Preparing students to work for sustainability: Teaching as if the earth's future mattered. *Journal of Teaching in International Business, 5*(1/2), 19–46.

Rands, G. P. (2007, August). *Principles for and desired attributes of management education for sustainability*. Academy of Management Annual Meeting: Doing Well By Doing Good, Philadelphia.

Robèrt, K.-H. (1997). *The natural step: A framework for achieving sustainability in our organizations*, Cambridge, MA: Pegasus Communications.

Robinson, J. (2004). Squaring the circle? Some thoughts on the idea of sustainable development. *Ecological Economics, 48*(4), 369–384.

Roome, N. (2005). Teaching sustainability in a global MBA: Insights from the OneMBA. *Business Strategy and the Environment, 14*(May/Jun), 160–171.

Roy, A. (2004). Peace and the new corporate liberation theology. The 2004 Sydney Peace Prize lecture delivered by Arundhati Roy: Seymour Theatre Centre, University of Sydney. Retrieved May 18, 2009, from http://info.interactivist.net/node/3723

Rusinko, C. A. (2005). Using quality management as a bridge in educating for sustainability in a business school. *International Journal of Sustainability in Higher Education*, *6*(4), 340–350.

Shephard, K. (2008). Higher education for sustainability: Seeking affective learning outcomes. *International Journal of Sustainability in Higher Education*, *9*(1), 87–98.

Springett, D. (2005). Education for sustainability' in the business studies curriculum: A call for a critical agenda. *Business Strategy and the Environment*, *14*(3), 146–159.

Standards Australia International Ltd. and Standards New Zealand (2004). AS/NZS 4360 Risk Management (3rd ed.). Sydney: SAI Global.

Stern, N. (2006). *Stern review: The economics of climate change*. Cambridge: Cambridge University Press.

Stubbs, W., & Cocklin, C. (2008). Teaching sustainability to business students: Shifting mindsets. *International Journal of Sustainability in Higher Education*, *9*(3), 206–221.

Sustainability Institute & Meadows, D. (2001). *The minitiature earth*. Retrieved September 10, 2008, from http://www.miniature-earth.com/me_english.htm

Svanström, M., Francisco, J. L.-G., & Debra, R. (2008). Learning outcomes for sustainable development in higher education. *International Journal of Sustainability in Higher Education*, *9*(3), 339–351.

Tighe, L. (2008). *Inspirational coaching*. Retrieved September 11, 2008, from www.icoachu.com.au

United Nations Environment Program. (2005). *One planet many people: Atlas of our changing environment*. Nairobi, Kenya: Division of Early Warning and Assessment (DEWA), United Nations Environment Programme.

United Nations Environment Program. (2007). *Insuring for sustainability: Why and how the leaders are doing it*. Genève: Insurance Working Group of the United Nations Environment Programme Finance Initiative.

Waterman, R. H., Peters, T. J., & Phillips, J. R. (1980). Structure is not organisation. *Business Horizons*, *23*(3), 14–26.

WGBH International (2001). *What's up with the weather? Screened on SBS Television*. Australia: Marcom Projects. Retrieved June 2, 2009, from http://www.marcom.com.au/product_details.php?prod=6SBWUW

World Commission on Environment and Development (1987). *Our common future*, Oxford; New York: Oxford University Press.

World Resources Institute. 2000. Water Quantity. Retrieved June 2, 2009, from http://www.wri.org/publication/content/8147

CHAPTER 15

GROUNDING SUSTAINABILITY IN REALITY

Encouraging Students to Make Their Own Case for Action

Kate Kearins and Eva Collins

This chapter encourages instructors to engage students in researching and writing their own sustainability cases, thus making 'the case' for and recommending specific action towards achieving sustainability. Personal engagement is shown to ground students' learning in actual organizational, industry, event or issue-based contexts. Students grapple with real-world tensions and challenges. They reflect on the relevance of classroom theory to practice. Examples are used to show how students apply, critique and sometimes even develop theory that yields insight into the situations they are analyzing. Students contribute to enhanced practice by presenting options and/or recommendations for the short, medium and even long term. To be successful, these options must take into account the complexities faced by the owner/managers, industry bodies, event organizers or relevant policy-makers in the case. A powerful learning experience can emerge for both the students and the organizations involved. Guidelines for implementing case-writing as a student learning and assessment exercise are offered.

Management Education for Global Sustainability, pp. 327–341
Copyright © 2009 by Information Age Publishing
All rights of reproduction in any form reserved.

INTRODUCTION

Our aim in this chapter is to encourage instructors to adopt a student case-writing project as part of coursework in a sustainability, social responsibility, or environmental management class. We advocate student case-writing projects primarily as a basis for the students themselves to learn about sustainability efforts and challenges in a real-world contex—not for our own or others' use as a teaching vehicle for the next class of students. Therefore, we concentrate in this chapter mostly on students writing what we call "case reports," rather than "teaching cases" which are a different genre with a different purpose. Case reports arguably take less time and are simpler to write. They enable students to focus in-depth on just one organization, industry or situation, evaluate for themselves the key issues and present an argument and/or a plan for working towards their resolution.

Our students generally like case-writing projects. Moreover, they usually consider they have learned a good deal from both doing the research, and writing it up in a format that is both professional and convincing. We tell them that the case reports should be able to be given to the case organization, or someone else with relevant industry or situational knowledge—and this approach further motivates them to be realistic in their evaluation of the situation at hand and reasonable about what they ultimately recommend. As our title suggests, we want our students to be able to make their own case for action, based on a real organization, industry or situation and the theoretical ideals and practical tools they have learned in our courses. A bonus—but also an important payback—is that often the case organization personnel or others involved get to learn about how they might move forward in embracing the sustainability challenge.

This chapter is structured as follows. First, we explain why, based on relevant literature and personal experience, it benefits students to write their own cases. Second, we demonstrate, through the use of examples, how researching and writing a case report allows students to reflect on the relevance of theory to practice. Third, we offer guidelines for implementing case-writing projects as a student learning and assessment exercise.

Rationale for Adopting a Student Case-Writing Project

A basic, but not uncontroversial definition of a case is offered by Naumes and Naumes (2006, p. 4): "A case is a factual description of events that happened at some point in the past." Whether there can ever be complete objectivity in selecting and presenting the "facts" is doubtful. Involving a degree of careful interpretation on the part of their writers, cases provide descriptions of actual situations faced by real people. They can be focused or more generally descriptive.

Cases of various lengths have come to occupy an important place in many business classrooms, particularly within management courses. Long advocated as a method of educating students, notably by Harvard Business School and the Ivey School of Business as early as the 1920s, cases are seen as being able to "breathe life and instill greater meaning into the lessons of management education" (Harvard Business School, 2008). Cases can allow students to appreciate the complexity and multidimensionality of management situations. Such complexity and multidimensionality is inherent in the sustainability challenge.

Porter (2006) reminds us that cases let those who write them pick up on what is happening in businesses or other organizations in ways we cannot capture in theoretical models, no matter how gifted we are. For example, sustainability case-writers are often confronted with one or more of the following difficult to resolve issues: tensions between sustainability and firm growth; reliance on the use of non-renewable resources; the far-reaching impacts of business operations across often very long product lifecycles; and the fundamental reality that despite the rhetoric, a truly sustainable business does not exist. It is relevant to consider these issues in the context of real cases where those involved are making choices and tradeoffs.

Cases can help overcome a disconnection between theory and practice that is increasingly the subject of concern (Bartunek, 2007; Van de Ven & Johnson, 2006; Van de Ven, 2007). As Gladwin, Kennelly, and Krause (1995, p. 874) lament, modern management theory suffers from a fractured epistemology, one that "separates humanity from nature and truth from morality." On the other hand, theories of ecological sustainability threaten business-as-usual. And to the extent these ideals have filtered down into business practice, they have largely morphed into the "business case" or what some have termed "corporate sustainability" where the environment in particular remains subordinate to the interests of business (Levy, 1997; Milne, Kearins, & Walton, 2006; Newton & Harte, 1997; Prasad & Elmes, 2005). Newton (2002) questions whether it is possible to create a new ecological order as seemingly promised by business's engagement with sustainability. Market-based environmentalism—being "green and competitive" (Porter & van der Linde, 1995)—may simply not take us far enough.

Letting students explore the disconnect between theoretical ideals and practical tools is important (see also Kearins & Springett, 2003). In our courses, which are admittedly elective courses, we have found it relatively easy to excite students about the vision of a sustainable future (albeit that the reality might indeed be less appealing in terms of material comforts).

Moreover, we see a clear role for universities in encouraging students to discuss theoretical ideals, and to consider and debate the nature and feasibility of the far-reaching and fundamental changes many commentators agree would be needed to achieve sustainability (Shrivastava & Hart, 1995; Welford, 1995). However, as instructors, we do feel a responsibility that our students leave our courses with the knowledge that business, in particular, has a crucial role to play in the transition to sustainable development (Hawken, 1993), together with a realistic sense of what businesses both can and should do going forward in that transition. For this reason, we use case writing projects as a way for students to bridge both a radical visionary approach, and a practical incrementalism one based on currently available frameworks and tools (such as, for example environmental management systems, social audits, life cycle and footprint analyses and eco-labeling).

We argue there is even greater potential for students themselves to learn useful skills when pitting their own idealism against the complex realism of currently unsustainable organizations, industries or situations, rather than their remaining mainly in the role of an analyst of cases written by others. Published teaching cases are already tidily structured, the information needed generally at hand, and the theoretical links if not transparent, the subject of someone else's intention and interpretation. They certainly have their place in the management classroom. But the analytic experience they offer is unlikely to be the same as first-hand engagement by students with the messy reality of unsynthesized, uneven and incomplete information. Add to that the difficulty of organizing the data so that it can be analyzed and then working out even small steps in a possible transition to an ideal sustainable state. Students learn that what they suggest as such steps are insufficient, but they nevertheless confront the dilemma of whether doing something is better than nothing.

Just as the case writing project tests the idealism of some students, we have also found the assignment helpful in breaking through other students' cynicism. Each semester, there are a few students who come into our courses with the idea that business should be focused only on the financial bottom-line. We have taught the case writing project for 11 and 7 years respectively, and invariably, we see that as students go into the field and talk to organizational or industry personnel, or examine a particular event in some depth, they begin to engage with sustainability issues at a more passionate level. On more than one occasion, the student who showed the most skepticism in class, became the biggest advocate for the need for business to engage with sustainability after talking to people actually involved in dealing with the issues in real situations—whether on a day-to-day basis or on a more strategic level.

More widely, the realism of student case-writing projects has been found to result in student engagement (Ashamalla & Crocitto, 2001). In addition, cases can be used to help novice professionals connect theory to practice and to develop better problem-solving skills, as noted by Kagan (1993). Cases provide unique avenues for generating insights based on the integration of course learning and actual opportunities and challenges. We believe that personal engagement better grounds students' learning about environmental management and sustainability in actual, organizational, industry, event, or issue-based contexts. In our experience, the real world is full of generally well-intentioned people struggling to understand sustainability concepts and put into practice even incremental changes—let alone the radical changes called for by some. For example in our country, the New Zealand economy is dominated by small and medium-sized enterprises (SMEs). In 2006, 96% of enterprises employed 19 or fewer people (Ministry of Economic Development, 2007). It is not uncommon for SMEs to have a passion for sustainability, but no systems and processes in place to support the stated commitment.

In summary then, we have claimed that student case writing projects can be an effective way to help students to bridge the divide between theory and practice. In addition, by getting students out of the classroom and into the field, student engagement with class content increases significantly. We next discuss how students are encouraged to make important linkages between theory and practice through case-writing projects.

Helping Students Relate Theory to Practice

Using examples, we show how students select (and sometimes develop) theory that yields insight into the situations they are analyzing. We also show how students can contribute to enhanced practice by presenting options and/or recommendations for the short, medium, and even long term. To be successful, these options must take into account the complexities faced by the owner/managers, industry bodies, event organizers, or relevant policy-makers in the case. A powerful learning experience can emerge for both the students and the organizations involved.

Regardless of the kind of practice exposed and the arguments and/or plans advanced, case writing projects have a role in providing both context-specific and more general lessons. To be convincing, students need to ground their evaluation, arguments, and/or plans in the realities of the organization, industry or situation they are examining. As discussed above, a small business will generally not have the resources for grand innovations, or often need an accredited environmental management system or ecolabel, or sustainability report, for example. But a larger business in the same industry or one with supplier or customer pressure will find it useful to make an assessment of these tools, based on the benefits and costs actually involved. Here the theory could be applied theory as to what constitutes an appropriate environmental management system or an effective ecolabel, and what the benefits and costs of accreditation are. Slightly different issues exist around the adoption of sustainability reporting—decisions need to be made on the extent and nature of reporting, appropriate measures and targets, as well as cost in time and resources and an evaluation of benefits in terms of hopefully enhanced firm reputation within its particular industry context. We might also expect some stretch in the student's recommendations as to what case personnel might consider doing beyond initial steps. Suggesting a progression of feasible steps would assist us to differentiate between an A and a C student in this particular class, as they would essentially be dealing with both the practical here-and-now, and the overall ideal of where particular organizations might ultimately head on their sustainability journey.

Students can usefully "benchmark" organizations against best practice within their own industry, or recommended best practice. One place to start background research is to see what an award-winning or leading organization in the same industry is doing. Another is the Global Reporting Initiative (G3) (2000) guidelines, including the sector relevant guidelines. Web-savvy students will find a plethora of additional information about what is considered best practice in particular industries around the globe, and what are signaled as the future industry trends.

A slightly different and more inductive approach is to start with the case organization, industry or situation and see what is being done by way of responsible management, what else personnel there think could be done to become sustainable (or less unsustainable) and to discuss the feasibility of different options. This approach allows students to drill down more into a case-relevant area they or the case personnel find interesting or important to know more about. They can then look for the theory that supports or helps explain or further thinking or application around that domain. A decision might need to be taken to invest in more environmentally-responsible plant or equipment, or to engage stakeholders more meaningfully. Motivations for such decisions can be explored with case personnel, and criteria for evaluating different options thought about both in light of the management style of the organizations concerned and different theories. These could be big picture theories such as political economy or legitimacy theory, or more immediately applicable theories such as stakeholder or strategic choice theory.

Very occasionally, existing theory is found to either not offer much or to be somehow deficient. Stakeholder theory is a case in point. Although much has been written about stakeholder theory, it can sometimes be seen as difficult to apply. The single case may itself contradict an aspect of theory. In this situation, a good student will want to discuss the anomalies and may even go on to suggest a potential modification or development of theory. A very good student will note the need to "test" the new theory with further examples. For more theoretically curious students (including in particular graduate students), Eisenhardt (1989) and Eisenhardt and Graebner (2007) offer sound advice on theory-building from cases.

In this section, we have taken a broad-brush approach to what constitutes theory—big picture theories and more applied theories that might be relevant to understanding particular case scenarios. Instructors and their students might like to substitute less daunting terminology for what we call "theory" by asking more generally: *what theories, concepts or techniques might be useful in the understanding or the resolution of issues identified in the case?*

Case-Writing as a Student Learning and Assessment Exercise

We reiterate here our focus on student case-writing projects with a 'case report' outcome. These reports are cousins of the typical teaching case that has a decision or evaluative focus. Like teaching cases, case reports provide a description of the case situation, gleaned from fieldwork interviews where possible and from secondary data about the case organization, industry or event scenario. But they differ in that they also provide in the same document, a clear definition of the issues, and a discussion of why they are important, as well as a plan or recommendations for working towards their resolution. In some ways, the additions are a little like what is in the typical instructor's manual or teaching note for teaching cases. They do not, however, focus students on worrying about pedagogical issues to do with teaching cases. We are not interested in this instance in teaching the students to be case teachers, or in teaching case-writers. It is more important that the format we have students write in is one that is useful for them to learn how to communicate relevant information in a professional and convincing way, potentially to case organization personnel, or people knowledgeable about the industry or situation under examination.

To write a good case, good research is fundamental. In our experience, students tend not to focus on a research method until they actually use it. For graduate students, the case-writing project provides an opportunity to go into more depth about case research in general and the methods used to gather and organize rich data. For undergraduates, it is less important to be concerned about the minutiae of particular research processes and better to focus them more directly on the task at hand which is gathering enough data to be able to make a reasoned assessment of the case situation.

Students can write cases from primary and/or secondary sources. Well-planned interviews with even one or two relevant case personnel can yield sufficient primary data for this project. Documentary research facilitated by internet access can be good as an additional data source—or sufficient on its own. There are likely to be students who don't have good access through friends, relatives, or cold-calling to a case site that they personally find interesting. We have found that this case-writing project can work well with access to secondary sources alone so long as students choose sites with sufficient relevant information and are prepared to dig for wider industry best practice information to draw on. They need information on the organization, industry or situation, the sustainability issues that are implicated, and the efforts made to date to address them.

Choosing a case that has meaning for the student at some level (whether they identify with the people involved or care about a particular issue or feel there is a case for action) is important. The case-writing project works best when student curiosity is piqued. Choosing an organizational, industry or situational context that opens up a whole new world to them, or maybe is somehow related to where they would ultimately like to work, certainly arouses their interest. Student case-writers often come to believe they have an important story to tell about an organization or an industry doing a lot more in the sustainability realm than they originally thought. They want to tell that story—or they want to help make a difference in some small way.

An important point to reiterate in this context, is that is very unlikely that any organization or situation is totally sustainable—in an ecological or social, let alone an economic sense. So any kind of organization or situation is a possible candidate for a case study. Our students have argued for the greening of legal firms, government audit offices and kindergartens. They have studied large firms, local manufacturing sites and waste dumps. There will almost invariably always be something more an organization can do to become less unsustainable, and that students can recommend. For the student, this learning itself may be one of the most important ah-ha moments. It can also be good for the organization concerned to receive this advice.

We do not allow students to make up cases—to write fictitious or composite cases. But we do acknowledge, both here and to them, that as case-writers they will be making choices about what to include and exclude in their case report, how to frame that information and inevitably, in doing so, they will be interpreting the information. To maintain a degree of objectivity, they need to be able to defend their choices both to us and to the parties concerned, as a fair representation of the case situation.

Early on, the instructor can obtain any ethical approval needed from their institution for their students conducting such research projects.

Because case organization personnel are often busy and/or have entirely different priorities from those of our students, the students do need to use the limited time they give you to best advantage. It is useful to do considerable background research on the circumstances and issues facing the industry/sector and case organization before conducting interviews. Internet sources can be very useful here. It is worth telling students to look at industry, professional association, and supporting organization Web sites as well as those of the focal organizations and similar organizations elsewhere. Advise them too, to investigate newspaper and magazine databases containing relevant articles and outsiders' views of events. From their background research, reading of the sustainability literature and discussions in class, they could come up with a topic they wish to explore more in the context of the case they are going to write. Or they might be going in with more general research questions in mind. It is unlikely that they will have no particular focus in mind as they enter a research situation (Strauss & Corbin, 1990), but they can benefit by being open to the possibility of something different from what they anticipated ending up being a more worthy focus. As Siggelkow (2007, p. 21) puts it: when entering the field, "an open mind is good, an empty mind is not."

Bear in mind some students may wish to tape record their interviews—although for the kind of case report we are expecting, direct quotes are not necessary. It is a good habit for students to write up notes after each interview and these might contain additional context for responses, references to interesting or problematic features of the interview, and reflections and theoretical hunches (Emerson, Fretz, & Shaw, 1995). But again, such a "rigorous" research approach is not essential.

Don't let the students forget to use the theory they have learned in class. They need to avoid the temptation to bung every little detail found about the case organization/industry or situation, or to use all the theories superficially rather than select the most appropriate theory to give insight. Enfolding literature is an important aspect of theory development. They need to give their case report a final read so as to be sure to focus squarely on the relevant case details and eliminate the superfluous is important for a polished result.

We encourage, but do not oblige students to give their case reports, or discuss their recommendations with the case organization. We see it as useful payback for the organization for the time its personnel may have spent being interviewed. Furthermore, good research, we believe, deserves an audience. Publication of student case reports, or further use of them, is not a priority for us. If students want to share them, we encourage it.

Feedback we have received from our students is that, at the beginning, the case report can seem an overwhelming assessment and the first place students can get stuck is choice of topic. It can be useful for students to see good examples of the kinds of case report we are looking for. We do generally offer a list of previous student case report titles like the one we give in Exhibit 1, so students get an idea of what others have chosen to study, how they oriented their case report and can consider whether it might be time for an updated case report on the same organization, industry or situation. Moreover the list reveals our openness to different kinds of cases, different levels of analysis and different ways of focusing a case report.

The case report is usually due at the end of the semester. On one occasion, the course was a week-long block course taught in Europe and the case report was due in lieu of an exam, a little while after the teaching had concluded. Having this assessment due at the end of the course means students can bring to bear a more considered view, based on an overview of the most relevant theory to apply, rather than just the ones they might have been taught up to any particular point in the course. Note, all but one of the international students in the Europe block course did their research from secondary sources, and most found cases from their country of origin that yielded fascinating insights into the application of theory. These particular students proved the transferability of the case-writing project by producing excellent reports on the whole, and themselves attesting to in-depth learning about environmental and sustainability matters in their home countries. Cases do necessarily provide a degree of contextualization, by their very nature.

Another approach that can be use to break the case research and writing task down into manageable pieces is to have a one-page paper due mid-way through the course, if taught over a whole semester. The one-pager identifies the organization, industry or situation, what data the student plans to collect and how they are going to collect it. The students share their one-pager with the rest of the class in a workshop-type session. This approach gets the whole class thinking about the assessment and sharing ideas and resources at the half-way point in the course instead of waiting until the very end. Near the end of semester, we have found it useful to have another workshop session on the case reports—but it is by no means mandatory. By this time students would have picked the topic, familiarized themselves with best practice for case research, and oftentimes some interviews have been attempted or completed. The second workshop allows students to brainstorm common difficulties, for example company representatives not returning phone calls, or a common problem in qualitative research, feeling overwhelmed by the amount of data collected and unsure how to write it up in a coherent fashion.

Exhibit 1: Sample Student Case Report Titles

Local SME/Organization-based Cases
Waikeria Prison Case Study: A Look at Sustainability
Frankton School's Battle against Childhood Obesity
Hamilton's MBS Balance Therapeutic Massage Clinic
An Assessment of Auckland Philharmonia's Ability to become a Sustainable Regional Orchestra

Local Issues-based Cases
'Spray It Ain't So' : Hamilton City Council, Graffiti Vandalism and a Time for Strategic Sustainable Thinking
Is Auckland Choking Itself? A Financial Capital's Air Pollution Problems from a Sustainability Perspective
The Dairying and Clean Streams Accord: What does the future hold for Waikato dairy farmers?
An Investigation into Ballast Contamination in the Whangarei Harbour

Larger / National and International Organization-based Cases
Incineration of Municipal Solid Waste: A Case of Shanghai Jiangqiao MSW Incineration Facility
Tasman Pulp and Paper Mill: Managing Environmental Impacts or in a State of Political Sustainability?
Trade Aid and the Environment
Sustainability at Shell: Investigating Sustainable Development in the Retail Oil Industry

Industry Issues-based Cases
Hamilton Restaurants and their Waste Initiatives
Environmental Concerns for the New Zealand Meat Industry
Sustainable Winegrowing New Zealand
How Environmentally Sustainable are New Zealand Supermarkets?

Events or Other Situational Cases
The Green Marathon
Green Events Management
What Lord of the Rings might have done for the New Zealand Environment
Getting the Right Kind of Road through the Forest

We have allocated 35% of the total course grade to this assessment. Appendix 1 details the full guidelines we give students for the assessment. We have previously allowed up to 8000 words but student feedback has consistently requested a shorter word length (4–5000 words), which also works well. We encourage students to be creative in the presentation of the reports with photos or even a different type of format, such as a film. The guidelines described represent a structure for the case report assessment that has worked well for us, but there are many possible variations from our guidelines (such as the length issue), which still achieves the learning benefits.

CONCLUSION

This chapter argues that student case-writing projects benefit students in making connections between real-world situations and theory in the sustainability domain. Making a theoretical connection with real organizations, industries and situations, 'good', 'bad' or just plain interesting, provides valuable learning opportunities for all concerned. It prompts students to think carefully about currently unsustainable practices and ways we might work towards changing them. And where case reports are given to the people involved in organizations, industries or other situations, those people get a payback for their efforts in sharing with our students and access to what we hope is best practice thinking in terms of the latest tools and frameworks and theory.

Encouraging students to write their own cases allows them to see the real-world tensions associated with the achievement of sustainability for themselves. It also avoids impressing students with professionally written best-practice examples, and the appearance of relative simplicity in working towards sometimes impracticable resolutions of complex sustainability issues. But perhaps, the biggest benefit we have found with the student case writing project is that students leave the course inspired to make change and to be change agents, but tempered in their idealism by having thought carefully about the practicability and the nature of needed changes in real-world situations. They are proven ready to make the case for action towards sustainability in terms of both the incremental and bigger strides, the world needs so much.

APPENDIX 1: SAMPLE INSTRUCTIONS TO STUDENTS

General Instructions

Produce a report on any organization, industry or situation impacted by environmental and/or social sustainability issues which illustrates the need for management strategy.

Research the case through direct access and/or through secondary sources. Use of original sources and direct access is much preferred. You will make contacts, you will learn, and if you do a good job, you stand to gain in credibility by helping others reflect on the latest thinking in the sustainability area.

Your case report should contain an analysis of relevant environmental and/or social sustainability issues facing the organization or industry, or management/policy bodies, an assessment of which issues are the most pressing in the short, medium and long term and a list of feasible options for dealing with at least the most urgent of these issues. You should distinguish between the activities that are already being undertaken and the options you recommend (which may include continued emphasis on similar activities or new areas of emphasis). Make a good case for action.

Your case report will be assessed on the following criteria: presentation of sufficient relevant and interesting information, integration of relevant theory from this course, evidence of critical thought and development of reasoned arguments and new insights for taking the organization/industry or situation forward, together with overall professionalism in presentation.

Hints on Choosing a Case

Find an organization, industry or situation which interests you. Sources of case situations include business newspapers, magazines, radio or TV news/documentaries, the web, and personal contacts. Think about the kind of organizations, industries or situations you might like to work in. It could well be worth your time choosing one of them and using this assignment to investigate it in some depth.

Assess the amount and quality of information available as to whether the case could be best written from secondary sources or with direct access. Original research is clearly better from both an academic point of view, and in terms of what you and the organization are likely to gain from the study.

If direct access is required, seek agreement from the organization concerned. Explain the type and extent of information you require, the methods you will use to collect information, and the organization's right to review the case report before submission or to ask for confidentiality agreements.

Focusing Your Case Study and Organizing Your Material

Reflect on the case situation in terms of relevant theory from the course and your further reading. The theoretical issues you raise in your case report should spring naturally from the case data. For example, in looking at a particular case, you might find packaging and labelling issues arising. In another case, stakeholder management may be more central, or effecting a culture change across the organization may be a critical area worth developing in your theoretical discussion.

Your case should be 4000–5000 words, include an interesting title and subheadings and be comprised of:

An introduction that names the organization, industry or situation being investigated and locates it within a particular place and time, and states the purpose and focus of the report;

a background section that gives relevant detail on the organization, industry or situation and describes current actions towards sustainability;

an issues identification and analysis section that describes key issues either grouped in paragraph form or introduced and listed in bullet points with appropriate discussion;

a theory integration section which shows how the latest thinking/theory is relevant to understanding the issues and working towards resolution where possible;

an argument and/or a plan, possibly including recommendations if appropriate that sets out what should be considered in the short, medium and longer term to move towards sustainability;

a short summary section to conclude the report;

a reference list and appendices (only include appendices if strictly relevant).

Make the case report interesting to read. Cite key figures in the case directly where they have interesting and pertinent comments. Consider including photographs and diagrams, constructing tables to display information, if appropriate.

REFERENCES

Ashamalla, M. H., & Crocitto, M. M. (2001). Student-generated cases as a transformation tool. *Journal of Management Education, 25*(5), 516–530.

Bartunek, J. M. (2007). Academic-practitioner collaboration need not require joint or relevant research: Toward a relational scholarship of integration, *Academy of Management Journal, 50*(6), 1323–1333.

Eisenhardt, K. M. (1989). Building theories from case study research. *Academy of Management Review, 14*(4), 532–550.

Eisenhardt, K. M., & Graebner, M. E. (2007). Theory building from cases: Opportunities and challenges. *Academy of Management Journal, 50*(1), 25–32.

Emerson, R. M., Fretz, R. I., & Shaw, L. L. (1995). *Writing ethnographic fieldnotes.* Chicago: University of Chicago Press.

Gladwin T, Kennelly J., & Krause T-S. (1995). Shifting paradigms for sustainable development: Implications for management theory and research, *Academy of Management Review, 20*(4), 874–907.

Global Reporting Initiative. (2000). *Global Reporting Initiative: A common framework for sustainability reporting.* Retrieved January 10, 2007, from www .globalreporting.org/

Harvard Business School. (2008). *The case method.* Retrieved 16 June 2008, from www.hbs.edu/case

Hawken P. (1993). *The ecology of commerce: How business can save the planet.* New York: HarperCollins.

Kagan, D. M. (1993). Contexts for the use of classroom cases. *American Educational Research Journal, 30*(4), 703–723.

Kearins, K., & Springett, D. (2003). Educating for sustainability: Developing critical skills. *Journal of Management Education, 27*(2), 188–204.

Levy D. (1997). Environmental management as political sustainability. *Organization and Environment, 10,* 126–147.

Milne, M., Kearins, K., & Walton, S. (2006). Business makes a "journey" out of "sustainability": Creating adventures in Wonderland? *Organization, 13*(6), 801–839.

Ministry of Economic Development. (2007). *SMEs in New Zealand: Structure and Dynamics.* Retrieved December 21, 2007, from www.med.govt.nz

Naumes, W., & Naumes, M. J. (2006). *The art and craft of case writing* (2nd ed.). Armonk NY: M. E. Sharpe.

Newton, T. J., & Harte, G. (1997). Green business: Technicist kitsch? *Journal of Management Studies, 34,* 75–98.

Newton, T. J. (2002). Creating the new ecological order? Elias and actor network theory. *Academy of Management Review, 27,* 523–540.

Porter, M., & Van der Linde, C. (1995). Green and competitive. *Harvard Business Review, 73*(5), 120–134.

Porter, M. (2006). On the importance of case research. *Case Research Journal, 26*(1), 1–3.

Prasad, P., & Elmes, M. (2005). In the name of the practical: Unearthing the hegemony of pragmatics in the discourse of environmental management. *Journal of Management Studies, 42,* 845–867.

Shrivastava, P., & Hart, S. (1995). Creating sustainable corporations. *Business Strategy and the Environment,* 154–165.

Siggelkow, N. (2007). Persuasion with cases. *Academy of Management Journal, 50*(1), 20–24.

Strauss, A., & Corbin, J. (1990). *Basics of qualitative research: Grounded theory procedures and techniques.* Newbury Park, CA: SAGE.

Van de Ven, A. H. (2007). *Engaged scholarship.* Oxford: Oxford University Press.

Van de Ven, A. H., & Johnson, P. (2006). Knowledge for theory and practice, *Academy of Management Review, 31*(4), 802–821.

Welford, R. (1995). *Environmental sustainability and sustainable development: The challenge for the 21st century.* London: Routledge.

CHAPTER 16

THE INTEGRATION OF REAL-WORLD STUDENT PROJECTS INTO A SUSTAINABLE MBA PROGRAM

Robert Sroufe

The Association to Advance Collegiate Schools of Business (AACSB) has accredited more than 550 degree-granting institutions in 30 countries. There are over 120,000 MBA degrees awarded each year in the United States. Only a small proportion of these newly minted MBAs will do more than read about a sustainable development issue during their graduate studies. The purpose of this chapter is to highlight how one business school has developed a fully integrated Sustainable MBA program featuring real-world student consulting projects that focus on ethical management of social, environmental, and financial resources. This case study can serve as a roadmap for how other business schools and faculty can develop their own approach to the integration of sustainability into student projects and curricula. It also describes how real-world projects present opportunities for cross-functional integration of an overall MBA curriculum and enrichment of individual classes.

Management Education for Global Sustainability, pp. 343–364
Copyright © 2009 by Information Age Publishing

INTRODUCTION

The Association to Advance Collegiate Schools of Business (AACSB) has accredited more than 550 degree-granting institutions in 30 countries. There are over 120,000 MBA degrees awarded each year in the U.S. (Moore, 2007). Only a small proportion of these newly minted MBAs will do more than read about a sustainable development issue during their graduate studies. This lack of exposure to a newly developing field can be attributed to a dearth of schools proactively integrating sustainability-focused, real-world projects into curricula, and in years past, a lack of MBA programs specializing in the emerging field of sustainable development. The tide has turned, and more recently the surge of interest in global warming, carbon trading, green buildings, and going green has brought many companies to the doors of business schools looking for help quantifying the business case for sustainability. Business managers are now asking for help in understanding sustainable development, measuring performance, and managing change. Other catalysts for the infusion of sustainability into academic institutions include the measurement and ranking of business schools along sustainability and service learning dimensions, a recent push for more corporate responsibility from special interest groups, and student career aspirations to work with more sustainable companies (Net Impact, 2007).

This chapter chronicles one business school's approach to the development and integration of real-world sustainability projects into curriculum, pedagogy, and research. The proposition is that relevant, contemporary projects present opportunities for cross-functional integration of an overall MBA curriculum, enrichment of individual classes, and development of student leadership and communication skills. While many schools are eager to hang the moniker of sustainability on some aspect of their program, this chapter provides a framework for meaningful projects with tangible impacts. It is intended to provide insight into what has worked and what has not with the hope of advancing service learning within business school environments. While opportunities abound, there are many challenges to developing successful service learning environments. The sections of the chapter address the catalysts for change; obstacles to creating an integrated service learning project management class; roles of faculty, students, and project clients; project selection; and evaluation of project and program success.

Primary criticisms of business education include the absence of realistic experience, applied learning, and grounded personal development (Mintzberg & Gosling, 2002; Pfeffer & Fong, 2002). Such concerns can be addressed in part by service learning courses. The American Association for Higher Education's definition of service learning is "that which helps promote both intellectual and civic engagement by linking the work students do in the classroom to real-world problems and real-world needs" (AAHE, 1997). Godfrey, Illes, and Berry (2005) argued that service learning projects create much needed breadth in business education programs, and that service learning pedagogy seeks to balance academic rigor with a practical relevance, set in a context of civic engagement, which furnishes students with a broader and richer educational experience". Unfortunately, graduate business students rarely have the option of taking a service learning elective.

The recent surge of interest in sustainable development presents a tremendous opportunity for business schools to get away from business pedagogy as usual, and instead design new curricula and course work that integrates global business priorities. A key part of this integration is the exposure of students to sustainability issues, local businesses, and problem solving. The MBA + Sustainability program at Duquesne University has developed a fully integrated graduate program that aligns pedagogy with the need for global sustainability. The program's administrators and faculty sought to develop a full-time 12-month MBA program with classes in sustainable theories and models, applications, and service-learning projects built into the core curriculum requirements. The faculty teaching these classes needed to go beyond the classroom recognition of sustainability opportunities to projects that include real consequences. In doing so, they have been adding a new dimension to their school's credibility in a developing domain.

Despite the school's relatively small size and resource constraints, Duquesne's business school was recognized as a top ten school internationally by the Aspen Institute's Beyond Grey Pinstripe Rankings in 2007-2008. The ranking process identifies innovative full-time MBA programs that are integrating social and environmental stewardship. In 2007-2008 the Aspen Institute reported a dramatic increase in MBA courses that focus on sustainability, from 13 in 2001 to 154 in 2007. Yet, according to the report, few of the courses were required of all students (Managan, 2007), and we can assume that an even smaller number involved service learning projects.

On the heels of the measurement and ranking of MBA programs, other nongovernmental organizations (NGOs) have devoted considerable effort in promoting corporate social responsibility. The United Nations has issued a call for business schools and academic associations to do their part to advance corporate social responsibility worldwide (Principles of Responsible Management Education [PRME], 2009). As signatories to PRME, Duquesne University and all other co-signing academic institutions are committed to and engaged in reporting on progress to all stakeholders, exchanging effective practices with other academic institutions, and continually seeking to align their actions with the six principles.

PRME is a framework for business schools to advance the broader cause of corporate social responsibility and a call for the incorporation of universal values in curricula and research. The use of real-world projects in any class or curriculum satisfies many of the PRME principles. The fifth principle explicitly focuses attention on the importance of partnering with managers of business corporations (See Table 16.1). Additional benefits of well-designed student consulting projects include the potential to develop students' leadership and communication capabilities, incorporate sustainable values into curricula, create processes and environments that enable effective learning, act as a pipeline for empirical research and case study development, and encourage students to interact with managers from a broad array of business and NGO environments. The interaction of project sponsors, faculty, and students extends our knowledge of the challenges businesses face in meeting social and environmental responsibilities while addressing the business case for developing and testing new approaches to sustainable development.

With many business schools clamoring to develop new course offerings, are students really interested in sustainable development? The answer appears to be: "Yes." Students have long been catalysts calling for the

Table 16.1.   Six Principles of Responsible Management

Principle 1. Purpose: We will develop the capabilities of students to be future generators of sustainable value for business and society at large and to work for an inclusive and sustainable global economy.

Principle 2. Values: We will incorporate into our academic activities and curricula the values of global social responsibility as portrayed in international initiatives such as the United Nations Global Compact.

Principle 3. Method: We will create educational frameworks, materials, processes, and environments that enable effective learning experiences for responsible leadership.

Principle 4. Research: We will engage in conceptual and empirical research that advances our understanding about the role, dynamics, and impact of corporations in the creation of sustainable social, environmental, and economic value.

Principle 5. Partnership: We will interact with managers of business corporations to extend our knowledge of their challenges in meeting social and environmental responsibilities and to explore jointly effective approaches to meeting these challenges.

Principle 6. Dialogue: We will facilitate and support dialog and debate among educators, business, government, consumers, media, civil society organizations, and other interested groups and stakeholders on critical issues related to global social responsibility and sustainability.

For more information on the principles see http://www.unprme.org/

integration of business management and sustainability. A quick look at information collected by the student organization Net Impact (2007) finds:

- The majority of MBA students surveyed (2,113 across all demographics) claim that social and environmental issues should be important considerations for business schools, career goals, and the private sector in general;
- In terms of their MBA education, 78% of those surveyed agree that corporate social responsibility is a topic that "should be" integrated into core curriculum classes at MBA programs;
- Of the students surveyed, 70% agree that business schools should place more emphasis on training socially and environmentally responsible individuals than they currently do;
- Overall, 79% of the students surveyed say they will seek socially responsible employment at some point during their careers, while 59% say they will do so immediately following business school;
- In terms of general perspectives on business, 81% of students surveyed believe companies should try to work toward the betterment of society, while only 18% think most companies are pursuing that goal currently.
- Finally, 90% of respondents say that business leaders should factor social and environmental effects into their business decisions, with 60% believing that this approach can be profitable.

The Net Impact (2007) study provides interesting insights for business school programs and for employers. For business schools, the survey results show that students today want to examine the social implications of business during their MBA programs, and universities should consider adding sustainability, corporate responsibility, and related topics to core and elective courses. Given the current environment and multiple catalysts, business schools have good reasons to support service learning activities that simultaneously achieve sustainability integration with core requirements, promote skill development, and engage business sponsors

The Net Impact (2007) study results also offer opportunities for businesses. Companies have an opportunity to retain employees if they can place more emphasis on environmental management, corporate responsibility, and the reporting of this information. Engaging student-led project teams is one way for a company to learn more about sustainable development as it launches its own sustainability initiatives. The project engagement process is an opportune time to screen potential hires and project the image of a preferred employer. Business sponsors improve their attractiveness as employers by addressing social responsibility issues in their workplaces and communicating their values to potential hires.

The pressures for corporate transparency are yet another reason for business schools and corporations to work together to address sustainability issues. The consideration of social and environmental impacts of business is now commonplace in much of the corporate world. A 2007 research study found 49 U.S. companies in the Standard & Poors 100 Index issued sustainability reports on their social, environmental, and governance practices for 2005-2006 (Social Investment Research Analysts Network [SIRAN], 2007). This number was a marked 14% increase in reporting from only the year before. The growth in environmental and social issues, corporate transparency, and the opportunity for multiple stakeholders to work together indicate that business schools who design the next generation of MBA programs to integrate service learning and sustainability will increase their value for their students and society, while also increasing their own programs' attractiveness, contributions to visibility, and brand.

CHALLENGES

The previous section highlighted catalysts for service learning and posited that we are now at a tipping point for improving management education through learning experiences outside the classroom. While there are ample opportunities for faculty to develop projects, the challenges to developing valuable projects are just as numerous. In their 1996 summary article, Kolenko et al. identified nine barriers to successful service learning integration. These included: (1) faculty resistance, (2) unsuccessful and/or negatively perceived project or program outcomes, (3) workload issues, (4) selfish "limelight" issues on the part of involved faculty, (5) insufficient institutional support, (6) liability issues, (7) student resistance, (8) personal agendas for faculty, and (9) on-site resistance from community organizations. We can attest to all of these barriers and would add (10) non-supporters of a program who feel left out of new developments. Additionally, Marshall and Harry (2005) remind us that we need to keep students in mind—that we have the challenge of making our courses relevant and meaningful for all students.

All business schools are trying to differentiate themselves. Some have established institutes, but many look like clones of the top schools with modest marketing and brand differences. Although a growing number of schools are attempting to develop proactive approaches to new sustainability programs (Aspen Institute, 2007; Shinn, 2008), the proportion of these schools to the overall domain of business schools remains small.

Why? It is because well established or large schools are not nimble. They cannot change their brand quickly. Looking at sustainability as a topic in an existing class, a new elective, or a series of electives is safer and easier. Despite the flurry of electives and new institutes, Stuart Hart, among others, believes business schools, due to "bureaucratic inertia," haven't done enough to integrate sustainable development concepts into core courses (Managan, 2007). Incremental approaches such as topic integration into classes will always be a starting point. What many schools may seek is a way to bridge the chasm between incremental change and a fully integrated business school curriculum. Real-world service learning projects have a significant contribution to make to such an endeavor. Service learning projects can integrate sustainability and new pedagogy into core classes, inspire faculty collaboration, and provide students with a unique academic experience that includes corporate stakeholders.

CREATING AN INTEGRATED SERVICE-LEARNING PROJECT MANAGEMENT CLASS

At Duquesne, we start the learning process locally. Every semester, we have area companies pitch their project ideas to our students and faculty. Students and faculty bid on the sustainability projects they find most appealing. Our semester-long projects in the fall involve audits. Spring projects involve process change. Summer projects involve change management. If a project does not have good fit with the MBA + Sustainability program, the projects are offered to faculty teaching in other classes in the business school. These real-world projects expose both students and faculty to current issues and problems, and provide an opportunity for students to apply classroom theory to solving sustainable development problems. The benefits of an integrated service learning class as part of the core MBA curriculum include not only engaging pedagogy and the development of solutions to real-world problems, but also include multiple opportunities for research and case study development (see Figure 16.1).

McCarthy and Tucker (1999) found that "incorporating service learning into the classroom mirrors the best practices found in organizations and thus prepares students for a productive and rewarding professional career." Duquesne's MBA + Sustainability degree builds on a solid foundation of core coursework in business fundamentals: accounting, finance, marketing, operations, information technology, and economics. What is different about it is the depth of knowledge—the "integrated sustainability" content delivered across required and elective courses. Designed from the ground up, the MBA + Sustainability curriculum goes beyond many programs, adding co-curricular experience and training to enhance class-

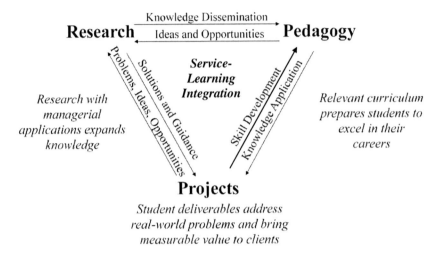

Source: Duquesne MBA+Sustainability Program.

Figure 16.1.   Service-Learning Project Triad.

room learning. Student engagements outside the classroom link faculty research, pedagogy, and consulting projects. The year-round program consists of three semesters.

THE THREE-SEMESTER PROGRAM

The fall semester examines how proven business models apply to managing financial, human, and environmental resources in a dynamic global economy. It has the following elements:

- Sustainable development theory and practice, merged with practical projects;
- Systems thinking;
- Applied Ethics: bedrock for future ethical decision-making;
- Value Chain & Operations Strategy: core course in cross-disciplinary integration in sustainability;
- Integrated case studies and a semester-long live corporate project.

The spring semester focuses on best practices in systems and processes, while continuing an integrative approach to learning:

- Emphasis on challenges organizations face in uncertain markets;
- Public affairs and change management issues;
- Two electives for students to pursue their concentrations;
- Concentrations in finance, environmental management, and supply chain management.

The summer semester calls upon MBA + Sustainability students to apply the full range of business management techniques and tools for leading systemic change:

- Emphasis on the role of strategic, ethical, and multi-disciplined leadership;
- Global Economic Systems; Strategy for Sustainable Enterprise; Leading Change for Sustainable Enterprise;
- Capstone experience: marketing seminar + strategic change management project.

For more information, this program's Web site can be found at: http://mba.sustainability.duq.edu/

The current curriculum model came about after some trial and error. The project-management-based core class was first offered as a non-credit class for students on a voluntary basis. This first option included scheduled meeting times throughout the semester, but lacked the integration and priority necessary to ensure appropriate student commitment. The class was offered concurrently with, and at times competing with, a full-time MBA schedule of coursework and evaluation.

The next step involved offering partial credit for an embedded project within a core required Sustainable Applications course. This option ran into workload issues, both within and outside of the assigned course, the third obstacle identified by Kolenko, Porter, Wheatley, and Colby (1996). The course, covering a litany of sustainable development topics, competed with the projects for student time.

Currently, the class is now a stand-alone class each semester. In its current state, the class has evolved into a formal team-based approach to project management with weekly milestones and deliverables. Each project has some ambiguity to it, and this lack of detailed project scope pushes students and faculty to think creatively and critically. Primary performance metrics are time and performance objectives that are developed and summarized in a project scope and objectives document. Planning the project format is facilitated through a communications document and a billable hours and project manager responsibilities worksheet (see Appendixes 1, 2, and 3 for blank examples of these documents).

Student teams are capped at five cross-functional members with the project manager responsibilities rotated for the project's duration. The project course teams meet on a bi-weekly basis with the instructor(s) during the fall and spring with weekly classroom sessions during the summer semester. Access to and use of Microsoft Project software is facilitated by professional development workshops outside of class time, and student teams go through the process of defining the work breakdown structure: developing Gantt charts, critical path models, and network diagrams.

Student teams are expected to have at least three on-site meetings with the client: kick off, mid-project review, and final presentation to the client management team. In addition to the final presentation, client deliverables include a written business report detailing the situation, research findings, analysis, and recommendations. Communication with corporate sponsors is filtered by faculty before release, and all documents are posted on group sites within Blackboard as a redundant system of document management and control.

Teams do not remain the same for all three semesters because we try to fit the best cross-functional composition of a team to our sponsors' needs. Student teams also prepare five-page pedagogical case studies with supporting materials. These case studies are further developed by faculty and, with the consent of the corporate sponsors, are used in the classroom as pedagogical tools.

Corporate sponsors are asked to provide written feedback on the project team with a 15-item questionnaire (Appendix 4) covering categories such as project management skills, quality of project deliverables, quality of business analysis, application of triple bottom line principles, and overall evaluation of project sponsorship experience. The survey also has open-ended questions asking clients to indicate the most challenging aspect of project sponsorship, any new information or insight provided by the student team, recommended changes for future projects, and any additional comments or suggestions for the students on the project team, faculty, or administrators.

FACULTY ROLES

Faculty have the ability to mediate the extended relationships of universities with business stakeholders. Basic roles for faculty instructors include: overseeing project objective setting, scope definition, communication, contracts, non-disclosure agreements, project timelines, student roles and responsibilities, billable hours, project termination, and project performance measurement. These factors culminate in individual student performance evaluations. When possible, projects are integrated into parts of other courses such as strategy, systems thinking, marketing research, ethics, and public policy. Students are expected to demonstrate an ability to apply theory and analytical tools for all of their business disciplines.

One or two instructors are responsible for the administration of the course for any given semester. Whenever possible, we would recommend having two instructors overseeing the course as it helps to divide responsibilities for both in-class instruction and for attending out-of-class project team meetings and/or on-site meetings. Each student team is tasked with seeking out at least one faculty sponsor from any discipline, but primarily within a discipline closely related to the projects' scope and objectives. Faculty sponsors receive no compensation for participation in the projects, but instead get to be on-site with the students, cultivate opportunities for new research, and incorporate practical problem solving into pedagogy. For some of us, the ability to work with managers and executives on real-world issues culminates in intellectual capital that in and of itself is priceless.

Project participants are sought through faculty networking with area business groups, NGOs, alumni, and other existing relationships. Benefits to the client include a low-cost approach to problem solving with minimal risk. At the time of writing this chapter, we are not charging clients for the opportunity to work with our student and faculty teams. We have found that NGO groups focusing on sustainability are a fertile network for locating potential project sponsors. Duquesne University's top ten ranking in the Aspen Institute's Beyond Grey Pinstripe Rankings survey has generated considerable interest in our school. Our region's transition from its rust-belt image toward a green collar job provider for the twenty-first century has also proven beneficial. Duquesne's business school, at the time of this publication, has also developed and successfully launched two annual sustainability symposia, drawing international speakers and regional business executives and managers. The symposium is one way to cultivate project opportunities and to showcase project success stories. Each semester we target up to five projects with area companies and have been fortunate enough to turn additional projects away for our full-time, daytime MBA + Sustainability program. Since we have a small selective program of fewer than 25 students, this approach fits our needs well at this time.

When a potential sponsor is identified, a project-specifications-and-implementation-guidelines document is sent by e-mail to the potential client. This document defines what the MBA students can do for the client, project selection criteria, and what types of projects are most suitable. Project selection criteria call for well-conceived projects that align with SMART objectives:

Specific ? tangible, clearly defined objectives, scope, scale, and deliverables

Measurable ? action-oriented outcomes with quantifiable returns

Achievable ? feasible for a team of 4-5 MBA students

Realistic ? expectations based on access to resources and information

Timely ? 6–12 week timelines

What types of projects are suitable?

- Development of models of innovation in technology, products, revenue models, and community competitiveness to support next generation business;
- Analysis of challenges of co-alignment among business, society, and environment;
- Development of alternative models of business and innovation for sustainable enterprises;
- Identification of best practices in leadership and transformation;
- Benchmarking—internal or external;
- Audit—documentation of current situation for use as baseline.

The information in the specifications-and-implementation-guidelines document also tasks sponsoring companies to provide written objectives, expectations, and deadlines. Sponsors should arrange for student access to information, resources, and personnel required to deliver the project on time. The sponsor is also required to assign an internal project manager who will meet with the students and answer their questions on a timely basis.

This same document defines the responsibilities for Duquesne professors and staff as coordinating the meetings and interfaces with clients, supervising student work, and assuring compliance with program requirements. Students recommend the approach and timetable, conduct the mid-term review, review progress versus milestones and metrics with the clients, and make the final presentation, including research, analysis, and recommendations.

Students and professors sign non-disclosure agreements for proprietary information. The sponsoring company is encouraged to camouflage highly sensitive data, and written approval by the corporation is required for publication of any learning or insights from the projects. Finally, we state that both the corporate partner and Duquesne recognize that the project is a learning activity which carries risk of error (and poor judg-

Table 16.2.   SMBA 521 Sustainable Projects I Syllabus Excerpt

Course Goals	Learning Objectives	Assessment
Ability to recognize common project management challenges, situation analysis	Participation in project layout and start up process, financing, post mortem	Participation; faculty sponsors; client evaluation
Apply project management planning and decision making to sustainability dilemmas	Know how to manage the flow of project information during various project phases	Participation; Group break-out sessions; PM weekly updates; MS Project software output
Implementation efficiency: Identify and evaluate organizational drivers within competing social, environmental, and financial issues	Identify organizational stakeholders, influences and risks for individual decision making processes; develop the business case for sustainability	Participation; working with instructor, client, and faculty sponsors; weekly project updates, stakeholder mapping
Apply decision-making and evaluation skills, tools as a project supervisor	Understand how project financing plays a role in project management and project cost control	Weekly updates; Final deliverables to clients and faculty; business case for project deliverables
Identifying, resolving, and making a case for project management practices	Coordinate the close out of a project. Understand how corporate practices and policies affect the management of projects and sustainability issues	Working with client; stakeholder mapping; final deliverables to clients and faculty
Professionalism	Communication, teamwork, interface with clients, presentation skills, final deliverables	Final deliverables to clients and faculty; individual participation; mid-term reviews

ment) from all participating parties. Students are not to be viewed as professional consultants or advisors, but their contributions and insight should be welcome and respected.

COURSE GOALS AND OBJECTIVES

The sustainability movement presents tremendous innovation opportunities for businesses. Managers now wrestle with a variety of pressures and make difficult decisions about how best to integrate the dimensions of social, environmental, and financial performance within business strategies, models, and management systems. During the semester, student teams help clients develop the business case for difficult multidimensional decision-making issues surrounding sustainability. Managing semester-long engagements provides all students in our program with tangible, hands-on experience with project management processes and tools. Not only do students gain marketable skills, they develop professional networks and hopefully good job references.

As project managers for Duquesne's School of Business Administration, students represent the University, School of Business, and the MBA+S program at all times. Therefore, student conduct must be professional and within the guidelines established in the University Academic Integrity policy and the School of Business Administration code of ethics.

Sponsors may ask student teams to sign nondisclosure documents, and this agreement needs to be taken seriously. Unless given consent from the sponsor, information from any team's sponsor engagements is NOT to be discussed with anyone in the public domain during or after the project.

The objective of the course is to build upon concurrent coursework to enable students to manage projects that meet and exceed client expectations. Table 16.2 shows the goals for the course, the learning objectives that match those goals, and the ways the students' success in achieving those learning objectives is assessed.

In 2008 alone Duquesne's MBA+S program students have worked with over a dozen corporations, manufacturers, service providers, and NGOs. Our students and faculty have helped their clients with decisions ranging from $15k to $40M. Projects to date include:

√ when and how to get involved in carbon trading
√ paper vs. plastic bags for consumers
√ promotion of green collar jobs
√ carbon footprint of the financial industry
√ criteria for sustainable business recognition for a regional NGO
√ HVAC decision support model
√ green flooring and landscaping options
√ value chain market research for an NGO working with the green building products
√ communication and transportation options for an NGO servicing troubled youth
√ risk management in banking
√ benchmarking and strategy development for an MNC's headquarters site
√ conversion of waste products to raw materials
√ profitable alternatives to bottled water
√ audit and management plan for sustainability in the service sector
√ market research for the launch of new green products

Table 16.3.   Stakeholder Benefits

Students:

• Gain practical job experience—accountability for deliverables and customer satisfaction
• Learn to apply critical thinking skills
• Develop time management skills
• Master project management skills and tools
• Improve written and oral communication skills

Faculty:

• Form /partnerships with organizations/executives who apply theories they teach
• Collaborate across silos (and it becomes contagious!)
• Work closely with students on challenges of mutual interest
• Develop respect for fresh innovative student thinking
• See first-hand how well what they teach can be applied to practical workplaces
• Learn to coach rather than teach to the test or direct students to do it the professors' way

University:

• Improves relationships with business, government and not-for-profit leaders
• Opens avenues for student job placement
• Opens opportunities for advancement and financial sponsorship of initiatives
• Develops networks of potential executive speakers
• Opens opportunities for applied research contracts with companies seeking cutting edge expertise
• Improves publication opportunities/status for case studies and applied research

Corporate Sponsors gain:

• Fresh, politics-free viewpoints and creativity
• Research via world-class e-resources and peer-reviewed journals
• Application of the latest tools, models, and theories
• Technological sophistication for a digital, global economy
• New insight into, and the start of, sustainability initiatives
• Insight of professors with application expertise who are up-to-date on cutting edge innovations and published research

PERFORMANCE EVALUATION

Performance evaluation on a microlevel is recorded as participation every time the students meet with their instructors or clients. Project managers are expected to set an agenda, run the meetings with clients, and report to their instructors during class time. Attendance and tardiness at classes, meetings, and off-site events are considered in team-member evaluations. Performance evaluation also includes an assessment of any individual's weekly deliverables on a (0 to 4) scale where (4) is highly professional, (3) has opportunity to improve, (2) is below expectations, (1) is inadequate, and (0) is unacceptable. Student performance evaluation is a combination of attendance, participation, and professionalism (25%); client evaluation (35%); mid-term presentation to faculty (20%); final presentation to faculty (10%); and instructor evaluation of the final written deliverables to the client (10%).

More often than not, the value of service learning cannot be measured by a student's grade. As Posner (2008) suggests, "We must assign students projects that require them to go out and lead, and then come back and reflect on that experience. Only then will they learn to be better leaders." Real value comes in the insights students get when they struggle with and make their way through a project. During the project, and even after they leave an MBA program, additional learning will come from reflection on their project experience. During the semester we try to use class meetings to reflect and share learning from team to team. Applied learning will come in the realization of what can be done differently when the next project opportunity occurs.

The combination of research, pedagogy, and projects should be a win-win for all parties involved (see Table 16.3). These opportunities do not come without some obstacles and the possibility that projects may fail to bring the desired value to a sponsor. Failure to meet expectations may be seen as something to avoid at all costs, but in reality it is part of learning. With this recognition in mind, the success of projects will always be critically dependent on the scope document for the project, managing sponsor expectations, communication, and real consequences for the actions recommended by students. While these requirements may take a tremendous commitment and bring significant coordination challenges, there are many benefits to all stakeholders involved.

For faculty who wish to implement successful service learning experiences, Godfrey, Illes, and Berry (2005) found four factors contributing to successful and sustainable service learning efforts: Centrality, Commitment, Community Engagement, and Continuous Improvement. When service learning activities are *central* to a course, that is, are part of the course objectives, the payoffs of the activity exceed the costs of implementation. Centrality also means that any sustainable development issues inherent in the service learning experience will be reviewed and discussed in the course or during concurrent courses. In our case, sustainability is central to the entire program. The application of the service learning experience into other courses and the development of pedagogy, such as case studies, helps to demonstrate an integrated and coordinated commitment to advancing business school education. This pedagogy works very well when engaging local businesses and expanding empirical research is central to a faculty member's agenda and/or university mission. As business school performance on social and environmental factors becomes increasingly important, the use of service learning offers a promising vehicle for developing programs that continuously improve and expand the minds of future business leaders and contribute to a more sustainable world.

CONCLUSIONS

Management educators face the continuing challenge of designing courses that transfer learning between the classroom, workplace, and global business domain. As we have learned, service learning is neither a simple nor easy pedagogy. Traditional classroom pedagogy cannot fully address the problems students will face after leaving MBA institutions. It is imperative that faculty and administrators consider the use of service learning within a sustainable development course, concentration, and/or curriculum. Our experience has taught us that service learning can improve and broaden our students' managerial understanding, skills, and technical knowledge. Service learning has the potential to instill within students a stronger sense of leadership and corporate social responsibility. As the needs of business keep changing, management faculty must continuously improve courses. Including multidimensional teaching and learning pedagogies is a vital part of the adjustment faculty members need to make.

At Duquesne, we build on the curriculum and local projects by integrating two required study abroad trips with students and faculty to Asia, Europe, India, or South America. These trips broaden the context of sustainable development from the microlevel at home to a macro level while abroad. International travel allows students and faculty to gain insight from academic engagement with global colleagues, students, and business leaders. These trips also present an opportunity for mini-projects with partnering universities and institutions. We encourage our students to become engaged members of their businesses and societies. In creating this type of engagement, we begin to "talk the talk" and "walk the walk" of corporate social responsibility and sustainable development.

Every day, students provide us with "gifts" in the classroom through their questions and comments. These gifts are in the form of learning opportunities that change the direction and outcomes of a classroom session. Companies are facing many tough issues regarding sustainable development, and when they come to management educators for answers, these same companies provide us with gifts that can take faculty and students outside the classroom. The timing is now for MBA program administrators and faculty to seek out these opportunities. While it may take some time for students to move into corporate positions that enable them to be more forceful with corporate social responsibility initiatives, now is the perfect time to engage these students on a different level. Students who have seen firsthand how companies grapple with quantifying social and environmental impacts will be better prepared to deal with ambiguities of the future. For programs wanting to differentiate themselves, service learning is a dynamic step in the right direction that builds capital for all stakeholders.

A special thanks to Diane Ramos and Marie Fechik for their help with this chapter. Diane Ramos is the Assistant Director of the MBA + Sustainability program and should be thanked for her help, commitment, coordination of our student projects, and for her help in reviewing this chapter. Marie Fechik is a current SMBA Fellow conducting research that aided in the research and writing of this chapter and other research projects.

Appendix 1

Scope Statement (Version xxx)

Project Title:
Date: **Prepared by:**
Project Justification:

Project Characteristics and Requirements:
   1.
   2.
   3.

Summary of Project Deliverables (to Be Determined)
Project management-related deliverables: business case, scope statement, schedule, cost baseline, status reports, final project presentation, final project report, lessons-learned report, and any other documents required to manage the project.
Project-related deliverables: research reports, business case, recommendations, risks, summary report, presentation, etc.
   1.
   2.
   3.
   4.

Project Success Criteria

Appendix 2

Communications Management Plan

Prepared by: **Date:**

1.   Introduction: (describe the project)

2.   Collection and filing structure for gathering and storing project information

3.   Distribution structure (what information goes to whom, when, and how)

4.   Format, content, and level of detail of key project information

5.   Production schedule and resources for producing key project information

6.   Technologies, access methods, and frequency of communications

7.   Method for updating the communications management plan

8.   Escalation procedures (how to address internal or external issues)

9.   Stakeholder communications analysis (who needs what and when)

Stakeholders	Document Name	Document Format	Contact Person	Due Date
Comments:				

Appendix 3

Project Manager Schedule
Responsibility Assignment Matrix for Project (XXXX)

Prepared by: Date:

	Week 1	Week 2	Week 3	Week 4	Week 5	Week 6…
Project Manager (insert name for each week)→						
Team Members (individual hours per week)						
A						
B						
C						
D						
E						

Each team should update this file weekly for changes in project managers, individual responsibilities, and billable hours. Put as much information as necessary into each cell to describe individual responsibilities.

Appendix 4

Client Evaluation of Projects
Duquesne University MBA + Sustainability Program

Thank you for serving as a consulting project sponsor for Duquesne University's MBA + Sustainability program. You can help us improve our educational preparation of next generation leaders by completing this project evaluation. Please return after receipt of the project's final deliverables.

Rate the quality of your project team's performance on the following dimensions:	*Type in your rating 1 (low) ←→ 10 (high) NA = Not Applicable*
Project Management Skills	
Establishing project goals, scope and timetable	
Keeping client team apprised of progress	
Managing meetings, timetable and interfaces	
Quality of Project Deliverables	
Correctly identified stakeholders and important relationships	
Presentation of findings, analysis, recommendations (oral communication skill)	
Written report and documentation (written communication skills)	
Response to questions (ability to think on feet)	
Quality of Business Analysis	
Demonstrated understanding of financial & return-on-investment requirements	
Identified and evaluated social responsibility factors	
Identified and evaluated environmental factors	
Demonstrated systems thinking balancing long- vs. short-term consequences	
Provided practical, well-thought-out solutions and recommendations	
Overall Evaluation of Project Sponsorship Experience	
How satisfied were you with the overall experience?	
To what extent did our students provide fresh insight to your challenges?	
How likely would you be to sponsor another project?	

Please write your answers below each question.
- *What was the most challenging aspect of sponsoring our student project?*
- *What new information, analysis or recommendations, if any, did our students offer that your organization hadn't already considered?*
- *What would you recommend be done differently?*
- *Do you have any additional comments or advice for the students on your project team? For our faculty and administration?*
  Your Name & Title:
  Organization:

*After completing this form, please return to Robert Sroufe. **sroufer@duq.edu** fax: 412.396.4764*

REFERENCES

Association to Advance College Schools of Business. (2008). Retrieved July 20, 2008, from http://www.aacsb.edu/

AAHE. (1997). *American Association for Higher Education's Monograph Series on Service-Learning in the disciplines* (Outreach Brochure). Las Vegas, NV: Author.

Aspen Institute. (2007). *Aspen Institution's Beyond Grey Pinstripes Rankings.* Retrieved August 1, 2008, from http://www.beyondgreypinstripes.org/rankings/topten.cfm's

Godfrey, P. C., Illes, L. M., & Berry, G. (2005). Creating breadth in business education through service-learning, *Academy of Management Learning & Education,* 4(3), 309–323.

Kolenko, T. A., Porter, G., Wheatley, W., & Colby, M. (1996) A critique of service learning projects. In A Decade of Service-learning Management Education: Pedagogical Foundation, Barriers, and Guidelines. *Journal of Business Ethics,* 15(1), 133–142.

Managan, M. (2007). People, planet and profit. *Chronicle of Higher Education.* 54(2), A14.

Marshall, R. S., & Harry, S. P. (2005). Introducing a new business course: Global business and sustainability, *International Journal of Sustainability in Higher Education,* 6(2), 179–196.

McCarthy, A. M., & Tucker, M. L. (1999). Student attitudes toward service learning: Implications for implementation, *Journal of Management Education, 23,* 554–573.

Mintzberg, H., & Gosling, J. R. (2002). Reality programming for MBAs. *Strategy and Business, 26*(1), 28–31.

Moore, T. E. (2007, July/August). Repositioning the MBA. *Biz Ed.,* pp. 50–56.

Net Impact. (2007). *New leaders: New perspectives,* A Net Impact survey of MBA student opinions on the relationship between business and social/environmental issues. Retrieved June 26 2007, from http://www.netimpact.org/displaycommon.cfm?an=1&subarticlenbr=80#undergrad

Pfeffer, J., & Fong, C. T. (2002). The end of business schools? Less success than meets the eye, *Academy of Management Learning and Education, 1*(1), 78–95.

Posner, P. (2008, May/June). The future is now. *Biz Ed.,* pp. 26–27.

Principles of Responsible Management Education. (2009). Retrieved June 2, 2009, from http://www.unprme.org/

Shinn, S. (2008, July/August). Sustainability at the core. *Biz Ed.,* pp. 30–38.

SIRAN. (2007, April 25). *Sustainability reporting moving into the mainstream. Social Investment Research Analysts Network. A study conducted jointly by the Social Investment Research Analysts Network (SIRAN) and KLD Research & Analytics, Inc.* Retrieved September 1, 2008, from http://www.siran.org/SIRANPR20070427.pdf

CHAPTER 17

TEACHING GREEN BUSINESS

How to Bring Sustainability Into a Capstone Business Class

Robert Girling

In chapter 18 "Teaching Green Business: How to Bring Sustainability Into a Capstone Business Class," Robert Girling describes why the issue of sustainability is an essential topic for students of business.

The article begins by explaining and illustrating with a series of examples what a range of companies are doing in order to minimize their environmental impact. Companies like Wal-Mart are beginning to make sustainability an integral part of their business plan. Meanwhile, few business strategy texts incorporate sustainability as a central theme. Girling explains how he introduces and includes sustainability into his capstone Strategic Management class by using "Current Issues", case studies and guest speakers to explain why and how specific companies consider the environment. The paper concludes with some examples of how two students see how they might apply the concepts in their current and future employment.

Management Education for Global Sustainability, pp. 365–376
Copyright © 2009 by Information Age Publishing
All rights of reproduction in any form reserved.

INTRODUCTION

Each passing week brings our attention to the growing list of environmental issues facing us. From melting glaciers, to natural disasters like the Katrina hurricane, we are awakening to the impact of our system of production and consumption on our environment. Companies around the world have been spurred to action by the Report of the International Panel on Climate Change (Climate Change 2007: Synthesis Report. Summary for Policymakers. UNEP http://www.ipcc.ch/pdf/assessment-report/ar4/syr/ar4_syr_spm.pdf), by a tightening regulatory environment in the European Union and in California, and changing consumer preferences to implement sustainable business practices. Moreover, corporate leadership organizations such as Business for Social Responsibility are working to promote and assist businesses to develop strategies for social and environmental justice.

More and more companies are coming to realize that they can benefit from a range of "green" business initiatives, which reduce costs or provide strategic advantages. Meanwhile, investors are increasingly finding a broad range of opportunities owning companies that look for environmental payoffs. The world's financial markets are demanding that businesses pay attention not only to the financial bottom line, or profit, but take into account risk factors related to the environment as well. For example, Innovest, which rates companies for investment banks, pension funds, and a range of public investment agencies, includes in its assessments information on emissions, hazardous wastes, energy efficiency, and global warming (Innovest, 2009)

Insurance companies, who have to pick up the tab for environmental disasters such as Hurricane Katrina and the Exxon Valdez oil spill, have moved to the forefront of those demanding sustainable solutions. The costs of ignoring sustainability principles can be high. In a Mississippi federal court, "plaintiffs are suing oil and coal companies for greenhouse gas emissions, arguing that they contributed to the severity of Hurricane Katrina" (Lash & Wellington, 2007, p. 98). As Jonathan Lash and Fred Wellington of the World Resources Institute point out "Companies that manage and mitigate their exposure to climate-change risks while seeing new opportunities for profit will generate competitive advantage over rivals in a carbon-constrained future" (p. 96).

Meanwhile, a range of new companies, such as New Leaf Paper, whose mission is to minimize the environmental impact of its customers' paper consumption and well-established companies like the global engineering firm CH2M Hill, are providing triple-bottom-line, environmentally sound solutions. General Electric has changed its strategy and is investing heavily to position itself as a leading innovator in a wide range of products from wind power and LED lighting to hybrid engines. A recent article in *Business Week* pointed to GlaxoSmithKline's discovery that, by investing to develop drugs for poor nations, it can more effectively encourage governments to make sure its patents are protected while Dow Chemical Co. is investing in R&D for a range of products including roof tiles that deliver solar power to buildings (Engardio, 2007). Even Wal-Mart is moving toward sustainability, working with the Environmental Defense Fund, which has set up an office in Wal-Mart's headquarters, and with Eaton, a manufacturer of power and drive trains for commercial trucks to back the development of a new generation of hybrid truck engines to improve the efficiency of Wal-Mart's fleet of over 7,000 trucks. (Walmart Tests New Trucks, surpasses fuel efficiency goals. Feb. 3, 2009. http://www.environmentalleader.com/2009/02/03/wal-mart-tests-new-trucks-surpasses-fuel-efficiency-goals/)

Emerging trends around the world and particularly within the European Community are setting new standards with respect to product design, waste treatment, and a host of other operational issues that most businesses will need to consider in developing their strategies. To respond to the changing regulatory environment, PriceWaterhouseCoopers has established a global environmental office in New York.

Financial giants like Goldman Sacks and HBSC are changing their business strategies and investing in a range of "green investments" as well as changing guidelines for lending to projects that entail social or environmental risks. In addition, mutual fund investments in socially and environmentally screened funds have soared from $12 billion in 1995 to $178 billion in 2005 (Social Investment Forum, 2005).

Clearly there is a sea of change in the business environment that mirrors the growing environmental awareness in our society. The question that faces professors and teachers of business is how best to bring this information into the classroom so that our curriculum reflects the changing reality while effectively preparing the next generation of managers, entrepreneurs, and societal leaders. Graduates need to be prepared to deal with the array of environmental as well as social risks and regulations and they need to be informed about the nature of sustainability as it pertains to business and society. But even more than these needs, they need to have a clear understanding of the tools they can use to make business sustainable, such that business moves from being part of the problem to seeing itself as a vital part of the solution. (Two valuable resources for learning about corporate best practices are Epstein 2008 and Erickson 2004.)

SUSTAINABILITY AND BUSINESS STRATEGY

For many business schools, a course in business strategy serves as the capstone to the undergraduate degree program. Typically such courses use a case method to examine the different approaches businesses use to develop and implement a strategy. However, few current textbooks incorporate any reference to environmental issues or a discussion of sustainability.

Yet, according to PricewaterhouseCoopers (2009),

> Making sustainability an integral part of a company's business strategy delivers the potential of very real bottom line benefits. Productivity improvements, cost savings, risk reduction, human resource gains, increased reputation and enhanced license to operate are all tangible outcomes cited by [sustainable] companies. At the same time, the insights that come from sustainable business practice give opportunities to reshape strategies for competitive advantage and growth. (PricewaterhouseCoopers, n.p.)

I have found that relatively few undergraduate business school students have given much thought to environmental issues. Consequently, I have found it helpful to begin with some visual images, to set the stage and engage the interest of the students, followed by a discussion of the meaning of sustainability. The concept of the "triple bottom line" and the Natural Step approach along with current articles from the press provide both a theoretical framework as well as evidence of the relevance and importance of the issues (Natrass & Altomare, 1999).

The concept of sustainability can be somewhat confusing as there are a host of competing definitions. One widely used definition is "Meeting humanity's needs today without harming the capacity of future generations to meet their needs." A more comprehensive definition is Herman Daly's proposal that (a) rates of use of renewable resources should not exceed their rates of regeneration, (b) rates of use of non-renewable resources should not exceed rate at which renewable substitutes are developed and (c) rates of pollution should not exceed the assimilative capacity of the environment.

Several videos illustrate the dimensions of the issues facing the planet. "The Eagle and the Condor" and "Awakening the Dreamer" are two DVDs available from the Pachamama Alliance (www.pachamama.org) which show the connection between those of us in global metropolises and the plight of the Amazon rain forest. The videos point out how we are damamging the earth and why we need to change our wasteful behaviors. Former Vice President Al Gore's documentary "An Inconvenient Truth," provides a comprehensive discussion of climate change replete with statistical data and charts. Visual images get the attention of students who may not have thought much about the environment.

It is not unusual for business students to wonder just what all these pieces have got to do with business. The approach I take is to say that while many business people may argue that it is their responsibility to make a profit—not save the world—the fact is that business needs stable markets, healthy consumers, and, uniquely, business has the technology, finance, and management skills needed to achieve a transition to sustainability. As Fiona Harvey (2006) points out:

> Financial institutions have begun to take action on environmental issues such as climate change, pollution, water shortages, and biodiversity. More than 40 banks have now signed up to the Equator Principles, which bind their signatories to standards governing the environmental and social criteria by which a project applying to the bank for funding should be judged. In part, banks have been driven by fear of reprisal from environmental groups if projects they finance turn out to be damaging, and by an increasing awareness of "green" issues among mainstream consumers. But they have also seen opportunities in areas such as renewable energy and low-carbon technology, and they are aware that the tide of government regulation is flowing in a "green" direction. (p. 19)

Business school faculty can use a combination of textbooks, lectures, and case studies to examine how companies have applied the concepts of sustainability in developing their business strategies. Sustainability also provides another avenue for teaching the concepts of corporate social responsibility. PricewaterhouseCoopers, in its Global Sustainability Report for 2006, put the case succinctly:

> Sustainability may sound like yet another corporate buzz word, the latest fad in a long line of management fads. But sustainability is serious business. A new standard of performance that measures the social, environmental, and economic effects of business activities—the so-called "triple bottom line"—it can mean the difference between a company's long-term success or failure. Alas, few corporations recognize the links between sustainability, reputation, and financial performance. However, without a sustainability risk management program in place, companies are flirting with disaster. A major misstep or miscalculation on triple-bottom-line issues can ruin reputations, jeopardize corporate financial integrity, and imperil relationships with customers, investors, and the banks.... Companies are converging in first generation sustainability themes like corporate governance, and transparency and accountability along the whole supply chain are increasingly visible through policies and control mechanisms.

While much of the recent movement toward sustainability has come as a result of skyrocketing world oil prices and related energy and transportation costs, it is helpful to point to additional factors driving business concerns with the environment. These include the problems of solid waste disposal, adequacy of water supplies, and aggravated health risks, to name a few. Collapsing aquifers and widespread contamination of water supplies add further risk factors, uncertainties, and costs, which challenge business planners (see UNESCO, 2006). A growing number of companies are concerned that we are approaching unmanageable levels of toxic, chemical, and hazardous waste. Case studies of what some companies are doing are articulated in *Walking the Talk: The Business Case for Sustainable Development.* (Holliday, Schmidheiny, & Watts, 2002) as well.

SUSTAINABILITY IN A BUSINESS STRATEGY: KEY CONCEPTS

What are some leading companies doing with respect to sustainability? I begin my discussion in class by examining some examples of strategic approaches that businesses around the world provide. Examples appear almost daily in the press. I begin each class with a discussion of "Current Issues" in which I bring in selected articles from the business press. For example, "Google's New Search." "Google Inc. says it will spend hundreds of millions of dollars to develop renewable energy as part of an ambitious plan to clean the environment and reduce the company's own power bill" (Google's New Search, 2007, p. 1).

Articles like "Wal-Mart backs drive for fuel efficiency" (2006) and "Ford Suffers Record Loss and Oil Shock Hits Industry" (2008) illustrate the pertinence of the issue as well as the conflicts and difficulties firms face in addressing issues such as climate change and conserving fossil fuels and other non-renewable resources.

I also include examples from company annual reports and mission statements. One example is that of Scottish and Newcastle, a British manufacturer of beer and cider, where they state in their 2005 Annual Report:

During 2005 we approved a new group environment policy which puts greater emphasis on engaging employees on environmental issues and will ensure that environmental considerations are seen as an integral part of our business management. The rapidly rising cost of energy and the introduction of the EU Emissions Trading Scheme have intensified the strategic importance of energy management to the business. Development of a more rigorous energy efficiency programme is well underway, to achieve further reductions in both energy costs and CO_2 emissions. We are also examining ways of generating our own energy to ensure that S&N is able to respond effectively to future cost and environmental pressures. In particular, we are evaluating the use of renewable energy. Bulmers has installed two micro wind turbines that provide electrical power to its orchard buildings. The installment is a modest start, but it reflects our intention to address the energy challenge as an opportunity to become a more efficient and innovative business. (p. 12)

CASE STUDIES

The detailed case studies contained in Brian Natrass and Mary Altomare's books, *The Natural Step for Business and Dancing with the Tiger* provide comprehensive analyses of how companies such as Nike, Starbucks, IKEA, Interface (carpets), and Whistler ski resort have become more sustainable (Natrass & Altomare 1999, 2002). Christine Arena's *Cause for Success*, (Arena, 2004) also provides a set of cases written in a more journalistic style. The cases help students gain insights into the strategies which some companies are using to design products as well as services that produce less waste, use fewer resources, and contain more recycled and less toxic components. Examples cited by Arena include the European Union's Directive on Waste Electrical and Electronic Equipment that requires producers, importers, and distributors to arrange take-back and recycling of waste for electrical equipment and how Dell Computer Corporation has responded by changing its production strategy in its worldwide operations.

The case study section of the curriculum is supported by local guest speakers like Michael Newell, director of a local business incubator for sustainable companies, Gary Barker, president of an industrial design firm, Jeff Mendelsohn, CEO of New Leaf Paper and Matt Reynolds, CEO of Indigenous Design, a producer of clothing. The speakers discuss their companies' strategies and respond to student questions. Each student is required to prepare a response paper, which answers the following questions:

- What is sustainability and what has motivated society to pay attention to sustainability?
- What do you think has led companies to integrate sustainability into their business strategies?
- What do companies do in order to build a sustainable business strategy?
- Identify three or more specific metrics or ways by which a company's performance could be measured with respect to sustainability.

APPLICATION OF THEORY TO PRACTICE

The next unit of the class involves an eight-week business simulation in which students operate a company. CAPSIM (Information about this simulation is available at www.capsim.com)is a problem-based learning simulation of a technology company in which teams of students design, produce, market, and finance high-tech sensors in competition with each other. It is an excellent vehicle for students who are completing their undergraduate university education or MBA and need to know how all the parts of business fit together.

CAPSIM is a challenging simulation, which engages student participants in designing, planning, and executing a strategy. It challenges them to put into practice, not just write about, all that they have learned in their college career. They must develop a strategy to restore their floundering company to financial health. Each week they practice applying management skills and building strategies, making about 125 specific business decisions ranging from handling inventories to the best ways to market their products. In the simulation, students learn:

- to weigh the advantages and disadvantages of Michael Porter's strategies;
- to position products to meet customer needs
- to develop and organize their team and how to provide support for each other
- to plan and to make decisions
- to implement their decisions and interpret the results
- to interpret financial results
- to research and develop an environmental management system (EMS)
- to respond to changes in the market and business environment.

As a component to the simulation, each student is required to apply the principles of sustainability to their company by researching current environmental regulations related to business and society on the Environmental Protection Agency (EPA) Web site (www.epa.gov) Using this information, they prepare a power point presentation of an Environmental Management System to enable their company to become more sustainable. The power point then becomes incorporated into each team's presentation to a "Board of Directors" comprised of outside experts drawn from the business community.

CONCLUSIONS

The above methodology provides students with an understanding of sustainability, which is grounded in the concept of business strategy. Students see a connection between business and the environment that is based in what specific companies are doing to develop strategies for sustainable production, purchasing, and operations. In addition they gain an appreciation for a sustainable vision of corporate social responsibility which:

- Focuses on outcomes over future generations;
- Builds upon an integrative approach to meet interdependent goals of social equity, environmental quality, and economic viability,
- Emphasizes a systems approach to problem solving and decision making, which incorporates full cost accounting in decision-making, including environmental and operating costs;
- Recognizes ecological limits as a fundamental business constraint.

In addition, students become aware of alternative strategies such as elimination of use of hazardous chemicals, redesign of products to make them more durable or easily repairable, the life-cycle design of products that can be recovered, and replacement of nonrenewable materials with more sustainable materials.

Some Results

Students in the Strategic Management class write about what they have learned and how they might apply their knowledge in their current or future employment as part of their final examination paper. The following are some representative responses:

I currently work for Marmot, a company that makes outdoor recreational apparel and equipment. Being a company whose sole purpose of their products is for outdoor recreation, the issues of sustainability greatly impact the success of the company. Consumers, athletes, and employees who buy and use their products extensively in the outdoors demand that what goes into the product has a positive impact on the environment that they cherish. Marmot contracts out all manufacturing overseas in India and China. Marmot must focus on Quality control in order to maintain their standards. Their current Vendor Code of Conduct states:

"Marmot considers workers rights, their well being and their working conditions to be paramount in the selection of all contractors. Marmot chooses to only nominate contractors who exhibit exceptional work environments and outstanding general well being programs such as on-site day care, on-site health care, on-site housing and/or meals, and who provide continuing educational programs. In additional Marmot nominated contractors must meet or surpass the national and local labor standards in terms of minimum age, hours of work, and work environment"

The company only uses dyes that are organic and vegan. Some outdoor apparel companies use a red dye that contain shell fish or a blue dye that is harsh on the environment and contaminates water. Marmot also only uses fabrics, cotton, and other raw material that were organically produced. The company also focuses on in-house operations. Employees are encouraged to conserve energy and water in the offices. The company even dropped producing catalogs, which they relied heavily on in the past, to eliminate paper waste. Marmot also has employee training programs and community volunteer work. The company is also big on giving back to the local community by participating and donating to local events, charities, and education. Marmot also works exclusively with nonprofit organizations such as the dZi Foundation. The dZi Foundation develops sustainable programs that positively impact individuals and communities located primarily within the Himalayan region. Their work is focused in the areas of education, health, and welfare. These programs are designed to serve within the existing social framework, maintaining particular sensitivity to local culture and tradition. Marmot also works closely with Business for Wilderness which focuses on Wild places providing high quality outdoor recreation destinations. (Karyn Pascal, quoted with permission)

I am going to work in the public accounting company in San Francisco-Grant Thornton LLP. Like every accounting company, in our company there is a lot of wasted paper. It is a big sustainability issue of how to save as many trees as possible on our planet by using less paper. I think a good resolution would be to try to put as much information as possible on the computer and accept all documentation from the companies only through PDF files instead of making copies and using a lot of paper. Another necessary commitment that a company should do is to implement an innovative recycling-based program. Also a good solution is to purchase recycled paper products.

Another big issue is energy. A lot of office buildings in San Francisco use so much energy, which I think should be reduced. It could be achieved by replacing it with renewable resources. It is a little difficult for the companies because a lot of the time they are renting only one or two floors in the building. As a result many companies occupy one big building, and each of them would have different strategies and goals. Our company should purchase only energy-saving computers, copiers, printers, and other office equipment that will serve us for many years. But the main principle to reach a sustainable future is that all of the companies and our whole community should come together and implement principles of sustainability. By doing this, we are going to survive in the future and be able to achieve a range of goals including profit target margins, high net income, and qualified employees...

It is very important that people who are working for the company support sustainable development, and be trained to focus on the specific problems and solve those problems.

Our company's primary strategy should ensure that sustainability is hard-wired into day-to day business management processes. Grant Thornton should make sure that it generates economic, environmental, and social value for our customers. Our customers would like to know that sustainability related issues connected with the business have been managed properly in our company.

I think another important issue, which our company really cares about, is to continue to succeed and develop new sustainable projects and attract bright young people to our industry that care about sustainability. Those people could bring a new fresh look on how to build a strong and healthy company that delivers a safe and rewarding workplace, and exceptional value to our customers for economic stability. I think Grant Thornton should identify strengths and weaknesses of its sustainability practice, and assess effectiveness of sustainable development of the company. Grant Thornton should have a long-term plan toward a sustainable future. Our company has a lot of customers from different industries around the world. It should work with its customers assessing sustainability management practices within their organizations. For example, utilize recycled paper, provide assurance for green house gas emissions, and make sure that all systems in place and properly managed. I think it will be a good idea for the company to establish ISO 14000 standards. It will help bring a worldwide focus to the environment, encouraging a cleaner, safer, healthier world.

It allows Grant Thornton measure environmental efforts against internationally accepted criteria and single standard will ensure that there are no conflicts between regional interpretations of good environmental practice. (Olga Gray, quoted with permission)

REFERENCES

Arena, C. (2004) *Cause for Success*. New World Library

Engardio, P. (2007, January 29). Beyond the green corporation. *Business Week*, pp. 50–64

Erickson, G. (2004) *Raising the bar: The story of Clif Bar, Inc*. San Fransisco: Jossey-Bass.

Epstein, M. J (2008). *Making sustainability work*. San Francisco: Berrett-Koehler.

Ford suffers record loss and oil shock hits industry. (2008, July 25). *Wall Street Journal*, p. 1.

Google's New Search. (2007, November 28). *SF Chronicle*, p. 1

Harvey, F. (2006, Sept. 18). Committed to the business of the environment. *Financial Times*, p. 19.

Holliday, C., Schmidheiny, S., & Watts, P. (2002) *Walking the talk: The business case for sustainable development*. San Fransisco: Barrett-Koehler.

Innovest. (2009). Retrieved May 31, 2009, from http://www.innovestgroup.com/

Lash, J., & Wellington, F. (2007, March). Competitive advantage on a warming planet. *Harvard Business Review*, pp. 95–102.

Natrass, B., & Altomare, M. (1999). *The natural step for business*. Canada: New Society Publishers

Natrass, B., & Altomare, M. (2002). *Dancing with the tiger: Learning sustainability step by natural step*. Canada: New Society Publishers.

Pricewaterhouse Coopers. (2009). *Integral business: Integrating sustainability and business strategy*. Retrieved May 31, 2009, from http://www.pwc.com /sustainability.

Scottish and Newcastle. (2005). *Annual Report*, p.12.

Social Investment Forum. (2005). *Report on socially responsible investing trends in the United States*. Retrieved May 31, 2009, from http://www.socialinvest.org/pdf/ research/Trends/2005%20Trends%20Report.pdf

UNESCO. (2006). *Water, a shared responsibility*. New York: United Nations.

Wal-Mart backs drive for fuel efficiency. (2006, July 19). *Financial Times*, p. 15

CHAPTER 18

TRAINING MANAGERS FOR SUSTAINABLE DEVELOPMENT

The Lens of Three Practitioners

Emmanuel Raufflet, Denis Dupré, and Odile Blanchard

How can we create a context in and around the classroom to motivate business students to become global citizens and managers aware of the issues around sustainable development that are usually ignored by traditional academic teaching? How can we make them aware of the issues, encourage them to take action, and enable them to act responsively?

This chapter aims to build on our experience as teachers and educators in business, economics and management education in our respective contexts—teaching sustainable development and management in a business school in Canada; global environmental and social issues in an MBA program in finance and in a business school in France; and environmental impact assessment in a department of economics at a French university. It comprises three sections. The first describes our three experiences "teaching" sustainable development in the classroom to business and economics students and to managers. The second section highlights how each of these experiences enhances the skills necessary for education in sustainable development based on Tilbury and Wortman's (2004) work. The last section sum-

Management Education for Global Sustainability, pp. 377–393
Copyright © 2009 by Information Age Publishing

marizes some of the lessons learned and proposes future directions for
research and practice.

INTRODUCTION

Management Education has been criticized from several angles over the
last decade, for being non-relevant and disconnected from practice (Mintzberg, 2004), and for training people from an economic perspective at
the expense of more integrated approaches (Ghoshal, 2005). Business
schools have lost their way in terms of giving managers the skill sets they
need to handle real-world problems and the issues they actually encounter in doing business.

Sustainable development is too often ignored by traditional academic
programs. Today, many institutions, be they corporations, non-govern-
mental organizations, or public agencies, have incorporated sustainability
goals into their strategies to be competitive, as well as for ethical, ecological, and societal reasons. Decision makers must therefore be trained to
deal with issues of sustainability. Today's management and economics students are tomorrow's decision makers. If they are to be able to meet the
needs of the business and financial world, they must learn to address the
complexity of sustainable development while at university.

This chapter focuses on teaching experiences where instructors tackle
sustainability issues in management and economics schools. It aims to
explore ways to create a context in and around the classroom to motivate
business and economics students to become global citizens and managers
aware of the issues around sustainable development, to encourage them
to take action, and to enable them to act responsively.

The chapter comprises three sections. The first section focuses descrip-
tively on our three experiences in "teaching" sustainable development in
the classroom. The second section highlights how each of these three
experiences enhances the skills necessary for education in sustainable
development, based on Tilbury and Wortman's (2004) work. The last section summarizes some of the lessons learned and proposes future directions for research and practice.

THREE CONTEXTS AND COMMON CHALLENGES

Teaching social responsibility, ethics, and environmental impact assessment to management and economics students is no easy task. Although
such courses are clearly part of business and economics syllabi, they face

common challenges, namely (1) a cross-functional challenge: sustainable management education is inherently transversal, although our institutions tend to be designed in functional silos; (2) an integration challenge: how to present and use a paradigm of complexity in a context which fosters linear thinking; (3) a problem-solving challenge: how to foster complex problem-solving approaches and skills acquisition in a learning agenda driven by instrumentalist values.

The next three parts of this section describe three teaching experiments we conducted in our graduate classes. It shows how we addressed the above-mentioned challenges.

TEACHING SOCIAL RESPONSIBILITY OF THE FIRM IN A BUSINESS SCHOOL IN CANADA (RAUFFLET)

Course Context

It has been difficult to integrate sustainability dimensions into existing courses in the MBA program. As of 2008, no attempt had been made to include sustainability issues in existing functional-based courses such as accounting, finance, or IT; sustainability issues have been added by developing new courses.

"Contemporary Issues and Responsibility of the Firm" *(Enjeux contemporains et responsabilité sociale de la firme)* is one course that has been added to the curriculum. It is scheduled at the end of a one-year, approximately 200-student, intensive MBA program at HEC-Montréal. It is usually taught in August over six sessions, with two sessions per week in a 3-week period. Several aspects make it difficult to teach this course: end of program, August, a 3-week time block that follows completion of a supervised project for many students and precedes the graduation ball, students actively looking for a job, and so forth.

Challenges

The first two years I taught this course (2005 and 2006), I introduced global issues such as poverty, inequality, and global climate change. I observed that after three sessions, students were uneasy, even angry at times, and often felt powerless. As a result, they disengaged from conversations, and some became cynical. Typical answers to questions in class were "What can I do about this?" or "This is not my responsibility." This uneasiness, anger, and frustration were reflected in tense conversations in the classroom, absenteeism, and negative course evaluations. In trying to understand why, I realized a couple things. This course was unlike most other courses in the program, which tend to make the students, as future managers, feel powerful—those other courses give them tools for action, increasing their sense of control in business organizations. In contrast, the emphasis on more global, and sometimes depressing, issues in this course made them feel less relevant and less powerful, and was clearly making them realize some of the limitations and dark sides of these tools.

Accordingly, I refocused the teaching on "issues" as well as on "realms of possibilities" in business sectors in each 3-hour session. Each session would be divided into two parts: (1) a *global panorama*, which introduces the global issues in layman's terms yet uses rigorously descriptive language (e.g., about poverty and inequality in developing countries and between developed and developing countries); and (2) *signs of hope*, which presents "new innovative approaches" such as bottom of the pyramid, microcredit, and innovative business models, and casts both an appreciative and a critical eye on these initiatives. This refocused approach reduces the feeling of powerlessness and increases the students' sense of their relevance as future business managers.

Overall, this course differs from other courses in the program in two important ways. First, students are invited to wear "different hats." Whereas most other courses consider management in terms of level of analysis and action, we try to make students actually think of themselves as managers. In addition, the course invites them to think, feel, and react as citizens and family members as well as managers. Second, the course asks them to redefine "success." Whereas most other courses in the program posit "success" in terms of short-term financial gain, this course highlights the coexistence of different foci, including interdependencies between societal groups (business, civil society, and government), and relations between different levels (managerial actions, effects of business in society, effects on businesses of the state, etc.).

TEACHING ETHICS AT THE UNIVERSITY OF GRENOBLE, FRANCE (DUPRÉ)

Course Context

Business Ethics is a course in the Master's in Finance program at IAE (Business Administration Institute) at the University of Grenoble, France. This course was created in 2002, following the introduction of similar courses at several other universities. I was asked to coordinate the course because I had edited an interdisciplinary book—D. Dupré (Ed.) 2002,

Ethique et capitalisme. Paris: Economica—on ethics and capitalism. The first 3 years were challenging on several counts. First, enrollment was very low, averaging 5 students per section. Second, as this new course was not compulsory, attendance was sketchy. And since no other course integrated any ethical aspect of management, it was seen as a fringe course—a "ghetto," separate from the other courses in the program. However, that situation has changed and the course is in high demand now, with high attendance as well.

In 2009, in response to the introduction of ethics courses in other master's degree programs, I was asked to open my course transversally; the challenge will be to bring other professors and practitioners into the initiative and to convince the institution to offer a transversal ethics course for the entire IAE program, with the possibility of one day extending it across the whole university. Since 2007, when it became compulsory, 45 students have registered for the course.

The course is composed of 8 sessions of 3 hours each. The first session takes place in January. Students then have several weeks to research a project that they have been assigned. The last 7 sessions take place over 7 weeks in April and May.

Challenges

I had complete freedom in designing the course, including defining its objectives and materials. Thematically, I decided to focus on Planet, People, and Profit, as opposed to business practices. This decision came from the fact that, in 2002, climate change, water crises, and food issues were not widely discussed. Students are required to adopt a scientific approach to the issues: I expect scientific rigor, academic honesty, and transparency in their use of sources and ideas; information has to be crosschecked and students have to evaluate information quality. This neutral position means that all positions can be argued and makes it possible to go beyond socially desirable statements.

My teaching approach focuses on three principles: freedom in thinking; openness; and integrating philosophy.

Freedom

I have realized that there are at least two possible ways to teach ethics: either by imposing formulaic constraints on students, or by creating a context to confront them with their freedom to think—which is, according to Rawls (1971), both an objective and a means to an end. Framed in this way, the path that leads the student to critical thinking is the only one that makes sense. In terms of project theme, students choose a topic based on their own interests (20% of choices) or from a list of topics I suggest (80% of choices). However, reports must be academically sound: I expect them to use data, cases, illustrations, and explanations of specific mechanisms such as the interaction of water and CO_2. I grade according to the quality of their report and the oral presentation. In 2008, for the first time, I suggested that they choose a concrete action on the campus. Thirty percent of the group followed this suggestion. The specific topic was open or chosen from a list of topics suggested by Odile Blanchard who does follow-up with some groups: recycling vending machine cups; purchasing fair trade coffee; installing solar panels on the roof of the IAE building. There were some positive outcomes, but in general, the debates that I tried to introduce over the 3 years I taught the course did not work: requiring students to think for themselves ("critical thinking") is not at all customary in the business education tradition.

Openness

I start by stating my choices and my limitations: I talk about what I do and write, as well as how I am involved in society in my different roles. I share my experiences with the students. More specifically, I explain my vision for the need to reduce consumption. For instance, I explain that my carbon dioxide emissions are four times over the Earth's carrying capacity. This exercise of openness and transparency is difficult to initiate but is indispensable for at least two reasons. First, it allows both teacher and students to engage in more personal conversations—from this, students understand that they are entitled to their choices and their limitations. Second, it eliminates inconsistency between speech and action—teacher and students identify what goals are realistic as well as what is beyond their scope.

Integration of Philosophical/spiritual Concepts

A constant source of surprise for me is students' fascination with what we might call philosophical or spiritual concepts, expressed in either formal philosophy or organized religions. I have used several videos in class including: an interview I did with Pierre Rabhi, a writer, farmer, and agroecologist; and one with René Girard, a French philosopher, who explains the notion of a scapegoat. The two best student reports in the last five last years of the course dealt with religious concepts. The first was written jointly by students from Muslim, Jewish, and Christian cultures. The second, written by a Chinese student, focused on what philosophy and religions have to say about the poor and their relationship to nature.

PROBLEM-BASED LEARNING IN AN ENVIRONMENTAL IMPACT ASSESSMENT COURSE AT THE UNIVERSITY OF GRENOBLE, FRANCE (BLANCHARD)

Course Context

The third teaching experience relates to a "Problem Based Learning" (PBL) experiment in a ten-hour introductory course on Environmental Impact Assessments (EIAs), offered to graduate students in Economics. The PBL course is a complement to a course on assessment of the economic impact of projects. The goal of the PBL course is to give students a broad knowledge of the legislation, stakeholders, assessment methodologies, and documentation involved in carrying out an environmental impact assessment.

The starting point involves dividing the class of around 40 students into groups of 10–12, then assigning a problem to each group. The 10-hour class starts with 2 hours of introduction to the course and PBL methodology followed by: two PBL group-sessions of 90 minutes each, conducted with an interval of a week between the 2 sessions; 2 hours to share the findings of the PBL sessions with the other groups; 2 hours devoted to complementary material and feedback on the PBL experience; and a final hour for evaluation.

The two PBL sessions form the core of the learning process. This teaching approach is used for a very short period of time in the EIA class as an innovation on the lecture-based approach. But it cannot be used in large-enrollment economics classes because the small size of the learning groups makes PBL too costly in large courses. (Additional information on PBL is available at: http://www.unimaas.nl/pbl/ the Web site for Maastricht University, a pioneer in PBL.)

The teaching material for the two PBL sessions is a paper handed out to students a week before the first PBL session. Each group gets a different paper to work on so that the class benefits from a broad range of problems raised. Students are assigned to read the paper very carefully before the first PBL session.

The four papers handed out in the most recent PBL session were all from the *Environmental Impact Assessment Review*. The papers were:

Public participation in EIA of nuclear power plant decommissioning projects: a case study analysis (Bond, Palerm, & Haigh, 2004).

EIA scoping in England and Wales: Practitioner approaches, perspectives and constraints (Wood, Glasson, & Becker, 2005).

EIA practice in India and its evaluation using SWOT analysis (Paliwal, 2006).

The quality of Portuguese Environmental Impact Studies: the case of small hydropower projects (Pinho & Monterroso, 2006).

The PBL instructional approach aims to make students independent thinkers, capable of solving complex problems similar to those they will encounter in their professional lives. Students are given a problem they are expected to solve by exchanging ideas with their peers and acquiring the necessary knowledge that they initially lack. Students are actors in their knowledge acquisition, responsible for it in at least two respects: first, they are responsible for being active participants in group discussions; second, they must sort out what they already know from what they need to learn to solve the problem. PBL depends on both group work and individual work. For the group, the work breaks down into three steps. The group completes the first step in the classroom with the instructor over a period of 90 minutes. The instructor presents the group with a question or a problem. In the EIA course, the question posed to one group, based on the paper they had read, was the following: "What are the success factors of EIAs?" The question is aimed at attaining goals which are set by the EIA course instructor but which are not revealed to the students. The first step is devoted to understanding the problem at hand, raising additional questions linked to the problem, identifying the knowledge needed to solve the problem, making assumptions about potential solutions, and deciding on the learning objectives each student will have to reach before the next session.

The second step consists of the individual work each student does during the week following the initial session. The student looks for answers to the questions identified in the classroom. Doing so involves acquiring knowledge the student may not yet have. Students may use any source including academic papers, journals, books, and Web sites, with the proviso that they read the source critically, evaluating its quality in terms of the ideology underlying the author's view, the relevance of the data, and so on.

The third step is the reporting back to the group, which takes place in the classroom for 90 minutes. The students share the information they found and their ideas for solutions to the problem with the other members of the group. Each student defends his or her views on the appropriate answer to the problem. Different views may be diametrically opposed. After potentially intense debate, each group must reach consensus, a common answer to the problem assigned by the instructor.

The two in-class sessions unfold in the same way: they depend on students sharing ideas under the authority of a discussion leader (a student) who structures the session and encourages participation from and cooperation between the group members. A secretary takes the minutes of the debates, and suggests diagrams or graphs to keep track of and summarize main points. The discussion leader and the secretary are student volunteers. All students are invited to participate fully in the discussions, identify assumptions, express their views, and test them by comparing them to other views. Discussions are the core activity in terms of helping students understand the problem and concepts and build their knowledge when they are unable to reach these goals by themselves.

As recommended by de Grave, Moust, and Hommes (2003), the instructor intervenes as little as possible in the classroom sessions. The instructor's role is to listen carefully to the debates, to check whether the discussions tend to go in a direction that will lead students toward the goals of the session, and, at the end of the first session, to validate the learning objectives that the students have collectively set. If the discussions appear to be moving in an inappropriate direction, the instructor will raise questions that bring students back on track. The instructor provides no answers to any answer at any time: students must rely on their own judgment. For further information on the instructor's role, see de Grave, Moust, and Hommes (2003).

Last, the evaluation of students in the EIA class is based on various criteria: (1) the quality of the students' participation in the PBL sessions, including their level of engagement, the relevance of their arguments, the value added to the group's discussion, and their cooperation skills (listening and tolerance); and (2) a short written exam based on a short case study. The goal of the exam is to check whether students have acquired the expected knowledge and understanding of EIAs.

Challenges

This course is innovative in two ways. First, it is part of an Economics graduate curriculum. The fact that an EIA course is part of an Economics graduate curriculum is unusual, since conducting an EIA in real life is usually the job of an environmental engineer rather than that of an economist. However, our decision to include the course in an Economics program stems from the fact that real-life problems are not bounded by academic disciplines. An economics expert on a consulting team hired to assess the impacts of an investment project will be expected to assess the economic costs and benefits of the project. Specifically, he or she will be expected to assess environmental impacts in economic terms to know whether an EIA is mandatory for the project under consideration, and, if so, to know how to use the EIA. Clearly, in that kind of situation, having a broad knowledge of EIAs will be a plus. The course is also innovative in its focus on concrete problem solving—the core of the PBL method. PBL is designed to prepare students for any professional context in which they will have to disentangle complex issues.

This section has focused on a description of three experiences of business educators in three different contexts. Raufflet's approach focuses on educating managers and graduate students of management about larger issues and providing them with examples to shift their thinking from a traditional business focus to a broader one. Dupré's approach uses personal involvement, open-ended dialogue, and the integration of philosophical concepts to teach ethics. Blanchard's approach focuses on problem-based learning and the solving of what are inherently concrete, interdisciplinary, and multi-level problems. Each of these three approaches operates in a different context; yet all aim to build five skills that pertain to education for sustainable development. Those five skills will be examined in the next section.

FOSTERING FIVE SKILLS IN ESD: ILLUSTRATIONS

In 2004, the International Union for the Conservation of Nature (IUCN) published a landmark report on ESD (Education for Sustainable Development) (Tilbury & Wortman, 2004). The report proposed that if ESD is to be an effective tool for engaging people in negotiating a sustainable future, making decisions, and acting on them, it should first address the way in which educators think about sustainable development *and* about education in general. The following five skills are critical for Sustainable Development: (1) Envisioning—being able to imagine a better future. The premise is that if we know where we want to go, we will be better able to work out how to get there; (2) Critical thinking and reflection—learning to question our current belief systems and to recognize the assumptions underlying our understanding, views, and opinions. Critical thinking skills help people examine economic, environmental, social, and cultural structures in the context of sustainable development; (3) Systemic thinking—acknowledging complexities and looking for links and synergies when trying to find solutions to problems; (4) Building partnerships —promoting dialogue and negotiation, learning to work together; (5) Participatory decision making—empowering different people and different groups. Tilbury and Wortman add that these skills should be learned and applied according to the cultural contexts of different groups and stakeholders. In this section, based on our three experiences, we illustrate how each of our approaches contributes to fostering one or more of these skills.

ENVISIONING

One of the challenges of education for sustainable development concerns its purpose: developing materials to educate for sustainable development requires instructors and administrators to rethink the purpose of education—especially in the context of business education. How can one judge ethical education? Diversity in teaching ethics is a reality, and the variety among our three practices leads to seek to clarify our targets. We propose to define two main ways of judging ethical education.

Table 18.1.   Five Skills for ESD and Examples

Skills	Description	Example
Envisioning	Being able to imagine a better future. The premise is that if we know where we want to go, we will be better able to work out how to get there.	Teaching freedom (Dupré)
Critical thinking and reflection	Learning to question our current belief systems and to recognize the assumptions underlying our knowledge, perspective and opinions. Critical thinking skills help people learn to examine economic, environmental, social, and cultural structures in the context of sustainable development.	Different hats (Raufflet) PBL: as many ways of thinking as students in the class. Students share ideas with peers to verify assumptions. This exchange of ideas leads to reflection (Blanchard).
Systemic thinking	Acknowledging complexities and looking for links and synergies when trying to find solutions to problems.	Making connections on the implications of business activities (Raufflet) PBL leads to higher-level thinking about complexity (Blanchard).
Building partnerships	Promoting dialogue and negotiation, learning to work together	Illustrate interdependencies, and their potentials (Raufflet). In-class discussions: students listen to their peers, and share ideas and opinions to construct a common answer to the problem (Blanchard).
Participation in decision-making	Empowering people.	Openness (Dupré) In-class conversations (Blanchard)

The first one could be called a consequentialist way of teaching ethics (to justify whether an act is morally right depends only on the consequences of that act: "the ends justify the means"). This approach is usually focused on the economic world and is the most widespread in the teaching of ethics at business schools. It is adopted when the main concern is the stockholder's point of view or when personal interests are at stake. Condorcet (1795/1988) dreamed of a system to educate the whole mass of people in home economics, which he felt they needed for knowing their rights and duties and for avoiding the charlatanism that set traps for their fortune, health, and freedom of opinion.

There is another more deontological way which is usually directed toward preparing future citizens. This approach consists of normative theories about which choices are morally required, forbidden, or permitted: the ones "we have a duty to perform." The Universal Declaration of Human Rights, written by Canadian John Humphrey and adopted by the United Nations in 1948, called for education to be "directed to the full development of the human personality and to the strengthening of respect for human rights and fundamental freedoms." Later in 1959, the United Nations proclaimed The Declaration of the Rights of the Child to promote general culture, a basis of equal opportunity, to develop abilities, individual judgement, and sense of moral and social responsibility, and so to enable each person to become a useful member of society.

Both approaches have pros and cons, advantages and disadvantages, but each requires the assertion of a vision of the world and the implementation of educational tools adequate to achieving that vision. Whatever the vision is, tools for improving critical thinking and systemic thinking are required. In the deontological way there is also an absolute necessity for building partnerships and for promoting participation in decision making.

CRITICAL THINKING

Critical thinking is fostered in PBL and in education for corporate social responsibility. When learning in a PBL context, students develop critical thinking in many ways. First, the content of the papers they are assigned and the problem they have to solve requires them to look critically at EIA. For example, a question as simple as "What are the success factors of EIAs?" implies that EIAs may fail in certain circumstances. The students have to disentangle which situations may lead to success from those oriented toward failure. Second, as we have already emphasized, each student is unique and has a unique way of reasoning. When students share ideas and viewpoints in the PBL sessions, they have to listen to others, argue their own positions, analyze their peers' positions, evaluate

Table 18.2. Two Cartesian Ways to Teach Ethics

	Consequentialism	Deontology
Means	Constraints	Freedom Awakening (create the interest)
Targets	Know the global stakes on the Planet	
	Serve the company and make a career by means of ethical reasoning	Adapt the ethics of the action to create a fairer world
Prerequisites	Theory of justice (Rawls, 1971) leads to the greatest system of freedom for each and every one of us	
		Experience freedom in the course itself
Interest	Follow societal choices	Possible conversion of society (citizens lead societal change)
Possible Limits		
From the firms' point of view	Not forward-looking: administrative vision which does not generate support in the company	Utopian: idyllic vision which does not take into account people and their contingencies
From the societal point of view	Focuses on results that are not as important as other urgent matters	Ineffective because it is not influential on companies

alternative solutions, and eventually rally around what is generally deemed to be the best approach. At the same time, they must test their own views against those of their peers and critically assess their own behaviors. Critical thinking is at the core of the skills required to do so.

Another kind of critical thinking is related to the requirement imposed on students to assume different perspectives. Raufflet introduces the notion of "wearing many hats" in his course on corporate social responsibility, where a "hat" is a role, which comes with a specific perspective or standpoint on a phenomenon or issue. Whereas most MBA programs ask students to wear the hat of a business owner or manager, a program that asks them to wear different hats simultaneously forces them to reframe their perspective and consider situations on different levels and from multiple angles. In adopting that multiple perspective, students develop critical thinking skills.

SYSTEMIC THINKING

In a traditional lecture-based course, an instructor passes knowledge on to students who are considered as "receptacles" or "banks" who store information for future use. In such a context, knowledge brought to the students is presented in a linear way, implicitly and explicitly formatted by the instructor's own mindset. Various studies have shown that the "banking" process is not effective because individuals learn according to their own individual "semantic network", not that of the instructor: each learner connects new information to information they have gathered in past experiences (Gijselaers, 1996). PBL acknowledges this process and enhances systemic thinking in the following ways. In the first PBL session, students face great difficulties in understanding the paper they are given, since they have not previously been exposed to what an EIA is. Often, they also find it hard to understand the question raised. They formulate group assumptions that may be dropped later in the session. No clues are given to them. Since all students are unique and bring individual knowledge and skills to their groups, cooperative work "magically" leads to answers that students initially thought out of reach.

Simple problems—such as building a chair—can be addressed using patterns and behaviors established by routine craft or commonly held knowledge; while complicated problems—such as building an airplane—require a high level of technical sophistication and precision, as well as tight coordination through rigid protocols. A complex problem—like raising a child—requires sensitivity to the uniqueness of the situation at hand, and recognition that approaches used to address simple or complicated problems may not work or may be counterproductive in such a context. Complexity involves thinking about the problem in a different way, both in terms of the connections that need to be made and in terms of the knowledge needed to address it. Using complex teaching cases in the classroom helps make students aware of the limitations of the methods used to solve problems that are only simple or complicated.

Building Partnerships

Two of our approaches emphasize building partnerships: Blanchard's use of PBL emphasizes interpersonal partnerships; and Raufflet's approach to Corporate Social Responsibility (CSR) emphasizes cross-sectoral partnerships. Poverty is not a simple issue. In recent years, several cross-sectoral initiatives have emerged to generate new thinking about poverty and potential solutions (Wankel, 2008). Discussion and evaluation of these new partnerships in class stimulate new ranges of possibilities for partnerships across society. For most business students, this leads to their adopting a perspective in which business is viewed not only as a wealth-creating activity but also as a potential agent for positive social and environmental change. Blanchard's use of PBL creates the partnership context in the classroom itself: by the very nature of the assignments, students become interdependent and must rely on each other to resolve the issue they are faced with. Even if the group comprises very different personalities, individual students have to work cooperatively, expressing their views, listening to each other, and learning from their peers' experience and knowledge in order to construct a shared answer to the problem. Student feedback on the PBL sessions emphasizes how beneficial teamwork is, both from a professional perspective and as dynamic learning. The discussion leader has a major role in building the partnership or failing to do so. A skilled discussion leader will get the most out of every student, however shy, reluctant, or friendly. Such a leader will enable the group to come up with a shared solution—a consensus—that has everyone's support. Conversely, a less skilled discussion leader may not enable the group to reach a commonly held position. As a result, students may leave the classroom with unanswered or unclarified questions.

Participatory Decision Making

Our experiences foster participation in decision making in two ways. First, Dupré's approach to openness, in which the instructor is transparent about his or her achievements and limitations and uses open-ended questions to nurture a conversational atmosphere, invites participation. The students themselves shape the classroom experience and learn to participate. Blanchard's PBL approach induces the students to make group decisions based on interactive discussions: in the first PBL session, they have to decide on their learning objectives for the next session; in the second session, they have to come up with a response/solution to the issue raised in the assignment. Every student is required to participate in the decision-making process.

CONCLUSION AND DISCUSSION

This chapter has focused on our three separate experiences in three contexts around the same broad structuring framework: (1) the context of our courses (both in relation to the rest of the curriculum and internal context we created in the classroom); (2) the challenges we faced and how we addressed them; and (3) how each of our courses has contributed to enhancing one or more of the five skills for sustainable development. In doing so, this exploratory study faces several limitations. First, even if we have overcome some challenges in the first years of our courses, none of us would feel comfortable asserting that our courses have been "successes." We prefer contending that they have been experiments in different contexts using different starting points, based on different pedagogical approaches, and that, as of 2009, they are still very much works in progress. Second, our evaluation of our approaches in introducing sustainability has not been guided by a scientific methodology of education evaluation. Rather, we have tried to compare our trajectories and experiences, then learn from them.

Doing so, we are proposing some preliminary conclusions for future research and practice. The first one concerns common challenges. In introducing dimensions of sustainability into the curriculum and into a course, we faced common challenges, namely (1) a cross-functional challenge: sustainable management education is inherently transversal, although our institutions tend to be designed in functional silos; (2) an integration challenge: how to enhance a paradigm of complexity in a context which fosters linear thinking; and (3) a problem-solving challenge: how to foster complex problem-solving approaches and skills acquisition in a learning agenda driven by instrumentalist values. In addition, our approaches identified common "paths" to make sustainability palpable and relevant, namely, learning-by-doing, experiencing, raising awareness, and grounding in local specificities and challenges. Second, we found the Tilbury and Wortman's (2004) framework very relevant as a way of organizing and comparing our experiences. As several courses and programs are being designed to integrate sustainability into the business education curriculum, this framework could be of help for program managers and scholars interested in going beyond more traditional discipline-based courses and seeking to foster new skills and competencies. This framework has the potential to enhance the integration of sustainability into specific courses on sustainability, which is a necessary stage, and for the real challenge ahead, which concerns the integration of sustainability in all courses of business education. Working toward this integration would lead us to rethink our assumptions and work for both implicit and explicit sustainability in business education.

REFERENCES

Bond A., Palerm J., & Haigh P. (2004). Public participation in EIA of nuclear power plant decommissioning projects: A case study analysis. *Environmental Impact Assessment Review, 24*(6), 617–641.

Condorcet, N. (1988). *Esquisse d'un tableau historique des progrès de l'esprit humain.* Paris: Flammarion. (Original work published 1795)

de Grave W., Moust J., & Hommes, J. (2003). *The role of the tutor in a problem-based learning curriculum.* Maastricht: Datawyse-Maastricht University Press.

ABOUT THE AUTHORS

Jill Bamburg is a co-founder of the Bainbridge Graduate Institute and served as the school's first Dean of the MBA program. She is the author of *Getting to scale: Growing your business without selling out* (Berrett-Koehler, 2006). Her academic experience also includes 7 years of teaching marketing, strategy, and entrepreneurship to mid-career managers in the Graduate Management Program at Antioch University/Seattle. Jill earned her BA at Washington University and her MBA at Stanford University. She currently serves on the Core Faculty of BGI.

Ralph Bathurst earned his PhD in Management from Victoria University, Wellington. Formerly a music educator and still a musician, Ralph's primary interests are in the arts and how arts organizations are managed. He currently lectures in management and leadership at Massey University. His research activities are in organizational aesthetics.

Odile Blanchard, is a graduate of the School of Management, École des Hautes Études Commerciales (HEC), France, and holds a PhD in Economics from the University of Grenoble, France. As an Associate Professor of Economics at the University of Grenoble, she teaches various courses relating to environmental economics, energy policies, and sustainable development. Her current research focuses on economic issues relating to climate change. She is also the director of a climate–friendly university initiative at the University of Grenoble.

Odile is currently co-editing the Proceedings of the conference on Sustainable Development Education that was held in June 2008 in Albi, France.

Jerónimo de Burgos-Jiménez earned a PhD in Management from the University of Almeria and a Bachelor's Degree in Business Administration and Management from the Spanish University of Education to Distance (UNED). He works as Reader of Operations Management at the University of Almería (Spain). His doctoral dissertation studied environmental management in hotels. He has participated in several research projects financed by the Spanish Government. His main research interests are related to environmental management, operations management, and stakeholder management.

Eva Collins, BS (Hons), MA, PhD, and Post Graduate Certificate in Tertiary Teaching, is a Senior Lecturer at the University of Waikato, New Zealand. She teaches Business Government and Society, Strategic Management, and a course entitled Strategies for Sustainability, which aims to enhance students' understanding of sustainability issues confronting today's managers. In 2003, she was awarded the outstanding teaching award for the Waikato Management School. She regularly contributes as a guest speaker to the University's Teaching and Development workshops. In 2005 and 2007, her coauthored cases (with Kate Kearins as one of the authors) were finalists in the international Oikos Sustainability Case Writing Competition.

Jose-Rodrigo Cordoba (MA, PhD) is a senior lecturer at the school of management, Royal Holloway, University of London. He is the director of the masters of science in business information systems and teaches courses related to the interface between organisations, people and technology. His current interests are in the use of systemic thinking to tackle complex problems in areas like sustainability and electronically mediated government. He has published several papers in internationally recognised journals both in English and Spanish. He is a core member of the Centre for Research into Sustainability (CRIS) at Royal Holloway and his first single authored book titled *Systems Practice in the Information Society* is to be released during 2009.

Denis Dupré (Engineer, mathematical thermodynamics, Ecole Nationale Supérieure des Mines de Paris; PhD, Finance, Paris-IX Dauphine University) is a Research Director at the University of Grenoble; Professor of finance and ethics at the IAE (University of Grenoble, France); and at ENSIMAG (INPG Grenoble, France); and in charge of seminars for researchers in finance at CERAG Research Center. He is the author of numerous economics texts in French, including *Ethique et capitalisme (Ethics and Capitalism: A Pluridisciplinary Approach)*, published by Economica in

2002; and *La planète, ses crises et nous* (*The Planet, Its Crisis and Us*) written with Michel Griffon, published by Atlantica (2008).

Margot Edwards earned a PhD in Management from Massey University, Auckland. Margot enjoys combining her background in zoological sciences with her strong interest in visual art to highlight sustainability issues in a management context. Her current research interests include leadership and aesthetics, and the management of arts organizations.

Mark G. Edwards is a lecturer at the Business School, University of Western Australia and John F. Kennedy University in California. He teaches in the areas of business ethics, organizational change and transformation and integrative metatheory. He has published in scholarly journals on a variety of topics including organizational development, organizational learning, sustainability, futures studies, cultural evolution, disability studies, metatheory development and integrative metastudies. Mark's PhD thesis was awarded with distinction and will be published by Routledge later in 2009 in a series on business ethics. The book will be titled, *Organizational Transformation for Sustainability: An Integral Metatheory*. His research interests include the development of global business ethics, metatheory building methods and the development of sustaining forms of organization and work life.

Robert Girling is a Professor in the School of Business at Sonoma State University where he teaches sustainable business strategy and social entrepreneurship. He received his PhD from Stanford University and has taught and consulted in 20 different countries. Recently he has served as a consultant to the Caribbean Development Bank on sustainable development strategies for the island of Dominica and as a founder and organizer of the Sustainable Enterprise Conferences on Tools for Sustainable Businesses and Communities series. His previous professional experience includes teaching at the Federal University of Bahia where he was co-founder of the LIDERE Project for School Improvement and International Project Director, at the Federal University of Minas Gerais in Brazil, the University of the West Indies and American University in Washington DC. He has consulted with the World Bank, USAID, the United Nations, and the International Center for Research on Women.Prof. Girling is the author of over 50 articles and books including *Structures of Dependency* (1973); *Multinational Institutions and the Third World* (1985); *Education; Management and Participation* (1990) and *A Escola Participativa* [in Portuguese] (5th ed. 2006). He is currently writing a book *Good Companies*. He is a member of Phi Beta Delta [The Honor Society for International Scholars] and has received awards for his teaching and research. He is currently a Fulbright Senior Scholar for the period 2005-2010.

Edeltraud Günther earned her doctorate in Environmental Accounting from the Universität Augsburg and holds the Chair in Environmental Management and Accounting at the Technische Universität Dresden. Since 2005, she has held a joint appointment as visiting professor at the University of Virginia's McIntire School of Commerce. Professor Günter teaches and researches extensively in the fields of environmental performance measurement, adaptation to climate change, public procurement, valuation of environmental resources, and hurdles analysis. She serves as a consultant to many businesses and government agencies, including the German Ministry of Environmental Affairs, the European Union and the German Organization for Standardization.

Mark Higgins, PhD, is the Dean and The Alfred J. Verrecchia-Hasbro Inc. Leadership Chair in Business at the University of Rhode Island. During his tenure at URI, he has served as the Director of the Master in Accounting Program, the Accounting Area Coordinator, and as the Associate Dean for Undergraduate Programs. He is the co-author with Kevin Murphy of *Concepts in taxation*, which is in its 16th edition. Mark earned a B.S. and M.S. in Accounting from the University of South Carolina and a PhD from the University of Tennessee. He is also a CPA.

John Hollwitz is Professor of Management Systems and University Professor of Psychology and Rhetoric at Fordham University. He holds doctorates from Northwestern University and from the University of Nebraska. He teaches at Fordham University, where he served for six years as Vice President for Academic Affairs. Before joining Fordham he was Dean of the College of Arts and Sciences at Loyola College in Maryland, and A. F. Jacobson Professor of Communication at Creighton University in Omaha, Nebraska. In addition to research articles on organizational behavior and communication, he is co-editor of *Psyche at work and Psyche and Sports*. In 1997, he began working with the Beijing International MBA program.

Vera Ivanaj is an Associate Professor of Management Science in the Chemical Engineering School (ENSIC) of the Institut National Polytechnique de Lorraine (INPL), University of Nancy, France. She received her MS in Economic Sciences, from the University of Tirana and her PhD in Management Science from the University of Nancy II. Recently, she worked on a major research project "Multinationals and Sustainable Development," leading to several publications: "Is Sustainable Development in Multinational Enterprises a Marketing Issue?" and "Sustainable Development and the Multinational Corporation as a Tool of Competitiveness" (*Multinational Business Review*, Special Issue, 2007), and others. She was co-editor of the Special Issue of *Multinational Business Review*, 2007.

Kirk Karwan is Chair of the Department of Business and Accounting, and the John D. Hollingsworth Professor of International Business at Furman University. He is a member of the University's Sustainability Planning Council and teaches a course entitled "The Sustainable Corporation." He received his PhD from the Heinz School of Public Policy and Management at Carnegie-Mellon University, and has BES and MSE degrees in Operations Research from Johns Hopkins University. He has been the recipient of federal grants from NOAA and the Departments of Transportation and Energy for work in environmental remediation management and has published in the *Journal of Environmental Economics and Management*.

Kate Kearins, BEd, MA (Hons), MMS, PhD, is Professor of Management at Auckland University of Technology, New Zealand, and for 2007–8, Visiting Professor of Groupe ESSCA, France. She was Chair of the Organizations and the Natural Environment Division of the Academy of Management in 2006-7, and has been active in teaching and writing about environmental and social issues since 1994, and specifically on education for sustainability since 2001. She was joint guest editor of a special issue of Business Strategy and the Environment on Education for Sustainability in 2005. Among Kate's other editorial board memberships, she serves on the board of the *Journal of Management Education*.

Ed Lockhart lectures in Corporate Sustainability in the Monash University's MBA program. He also lectures in two other Masters programs: Environment and Sustainability and Corporate Environmental and Sustainability Management. His research interests are in organizational creativity and business strategy development for sustainability. Given his broad commercial background, the focus of Ed's sustainability teaching is on the development of educational practices rooted in the context of what managers actually do. In particular, he has developed an approach to teaching and assessment that encourages learners to draw on what they have experienced as well as on their ability to think creatively

John R. McIntyre is the founding Director of the Georgia Tech Center for International Business Education and Research (CIBER). He is a Professor of International Management and International Affairs with joint appointments in the College of Management and the Sam Nunn School of International Affairs of the Georgia Institute of Technology, Atlanta, Georgia. He received his graduate education at McGill, Strasbourg, and Northeastern Universities, obtaining his PhD at the University of Georgia. Prior to joining Georgia Tech in September 1981, he was Research Associate for International Management at the Dean Rusk Center, University of Georgia School of Law. Among his more recent works is *Business and Management Education In China: Transition, Pedagogy, and Training*, Singapore: World Scientific, 2005.

Philip Mirvis is an organizational psychologist whose research and private practice concerns large-scale organizational change, corporate citizenship, and the character of the workforce and workplace. He is currently a senior research fellow of the Center for Corporate Citizenship, Boston College. He has authored or edited 10 books, including, *The Cynical Americans*, a U.S. national survey of corporate human resource investments, *Building the Competitive Workforce* and, covering 20 years of experience with mergers, *Joining Forces*. His latest works are about developing a leadership community, *To the Desert and Back*, and business in society, *Beyond Good Company: Next Generation Corporate Citizenship*.

S. Bradley Moran, is the Assistant Vice President for Research Administration and Professor of Oceanography at the University of Rhode Island. With over 50 oceanographic cruises completed to date, he maintains an active research program in Arctic oceanography, ocean carbon dynamics, coastal groundwater transport, and environmental radioactivity. Together with Mark Higgins and Deborah Rosen, he initiated the development of the Master of Business Administration-Master of Oceanography "Blue MBA" dual degree. Brad received a BSc in Chemistry from Concordia University and a PhD in Oceanography from Dalhousie University.

Claudia E. Natenzon earned a Bachelor Degree in Geography from the University of Buenos Aires and a PhD from the University of Seville. She works as Full Time Professor at the University of Buenos Aires. She has specialized in environmental risk, especially in diagnosis of social vulnerability due to natural catastrophes such as floods. She has collaborated with different international organizations including the UNESCO and has published more than 100 papers in peer reviewed journals.

José A. Plaza-Úbeda earned a PhD in Management and a Bachelor's Degree in Business Administration and Management from the University of Almeria. He works as Lecturer of Strategic Management at the University of Almería. He has participated in several research projects financed by the Spanish Government. His main research interests are related to stakeholder management, environmental management, and complementary assets. Recently he was granted, as the Spanish Coordinator, an international research project on environmental management, social vulnerability, and poverty by the AECI (Spanish Agency for the International Cooperation –Spanish Government).

Terry Porter is an Assistant Professor of Management at the Maine Business School. She received her PhD degree from the University of Massachusetts, where her research focused on bottom up strategic change and corporate environmentalism. Terry has published in the areas of complexity theory and coevolution in management inquiry, critical systems approaches to management education and practice, identity and sustainability, and strategic processes from a complex adaptive systems perspective. Her research interests include strategic processes, business and sustainability, complexity theory and sustainability, and organizational and personal identity processes in management.

Gordon Rands (PhD, Business Administration, University of Minnesota) is Professor of Management at Western Illinois University, where he teaches classes in business and society and organizations and the natural environment, is co-director of the Program for the Study of Ethics, and is co-chair of WIU's campus sustainability committee. Gordon worked on the National Wildlife Federation's curriculum development project, and is a co-founder and past chair of the Organizations and the Natural Environment (ONE) Division of the Academy of Management. Gordon holds a bachelor's degree in Natural Resources from the University of Michigan and a master's degree in Organizational Behavior from Brigham Young University.

Emmanuel Raufflet (PhD Management, McGill University) is an Associate Professor of Management at HEC Montréal. He published (with Pierre Batellier) *Responsabilité sociale de l'entreprise: enjeux de gestion et cas pédagogiques* (2008) and co-edited (with Albert Mills) *The Dark Side: Critical Cases on the Downside of Business* (Greenleaf Publishing, 2009) He received the Prix de Pédagogie—Assistant Professor, HEC Montréal in 2006, the Emerson Award for Best Case in Business Ethics at NACRA (North American Case Research Association) in 2005 and in 2007, and the Best case award (Bronze) at NACRA (2008). He is the pedagogical director of the Graduate Degree in Management and Sustainable Development at HEC Montréal.

Deborah Rosen, PhD, is an Associate Dean and Professor of Marketing in the College of Business Administration at the University of Rhode Island. Deborah is also Executive Director of the University of Rhode Island Transportation Center. Her research has appeared in the *Journal of Business Research*, *Journal of Electronic Commerce in Organizations*, *International Journal of Services Industry Management*, and *Academy of Marketing Science Review* and in conference proceedings. She received a BA in History from the University of Wisconsin-Madison and an MBA and PhD from the University of Tennessee-Knoxville.

Lorinda Rowledge, PhD, is Founding Provost of the Bainbridge Graduate Institute, a pioneering MBA program in Sustainable Business, and Co-founder of EKOS International, a consulting firm focused on helping companies integrate environmental and social sustainability into business strategy, product design, production processes, and supply chains. Lorinda was the lead author of *Mapping the Journey: Case Studies in Implementing Sustainable Development Strategies*, a book featuring global businesses leading in the application of sustainability (e.g., Sony, Volvo, and Patagonia) published in 1999 by Greenleaf Publishers, UK. Lorinda holds a PhD specializing in Organizational and Community Psychology, from the University of Oregon

Tom Smythe is an Associate Professor of Business and Accounting at Furman University. He. earned his PhD in Finance from the University of South Carolina, and holds a BS in Mathematics from Furman and an MBA from George Mason University. At Furman, he has served on the University's Environmental sub-committee for its Strategic Plan, and was a member of the University's Year of the Environment committee. Most recently, he participated in a feasibility study to examine the possibility of developing a Sustainability Center in Chile that integrates multiple disciplines ranging from science to business.

Robert Sroufe received his PhD in Operations Management from Michigan State University. He is an Associate Professor and the current Murrin Chair of Global Competitiveness in the John F. Donahue Graduate School of Business at Duquesne University teaching within the full time MBA + Sustainability program. He conducts research and consulting involved with sustainable theories and models, environmental management systems, and green supply chain management. He has published many research articles and pedagogical case studies involving the analysis and integration of environmental issues into business decision making.

Mark Starik is a Professor and the Department Chair of Strategic Management and Public Policy in the George Washington University School of Business. He researches, teaches, and advises organizations and individuals in the areas of strategic environmental management, environmental and energy policy, environmental entrepreneurship, and implementing solutions to climate crises. Mark is also the Director of the GW Institute for Corporate Responsibility Environmental Sustainability Program. Mark is a co-founder of several organizations, including the Academy of Management Organizations and the Natural Environment (ONE) Division.

James A.F. Stoner is Professor of Management Systems at Fordham University and Chairholder of the James A.F. Stoner Chair in Global Sustainability—a chair endowed in Jim's name by one of Jim's students (Brent Martini) and his father (Bob Martini). He earned his BS in Engineering Science at Antioch College and his SM and PhD in Industrial Management at MIT. He has published articles in journals ranging from *Academy of Management Review* to the *Journal of Experimental Social Psychology*, and has authored, co-authored and co-edited a number of books (approximately 16–20). Jim's current projects and interests include inquiring into new ways to bring about organizational and societal transformation to move toward a sustainable world and the role of spirituality in corporate excellence, and global sustainability. He has taught managers, executives, MBA, and undergraduate students in at least a dozen countries, won teaching awards at Fordham, and consulted with a broad range of companies.

Wendy Stubbs is a Senior Lecturer in the School of Geography and Environmental Science at Monash University in Australia. She coordinates the Master of Corporate Environmental and Sustainability Management program and teaches a corporate sustainability unit in the MBA program. Wendy's research interests include corporate social responsibility, corporate sustainability, sustainable business models, and systems sustainability. Her research explores new business models that are grounded in the principles of sustainability (environmental, social, and economic). Her research also focuses on systems sustainability—how organizations contribute to a sustainable socioeconomic system—acknowledging that organizations can only be sustainable if the system they reside in is sustainable.

Robert Underwood is an Associate Professor of Business and Accounting at Furman University. He earned his doctorate in marketing from Virginia Polytechnic Institute and State University (Virginia Tech), and holds a BS in Accounting and an MBA from the University of Alabama. His research has been published in a number of marketing and case study journals, and his teaching has focused on international and strategic marketing issues. He is currently involved in research projects that examine the challenges and opportunities of the corporate sustainable development integration process and how these issues can be incorporated into management curricula.

Diego A. Vázquez-Brust is a civil and environmental engineer from the University of La Plata, Buenos Aires. He earned an MBA and a PhD in Management from Royal Holloway, University of London. He is currently Research Manager/Senior Research Associate of the ESRC Centre for Business Relationships, Accountability, Sustainability and Society (BRASS) at Cardiff University, Business School where he leads the Poverty, Environmental Risk, and Business Responsibility Project. He is also Fellow Teaching Associate in International Business at Royal Holloway, University of London.

Charles Wankel, Associate Professor of Management at St. John's University, New York, earned his doctorate from New York University. Charles is on the Rotterdam School of Management Dissertation Committee and is Honorary Vice Rector of the Poznan University of Business and Foreign Languages. He has authored and edited numerous books including the best-selling *Management*, 3rd ed. (Prentice-Hall, 1986), eight volumes in the IAP series Research in Management Education and Development, the *Handbook of 21st Century Management* (SAGE, 2008), and *Encyclopedia of Business in Today's World* (SAGE, 2009). He is the leading founder and director of scholarly virtual communities for management professors, currently directing eight with thousands of participants in more than seventy nations. He has been a visiting professor in Lithuania at the Kaunas University of Technology (Fulbright Fellowship) and the University of Vilnius, (United Nations Development Program and Soros Foundation funding).

Mark White earned his PhD in Finance from Michigan State University and is currently Associate Professor of Commerce at the University of Virginia's McIntire School of Commerce and Visiting Professor for Environmental Economics at the Technische Universität Dresden. He has been teaching and researching in the field of business sustainability since 1992 and spent a year in Germany as a Fulbright Scholar studying German environmental management practices. In 2005, he and Prof. Günther were awarded a $150,000 grant from the Procter and Gamble Foundation to develop and deliver the innovative cross-disciplinary, cross-cultural course, "Investing in a Sustainable Future," described in their chapter.